Seize the Hour

Also by Margaret MacMillan

Women of the Raj

Canada and Nato (editor)

Peacemakers: The Paris Conference of 1919 and
its Attempt to End War

Parties Long Estranged: Canada and Australia in the
Twentieth Century (editor)

Seize the Hour

When Nixon Met Mao

MARGARET MACMILLAN

JOHN MURRAY

First published in Great Britain in 2006 by John Murray (Publishers)
A division of Hodder Headline

I

A CIP catalogue record for this title is available
from the British Library

Hardback ISBN-13 978-0-7195-6522-9
Hardback ISBN-10 0-7195-6522-7
Trade paperback ISBN-13 978-0-7195-6876-3
Trade paperback ISBN-10 0-7195-6876-5

Typeset in Bembo by M Rules

Printed and bound in Great Britain by William Clowes Ltd, Beccles, Suffolk

Hodder Headline policy is to use papers that are natural, renewable
and recyclable products and made from wood grown in sustainable
forests. The logging and manufacturing processes are expected to
conform to the environmental regulations of the country of origin.

John Murray (Publishers)
338 Euston Road
London NW1 3BH

To my sister Ann and
my brothers Tom, Bob and David

Contents

CONTENTS

Illustrations

The author and publishers would like to thank the following for permission to reproduce illustrations: Plate 1, NLNP-WHPO-MPF-C8473-16A; 2, NLNP-WHPO-MPF-C8598-35A; 3, NLNP-

WHPO-MPF-C8544(12); 4, NLNP-WHPO-MPF-C8521-08/photo Byron Schumaker; 5, NLNP-WHPO-MPF-C8487-02A/photo Ollie Atkins; 6, NLNP-WHPO-MPF-C8588-14; 7, NLNP-WHPO-MPF-C8487-16A; 8, Ollie Atkins Collection, Special Collections & Archives, George Mason University; 9, NLNP-WHPO-MPF-8649(01)/photo Rich Remsberg; 10, NLNP-WHPO-MPF-C8616-29; 11 and 20, Time & Life Pictures/Getty Images; 12, NLNP-WHPO-MPF-C8488(02A); 13, NLNP-WHPO-MPF-C8487-30A; 14, NLNP-WHPO-MPF-C8543-16A; 15, NLNP-WHPO-MPF-C8546-13A; 16, NLNP-WHPO-MPF-C8520(05A); 17, NLNP-WHPO-MPF-C8518-04; 18, NLNP-WHPO-MPF-C8549(25A)/photo Joe McCary; 19, NLNP-WHPO-MPF-C8530-13; 21, NLNP-WHPO-MPF-C8635(18); 22, Mike Lien/The New York Times/Redux.

Acknowledgements

In writing this book, I have accumulated many debts of gratitude. I have used, and probably abused, the wonderful libraries at the University of Toronto, especially Robarts and its inter-library loan facility, and the Graham Library at Trinity College. That College, of which I have been lucky enough to be the provost, gave me time and support to work on this book, and I am very grateful to its Board of Trustees, to my two marvellous assistants, Brenda Duchesne and Jean McNeill, and to my generous colleagues, in particular Geoffrey Seaborn, Derek Allen and Bruce Bowden, who took over my responsibilities when I went on research leave.

I have had outstanding research assistants, among them Erin Black, Jake Hirsch-Allen, Sadia Rafiqiddin, Rebecca Snow and Kate Snow. Early on Maria Banda did an invaluable search of the available literature. Wynne Lawrence carried on her work and wrestled my bibliography into shape. Matthew Hogan not only searched the National Archives in Washington for me but proved to be an inspired picture researcher. Andrew Galbraith was indefatigable in finding Chinese books in Beijing and Hong Kong and Tony Yixi Zeng and Jonathan Jen-fu Yang researched and translated Chinese sources. In Beijing, Joseph Caron, the Canadian ambassador, and his colleagues gave me invaluable assistance in making contacts with Chinese academics and diplomats, and the Chinese People's Institute of Foreign Affairs was gracious enough to be my host. Herbert Levin and Robert Edmonds, both of whom have first-hand experience of dealing with China as diplomats, gave me the benefits of their insights and helped me to make contact with several of those who participated in the events of the early 1970s. Thanks too to all those whom I list elsewhere who generously agreed to give up their time and allow me to interview them.

A number of friends have given me much valuable advice and help, and I would like to single out in particular Bernie Frolic, Blair Seaborn and Peter Snow. I have benefited greatly from my conversations over the years with Conrad Black, Bob Bothwell and Allan Gotlieb about international relations and American politics and with Tom Rawksi, Evelyn Sakakida Rawski and Alfred Chan about Chinese history and politics. I am also grateful to James Mann and Rosemary Foot for taking time to give me their insights and advice. Jennifer Polk kindly located the *Star Trek* quotation for me. If I were to list all those who fed me meals and gave me drinks and who put up with me when I was absent-minded, these acknowledgements would be very long indeed, but I hope they know how grateful I am.

This is the first book where I have worked closely with an agent, or rather agents; Caroline Dawnay, Emma Parry and Michael Levine not only give their profession a good name but they are full of wise advice and, when it is needed, encouragement. I have been equally lucky in my publishers and editors: Grant McIntyre, Peter James, Caro Westmore, Roland Philipps and Lucy Dixon at John Murray; David Davidar, Diane Turbide, Elizabeth McKay and Eliza Marciniak at Penguin Canada, and Gina Centrello, Kate Medina, Robin Rolewicz and Benjamin Dreyer at Random House, and all the efficient and nice people who work with them. Finally, as I always must, I thank my family: my mother who read everything with a kindly but critical eye, my brothers and sister to whom this book is dedicated, and my many nephews and nieces.

For their consent to quote from material in their collections or for which they hold copyright, I would like to acknowledge and thank the following: Dr Henry Kissinger for *The White House Years*; the Association for Diplomatic Studies and Training for the interviews in their Foreign Affairs Oral History Program; and the executors of the estate of Richard M. Nixon for *RN: The Memoirs of Richard Nixon*. Every effort has been made to trace copyright holders, but in the event of any omissions the author would be grateful to hear from them.

Note on Transliteration

Most Chinese names are now transliterated into English using the pinyin system. Hence Peking has become Beijing. I have kept the older system only for names which are very well known already: Mao Tse-tung (pinyin Mao Zedong); Chou En-lai (Zhou Enlai); Chiang Kai-shek (Jiang Jieshi); Sun Yat-sen (Sun Yixian).

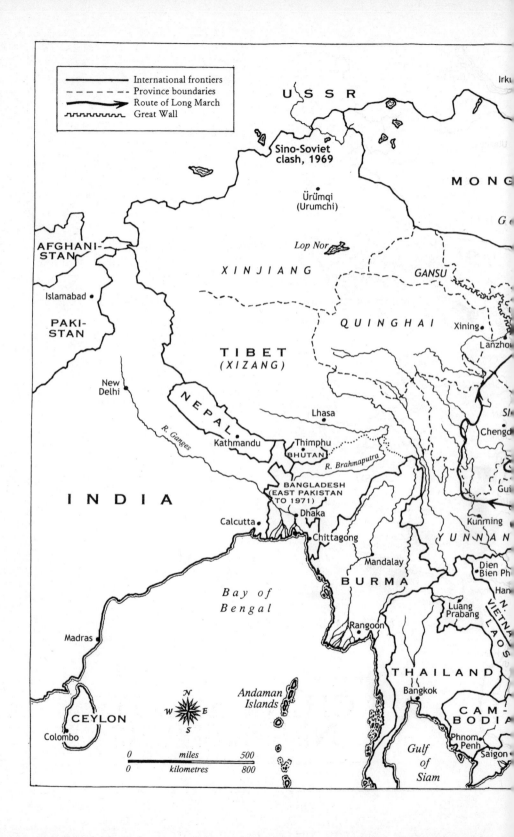

CHINA AND ITS NEIGHBOURS

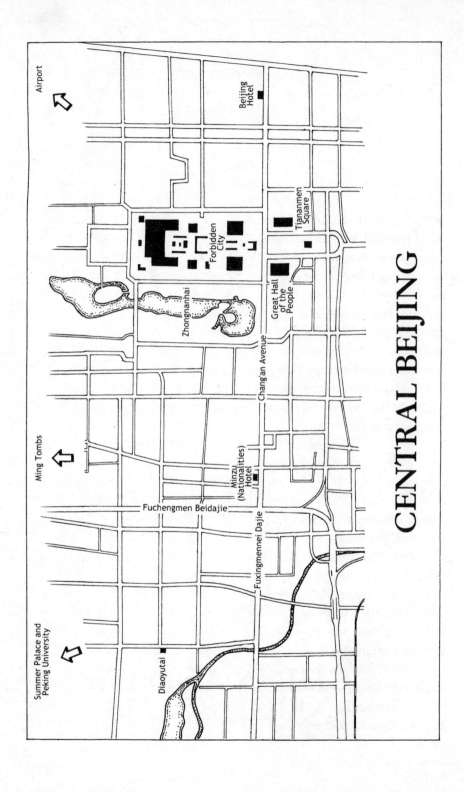

CENTRAL BEIJING

Introduction

ON A COLD February morning over a quarter of a century ago, Richard Nixon entered Mao Tse-tung's study in Beijing. The conversation that followed was slow and fitful because it went through interpreters. It was as one might expect of two people who were strangers but who had heard a lot about each other. They said how pleased they were to meet and exchanged polite compliments. They talked about mutual acquaintances: Chiang Kai-shek, the President of that other China in Taiwan, for example, or the former President of Pakistan, Yahya Khan, who had helped arrange for their meeting to take place. And they talked briefly about their mutual foe, the Soviet Union. They made some jokes, mainly at the expense of Nixon's companion Henry Kissinger, but they were generally serious.

Nixon tried to raise some matters which he felt were important. Mao waved him off and talked vaguely in what he called 'philosophical' terms. After about an hour, he looked at his watch and suggested that they had talked long enough. After a last exchange of pleasantries, Nixon took his leave. Neither man had said anything that surprised the other, and they had not come to any momentous conclusions. Yet their conversation was one of the most important occurrences in the recent past.

President Richard Nixon and Chairman Mao Tse-tung were well aware that they were making history that day in 1972. Both understood that their meeting and, indeed, Nixon's whole visit to China were important above all else for their symbolism. It was, after all, the first ever visit of an American president to China, an end to the long stand-off during which neither country had recognized the other. It was an earthquake in the Cold War landscape and meant that the Eastern Bloc no longer stood firm against the West.

I

One of the things the two men talked about was the past: particularly the events and the issues that had kept their two countries apart ever since the Communists took power in 1949. They also talked about politics, about Nixon's problems with his own right wing and the threat to his administration from the Democrats, and also about the recent upheaval in China when Mao's chosen successor, Lin Biao, it was claimed, had tried to stage a coup. They did not discuss the much greater turbulence of the Cultural Revolution which had started in 1966 when Mao called on the young to attack the old, whether values, traditions or people. Nixon, like an importunate guest, tried to bring the conversation around to his favourite topics, such as the future balance of power in Asia and in the world as a whole. Mao, the affable host, refused to be drawn and insisted on talking in vague generalities. They parted, with more polite words, both apparently expecting that they would meet again in a few days. They did not in fact meet again that time, although they were to do so on Nixon's subsequent visits to China.

International relations are about treaties, arms control, economic structures, courts, bilateral and multilateral deals, but they also involve gestures. Exchanges of ambassadors, public statements, state visits, these indicate the ways in which nations see themselves and how they see others. The meeting itself and Nixon's week in China which followed were partly about confirming what had already been negotiated, but they were also intended to underscore that there was a new era in the long and often stormy relationship between China and the United States and, indeed, between Asia and the West. The visit shook American allies such as Japan and Taiwan; it infuriated China's few friends in the world; and it worried the Soviet Union. We have been debating exactly what it really meant ever since.

The relationship between China and the West and between China and the United States more specifically has seen many stages. Long before the Thirteen Colonies had revolted against the British Empire, China had had indirect contact with the West in the shape of trade through Central Asia with the Roman Empire. In Europe's middle ages, a few brave or foolhardy travellers, Marco Polo among them, had managed to travel the overland route and see China for themselves. Later still, Jesuit missionaries had come to convert the Chinese court to Catholicism only to end up becoming quite Confucian in their outlook. They were followed by traders, impertinent bandits from the Chinese point of view, who clustered around the south coast of China to buy its silks, teas and porcelains – and eventually to sell the Chinese opium in return. American traders joined in enthusiastically. And missionaries, among them many Americans, arrived to save Chinese souls.

Until the start of the nineteenth century, the Chinese had dealt with Westerners, to their own satisfaction at least, as inferiors who were fortunate if they even had contact with the Middle Kingdom, the name the Chinese had for themselves, and enjoyed its high-quality products. That calm assumption of superiority was shaken and then shattered (although perhaps not irrevocably) when Western powers, strengthened by the products of the Industrial Revolution, forced their way into China and, in the end, helped to destroy the old order. By the end of the century, the ruling dynasty was on the point of collapse and China itself appeared to be on the edge of disappearing into one empire or another.

The United States had been part of that sorry story, but it had sometimes shown itself to be friendly. It had backed the continuation of a Chinese state. American missionaries who were actively founding schools and hospitals provided a growing constituency of support back home for a beleaguered China. There were other views of China in the United States, though, from the repository of the wisdom of the ages to the Yellow Peril, the source of powerful Oriental plots to overthrow American power and the American way of life. American attitudes to China continue to this day to oscillate between those two poles of fascination and sympathy on the one hand and fear and repugnance on the other.

Chinese attitudes have gone through similar evolutions, from suspicion and hostility to an admiration for American values such as democracy. The United States was China's ally during the Second World War, fighting Japan which had occupied so much of China. As the war ended, though, the United States slid from backing China to backing one faction, the Guomindang, against another, the Chinese Communists. When the Communists won the Civil War in 1949, they had every reason to fear and hate the Americans. That became open hostility during the Korean War when Chinese and American soldiers fought each other.

From that point on, neither side trusted the other and neither was seriously prepared to try to bridge the chasm between them. Chinese newspapers and Chinese officials railed against American imperialism. Chinese schoolchildren threw bean bags at an Uncle Sam whose long fangs dripped innocent blood, and Chinese streets and squares carried giant slogans of hatred and resistance. The United States reciprocated in full. It backed the Guomindang regime in Taiwan and its ludicrous claims to speak for the whole of China. It kept China – the People's Republic – out of the United Nations and other international bodies. At the Olympics, the Chinese athletes were those from Taiwan. American presidents referred contemptuously to the Reds and insisted that the capital of China was Beiping and not Beijing because that is what their allies in Taiwan still called it.

Occasionally there were hints that both sides would like to move away from what was becoming an increasingly tedious impasse, but something would always go wrong. An American pilot would be shot down on a spy mission over China; a Chinese diplomat would defect; and the insults would start up afresh. Then, in the 1960s, two events made the deep freeze even deeper. With Mao's Cultural Revolution, China virtually ceased to have a foreign policy at all as its diplomats were summoned home to be cleansed of imperfect attitudes. And the United States plunged headlong into Vietnam. With American troops pouring into South Vietnam and American planes bombing the North, China could not abandon its ally North Vietnam and engage in talks with its enemy.

The end of the 1960s brought shocks to both countries and their leaders, and, perhaps, a new sense of realism. The Chinese and, most importantly, Mao realized just how isolated they were in the world. Among China's neighbours only Pakistan was friendly and the Soviet Union was distinctly hostile, amassing vast armies along the common border and talking, none too quietly, about the possibility of a nuclear strike on China. The United States was not as friendless but it was newly aware of its own vulnerabilities. Vietnam had fuelled passionate debate and dissent at home, and, abroad, had made both American friends and enemies wonder just how strong the superpower really was.

President Nixon and Chairman Mao often take the credit for ending the absurd stand-off between their two countries, and they deserve it – but not all of it. The times were ripe for each side to make a move towards the other. In both countries there were influential voices saying that the advantages of a relationship, even a cool one, outweighed continuing non-recognition. For each the other was a card to play against the common enemy, the Soviet Union.

Bringing the United States and China together, though, was not easy. History, particularly recent history, stood in the way. National pride, too, was an impediment. The United States so often saw itself as the shining city on the hill, the repository of the right ways of managing a society and running an economy, its values those for all of humanity. The Chinese were not much different. If the old China of the dynasties had seen itself as the centre of the world and all other nations as subordinates, the new Communist one held itself out as the world's revolutionary vanguard with the thought of Chairman Mao as the only guide for the future.

Nixon's visit to China that February in 1972 had taken three years to arrange, three years of delicate feelers, of careful signals sent out and usually but not always received, of indirect contacts, of intense internal debates, and finally of direct negotiations. Henry Kissinger, Nixon's National Security Adviser, had made a secret trip to Beijing in the summer of 1971 and then a public one in the autumn to prepare the way for a visit by Nixon himself. He had discussed grand strategy with Chou En-lai, the Chinese Prime Minister, and, in sharp exchanges, the issues that still divided their two countries. Kissinger and Chou had also discussed the details of Nixon's coming trip. Was the American President a supplicant, asking to come to China, or were the Chinese inviting him? Such questions matter in international relations, especially between two countries each convinced that it is the more important.

The Chinese leadership, who had worked so hard to make China the centre of world revolution, now found themselves with the leader of the world's greatest capitalist nation coming to visit. The Americans, for their part, risked attacks from conservatives at home and possible humiliation in China. Both sides knew that they were taking a terrific gamble. On the one side lay a new relationship that would change the balance in international relations and, if all went well, produce great benefits. For the United States, a friendly China could put pressure on the recalcitrant North Vietnamese to negotiate an end to the war. For China, the relationship promised access to technology and vital strategic information. For both, the other provided a counterbalance to potential enemies, Japan and the Soviet Union in the case of China, the Soviet Union above all for the United States. If the trip went wrong, then the recriminations and the renewed suspicions would send Chinese–American relations back to where they had been at the start of the 1960s.

To the end of his life, through the long dreary years after the disgrace of Watergate, Nixon maintained that the opening of relations between the United States and the People's Republic of China was the high point of his time in office. Good relations between the two countries, so he held, were a way not only of keeping the Soviet Union under control but of bringing stability and peace to Asia and indeed to the world. As he prepared to leave Shanghai at the end of his momentous trip, he made a toast. 'We have been here a week. This was the week that changed the world.'[1] Typical bombast, one might say. Does it really matter now that Nixon and Mao chatted among the antimacassars and spittoons of Mao's study? That the Cold War, itself now vanished, saw a realignment of forces? Or that the United States and China finally began to trade with each other and exchange visitors?

Of course it matters. We worry, as we must about terrorism, about the potential for conflict between the values of liberal democracy and religious fundamentalism. We look at the instability in the Middle East with concern. We must not, however, forget Asia. With its vast population, its wealth and its extraordinary rate of economic growth, it promises to be the continent of the future. Already the edge in technology, and the lead in development and power, are shifting eastwards. Asia will be at the centre of the world again. Yet there will be no peace for Asia or for the world unless those two great Pacific powers, the United States and China, the one supreme today and the other perhaps tomorrow, find ways to work with each other. To understand their relationship we need to go back to 1972, to the moment when it started anew.

I

Setting Out

O N THURSDAY 17 FEBRUARY 1972, President and Mrs Nixon
came on to the south lawn of the White House where a
helicopter waited for them. A small crowd, among them the Vice-
President Spiro Agnew and his wife, Republican and Democratic
Congressmen and the two Nixon daughters Tricia and Julie, saw
them off as they started the first leg of their long trip to China. The
brief ceremony was carried live on American radio and television.
Nixon spoke briefly. He was making, he said, 'a journey for peace',
but, he added, he was under no illusions that '20 years of hostility
between the People's Republic of China and the United States of
America are going to be swept away by one week of talks that we will
have there'. Nevertheless, he was going in an optimistic spirit: 'if
there is a postscript that I hope might be written with regard to this
trip, it would be the words on the plaque which was left on the moon
by our first astronauts when they landed there: "We came in peace for
all mankind."'[1] It was classic Nixon, that mixture of pragmatism and
grandiloquence.

Inside the waiting plane at Andrews Air Force Base, the rest of
Nixon's party, which included his Secretary of State, William Rogers,
and his National Security Adviser, Henry Kissinger, watched the ceremonies on television. Winston Lord, a young aide to Kissinger, joked
nervously that if the plane blew up they would all see themselves
going sky high. As Nixon was boarding the plane, one of the waiting
reporters handed him an atlas of China which had the seal of the CIA
on its cover. 'Do you think they'll let me in with this?' asked the
President in a rare joke with the press, as he climbed aboard Air Force
One. He, the man who had made his name as a dogged and vocifer-
ous anti-Communist, was reversing two decades of American policy

by travelling to Beijing, into the very heart of Chinese Communism. As the plane climbed into the air, Nixon, so he said in his memoirs, felt like an explorer: 'We were embarking upon a voyage of philosophical discovery as uncertain, and in some respects as perilous, as the voyages of geographical discovery of a much earlier time period.'[2]

He was taking a considerable gamble, that conservatives at home would not attack him and that liberals would not be disappointed in the results of his trip. He was pleased by the many fervent messages he had received wishing him well – but also concerned. 'I told Henry that I thought it really was a question of the American people being hopelessly and almost naïvely for peace, even at any price.' Kissinger was, as always, reassuring. The Americans were excited by the boldness of Nixon's move.[3]

Nixon also did not know whether the Chinese themselves would overcome their decades of hostility to the United States and make his visit a success. Although every detail of his trip had been negotiated with the Chinese, he did not know, when he clambered aboard his plane, whether he would have a meeting with Chairman Mao Tse-tung, who, from his seclusion in Beijing, still controlled China. If he came back to the United States without meeting Mao, his trip would be regarded as a failure, and, worse, a humiliation for the United States.

After the trip was over, the Nixon people always maintained that they felt quite confident about a meeting. 'Well, we knew in our gut', said Winston Lord, 'that Mao would meet Nixon.' The Americans had no firm promise, though, only vague assurances from the Chinese. 'I know', Lord remembered, 'that we made unilateral statements that Nixon would, of course, be seeing Mao. We said that we would like to know when this would be, but we knew that this was going to happen. It would have been unthinkable if it didn't.'[4]

It was a gamble that Nixon was prepared to take because he felt that it was crucial for the United States. He had always taken risks, as a young soldier in the army when he passed the time (and made a lot of money) playing poker, and later as a politician. He had not spent those long and often difficult years making his way to the presidency to be a caretaker. And the United States needed some good news. The war in Vietnam had cost the country much, in lives, in money and in reputation. It had led to deep divisions at home and a loss of influence and prestige abroad. The failure of the United States to finish, much less win, the war had contributed to a decline in American power. But it had only contributed; the extraordinary military and economic dominance which the United States had possessed from the end of the Second World War to the start of the 1960s could not last for ever.

It had been in part the product of the times. In 1945, other world powers lay defeated or, like Britain, so weakened by the huge costs of victory that they could no longer play a world role. The Soviet Union had great military strength and, by 1949, its own atomic bomb, but it had to make good the hideous costs of Hitler's invasion and the war. By the end of the 1960s, however, Western Europe and Japan had revived. The Soviet Union, although it would never be an economic power to match the United States, was investing heavily in its military. Newly independent countries such as India were playing their parts in the world. China's potential remained a question mark; the Communists had brought unity, but for much of the time since 1949 Mao's policies had sent the country down wasteful and destructive paths. Yet, despite that, the Chinese revolution had become a model and an inspiration throughout what was coming to be known as the Third World, those undeveloped countries emerging from foreign empires or attempting to free themselves from foreign domination.

Throughout the 1960s, Nixon worked on a political career which most people thought was over after his defeat by John F. Kennedy in the presidential race of 1960 and his even more humiliating failure to win the governorship of California in 1962. And he continued to develop his ideas on his favourite area of public policy, international relations. In the summer of 1967, he was invited to California to give the Lakeside Speech at Bohemian Grove, an institution which could exist only in North America, where rich and powerful men enjoy the arts and the simple, contemplative life for a couple of weeks in carefully rustic luxury. Nixon later said that he got more pleasure out of his speech – 'the first milestone on my road to the presidency' – than any other in his career. In what would become known as the Nixon Doctrine, he argued that the United States could no longer afford to fight other nations' wars. Although the US would offer support, its allies must be prepared to stand on their own feet. On the other hand, there were encouraging signs on the world scene. The Soviet leaders were still striving for Communist domination of the world but they did not want war with the United States. Moreover the Communist monolith had broken apart and China and the Soviet Union were at loggerheads. Nixon had come to this realization, he told Chou when they finally met, in those years in the 1960s when he was out of office and travelling about the world.[5]

Nixon, it has often been said, especially by his supporters, was the only American president of the late twentieth century who could have taken advantage of the split in the Communist world and made the breakthrough in China–US relations. The man and the times were right for each other. As Nixon himself once told an interviewer, the mark of a leader 'is whether he can give history a nudge'. For the United States to refuse to deal with a major Asian power, one more-over which was the world's most populous country, had never made much sense. As Nixon himself had written in a 1967 article in *Foreign Affairs*, the leading American foreign policy journal, 'Taking the long view, we simply cannot afford to leave China forever outside the family of nations, there to nurture its fantasies, cherish its hates and threaten its neighbours.' In a revealing comparison, he said that deal-ing with China was like dealing with angry blacks in America's ghettos. 'In each case a potentially destructive force has to be curbed; in each case an outlaw element has to be brought within the law; in each case dialogues have to be opened.' In the short term, China would simply have to be contained; in the longer term, though, it ought to be brought back into the community of nations. His article did not show the slightest sympathy for Chinese Communism, nor did it hold out much hope for an immediate change in China's relations with the world. By the time he was president, though, he was starting to become more optimistic. In the election campaign, he repeated his warnings about the dangers of leaving China outside the international system and referred obliquely to it in his Inaugural Address in January 1969: 'We seek an open world – open to ideas, open to the exchange of goods and people – a world in which no people, great or small, will live in angry isolation.'[6]

By the early 1970s, both the United States and China realized that the world had changed and that they needed new friends. As Henry

Kissinger wrote years later, 'For both sides, necessity dictated that [a] rapprochement occur, and the attempt would have had to be made no matter who governed in either country.'[7] And while public opinion did not matter in China, it did in the United States, and Americans, by and large, no longer felt the same antipathy towards and fear of Chinese Communism that had been such a feature of American politics in the 1950s.

Moreover, Nixon had banked the political capital he needed at home. Dealing with Communists was always tricky during the Cold War. American public opinion had been slow to recognize the threat from the Soviet Union immediately after the Second World War, but, once convinced that the threat was real, it had become seized of the idea that Communists were very powerful and that they were everywhere, in Russia, of course, throughout Europe, in Asia and throughout American society. Nixon himself had ridden to power by calling to those fears, no matter how exaggerated they sometimes were. His anti-Communist credentials were beyond challenge. From the time he first entered politics in California, running against the liberal Democrat Jerry Voorhis in 1946, he had charged that his opponents were soft on Communism or worse. Nixon's campaigning, with its insinuation and accusation and its reliance on unproven statistics and stories, won him the name 'Tricky Dick', but it worked. Americans listened to his repeated and forceful warnings about the threat that Communism posed to the United States and to American society. They had watched as he stood up to Communists around the world, whether swapping boasts with the Soviet leader Nikita Khrushchev in Moscow or defying the mobs who spat at him and tried to turn his car over in Venezuela.

Nixon's other great advantage was that he had the determination, the intelligence and the knowledge to sense the currents in history and to take advantage of them. And he loved foreign policy. Indeed he much preferred it to dealing with importunate Congressmen and the minutiae of schools or highway building. 'I've always thought this country could run itself domestically without a President,' he told the journalist Theodore White in an interview during the presidential campaign. 'All you need is a competent Cabinet to run the country at home. You need a President for foreign policy; no Secretary of State is really important; the President makes foreign policy.'[8] While presidents always gave State of the Union addresses to Congress, Nixon started making annual reports on the world situation. And he made it quite clear from the moment he took office that he was going to use an enhanced National Security Council to run major foreign policy issues out of the White House. His first appointment the morning after his inauguration in January 1969 was with his National Security Adviser, Henry Kissinger. The first formal meeting he called was of his new NSC. Six weeks later, he was off on his first foreign trip, to see European leaders – among them a man he revered, Charles de Gaulle.

In the long and rambling conversations he had with his few intimates, Nixon returned constantly to the subject of the great leader, the man who boldly went on ahead, dragging his nation with him and changing the world. De Gaulle, of course. Winston Churchill, a favourite it seems with many American presidents including George Bush junior. Or General George Patton – the movie with George C. Scott was one of Nixon's favourites and he kept a biography of Patton beside his bed. Such great leaders, in Nixon's view, were usually lonely, often misunderstood, but they worked indefatigably nevertheless to advance the interests of their nations. 'There were never tired decisions,' he told Kissinger in one of their phone conversations, 'only tired commanders.'[9]

The world, with its great issues, was for Nixon where the leader could show what he was made of. He had prepared himself thoroughly for this moment. As vice-president, he had travelled more than any of his predecessors and, in the 1960s, before his run for president, when he was meant to be a private citizen, he had toured the world incessantly, meeting with local leaders and browbeating American diplomats as though he were still in office. A low-ranking foreign service officer who had to entertain him in Hong Kong remembered his 'tremendous intellectual curiosity'. Nixon asked question after question, 'picking my brain for everything and anything I could tell him about China'. Marshall Green, later Assistant Secretary of State with responsibility for East Asia during the Nixon administration, met Nixon in Indonesia in 1967 and had long conversations with him which Nixon tape-recorded for later reference. 'I remembered him as the best informed on foreign affairs of all the luminaries who visited Jakarta during my four years there.'[10] The result of all the travel and the hours of questioning and conversation was that Nixon was the best-prepared president on foreign policy until Clinton. He also knew many heads of state and foreign ministers personally.

Nixon has often been described as a realist, coldly calculating the best way to advance American interests in a dangerous and anarchic world. And indeed he could often sound like the great nineteenth-century British statesman Lord Palmerston, whose formulation remains the credo of realists: 'We have no eternal allies, and we have no perpetual enemies. Our interests are eternal and perpetual.' In 1970, in his report to Congress, Nixon explained that the first goal of his administration's foreign policy was to support American interests. 'The more that policy is based on a realistic assessment of our and others' interests, the more effective our role in the world can be. We are not involved in the world because we have commitments; we have commitments because we are involved. Our interests must shape our commitments, rather than the other way around.' Great powers always looked out for their own national interests, he told his White House staff just after the announcement that he was to visit China, 'or else they're played for suckers by those powers that do'.[11] Interests could coincide, and it was the wise statesman who could see this and be ready to negotiate.

Nixon chose the portraits of the three presidents he most admired for the cabinet office in the White House. Dwight Eisenhower was a revered leader in war and peace, loved by Americans as Nixon never would be. Theodore Roosevelt was the fighter, the man who willed himself to be strong and brave. Nixon often quoted admiringly his image of the bloodstained and weary man in the arena, 'who does actually strive to do the deed, who knows the great enthusiasms, the great devotions, who spends himself in a worthy cause, who at the best knows in the end the triumphs of high achievement and who at worst, if he fails, at least fails while daring greatly'. (Nixon used that in his resignation speech.) The one he identified with most, though, was the Democrat President Woodrow Wilson. Wilson was not only brilliant intellectually but 'a man of thought who could act'. Wilson, so Nixon saw it, had also worked for peace in the world. 'For the first time, because the people of the world want peace, and the leaders of the world are afraid of war, the times are on the side of peace.' Although the sentence comes from Nixon's inaugural address, it could just as easily have been uttered by Wilson himself. For his desk in the White House, Nixon chose Wilson's. Like others of Nixon's gestures, it went went slightly awry. The desk, it later turned out, had belonged to another Wilson altogether – Henry, a shoemaker who had risen to be Ulysses S. Grant's vice-president.[12]

Nixon, unlike many of his more conservative Republican supporters, was not an isolationist. He maintained that the United States should have joined the League of Nations in the inter-war years and that it had done the right thing in joining the United Nations after the Second World War. He had supported the Marshall Plan in the 1940s to aid Western Europe; he was in favour of committing American troops to the North Atlantic Treaty Organization; and in the 1950s he was prepared to see the United States join alliances around the world in order to contain Communism. Indeed he worried that the experience of Vietnam and the preoccupation of the country's elites with domestic problems would turn the United States inwards. He also believed that the United States was and ought to be a force for good in the world. As he told Kissinger, 'nations must have great ideas or they cease to be great'. His big idea was to lead the United States to build permanent peace in the world. In his inaugural address, which he largely wrote himself (as he did all his major speeches), he called on his fellow Americans and on the world: 'Let us take as our goal: Where peace is unknown, make it welcome; where peace is fragile, make it strong; where peace is temporary, make it permanent.'[13]

Then and since, his critics have dismissed such rhetoric as Nixon's cynical attempt to conceal his own moral vacuum. That is wrong. Nixon did many immoral things in his life but he longed to be good. In the notes which he wrote endlessly to himself on his favourite yellow legal pads, he exhorted himself to provide moral leadership, to be the national conscience of his country. If he often behaved like his father, who was a loud-mouthed and opinionated bully, he wished to be more like his saintly mother. A devout Quaker, she gave all her children a profoundly religious upbringing. For decades, Nixon carried a note in his wallet which she had given him in 1953 when he became vice-president. 'I know that you will keep your relationship with your Maker as it should be, for after all, that as you must know is the most important thing in this life.'[14]

Even historians who disapprove of psycho-history find themselves tempted irresistibly when it comes to Richard Nixon. It is partly that he inspired such strong feelings. It is partly the contradictions. The statesman of distinction who, as his tapes revealed, could talk with insight and understanding about the role of the United States in the world and then flail the next moment at his enemies, real or imagined, in crude, racist and scatological terms. (Thanks to those tapes, whose existence Nixon seems to have forgotten about from day to day, we know a lot about a deeply private and secretive man.) The man who wanted to be great, who told himself at the start of 1970 'Be worthy of 1st man in nation and in world', yet who was capable of such petty meanness and did so much to damage American public life. He was vicious and relentless in attacking others; in one of his first campaigns, he successfully painted Helen Gahagan Douglas as a Communist sym-pathizer, 'pink right down to her underwear'. Yet he later told a British journalist, 'I'm sorry about that episode. I was a very young man.' When the regret was reported, though, he denied it furiously.[15]

He came from small-town America and liked to see himself as an Horatio Alger figure, triumphing against all odds. He talked about the simple values of his youth: hard work, thrift, piety, sobriety, decency. Yet his own finances and his acquisition of properties in Florida and California raised many eyebrows, especially when he spent govern-ment money on refurbishing them. He spoke, so he always said, to ordinary American men and women, yet he could also say 'You've got to be a little evil to understand those people out there. You have to have known the dark side of life to understand those people.' He realized that middle Americans did not care about what he loved most – foreign policy. 'They don't know anything about what you're doing on SALT [Strategic Arms Limitation Talks] and all these other things,' he said more in amusement than anger, 'they just want things to simmer down and be quiet, and to them we have not accom-plished very much.'[16]

He loathed the hippies of the 1960s with their drugs, their rejec-tion of work and their sexual freedom. On the other hand, he was fascinated by the sexual peccadilloes of others. He ordered a round-the-clock watch on Senator Edward Kennedy in the hopes of catching him with, as Nixon put it, a 'babe'. He made clumsy jokes about Kissinger's reputedly extravagant sex life. He envied and even admired John F. Kennedy, but also railed against the East Coast establishment and the Georgetown intellectuals of Washington. His tastes remained resolutely middle brow. He loved American musicals and wept unabashedly at *Carousel*. (He was particularly moved by the song 'You'll Never Walk Alone'.) One of his favourite movies was *Around the World in 80 Days:* 'Watch – watch this!' he would urge the audience in the White House screening room. 'Here comes the elephant!'[17]

According to an aide who knew him well, he deliberately played down his own intellectual side to portray himself as a good old boy. He told bad locker-room jokes. He talked incessantly about sports. That part was not an act; he loved sports, especially football. When he was at college, he turned out for the team, year after year, although he rarely got to play. At practices a skinny Nixon would face much bigger players, but the coach would not let up on him or them. 'So I'd have to knock the little guy for a loop,' remembered another player who had been responsible for blocking. 'Oh, my gosh did he take it.'[18]

Nixon always prided himself on his iron determination and his capacity for work. Like the ninety-nine-pound weakling in the Charles Atlas advertisement, he had shown those who once laughed at or underestimated him. 'If you are reasonably intelligent,' he told an old friend from his law-school days, 'and if your anger is deep enough and strong enough, you learn that you can change those attitudes by excellence, personal gut performance, while those who have every-thing are sitting on their fat butts.' Kissinger, who came to know him well, said that Nixon always believed, though, that he was going to lose in the end. Once, as Nixon waited for a flight in Saigon, he told an American diplomat that it was sure to be late. 'If anything bad can happen to me, it will.' Tom Wicker, who wrote one of the more sympathetic biographies, watched him in the 1960 campaign: 'painfully conscious of slights and failures, a man who has imposed upon him-self a self-control so rigid as to be all but visible.'[19]

The career he had chosen placed a terrific strain on him, and, from time to time, it showed. When he was tired and tense, even one drink would tip him over into slurred and rambling speeches. He often had trouble sleeping, and his colleagues grew accustomed to the middle-of-the-night phone calls. Unsubstantiated rumours circulated for years that Nixon had seen a psychoanalyst or that his doctor had treated him for impotence. One of his doctors, in New York, talked mysteriously in his old age about Nixon's neurotic symptoms and how difficult it was to discuss them with a patient 'so very inhibited'. It is hard to know how seriously to take such stories. It is certainly true, though, that many people found Nixon puzzling. 'The strangest man I'd ever met,' said one White House assistant. Kissinger, usually cautious in public, once told a reporter that he found Nixon 'odd, artificial, and unpleasant'.[20]

'I do not recall a moment', said Herb Klein, his Director of Communications, 'when I saw him completely lost in happiness.' Nixon could never forget past humiliations and setbacks. As he told Chou En-lai when they finally met, 'an election loss was really more painful than a physical wound in war'. The former only wounded the body, the latter the spirit. On the other hand, adversity gave you 'strength and character'. All he wanted, so he told Chou, 'was a life in which I had just one more victory than defeat'.[21] It was a curious and revealing way to talk to someone he scarcely knew.

Nixon went through agonies even as vice-president and when he was running for the presidential nominations in 1960 and 1968, because Eisenhower, whom he admired so much, would never wholeheartedly support or endorse him. Although he prided himself on his self-control, there would be moments of uncontrollable rage or self-pity. He broke down famously in public in 1962 at the end of his unsuccessful campaign for governor of California; in a rambling statement he blamed the press for his loss. 'You won't have Nixon to kick around anymore, because, gentlemen, this is my last press conference . . .'[22]

It was not, of course. 'Once you get into this great stream of history,' he wrote in *Six Crises*, about what he considered the most significant incidents in his career, 'you can't get out.' Why would a man who was uncomfortable with strangers choose a life in politics? 'It doesn't come naturally to me to be a buddy-buddy boy,' he told a journalist, 'I can't really let my hair down with anyone.' What drove him on after so many setbacks: his narrow loss to Kennedy in 1960, his humiliating loss for the governorship of California and, of course, being driven from office by the Watergate scandal? Who or where was the real Nixon? Was it the man who barked orders at his aides to fire this son-of-a-bitch and to get that opponent? The man who wrote, in the same 1970 New Year's memorandum to himself, 'Cool – Strong – Organized – Temperate – Exciting'? Or, the man whom an aide, a liberal Jewish lawyer from New York, remembered for his 'intelligence, idealism and generosity' and whom, for all the ranting about Jews on the tapes, the aide never believed to be anti-Semitic? Russell Baker, the writer, once came up with a striking image: of Nixon as a row of suits which came out of the closet in turn and which ran from the demagogic anti-Communist to the elder statesman.[23]

When he was at college, Nixon loved acting. Many of the journalists who followed him over the years felt that he had never stopped. He could be brilliant, drawing crowds to their feet with his speeches. When he talked to his fellow statesmen, he was wise and dignified. But the acts were not always convincing. Eisenhower's secretary thought that Nixon 'sometimes seems like a man who is acting a nice man rather than being one'. In public appearances, he sweated too much, gestured stiffly, wrung his hands together until his knuckles went white. When he was president his staff tried to set up opportunities to show him being relaxed and spontaneous, as the Kennedys, who fascinated and infuriated Nixon, so easily were. Bob Haldeman, his chief of staff, got him an Irish setter but it had to be cajoled with a trail of dog biscuits to come near him. A scene staged to display to the press a rugged Nixon strolling by the Pacific Ocean somehow did not come off with polished leather shoes and dress trousers. When visitors came to his office, he tried to set them at ease, but when he brought out a memento, a pin or a pen perhaps, he thrust it out awkwardly with one of his unfunny jokes. 'He was a man totally lacking in personal grace,' said a senior State Department official, 'with no sense of the proper distance to keep in human relations.' Yet when he gave out posthumous Congressional Medals of Honor (something he shrank from doing), he was direct and simple with the families.[24]

He loved the idea of being president, although he found some of the reality such as cabinet meetings tedious. (He simply gave up holding them.) He loved being greeted abroad as a head of state. He loved living in the White House. He tried to enhance its already considerable pomp with new uniforms in white and gold for the White House police. (After press comment compared them to costumes in comic operas, the uniforms quietly disappeared; the elaborate hats popped up later at a rock concert.)[25]

He knew how he wanted to be seen: the charm of a Kennedy; the leadership of a Churchill or a de Gaulle. 'At his best in a crisis. Cool. Unflappable,' were the qualities he wanted the press to see, so he told Kissinger. 'Steely but subtle.' He must be mysterious: 'always like the iceberg, you see only the tip'. His staff had orders to stress how hard the man Nixon referred to as 'N.' or the 'P.' worked, how he needed only a few hours of sleep, how focused and energetic he was. This was true, but not always. Nixon was easily distracted. 'P. is all of a sudden enamored with the use of the Dictaphone,' Haldeman wrote in his diary one day, 'and is spewing out memos by the carload.' Nixon fussed endlessly about the details for state banquets or the latest story in the press.[26]

'All people think the P's doing an excellent job,' he told Haldeman in 1972 just before the China trip, 'but no one loves him, fears him, or hates him, and he needs to have all three.' He had the last two, at least in some circles. He suspected, though, that even his own staff did not take his orders seriously when, like the Red Queen, he demanded that this person be fired at once and that office be closed down immediately. If sheer hard work and attention to image could have done it, Nixon would have had love too, but he knew well and sometimes despaired that he was not naturally charismatic.[27]

He was generous to his staff, but he seems not to have known how to treat them as human beings. He never thought, for example, to ask Haldeman how many children he had. And although his chief of staff spent hours of every day with him, the President only ever invited him once with his wife to a purely social dinner with Mrs Nixon. But then Nixon had few purely social occasions or friends. Haldeman, who tried to anticipate everything, once tried to find a friend for him, someone he could confide in. Nixon was astonished. In any case, he already had the perfect friend in Bebe Rebozo, 'a genial, discreet sponge', who sat silently for hours while Nixon held forth.[28]

Otherwise it is difficult to know whom he was close to. His daughters certainly; perhaps his wife, Pat, although he rarely showed any interest in her after the first few years of their marriage. He had thousands of acquaintances but very few close friends.

He often talked about his mother, widely held to be a saintly figure, who suffered the early deaths of two of her children. But she was a cold saint, doing her duty uncomplainingly but never showing her children open affection and warmth. Nixon told his sympathetic biographer Jonathan Aitken that his mother had never kissed him. When Aitken seemed surprised, Nixon grew angry. Aitken's reaction, Nixon felt, was like something from 'one of those rather pathetic Freudian psychiatrists'. Yet he wept in Billy Graham's arms when she died. Henry Kissinger, who could be so cruel about Nixon, once said, 'He would have been a great man had somebody loved him.'[29]

The area where Nixon came closest to real greatness, in his own mind and those of his defenders, was foreign relations. As he took off from Washington that February day in 1972, he was flying not just towards China but towards, so he thought, a shift for the better in the United States' position in the world. Perhaps even more important to him was the historic nature of his trip. He talked about it incessantly in the months before his departure. He was the first American president ever to visit China and he was going to a country which was a mystery to most of the world. 'A trip to China', he told journalists, 'is like going to the moon.'[30] He was determined that it would go well.

'I know of no Presidential trip', wrote Kissinger in his memoirs, 'that was as carefully planned nor of any President who ever prepared himself so conscientiously.' Nixon summoned the venerable and mendacious André Malraux from Paris, who, after a brief encounter with Mao, claimed to be a China expert. Malraux assured Nixon that, if de Gaulle stood in his place, he would salute him as well for the step he was taking: 'You are about to attempt one of the most important things of our century.' Kissinger was less impressed. 'Unfortunately Malraux was grossly out of date about China.' He did admit, with the respect of a connoisseur, that Malraux was wonderfully eloquent. John Scali, a press adviser on foreign affairs in the White House, was blunt: 'I felt I was listening to the views of a romantic, vain, old man who was weaving obsolete views into a special framework for the world as he wished it to be.' Nixon, however, was enthralled, even though the sage's severe facial tic made his every statement painful to listen to: 'Time had not dimmed the brilliance of his thought or the quickness of his wit.'[31] And Malraux had been a friend of the Kennedys.

The CIA gave the President analyses of Mao's and Chou's personalities. Old China hands sent in lots of unsolicited advice. The State Department drew up background papers on all the outstanding disputes, on property for example, between the United States and China and on major policy issues. (It is not clear Nixon ever saw these, because they had to go through Kissinger who had no love for the Department.) Kissinger and his NSC staff prepared their own briefing books and sent the President extracts from books and articles which they felt he should read. Nixon did his homework meticulously, bearing down particularly hard in the week just before his trip.[32]

On the plane, Nixon and Mrs Nixon, along with his close advisers including Henry Kissinger, sat in comfort at the front; the State Department officials were relegated to the back of the plane. The flight to China was carefully planned so that Nixon would arrive as well rested as possible. He also took advantage of the time to go over his papers and practise using chopsticks. While two planeloads of journalists went on ahead to Shanghai, Air Force One (or, as Nixon preferred to call it, especially for this trip, the Spirit of '76) stopped in Hawaii at an air force base for a couple of days. The President's party, including Kissinger, went off to stay with the commanding officer while the lower ranks stayed in the greater comfort of a local luxury hotel. Clare Boothe Luce, who with her husband Henry Luce had used their publications such as *Time* to support the other China, the one in Taiwan, gave a dinner for some of the party at her spectacular house overlooking the Pacific. 'You liberals', she said, 'don't really understand this trip.' But, she added, times were changing and the Communist Chinese would recognize that the United States had always been a friend to China.[33] On 21 February, with military music and hula girls, the plane took off for Guam, where there was another overnight stop. That left a short flight to Shanghai for the next day. In Shanghai, after a brief welcome and a rapid breakfast, Chinese pilots came on board (this had been the subject of intensive negotiations) and piloted the plane for its final leg.

The presidential plane landed at the civilian airport in Beijing at 11.30 a.m., an hour chosen carefully to ensure that Nixon's arrival would make prime-time television news in all time zones back in the United States. Nixon had been worrying about his first moments in China for days. On the flight earlier that day from Guam to Shanghai he had gone over the details yet again with his chief of staff. 'He's very concerned', wrote Haldeman in his diary, 'that the whole operation at Peking airport be handled flawlessly since that will be the key picture of the whole trip.'[34]

2

Arrival

O N THE MORNING of Monday 21 February 1972 Air Force One flew northwards from Shanghai towards Beijing. Nixon anxiously went over the arrangements for his arrival and pestered Kissinger with questions about the Communist Chinese. In the heart of Beijing, an old and sick Mao Tse-tung woke up early and had his first shave and haircut for months. As the plane neared the Chinese capital, Mao's subordinates phoned him repeatedly to report its progress.

The morning was cold and grey and slightly hazy. At the last moment before the plane's wheels touched down, Chou En-lai, China's Prime Minister, dressed in a dark-blue overcoat over a grey Mao suit, appeared on the runway with a party of about twenty-five officials. An honour guard, some in the drab green of the People's Liberation Army and others in the blue of the navy, marched out to join them together with a military band. The red stars which glinted in their caps were the ubiquitous symbol of the new order in China. Two solitary flags, one the American, the other the Chinese, hung limp in the still air. The only other witnesses to the historic arrival were American journalists, who had been sent on ahead. Otherwise the airport was largely empty. A Canadian diplomat, one of the handful of foreign representatives in Beijing, had asked whether he could attend the welcoming ceremonies. A Chinese official told him that it would be necessary to get a special pass. How, asked the Canadian, was he to get his pass? 'Special passes will not be issued.'[1]

On the terminal building, one of the ubiquitous big character signs carried a famous phrase from an article Mao had written in 1949 attacking the United States: 'Make Trouble Fail, Make Trouble Fail Again, Until their Doom / This is the nature of all imperialists and capitalists and they cannot go against it.' Another said simply, 'China 5, US 1'; it was not clear whether this referred to war or to the recently completed ping-pong tournament which had been held in Beijing. From inside the plane, the head of the President's security radioed his agent who had come with the advance party to ask his usual question on presidential visits: 'What about the crowd?' The answer came back, 'There is no crowd.' 'Did you say, "No crowd"?' 'That is an affirmative.' Nixon, joked one reporter, was enjoying his best reception since he went to the annual meeting of American trade unionists.[2]

The Chinese were making a point, but what it was remained obscure. Perhaps it was to show that even the head of the most powerful nation in the world did not impress them. Perhaps because they feared that the Americans would be cool. Perhaps to demonstrate that the trip was strictly about business and not friendship. After all, the authorities could summon up pliable crowds when they wished. Haile Selassie, soon to be deposed from the throne of Ethiopia, had visited Beijing in October 1971. For him, the airport had been alive with dancers and workers and schoolchildren, all waving enthusiastically. The Emperor's drive into the city had been seen by some 250,000 people waving Ethiopian flags and the Little Red Books which contained Mao's wisdom, banging drums and clashing cymbals, and cheering as though they actually knew where Ethiopia was and why its friendship mattered to China. Tiananmen Square, the monumental parade ground in the heart of the city, had been draped with banners of welcome in English and Chinese and in the stands teenagers had spelled out Haile Selassie's name in red and yellow paper flowers.[3]

Inside the plane Nixon's staff peered out to see whether Chou En-lai was wearing an overcoat. When they reported to Nixon that indeed he was, the President kept his own coat on. It would not do to appear to be trying to show American superiority in braving the cold. The door of the plane opened and the President emerged to faint applause from the small crowd on the ground. Partway down the steps, he paused and briefly returned the claps. Inside the aircraft, Haldeman and the Secret Service men held everyone else back so that Nixon would savour this moment by himself – and so that the American newsmen assembled on the ground would catch it. Nixon, in a dark-blue suit and grey overcoat, looked solemn. What one journalist called 'those famous twitching hands' were for once still.[4] Nixon's wife Pat then emerged, wearing a vivid red coat. She had ignored the warnings of American China specialists that only prostitutes wore red in China; but then their knowledge, like so much of what Americans knew about China, was probably out of date. Mrs Nixon gave a tentative little wave at the top of the steps and hastened down to join her husband.

As Nixon reached the last steps, he thrust his arm out towards Chou and the two men shook hands, seemingly for longer than usual. The press cameras homed in on the clasped hands. Chou, who spoke several languages, said a few words to Nixon in English. How was Nixon's flight? 'Very pleasant,' said Nixon. As the rest of the American party clambered down, Chou noticed Kissinger and said, with what seemed like genuine warmth, 'Ah, old friend.'[5] The two men had met twice already when Kissinger had come to pave the way for Nixon.

Everyone stood to attention while the band played the national anthems of China and the United States, and then, while it moved on to revolutionary favourites such as 'A Song to our Socialist Motherland', Chou and Nixon inspected the honour guard. Mrs Nixon came in the rear with her escort, an American military aide. It was the first time since 1950 that an American in uniform had walked freely in the People's Republic of China. They were trailed by a group of American and Chinese officials: the American Secretary of State William Rogers and his aides; Kissinger and his staff; Marshal Ye Jianying, one of the old heroes of the Communist victory; Ji Pengfei, the Chinese Foreign Minister; and their Chinese colleagues. Joseph Kraft, the distinguished journalist, noticed how many acting and deputy ministers there were among them, filling in for all those officials who had lost their jobs during the recent Cultural Revolution.[6]

The airport ceremonies, perfunctory by Chinese standards, were over in fifteen minutes. The party climbed into big black Chinese limousines with lace-curtained windows and disappeared towards the city with the press following on in buses. The Americans had a brief glimpse of the north China countryside. The shabby farm buildings, the peasants and their animals brought home China's poverty and weakness. There were no other cars on the roads, only buses and hordes of bicycles. The photographers leaned out of the windows to snap workers sweeping up fresh snow and passers-by, who seemed curiously uninterested in the convoy dashing past. The convoy passed the diplomatic quarter, where the Chinese authorities kept foreign diplomats carefully segregated, and turned left at the Workers' Stadium. Some of the more observant Americans caught sight of barricades holding back traffic in the side streets and police discouraging pedestrians from taking a closer look. Haldeman, himself a master of stage management, wondered whether the Chinese authorities had chosen not to assemble a huge crowd in Tiananmen Square in the heart of Beijing as a dramatic display of the indifference of the Chinese people to their foreign visitor. Diplomats in the British mission learned that the Communists had given extensive briefings; the locals were told to ride their bicycles or walk by without showing any curiosity. That night on the Chinese news the lead item was about a group of women workers. The last item mentioned that the American President had dropped by.[7]

As they entered Beijing, the Americans were struck by the ubiquitous smell of burning coal and by how drab it all was, from the buildings to the monotonous blue of the locals' clothing. Most of the Americans had read their briefing notes and their guidebooks on the plane and they knew that they were entering one of the great cities of the world. For seven centuries, China's rulers had made it their capital, erecting its massive walls and gates, dotting it with monuments, and, in its heart, creating the series of palaces, temples and courtyards which made up the Forbidden City. Chinese noblemen, bureaucrats, merchants and scholars had built their own palaces, arranged around a series of courtyards, and the lower classes had followed suit in their own more modest dwellings. Ceramic dogs stood guard outside the entrances to important houses and smaller dogs and other beasts fixed on the points of the tiled roofs warded off evil spirits.

Beijing was a network of alleyways – the *hutong* – whose walls hid both crowded slums and serene gardens. In the spring, if you stood on one of Beijing's few hills or climbed a pagoda, you could see a forest of soft green and flowering trees. Running north and south through the city, a series of lakes brought fresh water in from the hills to the north and helped to keep the city cool in the summer. Beijing's climate was as extreme as Chicago's or Toronto's: stiflingly hot and humid in the summer and bitterly cold in the winter. Because of earthquakes, most buildings were only one storey.

Foreign incursions, invasion, civil war had all taken their toll on the city, but it had survived largely unchanged into the twentieth century, with only a few signs of the new world in which China found itself: a railway station, a handful of Western churches and embassies, a few universities, some office buildings. In 1949, when the People's Republic was proclaimed, Beijing had the largest area of medieval buildings in the world. The new Communist rulers were indifferent both to the city's charms and to its past. They were revolutionaries, who had spent the past two decades in the countryside. Many of them had never seen a city before and what they saw they did not approve of.

What the Nixon party saw was an ancient city in the process of being turned into a new, Communist one, worthy of a centre of world revolution. Beijing was to become modern, and the model the Communists had first had in mind was the capital of the Soviet Union, in those early days one of the new China's few friends. And so the arches over the main streets which had been erected over the centuries to virtuous people – upright civil servants, for example, or loyal widows – were removed. Acres of the old city were bulldozed to build gigantic avenues and immense squares. Tiananmen Square itself was laid over the ruins of part of the Forbidden City. The great walls which had encircled the city for centuries were torn down to make a multi-lane ring road. Their magnificent gates went as well.

The Americans were also struck by the silence. Bicycle bells tinkled gently and occasionally a truck or bus honked its horn, but there was none of the usual hubbub of a great city. John Holdridge, from the State Department, who had known Beijing before the Second World War when it was, like all Chinese cities, noisy and bustling, was startled at the change: 'When I peeked at Beijing through the car curtain, it appeared to be almost a ghost city. The few pedestrians moved slowly, their faces impassive, as if they were suffering some form of combat fatigue as a result of the Cultural Revolution, which was then winding down.'[8]

Few outsiders knew much about the Cultural Revolution. China had virtually shut down for three years between 1966 and 1969. Most of its embassies were closed or scaled back as Chinese officials were summoned home to get their thoughts purified. Foreign visitors were discouraged, apart from a handful of sympathizers like the ever adaptable writer Han Suyin, who wrote admiringly of the wonderful way the Chinese were throwing off old, outmoded ways of thought and launching themselves enthusiastically into the future. The young were challenging their elders and all were working together, or so official propaganda said, to build a truly democratic and socialist China. Only a handful of foreign journalists and diplomats had remained in Beijing and their movements had been severely limited, or worse. The British mission was ransacked and burned by Red Guards. Soviet diplomats were penned in their embassy by days of demonstrations; when the Soviet Union finally withdrew their families in 1967, women and children were beaten or forced to crawl under pictures of Mao on their way to their planes.

The Chinese press was filled with wild attacks on some of the leading figures of the Revolution. Could it really be true that the President, Liu Shaoqi, had been planning to restore capitalism in China? That the great revolutionary general Peng Dehuai had spent years plotting against the Revolution? Glimpses of curious events reached the outside world: millions of ecstatic Red Guards jamming Tiananmen Square to wave their Little Red Books, weeping and cheering as their idol, Mao, appeared on the reviewing stand; mass rallies to denounce elderly men and women; provincial governors paraded through the streets with dunces' caps and placards around their necks; a steady stream of vitriol against the enemies of the Revolution from Chinese radio, along with extraordinary claims of miracles performed by Mao's words. Party officials, it was announced, were being re-educated in factories or on farms. The universities and many of the high schools were closed so that the students could take part in the new revolution and their teachers go off for their own re-education.

Then, suddenly it seemed, the whole thing was over. In the autumn of 1968 the authorities ordered the students to stop rampaging about and head for the countryside. Slowly and cautiously the schools and universities reopened. Mao remarked, with his customary insouciance, that it would probably be necessary to have another cultural revolution 'in a few years'. In the event, the factional fights let loose by the years of turmoil went on, in some cases until Mao's death seven years later. In 1969, the Ninth Party Congress officially ended the Cultural Revolution, declaring it a triumph.

The Chinese who had suffered through the Cultural Revolution had a different view. The bill for that hideous event is still being totted up and may never be completely known. An entire people were encouraged to turn on their own society and culture, and on each other. Any cruelty, any excess, was permitted as long as it was done in the name of Mao and the Revolution. Being descended from the wrong class – being a landowner, for example – owning a foreign book or old porcelain, or saying something that appeared to criticize Mao, all were grounds for persecution. Teachers, blamed for transmitting old values, were arrested by their students and, in many cases, tortured to death. Children were told to denounce their parents. Neighbours and colleagues turned on each other.

It was dangerous to work for the government or to be a member of the party, and it was particularly dangerous at the higher levels. Marshal Peng, who had contributed so much to the Communists' survival and eventual victory, was beaten until his ribs broke and he could no longer lie down; his lingering death was made worse because he was denied medical treatment until it was too late. Liu Shaoqi was publicly humiliated and tormented, and then placed in solitary confinement where his guards and medical attendants had strict orders to treat him harshly. He went mad and died in squalid misery. The persecution did not spare family members. (Deng's son was thrown out of a window and became a paraplegic. Deng Xiaoping would later recover his position and, after Mao's death, become the most powerful man in China, and his son received medical treatment in Canada.) Young children were turned out of their homes and left to wander the streets. All over China, at all levels of society, there were similar tragedies. A recent estimate is that between 1966 and 1976 three million Chinese died as a result of the Cultural Revolution. That is not counting the many millions more, by the admission of the Chinese authorities themselves, who were brutalized and victimized. An Italian psychiatrist who visited China shortly before Nixon's visit was astonished at the prevalence of facial tics.[9]

In 1972 the American visitors did not have any idea of the extent of such horrors. Their Chinese hosts were unfailingly helpful and polite but simply ignored awkward questions. The journalists had hoped for man-and-woman-in-the-street interviews, but found them impossible to arrange. When owning a book published outside China could be enough to ruin a family, it is not surprising that no Chinese would take the risk of talking to foreigners, especially those who, until so recently, had been portrayed as China's bitter enemies. The day Nixon arrived in Beijing, a Chinese women had been arrested by plainclothes police for waving at his motorcade; it turned out that she had seen her niece, who was an interpreter for the journalists. The only Chinese the Americans were going to meet were officials and a few carefully selected individuals, writers or academics for example, who were always brought out to greet foreign visitors. 'Pathetic mummies' was how Pierre Ryckmans, the Belgian China expert who wrote as Simon Leys, described them. 'Out of eight hundred million Chinese, foreigners meet about sixty individuals.'[10]

In 1972 there were very few foreigners living permanently in Beijing or indeed in China. The Chinese Communists had moved quickly after they seized power to drive out foreign businesspeople, missionaries and teachers, all of whom were lumped together as imperialists. A few enthusiasts for Communism – 'our foreign friends' – had chosen to stay on after 1949 and, at least until the 1960s, had lived privileged lives. 'The Three Hundred Percenters', as a British diplomat called them, were trotted out to laud the glories of the Revolution and Mao and to condemn the inequities of the West. During the Cultural Revolution even they came under attack, much to their bewilderment. Chinese universities, as part of the attempt to position China as the leader of revolution for the Third World, took in some foreign students, but this foundered when African students complained that they were looked down upon by the Chinese; after a brawl at the Peace Hotel, most of them left.[11] A handful of foreign journalists from China's fellow Communist republics or from countries such as France and Canada which had already established relations with China tried – usually unsuccessfully – to find some real news.

Only forty or so countries had any sort of relations with China, and the lives of their diplomats, even those from friendly countries, were severely circumscribed. There was little to see in Beijing; most of the famous sites had been badly damaged during the Cultural Revolution and remained closed. Foreigners could visit the Temple of Heaven and one street to look for antiques. Most restaurants did not serve foreigners at all and those that did had a special room set aside. Travel outside Beijing, except to the Ming Tombs, required a special permit, and permits, usually, were not forthcoming. Most diplomats had to live in the Diplomats' Big Building, the Communists' equivalent of the old imperial Barbarian Hostel which had once housed foreign emissaries. Their servants, supplied by the Chinese authorities, were undoubtedly spying on them.[12]

When the Communists took power in 1949, their fellow Communist regimes, led by the Soviet Union, had moved quickly to recognize them as the new government of China. So too had a number of newly independent Third World nations such as India and Indonesia. The Japanese, who accepted American influence over their foreign policy, had only been able to move cautiously to re-establish trading relations. By the time Nixon visited China, though, a number of American allies had already established diplomatic relations. The British had recognized the People's Republic in January 1950, partly because they had extensive interests to protect in the East, most notably Hong Kong, but also because their longstanding policy was to deal with governments that had established control. Several of the smaller European countries followed suit, although France held back, partly because it feared the Communist Chinese threat to its position in Indochina. The People's Republic accepted a British representative but did nothing to send its own to London. The outbreak of the Korean War later that summer precluded any further improvements. Chinese entry into the war in the late autumn of 1950 hardened American attitudes, both towards the Chinese Communists and to having any dealings with them. For their part, the Chinese Communists showed no inclination to deal with any imperialists. In 1954, a year after the Korean armistice, there was a sudden thaw when Chinese Foreign Ministry officials in Beijing unexpectedly accepted an invitation from the British chargé d'affaires to see a film of the coronation of Queen Elizabeth II. In September the Chinese government sent its first representative to London. French recognition came ten years later in a sudden move by de Gaulle, which his defenders claimed was to exploit the differences between China and the Soviet Union but which was in fact designed to demonstrate his and France's independence from the United States. De Gaulle hoped to be the first major Western leader to visit China, but he was driven from office unexpectedly in the turmoil of 1968. By the late 1960s, Belgium and Italy were moving towards recognition and so was Canada, whose foreign policy usually meshed with that of the United States on major issues. The United States was finding itself increasingly alone in its insistence that the Communists not be recognized as the legitimate government of China.

Because the diplomatic corps was so small, diplomats from different blocs who normally would have seen little of each other tended to get together. Only the North Vietnamese, the Albanians and the North Koreans kept themselves aloof. The Finns had a sauna club. The Soviets built an ice-hockey rink at their embassy and had games every Sunday morning featuring the Soviet Union against a World team made up mainly of Canadians and the Mexican ambassador, who played enthusiastically but very badly. The British brought movies in once a month from Hong Kong. To pay for shipping they held 'girl-racing evenings' where the prettiest British secretaries jumped ahead at the roll of dice; the Soviets adored these and were morose when a temporary freeze in relations between the Soviet Union and the West obliged them to boycott the British embassy.[13]

Now, as the Nixon motorcade sped through Tiananmen Square, where a giant portrait of Mao gazed down on vast empty spaces, almost the only spectators were a small crowd of foreign diplomats hoping to get a glimpse of the momentous visit. A small Canadian girl puttered about on a miniature motorcycle and a couple of the British men climbed lampposts to snap pictures of the cars. For the isolated little diplomatic community in Beijing, this was a rare break in their usual routine.

3

Chou En-lai

IN THEIR CAR on the drive from the airport, Chou turned to Nixon and said, 'Your handshake came over the vastest ocean in the world – twenty-five years of no communication.'[1] It had crossed over much more than that: the long years of humiliation that the Chinese had endured at the hands of the outside world; the Americans' own memories of retreating in Korea in the face of Red Chinese attacks; and the decades of fear and suspicion on both sides since the proc-lamation of the People's Republic in 1949. The handshake also had to make up for one that had never occurred. In 1954, at the Geneva con-ference which was trying to wind up the Korean War and deal with the French defeat in Indochina, the American Secretary of State, John Foster Dulles, had publicly brushed pass Chou En-lai's proffered hand. The Chinese had not forgotten the incident – indeed they remem-bered it vividly, just as they remembered the sign that was said to have been placed at the entrance to the park in the foreign quarter of Shanghai, 'No dogs, no Chinese'. For them, though, the handshake now was not just about making up for a past slight. Its real significance was that China was being treated as an equal by a great power. Nixon's first moments in China had been worrying both sides ever since the trip had been arranged. The Americans feared that Nixon might forget to shake hands with Chou, the Chinese suspected that he might repeat Dulles' snub.

The Chinese had a good memory for slights and grievances. The decades before the Communist takeover of power, during which China had been exploited and invaded by foreigners, were kept fresh in the national imagination as 'the century of humiliation'. China's history had not prepared it to be humiliated by outside powers. Two hundred years before Nixon's arrival, when there was not yet a United

States, Beijing had been the capital of a self-confident and powerful country. Under the great Qianlong Emperor who reigned from 1736 to 1799, China had expanded its borders in the west, doubling in size. The Emperor had added new courtyards and buildings to the Forbidden City at the heart of Beijing, and built a magnificent new Summer Palace just outside the city walls. He was a patron of the arts and learning. Chinese arts – the magnificent porcelain, for example – had reached new and more elaborate heights. When the British sent an embassy under Lord Macartney to ask for rights to trade freely, as equals, and to send diplomats, again as equals, to Beijing, the Qianlong Emperor received him as the representative of an inferior ruler, bearing not gifts but tribute, and with sublime condescension brushed off the requests. Over the ensuing decades, China stood still, secure in its old civilization. The outside world, especially Europe, moved on, into the Industrial Revolution. Western science, industry and technology jumped far ahead of the rest of the world to produce, among much else, ships and guns better than anything the Chinese had.

By 1872, eighty years after Macartney's mission, the Summer Palace lay in ruins, looted and burned by foreign troops, and the young Emperor was a cipher, dominated by his ruthless and ignorant mother. China had been racked by massive peasant rebellions which had left great stretches of the country depopulated. And, to add to China's misery, foreigners, greedy, demanding, unreasonable and regrettably powerful, were tying up a weak Chinese government with a series of treaties, remembered to this day by the Chinese as 'the unequal treaties'. Chinese territory and Chinese independence were slowly being sliced away. Foreign businessmen were setting up shop on Chinese soil, protected by their own consuls, their own laws and their own soldiers. The United States, newly reunited after the Civil War, had not yet become a major player in the Far East, but American businessmen and American missionaries were busily establishing footholds. With missionaries came schools and printing presses and, perhaps most dangerous of all, ideas which began slowly to undermine the old order.

Thoughtful Chinese grappled with ways of dealing with the challenges that came from within and without. How could the Qing dynasty and its administration revitalize itself? How could China take the foreigners' technology and perhaps even some of their techniques, as Japan was starting to do, and use them to fend off the outside powers? Yet to turn around a huge China, with its deeply conservative society, was not an easy task and there was little will to attempt it from the regime itself. So the catastrophes continued to pile up: the French defeated a Chinese fleet in 1884 and confirmed their hold over Indochina; in 1894–5, Japan destroyed two Chinese navies and took control of Korea and possession of Taiwan; and in 1898, the Boxer Rebellion brought more misery to north China and provided the foreign powers with yet another excuse to invade.

Chou En-lai was born in that last year, in a prosperous town in Jiangsu province, north of the great trading port of Shanghai. When he was two, foreign troops marched into Beijing to rescue fellow nationals besieged by the Boxers. The Chinese signed yet another humiliating treaty which allowed outside powers to station their troops in China permanently to protect their citizens. Chinese patriots wondered how much longer their country would survive before it was parcelled out among its enemies. The outlook was grim, with the Russians pressing in from the north and the west and the French from the south. The British were moving up the Yangtze valley and the Germans had established themselves in Shandong. Perhaps the most dangerous of all, the Japanese had seized the island of Taiwan and clearly had their eyes on Korea and the even richer prize of Manchuria. Chou grew up at a time of mounting nationalist fervour and debate. What was wrong with the old order if it allowed China to grow so weak? How could China be saved? Western science? Western democracy? Or both?

Chou's family were part of a vanishing world, their position in society tied to the old regime and the old order. They were scholars, part of the elite who provided the bureaucrats to run China. Men like them studied the great Chinese classics, the works of Confucius among them, so that they could take the government examinations and enter the civil service. Chou's grandfather had been a distinguished scholar and civil servant, and several of his uncles had passed their examinations. His own father, however, only ever held a minor government post and seems to have spent his days in genteel idleness.

Chou was brought up by his extended family, partly in his father's household, partly in those of his uncles. The main influence on him seems to have been the widow of one of his uncles, a woman he always called mother. 'Without her care I would not have been able to cultivate any interest in academic pursuits.' In 1907, when he was nine, his natural mother died after an illness which drained his father's modest savings. Chou was sent out to take family treasures to the pawnbrokers.[2]

Chou was later dismissive of his 'bankrupt mandarin family', which clung to the old ways when the world was changing around them. Yet he kept something of their manners and their deep appreciation of the arts and learning of the old China. His own education was a mix of the old and the new. He studied the classics but his adopted mother also hired a foreign missionary, a woman, for the 'new learning' – Western chemistry or mathematics, for example. In 1910, he went north of the Great Wall, to Manchuria, to live with one of his uncles. Although he was a small man, Chou attributed his toughness and his formidable capacity for work to the bracing climate and the standard diet of grain in the north. His new home of Shenyang (known to generations of foreigners as Mukden) was a major railway junction where Chinese mixed with foreigners from all over the world. In the five years since Russia's defeat by Japan, Japanese power had started to replace Russian in Manchuria. A weak China could only watch from the sidelines as its territory was fought over. In Shenyang, the young Chou became a nationalist, reading radical journals and the works of prominent reformers. It is said that when a teacher asked his students why they were studying, Chou answered, 'So that China can rise up.'[3]

The moribund Qing dynasty finally collapsed in 1911 and China became a republic. For a brief period, it looked as though the Chinese might be able to pull themselves together to deal with the twin evils of internal decay and external menace. Perhaps, thought the growing numbers of Chinese nationalists, a new form of government would bring rulers and ruled together to create a strong China. Chou celebrated by cutting off his pigtail, which had come to symbolize the old ways and subservience to the Qing.

Two years later he moved to a high school in Tianjin, the main port for Beijing, and another city where Chinese came into daily contact with large numbers of foreigners. By this stage, the adult Chou was starting to emerge. He was an outstanding student, and also good looking and charming, with an ability to inspire tremendous loyalty. When he needed money for further studies, four of his friends pledged him a share of their tiny scholarships. Chou was also learning to conceal what he was really thinking. Over the years his gentle courtesy, his patience and his good humour almost invariably won the praise of foreign statesmen, even when Chou was quietly working against them. 'We all considered him', said Nikita Khrushchev, 'a bright, flexible, and up-to-date man with whom we could talk sensibly.'[4] Chou was a talented actor; at Tianjin, he normally played women's parts because he had the necessary delicate looks and build and a light voice. When Nixon and Kissinger met him, they discovered a man who could be the fiery Communist revolutionary at one moment and the urbane man of the world the next.

The young Chou not only finished his schoolwork more quickly than his classmates but took on extra responsibilities, whether organizing debates or lectures or putting out student magazines. His essays frequently won prizes. In them he showed what was to be a lifelong preference for empirical knowledge. In the turmoil of the last years of the Qing, there was a renewed interest in the scholars who had unsuccessfully resisted the invasion of China in the seventeenth century by these Manchu foreigners from north of the Great Wall and who had tried to understand why the preceding Chinese regime, the Ming, had collapsed. Chou was particularly influenced by those scholars who argued that Chinese learning had become too abstract and speculative and who called for 'practical statesmanship' and 'practical learning'. Like many nationalist Chinese of his time, he was also drawn by the ideas of Darwin and Herbert Spencer, which seemed to promise that China might evolve out of its present miserable state.[5]

Exactly how that was to happen did not seem at all clear in the second decade of the twentieth century. The republic was a disaster, with its first president trying to make himself emperor. After his death in 1916, China slipped into warlordism, where strong men and their armies controlled their own fiefdoms and competed with each other to gain control. Japan took advantage of the breakdown of the

Chinese state and the preoccupation of the other powers with the First World War to present demands which would have turned China into its protectorate. Only a public outcry and pressure from the rest of the other powers made the Japanese back off, and even then only temporarily. Chou, in the ancient tradition of China's scholar–bureaucrats, wrote a sad poem:

> A whirlwind pounds
> Our heartsick land.
> The nation sinks
> And no one minds.
> Compounding heartbreak,
> Autumn is back:
> Its horrid insect chorus
> Blasts our ears.[6]

In spite of the threat from Japan, Chou, like a number of other young Chinese, decided in 1917 to study in that country on the ground that it was showing China the way to become modern and powerful. When he arrived, however, he found himself part of a beleaguered Chinese community, despised by the nationalistic Japanese and uncomfortably aware that their homeland needed them. Chou, who rarely went to classes, increasingly devoted himself to radical émigré politics. And, apparently for the first time, he encountered the ideas of Karl Marx.

Marxism, with its claims to be scientific and its promise of a glorious socialist world to come, was immensely appealing to radical Chinese intellectuals. At a time when they were engaged in attacking the old values and institutions which had held China back and made it so weak, it was modern and revolutionary. During a drunken evening in Tokyo, Chou told his friends that students, workers and peasants must work together. 'You have to have them all with you before you can push a revolution to a successful conclusion. And without a revolution China cannot be saved!'[7]

A future in which there would be no more private property and no more conflicts between classes and nations had a particular appeal, perhaps without their realizing it, to Chinese brought up in a world where the Confucian values of order and harmony and of disdain for business were still powerful. Moreover the Bolshevik Revolution of

1917 in Russia provided an encouraging example. What also impressed the Chinese was that the new regime in Russia, alone among the powers, proposed to hand back land taken from China in the previous century. That the gesture would prove to be an empty one was something the Chinese could not then know.

Chou went back to a China full of anger directed against the Western powers for, as the Chinese saw it, betraying them. The end of the First World War, in which China had participated on the victorious Allied side, had brought hopes that the great powers would be true to their own publicly stated principles and help China to rule itself and safeguard its territory. Instead the Allies had decided, at the Paris Peace Conference of 1919, to award former German possessions in China to their ally Japan, despite the fact that China had also been an ally of the victorious powers, and that the West had repeatedly professed to be fighting for democracy and justice. The decision was based on cold calculation: China was weak and Japan was strong. It produced huge anti-Western and anti-Japanese demonstrations in Beijing on 4 May 1919 which then spread across China.

The collapse of the 1911 republic into warlordism and the burgeoning threat as Japan tried to bring China under its control stimulated an intense artistic and political ferment which came to be known as the May Fourth Movement. Writers and scholars moved beyond criticizing their leaders and attacked the whole of the old order, which, so they argued, had got China into its present miserable straits. Reverence for the past and obedience for authority had trapped the Chinese in outmoded and useless ways of thinking and acting. The time had come, so the radicals argued, for China to become modern, to follow, in the language of the time, Mr Science and Mr Democracy. The Allied betrayal of China at the Peace Conference helped to persuade many that Communism and its promise of a classless democracy, not capitalism and liberal democracy, offered the best hope for China. Moreover, radical change at home, so they hoped, would make China stronger abroad.

Chou enrolled at university in Tianjin but spent most of his time on political work. His revolutionary activities brought him his first term in jail and his first encounter with a fifteen-year-old who was one of the leading lights of the local Girl Students' Patriotic Association.

Deng Yingchao would become his wife seven years later. Chou may also have met at this time another, slightly older revolutionary: Mao Tse-tung, the man whose faithful subordinate he would one day become.[8]

In 1920, Chou sailed for France on a work-study programme to learn more about the world outside China. For the next three years, he eked out a living, writing articles for Chinese papers and working at menial jobs. He also wrote faithfully to Deng. 'I haven't made a single female friend,' he assured her, 'and I have no intention of having one in the future.' From his base in France, he managed a considerable amount of travel, to London, which he did not like, and to Germany, which he found more congenial. Increasingly he made a name for himself among his fellow Chinese, as an organizer, writer and revolutionary. (The French police eventually got wind of his activities, but not until six months after he had returned to China.) In the summer of 1922, he helped to found a European branch of the new Chinese Communist Party. Although he could not know it, he was preparing himself for his future management of China's foreign affairs.[9]

Chou came home to China in the summer of 1924. Warlords were running the country, but in the south a new political movement was growing. Sun Yat-sen's National People's Party, the Guomindang, was, as its name suggested, nationalist and in those days a mix of radicals and workers on the one hand and the propertied classes on the other. The party was building new branches and creating its own army with support from the Soviet Union, which saw this as a way to strike at the imperialists. The Soviets ordered the tiny Chinese Communist Party to co-operate faithfully with the Guomindang. Let them unite China and kick out the Western powers, and then the Chinese Communists, so the revolutionary experts in Moscow asserted, could overthrow the bourgeois forces represented by the Guomindang and have a proper socialist revolution. Chou, although this was later played down in accounts in China, worked tirelessly for the coalition and indeed ended up virtually running the Guomindang's military academy.

He also found time to marry Deng Yingchao, herself by now an experienced revolutionary. Perhaps there was some love involved, but their relationship seems to have been more a political partnership.

Chou apparently told a niece years later that he had given up a woman he loved because he needed a revolutionary comrade: 'And so I chose your aunt.' Deng, like Chou himself, was prepared to commit herself wholeheartedly. When she became pregnant shortly after their marriage, she had an abortion. 'We felt', the couple said later, 'a child would interfere with our work.' She had miscarriages later but never her own children. Like many of the revolutionary wives, she paid a price. In the early 1930s, she came down with tuberculosis and had to be carried on a litter for much of the Long March when the Communists fled through the Chinese countryside from their former allies, the Guomindang.[10]

At the end of the 1920s there seemed to be a moment of hope for China when the Guomindang, now under the leadership of Chiang Kai-shek, managed to bring most of the country under at least nominal control. China at last had a central government that worked. In response, possibly because they felt guilty about their years of exploitation, most of the foreign powers started to give back the concessions they had wrung out of China over the previous century; Japan alone held back. The Communists were not there to share in the triumph because Chiang turned on them as soon as he no longer needed their help. By the end of 1927, the Communist organization, which had been strongest in the cities, was shattered and thousands of Communists had been killed or thrown in jail. A few scattered groups remained at large, out in the countryside where they lived hand to mouth like bandits. Chou, with a substantial price on his head, went underground in Shanghai and, with what was left of the Communist Party's organization, managed to escape the Guomindang's attentions until the start of the 1930s.

The Communists' disaster was made worse by incompetent and unworkable instructions from Communist International headquarters in Moscow. The Soviets, however, invariably laid the blame on the Chinese Communists themselves. Chou somehow managed to avoid the repeated purges of the Chinese leadership. He made abject self-criticisms whenever necessary. In 1931, as the Guomindang hounded the remaining Communists, he and his wife abandoned Shanghai for the relative safety of a Communist guerrilla base in south-central China where Mao and others were trying to hang on. Over the next four years, as Guomindang troops closed in, Chou manoeuvred adroitly through the shoals of vicious internal party struggles, managing to choose the winning sides. At the beginning of 1935 he threw his support behind Mao. Perhaps he did so out of conviction, or perhaps, as a recent biography of Mao suggests, because he was blackmailed. In 1932 Guomindang newspapers had published a notice in which Chou renounced Communism. Although Chou denounced it, almost certainly truthfully, as a fake, Mao held it over him for the rest of his life. Chou became Mao's faithful lieutenant, never bidding for supreme power himself nor joining with those who dared to disagree with Mao. As he said in 1972, in one of his last and most humiliating self-criticisms, 'I have always thought, and will always think, that I cannot be at the helm and can only be an assistant.' Towards the end of his life in 1976, when the attacks from the radicals around Mao were mounting, he refused to go into the operating theatre until he had finished a letter to Mao saying that he had never betrayed the party.[11] His survival in the recurrent savage and bloody intra-party struggles won him a comparison to a popular Chinese doll which always righted itself when it was knocked over.

While the Communists struggled to survive, the Guomindang appeared to be consolidating its power and starting to build a new China. Chiang Kai-shek and the Guomindang might have brought the remaining warlords under control and finished off the Communists; they might have built a proper infrastructure for China, with roads, airfields, railways, heavy industries and a sound education system; they might in time have been a good government. They never had the chance. At the start of the 1930s, the Great Depression hit the world. China itself as a largely agricultural economy was spared the worst of the economic downturn, but it could not escape the impact on international relations. The Western democracies including the United States, which had helped to maintain a stable international order in the 1920s, turned inwards, preoccupied with their own problems. Unfortunately, other nations like Germany and Italy took a different tack to secure what they needed, whether territory or influence, and by force if necessary. The Japanese too adopted an increasingly nationalistic and militaristic route – necessary, so many of them thought, to protect Japan from the indifference of the great powers. In 1931, Japanese militarists seized Manchuria outright, and the world did little to stop them. From then on, the Japanese man-oeuvred to extend their sway into the parts of China south of the Great Wall. The Guomindang was forced to divert its resources to dealing with the threat.

In 1937, Japanese armies invaded China proper, eventually bringing the whole of the rich coastal area into a new Japanese empire. The war with Japan, which was in time absorbed into the Second World War, cut short the prospect that the Guomindang would bring stability and prosperity to China. It also opened the door to the rapid growth of the Chinese Communist Party. Without meaning to, the deeply conservative Japanese militarists saved Communism in China. The Guomindang was distracted from what was an increasingly successful campaign to wipe out the Chinese Communist Party, and the Communists themselves were able to tap into a burgeoning Chinese nationalism. When the Second World War was over, the Communists controlled much of the countryside north of the Yangtze and had a formidable army. In 1946, after fruitless talks brokered by the United States, the two sides embarked on a civil war which ended with the victory of the Communists in 1949. Mao Tse-tung proclaimed the People's Republic in Beijing and the defeated Chiang set up an alternative government on the island of Taiwan.

In 1949, at the age of fifty-one, Chou became the new China's first premier as well as its foreign minister. (Although he gave up the second post in 1958, he continued to supervise China's foreign relations until his death.) He was as charming as ever. He lived austerely and simply, darning, so legend had it, his own socks. He worked constantly, well into the night. No detail was ever too small for him. When he set up his new foreign ministry, he did his best to ensure that China's freshly recruited diplomats, most of whom came from the military, acquired the knowledge and the skills they now needed, whether it was through lectures on international law or diplomatic protocols. The trainees had lessons from the Soviets on how to wear suits and ties and how to dance, and sessions in a Beijing restaurant to practise eating Western food with Western-style utensils. Those who worked for Chou usually adored him. 'He worked so hard,' remembered one of his interpreters, 'paid attention to every detail, read all the reference materials so carefully.' It was not fair to blame him for supporting Mao, even in his more outrageous policies. 'What could he have done otherwise?'[12]

Foreigners who met him generally found him delightful and deeply civilized. UN Secretary General Dag Hammarskjöld thought he had 'the most superior brain I have so far met in the field of foreign politics'. Henry Kissinger, unusually in someone so critical, was completely entranced. 'He moved gracefully', said Kissinger of their first meeting, 'and with dignity, filling a room not by his physical dominance (as did Mao or de Gaulle) but by his air of controlled tension, steely discipline, and self-control, as if he were a coiled spring.' Kissinger, who was to have many hours of hard negotiations with Chou, found him 'one of the two or three most impressive men I have ever met' – and a worthy adversary. 'He was a figure out of history. He was equally at home in philosophy, reminiscence, historical analysis, tactical probes, humorous repartee.'[13] Kindness, compassion, moderation, these were qualities both Chinese and foreigners saw in Chou.

Yet he could also be utterly ruthless. He had become hardened during that long climb to power, as they all had. Chou had seen close friends die and he had condemned others to death. As early as 1931, he ordered the execution of all the immediate relatives of a Communist who had given up information in a police interrogation. He was not just complicit in the repeated purges and killings in the Communist base areas, he helped to organize them. At the start of the Long March in 1934, when the Communists fled the Guomindang, it was Chou who decided who should be weeded out and executed as unreliable, and who should be left behind to the mercies of the enemy. In 1955, the man who always thanked the crews on his planes let a whole flight be blown to pieces to flush out the Guomindang agents who had placed a bomb on board. During the Cultural Revolution, when his longtime bodyguard fell foul of Mao's wife, Chou did not lift a finger to protect him. The man who was so gentle with children did not intervene when his own adopted daughter was carried off by Red Guards during the Cultural Revolution. She died of her beatings in prison.[14]

Did he really have no choice, as his interpreter suggested? Did he remember the advice of the scholar two millennia earlier who had said the small craft that comes close to the great barge should be empty so that the crew on board the bigger vessel will leave it alone to bob on top of the waters?[15] Or did he decide that he must survive for China's sake? Throughout the calamitous attempts by Mao to transform China, Chou En-lai remained at his post. He worked extraordinary hours and kept a grasp on an extraordinary range of issues. Perhaps without him China would have gone even further into anarchy than it did during the Cultural Revolution.

The Chinese as well as foreigners tended to see Mao as the radical and Chou as the moderate, Mao as the one who caused the damage with his wild policies and Chou who picked up the pieces. There was much truth in this, but it is not all the truth. Chou was also a revolutionary, determined to transform China's society so that it could become strong and take its rightful place in the world. For him as for the other Chinese Communists, revolution and nationalism were intertwined. Mao spoke for them all on 1 October 1949 when he proclaimed the People's Republic of China from the great Gate of Heavenly Peace overlooking Tiananmen Square. 'We, the 475 million Chinese people, have stood up and our future is infinitely bright.'[16]

In November 1949, at the first meeting of China's new Foreign Ministry, Chou told his colleagues that the century of humiliation was over. The new regime had nothing to learn from its predecessors, such as the Qing or the Guomindang; 'all dealt with foreign affairs with their knees on the ground'. The new China must approach the other powers as an equal. 'We should have an independent spirit. We should take initiatives and should be fearless and confident.'[17]

Both Mao and Chou also saw the world through eyes which had been shaped by their study of Marxism. There were the capitalist powers, led after 1945 by the United States, and there were the socialist ones, their number greatly increased with the spread of Soviet power into Central Europe and then the victory of the Chinese Communists. The two camps were doomed to struggle until one, socialism if you believed Marx, was victorious. Communist diplomacy should be at the service of the final victory. Nations, Chou told the novices at the new Foreign Ministry in 1949, must always be ready to fight. 'There may not be a war of swords every year, but as sure as day turns into night, there will be a constant war of words, every day of the year.'[18]

With his deep-seated preference for what was practical over what was purely theoretical, Chou insisted that China's foreign policy must always take into consideration actual conditions, exploiting the differences between the capitalists, even making compromises with them, and so win time. As he pointed out, in a major statement on foreign policy in 1930, the Soviet Communists had saved their regime by submitting to a punitive treaty with their enemy Germany in 1918. Fortunately, since Chou was obliged to operate within guidelines laid down by Mao, the Chairman took the same approach: 'What we call concrete Marxism is Marxism that has taken on concrete form, that is Marxism applied to the concrete struggle in the concrete conditions prevailing in China . . .' In his management of China's foreign relations, Chou was flexible over tactics, seeking, as he put it, 'concurrence while shelving differences'. He told Kissinger, in one of their many talks, 'One must be cool-headed and analyze things.'[19] Chou had been responsible during the Second World War for negotiating a common front with the Guomindang against the Japanese; he was prepared to compromise even with enemies in order to safeguard the party and its China. Perhaps, too, as his enemies suggested from time to time, he betrayed the influence of his early classical education. In traditional Confucian thought, harmony and the golden mean were valued above conflict and disagreement.

Over the years, Chou became a great negotiator. One of his early heroes, when he lived in Europe in the early 1920s, was David Lloyd George, the British Prime Minister of the time. Chou admired him for his realism, his understanding of the contemporary scene, and his ability to bring different sides together in a way that benefited Britain. Lloyd George, he said, was 'cunning'. Everyone who dealt with Chou found the same thing. 'He shifts his line so subtly', wrote a Guomindang official, 'that it often escapes your notice. Of course he makes compromises, but only minimal and nominal compromises at the very last moment just to keep the negotiations going. When you study his statements afterwards, you realize that he hasn't made any substantial concession on any important issue at all.'[20]

4

Diaoyutai

NIXON'S MOTORCADE SWEPT on through Tiananmen Square to the west of the city. Important foreign visitors to Beijing stayed, as they still do today, in a special, heavily guarded compound. The Diaoyutai had been created at the end of the 1950s for the celebrations of the tenth anniversary of the founding of the People's Republic. Most of its villas were new but the site itself was very old. Generations of scholars had loved its lakes and groves. A famous Chinese poem talked of its weeping willows against the darkening hills to the west: 'Peach blossoms float on the water at sunset.' Emperors and noblemen built their pavilions there and fished from its terraces and the great eighteenth-century Qianlong Emperor, renowned among much else for his calligraphy, wrote out its name – the Fishing Terrace or Diaoyutai – for a plaque which is still by one of the gates. The Communists had surrounded the area with barbed wire, searchlights, high walls and armed guards, and appropriated it for themselves and their friends. Mao and his wife each had villas there which they used from time to time. Kim Il Sung, the dictator of North Korea, Nikita Khrushchev and Che Guevara had all preceded Nixon there. So, several months earlier, had the Prime Minister of North Vietnam. The US press corps heard rumours that Prince Sihanouk of Cambodia, whose clever balancing act between the Communists and their American enemies was finally over, had just moved out of Villa 18 where Nixon and his immediate entourage were housed. (Today, in the new China, it can be rented for US$50,000 a night.)

In that nineteenth-century bourgeois style so loved by the Soviet and Chinese Communists, its rooms were filled with over-stuffed armchairs and sofas, each with its antimacassar. Nixon and Chou En-lai sat side by side on a sofa in the main reception room while the other Americans and Chinese sat in a semi-circle drinking tea and listening to their exchange. (Although the Americans had brought their own interpreters, they had agreed to use Chinese ones for most meetings.) 'Both seemed to be very friendly, but noncommittal,' Haldeman recorded in his diary. 'They didn't get off of the trivial ground at all during the session.' Dwight Chapin, Nixon's appointments secretary, watched the body language. 'I found it extraordinary that Chou Enlai would be focused on the President, would drill in on him, but the President kind of would look off or look down on the floor and would not focus directly on Chou Enlai . . .' Kissinger found the conversation itself troubling. Nixon, he complained later to Haldeman, had responded to Chou's compliments about Kissinger's work in getting the trip organized by saying that other Americans had done the advance work, 'which had Henry disturbed that it would put him down in the eyes of the Chinese'.[1]

It was not unusual for Kissinger to be worried about his position. His time in the Nixon administration, first as National Security Adviser and then, after the 1972 election, as Secretary of State, was punctuated by complaints, about his rivals, his subordinates, his colleagues. He repeatedly accused William Rogers and the State Department of stabbing him in the back and moaned that the President did not do enough to defend him. Nixon in turn worried about his mental state. As Raymond Price, one of Nixon's speechwriters, put it, 'The care and feeding of Henry was one of the greatest burdens of his presidency, but he was worth it.'[2]

He was worth it, in Nixon's view, for his brains and his enormous knowledge of the world and because he represented the East Coast intellectual establishment of which the President was secretly in awe. Although Nixon was grudging with his praise, his memoirs grant that Kissinger had 'intensity and stamina' and was 'so enormously endowed with extraordinary intellectual capacity'. In the end, though, Nixon valued Kissinger because he found in him someone who saw foreign policy as he did. 'I knew', Nixon wrote in his memoirs, 'we were very much alike in our general outlook in that we shared a belief in the importance of isolating and influencing the factors affecting worldwide balances of power.'[3]

Like Nixon, Kissinger recognized that the United States had lost ground internationally in the 1960s, partly because of Vietnam and partly because other nations had grown in power. 'In the forties and fifties', Kissinger wrote in a 1968 essay, 'we offered remedies; in the late sixties and in the seventies our role will have to be to contribute to a structure that will foster the initiative of others. We are a super-power physically, but our designs can be meaningful only if they generate willing cooperation.' Like Nixon, too, he believed that the United States needed to look to its friends and allies to share the burden of maintaining international order. He also saw the world as a series of overlapping relationships. Statesmen should always be aware of the ways in which issues were linked and be prepared to use that linkage. If China wanted better relations with the United States, then it could be asked to put pressure on the North Vietnamese to come to an agreement with the Americans.[4]

Nixon and Kissinger did not always see eye to eye. Nixon was more American, more optimistic. He believed that the United States, by its very nature, was a force for good. Kissinger was deeply suspicious of talk of morality or principles in foreign relations. 'It is part of American folklore', he wrote in the same 1968 essay, 'that, while other nations have interests, we have responsibilities; while other nations are concerned with equilibrium, we are concerned with the legal requirements of peace.' He was inclined to be pessimistic and to see the international arena as an anarchic, savage place, where nations struggled in an endless Darwinian competition for survival. What Kissinger valued was stability and peaceful change. What he feared were active, revolutionary nations which wanted to overturn the existing order. Nevertheless, in the pursuit of stability, he argued, statesmen should be prepared to deal with any power. 'Our objective', he said of himself and Nixon, 'was to purge our foreign policy of all sentimentality.' American policymakers should always ask themselves two questions: 'What is it in our interest to prevent? What should we seek to accomplish?'[5]

American statesmen did not usually talk in such terms because they smacked too much of the old Europe, and Kissinger often used circumlocutions such as 'geopolitics' or the 'rules of equilibrium'. European alliance systems – often referred to as 'entangling' – spheres of interest and balances of power were all part of the bad old game of politics which, in the eyes of many Americans, led to wars. European statesmen such as Metternich, Bismarck and others who practised Realpolitik (a practical policy based in reality) were seen on the other side of the Atlantic as cold-hearted operators who sought power for their own countries at the expense of others. The United States ought to be wary of being drawn into their destructive games. In his farewell speech in 1796, George Washington famously warned against 'the insidious wiles of foreign influence' and asked, 'Why, by interweaving our destiny with that of any part of Europe, entangle our peace and prosperity in the toils of European ambition, rivalship, interest, humor, or caprice?' Over a century later, as his country stood poised to enter the First World War, Woodrow Wilson told the Senate that the United States had war aims unlike those of any other nation. 'I am proposing that all nations henceforth avoid entangling alliances which would draw them into competitions of power, catch them in a net of intrigue and selfish rivalry, and disturb their own affairs with influences intruded from without.'[6]

As a graduate student at Harvard, Kissinger had written his thesis on that classic period after the French Revolutionary Wars when the peace of Europe depended on the balance of power and when those great practitioners of diplomacy, Lord Castlereagh and Prince Metternich, had made the system work. 'Their goal', wrote Kissinger approvingly, 'was stability, not perfection, and the balance of power is the classic expression of the lesson of history that no order is safe without physical safeguards against aggression.' The best and most effective statesman, in his view, was the one who understood the world and that other nations than his own had interests and goals. Such a person worked with the world as it was, not as he hoped it might be. 'His instrument is diplomacy, the art of relating states to each other by agreement rather than by the exercise of force, by the representation of a ground of action which reconciles particular aspirations with a general consensus.'[7]

For Kissinger, diplomacy was a marvellously enjoyable art, and a very important one. The great statesmen, he believed, embraced their calling, even the moments of crisis. 'The few prepared to grapple with circumstances are usually undisturbed in the eye of a hurricane.' He admired, of course, both Metternich and Bismarck, and, like

Nixon himself, Churchill and de Gaulle. When necessary, they had boldly gone against conventional wisdom. Such statesmen, Kissinger complained, often went without honour in their own countries because it was difficult to get domestic support for policies which appeared to require compromises, with other powers or of a nation's own dearly held principles. In what became a notorious interview with the Italian journalist Oriana Fallaci in 1972, the short, plump Kissinger compared himself to that American icon, the cowboy. 'Americans like the cowboy who leads the wagon train by riding ahead alone on his horse,' he told her. 'He acts, that's all, by being in the right place at the right time.'[8]

Nixon knew something of Kissinger's ideas but not the man himself when, in late November 1968, after the Presidential election, he sounded him out about becoming National Security Adviser. It was, as Nixon himself said, 'uncharacteristically impulsive'. Kissinger had worked for a rival Republican candidate, Nelson Rockefeller. What is more, it was well known that Kissinger was not a Nixon fan. 'The man is unfit to be president,' he had said repeatedly during the primaries.[9] Nixon was forgiving. 'I expected this from a Rockefeller associate, and I chalked it up to politics.' On 25 November, as Nixon was putting together his new administration, he summoned Kissinger to meet him in New York in order to invite him to be his National Security Adviser, a post first created by Harry Truman in 1947 to provide the President with comprehensive advice on American foreign affairs. Both the position and the National Security Council itself had been sidelined in earlier administrations. Nixon was determined to make the NSC the vehicle for his foreign policy.

It was only the second time the two men had met. Kissinger found the conversation interesting but unsettling. Nixon, as he usually was with unfamiliar people, was shy. He avoided small talk and plunged straight into a discussion of foreign affairs. He wanted, he told Kissinger, to avoid Johnson's trap of devoting all his time and energy to the Vietnam issue. The United States must concentrate on the longer-term problems that threatened its very survival: disunity in the North Atlantic Alliance, the Middle East, and relations with the Soviet Union and Japan. Nixon also mentioned one of his major preoccupations – the need to look again at American policy towards the

People's Republic of China. 'We also agreed', said Nixon, 'that what-ever else a foreign policy might be, it must be strong to be credible – and it must be credible to be successful.'[10]

The conversation ended without any mention by Nixon of a post for Kissinger. 'After frequent contact,' Kissinger later wrote, 'I came to understand his subtle circumlocutions better; I learned that to Nixon words were like billiard balls; what mattered was not the initial impact but the carom.' Nixon also hated being turned down, so, as much as he could, he avoided being put in a position where that might happen. Kissinger went back to Harvard, intrigued but uncertain about where he stood. Two days later, he was asked to come back to New York for a meeting with Nixon's friend John Mitchell. What, asked Mitchell, had Kissinger decided about the national security job? Kissinger replied that he had not been offered it. 'Oh, Jesus Christ,' said Mitchell, 'he has screwed it up again.' Kissinger, after some thought, accepted. He had now, he wrote in his memoirs, changed his mind about Nixon. 'I was struck by his perceptiveness and knowledge so at variance with my previous image of him.' Just after the new President's inauguration, Kissinger made sure that Haldeman knew how enthusi-astic he now was about Nixon. 'K. is really impressed with overall performance,' Haldeman recorded in his diary, 'and surprised!'[11]

'The combination was unlikely,' Nixon himself admitted, '– the grocer's son from Whittier and the refugee from Hitler's Germany, the politician and the academic. But our differences made the partnership work.'[12] And Henry Kissinger, the chubby professor with the thick glasses, the heavy German accent and the fingernails bitten to the quick, was an unlikely American statesman. Yet although Nixon and Kissinger had followed very different paths to power, the two also had much in common. Nixon was a politician through and through, but he was also a highly intelligent and reflective man. Of all American presidents, with the exception perhaps of Bill Clinton, he had the best grounding in foreign relations. He had been preparing for years. Kissinger, it is true, was an academic, but he had a tremendous instinct for power. He knew how to get it and how to use it. Even as a pro-fessor, at Harvard, he had shown himself adept at attaching himself to powerful patrons. Every summer he had run a special international seminar which brought together young leaders from the United States and its allies. Over the years that gave him a network of contacts which included prime ministers, presidents and foreign ministers around the world.

That Kissinger was at Harvard at all is an indication of his extraordinary talent and determination – and perhaps some luck as well. Born in 1923 into a solid middle-class Jewish family in a small Bavarian town, his happy and secure childhood had been overshadowed by the rise of the Nazis to power at the beginning of the 1930s. Like other Jewish children in Germany, he found himself forced out of the local school and barred from ordinary activities, whether sports or dances. Jews were taunted in the streets and beaten up. Kissinger's gentle, scholarly father was shattered by the change in the Germany he loved. His energetic and practical mother decided in 1938 that the family should leave for the United States, where her cousin was ready to welcome them. The Kissingers, parents and two sons, were among the fortunate ones; many of their relatives and friends died in the concentration camps. Kissinger rarely talked about that period in his life, but it is hard not to imagine that it had something to do with his antipathy to revolution and revolutionary ideologies and with his insecurities as an adult. His first significant mentor, a Prussian called Fritz Kraemer, who fought for the Americans in the Second World War, believed that 'It made him seek order, and it led him to hunger for acceptance, even if it meant trying to please those he considered his intellectual inferiors.'[13]

And most people were Kissinger's intellectual inferiors. He was a brilliant student. In his American high school, his unfamiliarity with English scarcely held him back at all. His grades were virtually all 90s or higher. (Unlike his younger brother Walter, though, he always kept his pronounced German accent. In Walter's view, it was because he listened to others where Henry did not.)[14] He sailed into the City College of New York and was doing equally well there when, at the start of 1943, the draft took him into the army and a new life.

Kissinger learned much in the army, both on special courses for particularly bright soldiers and from his fellow conscripts, most of whom came from very different backgrounds to his own. He began to develop his famous charm and his ability to laugh at himself. Thanks to a chance encounter with Fritz Kraemer, who had a keen eye for talent, he soared out of the ranks to become a counter-intelligence officer in occupied Germany at the end of the war. He did a superb job, rooting out senior Nazis and getting local administrations running again, and he did so without vindictiveness. Thanks to Kraemer again, he decided to apply to Harvard when his military service finished in 1947.

The Henry Kissinger who joined the faculty at Harvard in 1954 was a mature intellectual who had already seen much of the world. He was drawn by academic life, but even then he found it limited. Early on, he developed contacts in the centres of power in New York and Washington. In 1955 he took a leave from Harvard to research and write a book on nuclear weapons for the Council on Foreign Relations, the pre-eminent foreign policy forum for the East Coast establishment. The project brought him into contact with a number of powerful people, among them Nelson Rockefeller, who was to become another Kissinger patron. The resulting book, *Nuclear Weapons and Foreign Policy*, surprised everyone, including Kissinger himself, by becoming a bestseller. Richard Nixon read it and was impressed. The book also made his name outside the university world as someone to watch and, for his critics, as a cold and calculating strategist who talked calmly about using nuclear weapons in limited wars.

Kissinger spent much of the next decade at Harvard, broadening his already wide range of acquaintances and burnishing his academic reputation with articles and lectures. Increasingly he used the university as a base. In the 1960s he spent much time in New York and Washington, working as a consultant on and off for the Kennedy and Johnson administrations. Politically, though, he was finding that his natural home was with the Republicans. In personal terms, he was drifting away from his first wife, a childhood sweetheart whom he had married in 1949. In 1964, they divorced and he became, for a few years, a dashing bachelor. In the White House, Nixon loved the stories of Kissinger's reputed girlfriends and made ponderous jokes about his sex life.

Although they had much in common and were going to spend huge amounts of time together while Nixon was president, the two men never became real personal friends. 'A marriage of convenience' was how Pat Nixon described it. The two men did not watch football together like President Bush and Condoleezza Rice. They rarely socialized with each other. John Holdridge of the State Department, who came to know both men well, was once struck by a photograph of Thanksgiving dinner at Nixon's western house at San Clemente. 'Here were the Nixons with the people who were invited in to have Thanksgiving dinner, and Bob Haldeman, [John] Ehrlichman [Nixon's domestic affairs adviser], those two principally, and some other people from the White House staff, all more or less informally dressed. And here was Kissinger looking very German with a coat and a tie and with kind of a frozen expression on his face, and I thought, my God, the sort of unlikeliest guest.'[15] After Nixon left office, he and Kissinger met only infrequently.

'Each of them', said a diplomat who worked with them, 'saw the other as a friend poised with a potential dagger in his back; there is a little paranoia in both men.' In his own way, Kissinger was as insecure and as suspicious as Nixon. He was as sensitive to slights and criticism. It was not easy to be Henry Kissinger, the professor and the son of Jewish refugees, in Nixon's White House. He was treated, said Leonard Garment, a New York lawyer who became a special adviser in the White House, and himself a Jew, 'as an exotic wunderkind – a character, an outsider'. His colleagues admired him but also laughed at him with his thick German accent and his glasses. He had to endure, said Garment, 'the railings against Jewish power which were part of the casual conversation among Nixon's inner circle'.[16]

Leslie Gelb, who knew Kissinger well from their Harvard days and who also became part of the foreign policy establishment, saw him as 'the typical product of an authoritarian background – devious with his peers, domineering with his subordinates, obsequious to his super-iors'. Where Kissinger was different from Nixon, though, was in his ability to see himself from outside. 'I don't want you to get the wrong idea', he told a reporter when he took a call from Nixon, 'just because I was on my knees when I answered the phone.'[17]

Perhaps he had to be a courtier because he had no independent power base; he was Nixon's appointee and Nixon knew that. 'Henry is a genius,' Nixon told Gerald Ford as he was preparing to hand over the presidency, 'but you don't have to accept everything he recommends. He can be invaluable, and he'll be very loyal, but you can't let him have a totally free hand.' He advised Ford to keep Kissinger on as his secretary of state but hoped, he told an aide, that the new President would be tough enough. 'Ford has just got to realize that there are times when Henry has to be kicked in the nuts.' At other times, though, 'you have to pet Henry and treat him like a child'.[18]

Nixon, who was determined that American foreign policy should be run through the White House and not by the State Department or any other government arm such as the Central Intelligence Agency, knew that in Kissinger he had the subordinate he needed. With Kissinger's encouragement and advice, he gave approval to a new committee, to be chaired by the National Security Adviser himself, which would review and approve all policy papers sent by the various branches of government, including the State Department, before issues and recommendations went on to the President. Kissinger also had the power to order major studies on important issues from any department. Richard Helms, the experienced head of the Central Intelligence Agency, was startled to be informed by Kissinger that from then on all intelligence reports, even oral briefings, were to come through the National Security Adviser. Furthermore Nixon had decided that Helms was to attend meetings of the National Security Council but leave before the policy discussions started. (Nixon later forgot that he had given the order.) Kissinger became the doorkeeper in all matters that went up to the President for decision.[19]

The National Security Council itself became like a second State Department. Kissinger brought in bright young men from the universities and ransacked State for experts. It was an exhilarating and challenging experience to work for someone so intelligent and so demanding. He threw memoranda and reports back until they were right, yet rarely praised the final product. 'One of the most mercurial and difficult bosses it has ever been my pleasure or peril to know,' said Robert McFarlane, who became Kissinger's military assistant in 1973. His temper was famous and, being Kissinger, he made fun of it. 'Since English is my second language,' he said, 'I didn't know that *maniac* and *fool* were not terms of endearment.' To his credit he never minded a good argument; on the other hand, he watched his staff carefully to make sure they did not outshine him. When he became Secretary of State in Nixon's second term, a sour joke ran round the State Department about why working for him was like being a mushroom: 'Because you're kept in the dark all the time, because you get a lot of shit dumped on you, and, in the end, you get canned.'[20]

In a very short time, Kissinger became virtually indispensable to the President. He was prepared to sit for hours, if necessary, while Nixon, as was his way, worked out his ideas in rambling conversations. As he told a journalist, 'If I'm not in there talking to the President, then someone else is.' In Kissinger, Nixon had found someone who was his intellectual equal, who understood his policies and who could carry them out. Haldeman, who never much liked Kissinger and found his repeated outbursts and threats to resign tiresome, nevertheless concluded early on that he was 'extremely valuable and effective'. In August 1970, when Kissinger was in yet another state about a perceived slight, Nixon wondered about letting him go. Haldeman disagreed: 'we have to recognize this weakness as the price we pay for his enormous assets, and it's well worth it'.[21]

Most observers agree that it was Nixon who set the strategic directions for the United States and Kissinger who worked out the tactics. 'It was understood', said Viktor Sukhodrev, who interpreted for Leonid Brezhnev, the Soviet leader, 'that while Kissinger was playing a major role, I would have to say that in all the negotiations with Nixon, he [Nixon] was very much in command.' Nixon, in the view of one of his closer associates, the speechwriter Raymond Price, created the framework within which Kissinger operated. 'In the final analysis, each major turn got down to a presidential decision, and Nixon gave more care to these decisions than to anything else in his presidency.'[22]

Although Kissinger has since maintained that he and Nixon were always as one on the opening to China, the initiative clearly came from Nixon. Kissinger, it is true, had considered the possibility that one day the United States might be able to improve its relations with China. In a speech he wrote for Nelson Rockefeller in the 1968 campaign, he included a phrase about 'a subtle triangle with Communist China and the Soviet Union', but his main concern in his first months as National Security Adviser was improving America's relations with its European allies, and dealing with the Soviet Union. By temperament and background, he was firmly focused on Europe and the great struggle between the two superpowers, not on Asia. Vietnam had to be dealt with, of course, because of the damage it was doing to the United States in other areas. Although he came to support Nixon's opening to China loyally and indeed enthusiastically, he still tended to see it in terms of what it could do for relations with the Soviet Union.[23]

When Nixon first told Kissinger in February 1969 that he wanted to open up relations with China, Kissinger, according to Alexander Haig, who was then his aide, was dumbfounded. 'Our Leader has taken leave of reality,' he told Haig. 'He has just ordered me to make this flight of fantasy come true.' In a discussion a few months later at the National Security Council, he wondered about the consequences of bringing China out of its isolation, 'whether we really want China to be a world power like the Soviet Union, competing with us, rather than their present role which is limited to aiding certain insurgencies'. In the late summer of 1969, when Nixon had already sent word indirectly to the Chinese that the Americans would like to establish contact, Kissinger remained sceptical. As the President and his party were flying back from a world tour, Haldeman sat down beside Kissinger on Air Force One and remarked that Nixon intended to visit China before the end of his presidency. Kissinger smiled: 'Fat chance.'[24]

In his memoirs, Nixon talks of 'the China initiative' and makes it clear that he was in control, giving Kissinger his instructions to pursue it. Kissinger, by contrast, refers to 'our China initiative' and claims that he and Nixon came to believe in the importance of the China opening independently. It is no wonder, of course, that both men would want to take full credit for a bold move that transformed international relations – and which was one of the good news stories of a troubled presidency. It was, moreover, a pattern in their relationship. 'P realizes K's basically jealous of any idea not his own,' wrote Haldeman in his diary. According to John Ehrlichman, one of the reasons Nixon taped his own conversations was to leave a record that his ideas were his own. Nixon was livid when he had to share *Time*'s Man of the Year with Kissinger in 1972, and was jealous and hurt when Kissinger won the Nobel Peace Prize for his work in ending the Vietnam War. He resented the way the press paid attention to Kissinger. 'H,' he scribbled in one of his daily notes to Haldeman, '*Again* the theme of K's power – Not helpful!' From time to time, he issued orders, which he must have known would never be carried out, telling Kissinger not to give interviews to the press or appear on television.[25]

With Nixon, Kissinger was always deferential, sometimes to a fault. 'When I'd be talking to Henry', a friend of Nixon's remembered, 'and the president would telephone, his voice would shake; the whole tone of his voice would change.' Kissinger understood better than most the President's insecurities and his insatiable need for reassurance. He assured Nixon that he was a tough leader. 'It was extraordinary!' he told Nixon in his first year in office, after the President met with the Soviet ambassador. 'No President has ever laid it on the line to them like that.' Nixon, Kissinger insisted, was a success. In 1971, for example, the President gave one of his talks to the American people about Vietnam. The broadcast was at 9 p.m. and at 9.35 Kissinger's first phone call came in. 'This was the best speech you've given since you've been in office.' Kissinger's second call was at 10.21, then another at 10.35 and yet another at 11.13. There were more the next day. This was not unusual; there had been many other Nixon speeches and equally fulsome praise. Kissinger knew what Nixon wanted to hear: that he was wise and statesmanlike and, as important, that the public was aware of it. In 1982 Kissinger ran into John Ehrlichman in Los Angeles while the legal struggle over access to the Nixon tapes was still going on. 'Sooner or later those tapes are going be released, and you and I are going look like perfect fools.' Speak for yourself, Ehrlichman thought to himself.[26]

Away from Nixon, Kissinger was less polite. 'The madman' or 'our drunken friend', he would say when Nixon had been especially rambling. At Georgetown dinner parties, Kissinger would poke fun at Nixon's foibles and give the impression that he was trying hard to rein in the administration's wilder policies. He was a hawk in the White House, Haldeman later wrote, but a different person in the evenings. 'Touching glasses at a party with his liberal friends, the belligerent Kissinger would suddenly become a dove.' Nixon knew it was happening but he was forgiving. 'I know this. Kissinger likes to be liked. I understand that.' Even years later, when Kissinger had published some harsh comments about him, Nixon would only say to the historian Joan Hoff, 'I will be fair to Henry, even if he isn't always to me.'[27]

For all the tensions between them, the two men made one of the most influential foreign policy teams in American history. 'Nixinger diplomacy', one academic has called their tenure. Not only did they have the same perspective on international relations, they believed in keeping all major policies and initiatives in their grip. They shared a penchant for intrigue and secrecy. Both had trouble trusting people, even their own staffs. Both spent much time and energy worrying about leaks. 'They developed', said Lawrence Eagleburger, a Kissinger aide who later became Secretary of State for the first President Bush, 'a conspiratorial approach to foreign policy management.'[28]

It was on some issues, such as the breakthrough with China, a very effective approach because they cut through the bureaucratic thickets of precedence and caution which have hemmed in so many leaders. It did not always work when they did not keep the rest of the American government, especially the State Department, up to date on what they were doing. And it did not work when they tried to do too much themselves or when they simply ignored issues, such as economic ones, which did not interest them.

Kissinger, who Nixon later said admiringly was a 'very good infighter', took full advantage of his position to consolidate his power. He made good use of the new structure set up by Nixon for foreign affairs to ensure that he had the ultimate right of access to the President. Much to the annoyance of the State Department, he also started dealing directly with foreign representatives in Washington and abroad. After Nixon indicated to Anatoly Dobrynin, the Soviet ambassador to the United States, that he should work through Kissinger, the two men met regularly in Kissinger's office without anyone else being present. Dobrynin came and went at the White House by the service entrance. In time a private telephone line linked Kissinger's office directly to the Soviet embassy. At Foggy Bottom, as the State Department building was known, they had only the vaguest idea of what Kissinger and Dobrynin were discussing, or even when their meetings were taking place.[29]

That was how both Nixon and Kissinger wanted it. They were at one in their contempt for the State Department, filled with egghead liberals and, from Kissinger's perspective, rivals. 'Our basic attitude', said Kissinger as he and Nixon discussed the major crisis in South Asia in 1971, 'was the hell with the State Department; let them screw around with the little ones.' Major diplomatic secrets and initiatives could not be entrusted to the State Department, so Nixon and Kissinger believed, because it was incapable of moving rapidly and in any case was bound to leak information. It was, in their view, an incompetent, ineffective and over-staffed bureaucracy. 'I opened up China with five people,' Kissinger liked to say. In his first year in office, a senior State Department official remembered, 'Nixon gave us a little harangue about what our jobs were and how, by God, he was going to run foreign policy.' What is more, the President added, 'If the Department of State has had a new idea in the last 25 years, it is not known to me.' It was a view that Kissinger both shared and encouraged. 'The spirit of policy and that of bureaucracy are diametrically opposed,' he had written in his book on Metternich and Castlereagh. Policymakers had to take chances, while the whole instinct of bureaucracy was to seek refuge in routine. Kissinger kept the State Department out of the plans for Nixon's trip to China as much as he could and he was determined to make sure that its representatives stayed on the sidelines during the visit itself. The one thing he had not yet worked out, he told Dwight Chapin, during his October 1971 visit to Beijing, 'was how he was going to be able to keep Secretary of State Rogers from attending various meetings . . .'[30]

Now, at the Diaoyutai that February day, William Rogers, the Secretary of State, and his assistants were housed several hundred yards away from Nixon's villa in a smaller building. As Kissinger, who was in Nixon's villa, remarked in his memoirs, 'The Chinese well understood the strange checks and balances within the Executive Branch and had re-created the physical gulf between the White House and Foggy Bottom in the heart of Peking.' If the Chinese had not been aware of the tension between the State Department and Kissinger, he obligingly let them know about it on every possible occasion. In his talks with Chou En-lai on his trips to China in 1971, he had lamented the difficulties of dealing with American officials. 'We have not had the benefits of the Cultural Revolution,' he complained jokingly. 'So we have a large, somewhat undisciplined and, with respect to publicity, not always reliable bureaucracy.' The Chinese, he advised, should discuss the important issues such as Taiwan and relations with the Soviet Union with him and not with representatives from the State Department. It was also not necessary for the State Department to be involved in the crucial meetings between Nixon and Mao. As he told Chou, 'If those people who will not be meeting with Chairman Mao and the President could be separated from them in the most delicate way possible, it will help me tremendously.'[31]

Members of the State Department were torn between admiration for Kissinger's intelligence and his abilities as a negotiator and resentment over his determination to keep their department out of all important areas. As one said, 'if Henry Kissinger is not the bride, there's going to be no other wedding anywhere else'. Kissinger, at his best, was 'astute, articulate, a master of manoeuvre' in the view of Marshall Green, who was the senior person responsible for East Asia and the Pacific during the Nixon presidency.

> But he was also a megalomaniac, and as long as he was in the White House he lost no opportunity to build his power base at the expense of the State Department, undercutting the Secretary of State and shamelessly exploiting President Nixon's long-standing suspicions and prejudices against careerists in the State Department (despite our loyalty to all Presidents and our high respect for Nixon's extraordinary grasp of strategic issues).[32]

Unfortunately the man that Nixon chose to be his Secretary of State was no match for Kissinger. William Rogers, a handsome, affable and well-connected Republican from the East Coast, chafed at times but he was too gentlemanly to protest openly. 'A very nice man,' said a diplomat who knew him, 'a lawyer whose proudest achievement was some product-liability suits that he'd engaged in to defend Bayer Aspirin and other miscreants of great renown, and who was intensely loyal to the president on a personal level.' He and Nixon had worked together in politics for years; indeed Rogers had stood by Nixon during the 1952 campaign when the future President was accused of using a secret slush fund for his own benefit. Yet, like so many others who spent a lot of time with the man, Rogers always found the real Nixon elusive. 'His personality is more outgoing in his public appearances than in his private appearances,' he told one of Nixon's biographers. Nixon, for his part, seems to have regarded Rogers with mingled envy, admiration and contempt. In his memoirs, he praised Rogers' abilities as an administrator and negotiator, but to his White House aides he described him as 'ineffectual, selfish and vain'.[33]

Rogers had few obvious qualifications for his position as Secretary of State. He could not, said a leading conservative journalist, 'find the State Department in broad daylight with a flashlight'. He had not shown much interest in foreign affairs before he was appointed and, according to some of his critics, never developed any. In the State Department, where he was regarded with a sympathy tinged with disdain, he had the reputation of never reading anything that was more than three pages long. When Charles Freeman, from the China desk, tried to brief him during the layover in Hawaii on the trip out to China, Rogers was his usual courteous self. He was, Freeman recalled, 'able to sustain some interest in the trip for a while, but, as others seem to have remarked, did not have a great attention span for such matters and quickly drifted off and went off to play golf'.[34]

Nixon frequently complained about the tension between Kissinger and Rogers, but he also deliberately stirred it up. He would invite Rogers to private dinners in the White House, for example, something he rarely did with his National Security Adviser. Kissinger would stay in his office, checking with the Secret Service agents to see if Rogers had left yet. 'He would seem paranoid,' said Haldeman, 'ranting that he couldn't understand why the president would want to talk to Rogers.'[35]

Nixon may have seen Rogers' inexperience as an asset. 'I recognized', Rogers told the journalist Seymour Hersh, 'that he wanted to be his own foreign policy leader and did not want others to share that role.' Rogers' deputy, Elliot Richardson, felt that Rogers was not prepared to try to work seriously with Nixon in the making of American foreign policy. 'Rogers felt that in terms of character and judgment he was a better man and he could not subordinate himself, which an effective Secretary of State must do.'[36] He had not perhaps counted on having to subordinate himself to Kissinger as well.

Rogers allowed himself and the State Department to be outmanoeuvred in the early days of the Nixon presidency when Kissinger and the National Security Council became the centre of policymaking and, although he came to resent it, he never managed to recover what had been lost. He complained frequently to Nixon himself and to Nixon's aides that the President did not trust him and that Kissinger did not treat him properly. 'It would be goddam easy to run this office', said Nixon after one conversation with Rogers, 'if you didn't have to deal with people.' Nixon tried to reassure him but, in the end, perhaps he did not entirely mind seeing Rogers humiliated by Kissinger. Rogers had helped him over the Checkers scandal, when Nixon was accused of accepting presents from lobbyists, but, as a result, had also seen him at a low point in his life. The President was clear, in any case, that Kissinger was the indispensable one. 'If we got to the stage', he told Haldeman, 'where somebody had to fall on a sword in order to save the P, Henry would do it, but Rogers wouldn't.' Haldeman agreed but added, 'if Henry did do it, he would do it with loud kicking and screaming and make sure that the blood spurted all over the place so he got full credit for it . . .'[37]

After their welcoming remarks, the Chinese gave the Americans a lavish lunch and left them to settle in. Kissinger wandered about aimlessly waiting for his scheduled meeting with Chou at 3 p.m. The three American interpreters were called in to see Nixon to go over arrangements for the banquet that night. Charles Freeman, from the State Department, remembered being struck by Nixon's pancake makeup. 'There was a large glob of Max Factor hanging from a hair in the middle of the groove at the end of his nose.' (Ever since the debates with Kennedy when his five-o'clock shadow had given him a sinister cast, he had taken care to wear heavy makeup when there were cameras about.) The President merely shook hands and said how delighted he was to meet his interpreters but did not give them any instructions. He also called Haldeman up to his room to go over the low-key welcome. 'We talked a little', Haldeman said, 'about getting out the line that we weren't concerned at all about the lack of people in the streets and so forth.' It was just what they had expected, Nixon insisted. What was more important was that the Chinese had played the Star-spangled Banner at the airport.[38]

The Americans still had not had word on the crucial encounter between Nixon and Mao. In the discussions Kissinger had had with him in 1971, Chou had suggested that there might be two meetings: perhaps a first formal one with an American party including the President and the Secretary of State and then one with just Mao and Nixon and possibly Kissinger. 'You recommend early in the visit?' Kissinger had asked. 'Not the first day,' Chou replied. 'There are a lot of formalities on the first day.'[39]

5

Meeting with Mao

To the south of the Diaoyutai, in the Zhongnanhai compound where the top Communist leadership lived, the most powerful man in China sat propped up on a sofa, in a new suit and shoes made especially for the occasion, waiting anxiously for news of Nixon's arrival. Although the Americans did not know it, Mao was barely well enough to be seen. He had been sick for months with congestive heart failure. His legs had swollen; his blood pressure was dangerously high; and his lungs were filled with fluid so that he coughed incessantly.

The top leadership and Li Zhisui, his long-suffering personal doctor, urged him to receive treatment, but Mao, with a stubborn peasant suspicion of medicine, generally refused. He did not, he told his doctor, believe in traditional Chinese remedies and he would not have injections. On the rare occasions when he consented to take antibiotics in the shape of pills, he stopped as soon as he felt better. At the start of 1972, he had insisted on going out in the bitter Beijing winter to the funeral of an old comrade, Chen Yi. The result was pneumonia. Mao spent the next weeks in bed, growing increasingly weak and disoriented. On the morning of 18 January, a month before Nixon was due to arrive, one of his nurses panicked when she could no longer find his pulse.[1]

Beijing's top medical specialists examined him and prescribed a course of drugs. Mao agreed, reluctantly, to try antibiotics again but refused all others. At his bedside, Chou and Dr Li tried to make him aware of how sick he was, while Jiang Qing, Mao's estranged wife and no friend to Chou, accused Li of trying to poison her husband. Mao rallied briefly to tell her off and then murmured to Chou that he was done for and that Chou must take over after his death. A furious Jiang

Qing, making dark references to spy rings, rushed outside to summon a meeting of the Politburo, the inner party council. In spite of hours of high-level debate and entreaties from his colleagues and doctor, Mao continued for days to refuse all treatment. Suddenly on 1 February, with three weeks to go before Nixon arrived, Mao asked his doctor whether he could make him better.[2]

The Zhongnanhai clinic was stripped of its emergency equipment. The United States' government made an unwitting contribution as well; oxygen tanks and a respirator which had been sent on ahead in case Nixon fell ill were moved into Mao's bedroom. Dr Li and his team worked round the clock to get the Chairman well enough to receive Nixon. They managed to get his heartbeat under control and started him on diuretics. By the third week of February, Mao could get out of bed and walk a few steps. He was still bloated – the new suit and shoes were in fact essential – and had trouble getting his words out, but he was well enough to show to the Americans. The emergency medical equipment, including that from the United States, was hidden in a giant lacquer chest or behind potted plants, and Mao's hospital bed was taken away.[3]

On 21 February, Mao was 'as excited as I had ever seen him', remembered Li. As soon as Air Force One landed, he had ordered Chou to bring Nixon around at once. Chou urged that Nixon be taken to his villa first. Mao reluctantly agreed. By 2.30 he could no longer wait and called Chou again at the Diaoyutai. Chou went immediately to call on Kissinger to tell him that Mao wanted to see the President and 'fairly soon'. Like those other great dictators, Stalin and Hitler, Mao was used to making others fit his timetable. His colleagues had long since grown accustomed to sudden meetings in the middle of the night. Mao was also a master at keeping his friends and enemies off balance. So too had been generations of Chinese rulers before him. To Winston Lord, this was 'a typical example of the Chinese style, where the Emperor used to keep visitors on edge, and the schedule was never fixed until the last minute'. The purpose, he thought, was 'partly to make us feel grateful when the actual meeting took place and that it did take place'. It also reminded Lord of the traditional Chinese approach to the world: 'it was typical of the Chinese Emperor indicating that he was the head of the Middle Kingdom and that we were showing obeisance'.[4]

It was tempting to assume, and many foreigners did, that the Chinese remained Chinese in some essential and timeless way whether they were Communist, nationalist or something else. After all, China had over 2,000 years of virtually continuous existence as a state and 2,000 years of dealing with the outside world. History, as a source of lessons and analogies, had tremendous power over Chinese thinking. As one American scholar said, 'It was as if the Egyptians at the beginning of the twentieth century still wrote in hieroglyphics, studied in their schools a variant of the ancient cults of Isis and Ra, and were still ruled by a dynasty modeled after that of the Pharaohs.'[5] When the Communists debated policy among themselves, they drew as easily on the events of the third century BC as on those of the Russian Revolution of 1917.

Whoever led China had inherited deeply rooted ways of looking at and dealing with foreign powers. What this meant, or so observers like Lord argued, was that the Chinese still saw China as the kingdom at the centre of the world and the ruler of China as superior to all other rulers. While the Chinese possessed civilization, others were merely barbarians. For much of its history, certainly, China had been the dominant civilization and the dominant power in its world. Geography – seas, deserts, mountains, wastelands – had combined to insulate it from sustained contact with other great civilizations. Those peoples the Chinese knew well were at lower stages of development; they looked to China as the model of civilization. And so the Japanese, Koreans, Vietnamese, Mongols and Tibetans borrowed from China, whether it was a written language, religion, manufacturing techniques or philosophy.

The idea that China was merely a nation among other nations was not an easy one for many Chinese to absorb and the country's first steps into international diplomacy in the nineteenth century were often difficult. When the Qing dynasty finally decided to send scholars abroad to report back on other countries, it had trouble finding anyone who would agree to go. One man resigned his official position rather than suffer the shame of being sent among barbarians. A scholar who did tour foreign countries and who sent relatively favourable reports back was accused of losing his senses. Conservatives at court tried to prevent his reports being disseminated. A hundred years later, when the People's Republic of China was established, Mao reacted with fury to a suggestion that China might act as a bridge between the Soviet Union and the United States. 'This is nonsense! That means the Chinese people should bend their heads down to allow Americans to walk to the Soviet Union and to allow Soviets to walk to the States on our back. Can we do this?'[6]

At times, the Communists reflected, perhaps without their realizing it, the old assumptions about China being the centre of the world. In 1936, a young left-wing American writer, Edgar Snow, was granted one of the most dramatic scoops of twentieth-century journalism when he was able to interview Mao and the other top Communist leaders just after they had finished the Long March. In an exchange which Snow did not include in his famous book, *Red Star over China*, he asked Mao what effect a successful Communist revolution in China would have elsewhere. 'The Chinese revolution', replied Mao without hesitation, 'is the key factor in the world situation, and its victory is heartily anticipated by the people of every country, especially by the toiling masses of the colonial countries.'[7] It was an attitude that infuriated the Soviets and contributed to the split between them and the Chinese at the end of the 1950s.

Yet to see China as locked into such a limited sense of itself as the Middle Kingdom overlooks the richness and variety of the Chinese past.[8] The Chinese had many different traditions to draw on and a great many centuries. Their history had other lessons to offer. In the Warring States period, before the Qin Emperor united China in 221 BC, or in the Three States period of the third century AD, statesmen saved their nations through their skills in fighting and negotiating. The lessons from those years sound like ones that Machiavelli could have taught, about how to manoeuvre in an anarchic world. Even when it was united, China had not always been strong. Chinese rulers may have claimed to have the Mandate of Heaven to rule the earth, but for much of the time they knew it was not true, that other rulers did not obey the Chinese Emperor. China had suffered invasions by the same peoples it sometimes patronized. It had been obliged to make deals and bargains with powerful leaders on the periphery. In its turn, it had learned from others. As a much watched Chinese documentary of the late 1980s on the Yellow River put it, China always had the choice before it of looking inward or turning outward and embracing the world. In the nineteenth and twentieth centuries, as China's rulers tried to come to grips with outside powers, the same choice came up repeatedly: should China seek its security by dealing with other powers and manoeuvring through the complex world of international relations or should it rely only on itself and, as much as possible, shut the world out? Such questions have also occurred to Americans over the centuries.

The Chinese Communist Party reflected the tension in that choice. It had its genesis in the fury of Chinese nationalists at the depredations of the outside world, yet it drew its inspiration from a foreign ideology. It belonged to a worldwide movement but it also had moments of profound chauvinism. To Chinese Communists, as to other Chinese nationalists, the record of past humiliations at the hands of foreigners was a painful and a living one. In their conversations on Kissinger's first two trips to China, Chou En-lai returned again and again to past injuries at the hands of the Americans. On the other hand, the Chinese Communists knew that China needed alliances and friendships. One of China's first acts after 1949 had been to obtain a treaty with the Soviet Union and, in the 1950s at least, it had participated energetically in international bodies, from the Geneva conference of 1954 to the non-aligned movement of Third World countries. In 1972, Mao had decided on a radical new friendship.

When Chou brought Mao's summons to the Diaoyutai that February afternoon, Kissinger, or so he claimed in his memoirs, remained 'somewhat cool' and asked Chou about a few minor details for the banquet scheduled for that evening. In fact the news was intensely exciting and a relief to both Kissinger himself and Nixon. Lord recalled their reaction: 'It was going to send a clear signal to the world and to the Chinese people that Mao personally was behind this visit and the historic importance of the event. So this was obviously very good news, even if it was a somewhat unorthodox way to proceed with the leader of the Free World.'[9] American conservatives, many of whom were already unhappy about the trip, would have been incensed if the Chinese had appeared to insult their president – and they would have blamed Nixon for putting himself in such a position.

Kissinger darted upstairs to get Nixon and the two men piled into a Chinese limousine along with Chou En-lai, Lord and a Secret Service agent, leaving consternation in their wake. The agent, torn between following his orders not to tell anyone where he was going and his responsibility to protect the President, managed to alert Dwight Chapin, the man responsible for Nixon's schedule, on the way out. Chapin consulted Haldeman, who in turn called in Ron Ziegler, the press secretary, and the three men spent what Haldeman described as 'a very long hour and a half trying to figure out what the various contingencies were'. There was a moment of panic when the agent's radio went dead. (It turned out that the tin roof on Mao's house briefly blocked communication.) He could not avoid, Haldeman admitted, 'all the wild range of possibilities you have when you're sitting in a Chinese guest house with Red Army troops guarding you outside and you kind of wonder if the P's taken off alone with no staff, no security, except one agent, no doctor, etc.'.[10]

Haldeman, as always, also worried about press coverage. No one knew when Nixon would be back, and in the meantime a plenary session between the Americans and the Chinese had been scheduled for 4.30 p.m. The American press corps were already being assembled at the Great Hall of the People in preparation and the networks were planning for live coverage. (When Haldeman and Ziegler postponed the start of the plenary, there was eager speculation among the journalists but most dismissed the outlandish rumour that Nixon was meeting Mao.)[11]

The car bearing Nixon towards his momentous meeting turned in at the gate of the walled Zhongnanhai, named after the two man-made lakes, the Central and the Southern, which separated it from the Forbidden City. Just as the old imperial complex had been 'forbidden', off-limits to anyone except the imperial family, their court and their servants, so too was the Zhongnanhai. Very few foreigners and few ordinary Chinese had ever been allowed past its ubiquitous special guards. It was impossible even to peer into its extensive grounds, where the top Communist Party leadership lived in their special villas. Many of the Zhongnanhai's buildings dated back to the time of the Qing emperors, and it was as secluded and remote a seat of power for China as the Forbidden City had once been. Special farms all over China provided supplies for its inhabitants. Mao's food was treated with particular care; it went first to a laboratory in Beijing which checked on its freshness and tested for poison. Special food tasters then did another check.[12]

At first, Mao had lived in the Hall of Beneficent Abundance, a library built in the eighteenth century by the Qianlong Emperor. Its main entrance still bore a sign in the Emperor's own calligraphy. From its chambers and courtyards, Mao had planned the disastrous Great Leap Forward of the 1950s and had laid the groundwork for the Cultural Revolution. After he had discovered that his study had been bugged by overzealous colleagues, he never lived there again. In 1966, he had his private indoor swimming pool converted into a house.

Nixon's car was waved through the red walls and drove for a mile past walled houses, past the lakes and past groves of trees. Mao's house stood alone, 'simple and unimposing' in Kissinger's words. 'It could have belonged to a minor functionary.'[13] There did not appear to be any special security as the car halted at the front door. In fact, Mao and all the top leaders were constantly under an elaborate and intensive guard.

The Nixon party walked into a hallway which contained a ping-pong table. Mao's doctor motioned them towards the Chairman's study and then waited anxiously outside the open door in case his patient collapsed again. Only Chinese photographers were on hand to record the scene as Nixon and Mao met for the first time. Mao shuffled towards Nixon, supported by one of his corps of pretty young assistants. He took the President's hand in his own and shook it warmly for a long time. The photographers made sure that they caught this handshake too.

Another photograph shows the party seated with piles of Mao's books around them and, on the floor, white porcelain spittoons, standard furnishings in many Chinese offices to this day. Chou and Kissinger sit attentively on the edges of a semi-circle, overshadowed now by their masters. Although the photograph does not show him, another man sat beyond Kissinger. Winston Lord had worked on the China file at the National Security Council and had been on Kissinger's earlier trips to China. Kissinger brought him along to this historic meeting, so Lord thought, as a reward for all his hard work. Since even Kissinger realized that taking along a junior official rather than the Secretary of State was odd, he asked the Chinese to crop Lord out of any photographs.[14] In order to keep the discussions from leaking to the press or to the rest of the United States' government, the only interpreter was the Chinese one. Beside Chou in the photograph is a demure young woman, Tang Wensheng, Mao's interpreter, who was able to make sense out of his slurred speech and heavy Hunanese accent. She was also an influential player in the dance to gain his ear. The Americans knew her better as Nancy, the name she had acquired when she lived in Brooklyn as a child. In the middle a beaming Mao sits back, looking supremely comfortable. On his left, Nixon leans forward with an intent expression.

The conversation, which was originally meant to last for fifteen minutes, continued for just over an hour. The tone was amicable and, at times, jocular. Mao spoke with difficulty; his words came out in harsh bursts. The Americans assumed that he must have had a stroke. Partway through, Mao seized Nixon's hand again and held it for almost a minute. Nixon was delighted. 'The most moving moment,' he told his diary. The President started by praising Mao's impressive learning: 'You read a great deal.' He expressed his admiration for Mao's essays and for his poetry. 'Those writings of mine aren't anything,' Mao said. 'There is nothing instructive in what I wrote.' (Yet millions of copies of Mao's collected works, and even more millions of the Little Red Book which contained his aphorisms, had been printed during the Cultural Revolution.) Nixon insisted: 'The Chairman's writings moved a nation and have changed a world.' Mao demurred: 'I've only been able to change a few places in the vicinity of Beijing.' That remark, Kissinger thought, was 'not without pathos'. Did Mao fear that China was slipping back into its old bureaucratic ways? 'The aging Chairman railed against a fate that so cruelly mocked the suffering and meaning of a lifetime of struggle.'[15]

Of Nixon's own writings, the Chairman said generously, 'Your book, *The Six Crises*, is not a bad book.' And of Nixon himself he remarked, 'I voted for you during your election,' and added, 'I like rightists.' In 1793, the Qianlong Emperor, whose grounds they were in, sent a letter to George III of England via Lord Macartney replying to the English request for diplomatic and trading relations: 'On perusing your memorial, so simply worded and sincerely conceived, I

am impressed by your genuine respectfulness and friendliness and
greatly pleased.' He went on to instruct George III on proper behaviour. Two hundred years later, Mao dealt briskly with Nixon's
complaint that American backing for Pakistan in the recent war with
India had cost the Republicans politically: 'As a suggestion, may I suggest you do a little less briefing!' When Mao reminded Nixon that the
Democrats might well come into office again, there was perhaps a hint
that his own position was much stronger than the President's.[16]

Nixon, who had prepared carefully for this moment, did his best to
talk about the relations between their two countries and about the
international scene, but Mao waved him off. 'Those questions are not
questions to be discussed in my place. They should be discussed with
the Premier. I discuss philosophical questions.' When Nixon tried
to bring the conversation around to the specific issues affecting the
United States and China such as Taiwan, Vietnam and Korea, Mao
was dismissive: 'all those troublesome issues I don't want to get into
very much'. On Taiwan, he would only say that Chiang Kai-shek,
'our common old friend', did not approve of his meeting with Nixon.
Mao also brought up a popular Chinese theme, that China was never
an aggressor. 'You want', he said pointedly to Nixon, 'to withdraw
some of your troops back on your soil; ours do not go abroad.'[17]

Both men had fun with Kissinger. 'What about asking him to be
the main speaker today?' asked Mao. The doctor of philosophy ('a
doctor of brains' interjected Nixon) should be ready to discuss the
philosophic questions. 'We two must not monopolize the whole show.
It won't do if we don't let Dr Kissinger have a say. You have been
famous about your trips to China.' When Kissinger replied that he was
only doing as the President wished, Nixon got a laugh from Mao and
Chou by describing him as a 'very wise assistant'. Kissinger, Nixon
added, was the only man who could make secret trips to Paris and
Beijing without anyone finding out beyond a couple of pretty girls.
When Kissinger replied that he had used the girls as a cover, Mao was
intrigued: 'So your girls are often made use of?'[18] Was it significant
that, although Mao asked Kissinger for his opinion a couple of times,
he did not do likewise with his own subordinate Chou? Was it perhaps
a subtle way of undercutting Nixon?

In the record made by Lord, which is the only one so far made public, there is only a fleeting reference to the thorny issues of Taiwan and of the Soviet Union. Dr Li, who heard everything from his post outside the door, thought he heard Mao say that Taiwan would be a continuing problem. According to Li, as well, Mao warned the Americans that the Chinese press would continue to have articles attacking the United States and he expected that American papers might do the same to China. It would take time for the peoples of their two countries to become friends.[19]

As the hour went by, Chou kept looking at his watch. Nixon made one last attempt to get Mao to talk about the big issues. Neither China nor the United States, he said, had plans to dominate the world or each other. 'Therefore we can find common ground, despite our differences, to build a world structure in which both can be safe to develop in our own ways on our own roads.' The same, he added pointedly, could not be said about 'some other nations'. Mao said merely that China did not threaten Japan or South Korea and then turned to Chou. 'Do you think we have covered enough today?'[20]

Nixon hastened to add a few last warm sentiments. Mao had taken a great risk in inviting him to China. And, he pointed out, it had been a difficult decision for the Americans as well. The Chairman was the sort of person who could see an opportunity. As Mao himself had written, 'You must seize the hour and seize the day.' The President wanted Mao to know that Richard Nixon was a man of his word – and more. 'You will find that I never say something I cannot do. And I always will do more than I can say.' Mao gestured at Kissinger and repeated enigmatically, 'Seize the hour and seize the day.' It was true, he admitted, that he made a lot of noise about overthrowing reactionaries and establishing socialism, but he hoped that Nixon himself would not be overthrown. Mao's last statement was equally enigmatic: 'It is all right to talk well and also all right if there are no agreements, because what use is there if we stand in deadlock? Why is it that we must be able to reach results?' People might say they had failed, but if they succeeded in getting agreements on a second attempt, what then?[21]

As they parted Mao told Nixon that he was not very well. Nixon reassured him that he looked good and Mao replied that appearances could be deceiving. A Chinese cameraman who had been filming the meeting had been worried about Mao's unhealthy pallor at the outset but was delighted to notice that, as the conversation went on, his face glowed to give the appearance of good health.[22] With a last round of handshakes and photographs, the Americans took their leave. The historic conversation had been a curiously inconclusive one, with Nixon trying to lay the groundwork for future talks and Mao meandering about.

Once Nixon had gone, Mao changed out of his new suit into his dressing gown and chatted happily with his doctor, who checked his pulse to find it steady and strong. Mao approved of Nixon: 'He speaks forthrightly – no beating around the bush, not like the leftists, who say one thing and mean another.' He liked the way Nixon talked frankly about the benefits to the United States of an improved relationship with China. And, in a reference to his estranged Communist ally, the Soviet Union, he said, 'He is much better than those people who talk about high moral principles while engaging in sinister intrigues.' In their subsequent meetings, Mao's admiration increased. '*There* is a man who knows what he stands for, as well as what he wants,' he told the British Prime Minister, Edward Heath, in 1974, 'and has the strength of mind to get it.' He was never as impressed by Kissinger. 'Just a funny little man. He is shuddering all over with nerves every time he comes to see me.'[23]

The Americans were equally, if not more, pleased. 'The P called me up,' Haldeman wrote in his diary. 'Obviously, he was very impressed with the whole thing, but didn't get into any details at that time.' What Nixon did want to talk about was how to deal with Rogers. He asked Haldeman to say that Chou had come by unexpectedly and asked specifically for Nixon himself and Kissinger to have a chat with Mao before the plenary session scheduled for later that afternoon. Lord later claimed that Nixon and Kissinger had assumed that there would be a second meeting with Mao so that there would be an occasion for Rogers to meet him. Whether any of this convinced Rogers is doubtful. He was very angry and humiliated but took the attitude, according to one of his State Department subordinates, 'Well, the president needs this, and he can decide who he wants.' Kissinger in his memoirs admitted that he should have insisted that Rogers be included. 'The neglect was technically unassailable but fundamentally unworthy.'[24]

The Americans were deeply impressed with Mao. In his memoirs Nixon talks about his 'remarkable sense of humour' and how his mind was moving 'like lightning'. Mao was a man, Nixon told White House staff on his return, 'who sees strategic concepts with great vision'. Kissinger was even more effusive. Mao was a colossus among men. 'I have met no one, with the possible exception of Charles de Gaulle, who so distilled raw, concentrated will power.' As both Kissinger and Lord were fond of saying later, if they had walked into a cocktail party they would have known at once that Mao was the most important man in the room.[25]

Although the Americans were at first a little disappointed with the actual conversation, as time went by it began to take on mythic proportions and even the most commonplace of Mao's observations seemed to have a deeper meaning. 'The more we began to think about it,' Lord recollected, 'the more we examined the transcript of the meeting, we realized that Mao had hit the key issues – the Soviet Union, Taiwan and Vietnam – in just a few sentences, sometimes directly and sometimes in an allegorical way, stating the basic Chinese positions, which gave us a framework to enlarge and flesh out over the next few days.' For Kissinger, Mao's scattered remarks were like the composer Richard Wagner's use of motifs in his overtures which he intended to develop later on. Or like the heart of China itself. 'Later on, as I comprehended better the many-layered design of Mao's conversation, I understood that it was like the courtyards in the Forbidden City, each leading to a deeper recess distinguished from the others only by slight changes of proportion, with ultimate meaning residing in a totality that only long reflection could grasp.' Mao, he told one of his biographers, was a visionary and Nixon a pragmatist, but those differences had faded into insignificance.[26]

6

Mao Tse-tung

J UST BEFORE HIS meeting with Mao ended, Nixon paid one last carefully crafted compliment. 'The Chairman's life is well known to all of us. He came from a very poor family to the top of the most populous nation in the world, a great nation. My background is not so well known. I also came from a very poor family, and to the top of a very great nation. History has brought us together.' Nixon liked to stress how he and Mao came from similar humble origins. Like Mao, it is true, he was a consummate politician. Like Mao, too, he liked the great policy issues and was bored by day-to-day administration. When he saw in a memorandum that a Washington paper had compared him to Mao, Nixon scrawled a delighted 'K – Note!'[1]

Nixon might not have been as pleased at some other comparisons that could have been drawn. The difficulties both men had, for example, in dealing with people, especially as equals. Where Nixon was most at ease with the attentive Bebe Rebozo, Mao seemed happiest with his undemanding and unsophisticated bodyguards and nurses. Both had difficult relationships with their wives. Nixon usually ignored Pat; Mao gave orders that his wife was not to be admitted to his presence. And both men were deeply suspicious, even paranoid. The Nixon tapes reveal a man who peered out to see a world full of enemies – Jews, liberals, homosexuals, the establishment, the press. Mao also saw threats everywhere, whether from Taiwan or the Soviet Union or from inside his own party. By the 1960s, although he was surrounded by layers of protection, he was convinced that unnamed enemies were trying to poison him. As a consequence, he moved restlessly around China from one house to another.[2]

There were also profound differences between the two men.

Nixon, for all the abuses of office, accepted and believed in democracy; Mao was a dictator. And the two men's paths to their momentous meeting had been very different. When Nixon was born in his quiet California town in 1913, Mao was twenty years old. He had already taken part in a revolution, when China got rid of the Qing dynasty to become a republic. While Nixon was going to college in the 1930s, Mao was manoeuvring his way into power in the internecine struggles of the Chinese Communist Party and trying to stay out of the clutches of the Guomindang. In 1937, the year Nixon started practice as a lawyer in the placid town of Whittier, near Los Angeles, Mao was living in a cave in north-west China and consolidating his hold over the party. That year, the Japanese invaded China. While Nixon laid the foundations for a career in politics by talking to local service clubs, Mao dealt with great strategic issues and negotiated with the Guomindang for a common front against Japan. Nixon spent most of the Second World War as a supply officer in the Pacific; Mao was positioning the Communists to seize power in the aftermath of Japan's defeat.

As Nixon was laying the foundations of his political career, Mao was leading the Chinese Communists in a civil war against the Guomindang. By 1949, as the new Congressman Richard Nixon was making a name for himself as the scourge of Communists, Mao was the undisputed leader of both China and his party. When Nixon was going after Alger Hiss in the early 1950s as a suspected Communist, Mao was purging and killing millions of landlords, Guomindang supporters and – a usefully vague term – 'rightists'. By the time Nixon finally achieved the presidency of the United States, Mao had been ruler of China for two decades.

Five years after Mao's death, in 1981, his own party ruled that he had been correct 70 per cent of the time and wrong for the other 30 per cent, and that most of his mistakes had occurred after 1949. It was a way of, or at least a start at, trying to deal with his legacy. On the one hand, there was the triumph of the Communist Party over the Guomindang and the unification of China under one rule; on the other, the secret police, the purges, the destruction of many of China's cleverest and most talented people, and, above all, the dreadful cost of his utopian schemes. The Great Leap Forward in the late

1950s, which was supposed to turn China into a developed country right away, ruined much of China's agriculture and industry and led to a famine which may have killed as many as 40,000,000. Then, as China was recovering from that horror, Mao visited the anarchy and cruelty of the Cultural Revolution on its people.

He was not born a ruthless dictator but his background, the times and his own character combined to make him one. By nature self-absorbed, headstrong and impatient of authority, whether that of his father or of the government, he lived in a time in China's history when such qualities were useful. As the old order disintegrated, partly under its own weight but also because of the challenges from the outside world, those who were bold and iconoclastic had the best chance to survive and flourish. In 1917, in one of his earliest published articles, Mao wrote: 'A long period of peace, pure peace without any disorder of any kind, would be unbearable.' History, he said, taking a theme popular in Chinese traditional historiography, alternated between order and chaos. 'It is the times when things are constantly changing and numerous men of talent are emerging that people like to read about.' He had never intended to become a Communist or make revolution, he told his old friend the American journalist Edgar Snow in a conversation in 1964, but China was oppressed and in turmoil. 'In short, this was independent of our will.' The fact that he survived at all helped to persuade him that he had been chosen by fate. 'On many occasions death seemed to be at my elbow.' Often he had narrowly escaped. 'Once a guard who was at my side was killed by a bomb and his blood splashed on me.'[3]

Like his colleagues in the Communist Party, Mao's rise to power was against a background of instability, violence and misery. Before he was out of his teens he had taken part in a revolution and seen headless bodies lying in the streets. He had seen pitched battles between reformers and conservatives trying to restore the old order. He had seen soldiers terrorizing the local population, mass arrests and executions. By the time he was thirty, he was a hardened revolutionary. He had experienced treachery, cruelty and betrayal, and inflicted the same things on others. He had already lost many friends and comrades, and his wife and two brothers had been executed by the Guomindang. He himself had fled into a precarious refuge in the hills of south-central

China. He had learned, through it all, to understand power and to trust no one. He had also learned how to survive in the savage internal struggles of the Chinese Communist Party, playing off one faction against the other and quietly undermining his rivals. In 1971, as Mao was turning his anger on Lin Biao, his Defence Minister, Lin's son said ruefully: 'Today [he] uses this force to attack that force; tomorrow he uses that force to attack this force. Today he uses sweet words and honeyed talk to those whom he entices and tomorrow he puts them to death for some fabricated crimes.'[4]

Like many other rebels in China's long history, Mao came from the countryside. His province, Hunan, had a long history of providing grand civil servants and also bandits who took advantage of its rivers and mountains. The Hunanese, who loved hot red peppers, were always said to have a temperament to match their cooking. They were stubborn and deeply suspicious of outsiders, whether their Manchu rulers or the foreign missionaries who started to appear in the nineteenth century. 'China can only be conquered', a proverb had it, 'when all the Hunanese are dead.'[5]

Mao was born a peasant, into a small village where life went on as it had for centuries. Only a few rumours of the outside world drifted in: of the upheavals of the Taiping Rebellion which convulsed so much of China in the mid-nineteenth century, and then the Boxer Rebellion at the end of the century which brought Western troops into the capital itself. Like Nixon, Mao later exaggerated his humble beginnings. His hardworking and thrifty father had grown more prosperous than many of his neighbours, partly through moneylending. He was able as a result to educate his sons, a move which, in a society which valued education highly, was the usual route out of the peasant class.

Mao went to a traditional village school where the pupils memorized the old characters and some of the classics of Chinese civilization. He also learned to write poetry in the classical forms, as Chinese scholars had done for centuries. By the time he was ten, he began to understand some of the key ideas of Confucianism, that legacy which underpinned so much of traditional Chinese culture. The Confucian ideas of individual virtue and of the need for leaders to be virtuous and Confucianism's faith that humans could be improved later mingled with his Marxism to produce Mao's beliefs that China needed the moral leadership of the Communist Party and that human nature was infinitely malleable. And, as Chinese had done for centuries, he looked to history for lessons and guidance. By the time Mao was in his teens, though, the changes in China and the wider world were starting to press in on even his small village. He came across a pamphlet which warned that China was going to be divided up by the outside powers. 'After I read this,' he remembered, 'I felt depressed about the future of my country and began to realise it was the duty of all the people to help save it.'[6]

As a young man, he also read the great novels with their upright heroes who defied corrupt and incompetent officials. Mao's favourite, *The Water Margin*, is a Chinese *Robin Hood*, with a brotherhood of bandits and rebels who swear to each other to protect the poor and avenge injustice. Within his own family, he practised rebellion by defying his father. (Like Nixon, he loved his mother deeply.) When his mother, a gentle Buddhist, tried to make peace between them, Mao, according to his own later account, was immoveable. 'I learned that when I defended my rights by open rebellion my father relented, but when I remained weak and submissive, he only beat me more.'[7]

When his father pulled him out of school to work on the farm, Mao dawdled in the fields and spent as much time as he could reading. A year later, when Mao was fourteen, his family, as was the custom, found a wife for him. Mao refused to accept the girl and left home. 'My father was bad,' he said many years later during the Cultural Revolution. 'If he were alive today, he should be "jet-planed" [a favourite torture of the Red Guards where the victim's arms were yanked up behind his head].'[8] While Mao may have been bolder than other young men his age, such conflicts between the generations were not unusual and are not sufficient to explain the man he became. His father, moreover, continued to support him when he resumed his education, trying first one school and then another.

At sixteen, Mao left the countryside behind – as it turned out, for ever. His father, with some reluctance, agreed that he should go to school in a nearby town. Some of the characteristics of the later Mao were becoming apparent by this stage. Among his new classmates he stood out as arrogant, stubborn and also sensitive to slights. 'Many of the richer students despised me,' he told Edgar Snow, 'because usually I was wearing my ragged coat and trousers.'[9] Two years later, he moved on to another school in the provincial capital of Changsha, just in time for the revolution of 1911, when China became a republic. Mao, like Chou and many other Chinese, cut off his pigtail as a sign that the world had changed. When some of his fellow students proved reluctant to follow his example, he and his friends seized them by force and chopped theirs off as well.

In those early years, he was finding his heroes: among them the tyrannical Qin Emperor who first united China in 221 BC and who burned books and buried scholars alive to make sure that nothing or no one could challenge his version of reality. He also admired Sun Yat-sen, the father of modern Chinese nationalism, and George Washington, who outlasted the British to win independence for the Thirteen Colonies. He even defended an unlikely figure, 'Butcher Tang', the general who imposed a harsh rule on Changsha in the years after 1911. Although Tang closed schools, banned newspapers and executed 5,000 people in his three years in power, often in the most brutal ways, Mao approved of his strong government. 'Without such behaviour, the goal of protecting the nation would be unattainable. Those who consider these things to be crimes do not comprehend the overall plan.'[10] The belief that firm, even harsh government was necessary for the Chinese people was to stay with Mao all his life.

In the years after 1911, Mao drifted from one thing to another. He served briefly in one of the new revolutionary armies, then decided to go back to school again. His long-suffering father agreed to pay his fees. He toyed with the idea of police school. Then he decided he would rather learn to make soap or perhaps how to be a lawyer. Then it was a business school. He finally ended up in a Normal School, for training future teachers. All the while, however, he was reading and learning. By this time, he was encountering some of the new ideas and knowledge that were challenging the traditional learning. He read Western thinkers, such as Adam Smith and Rousseau, in translation. Like others of his generation, he turned away with contempt from traditional Chinese learning. Centuries of tradition, he told a friend, had made the Chinese people slavish and narrow-minded.

'Their mentality is too antiquated and their morality is extremely bad.' The old ways of thought could be removed only 'with tremendous force'.[11] Unlike others of his generation, however, Mao never entirely repudiated the past. He continued throughout his life to refer to the classics in his writings and his conversation.

Mao also never thought that China should blindly imitate other civilizations. Like the passionate Chinese nationalist he was, he always had a mixed reaction to the outside world. He recognized that China needed to learn, at the very least, modern technology from the West, but he also resented that fact. He once told a friend to stop wearing Western-style clothes. Mao hated what he saw as a fawning admiration of all things foreign. 'If one of our foreign masters farts,' he wrote in 1923, 'it is a lovely perfume.'[12] On the other hand, like many other young Chinese nationalists, including Chou En-lai far to the north, he was impressed by Japan and by its rapid success in modernizing. He also shared their despair at the ineptitude of the new republic and the continued pressures from foreign powers.

By now he was also developing his own ideas. He kept a journal for a time and started to write articles. Like many of his contemporaries he was impressed by the Darwinian notion of the survival of the fittest which held out both promise and threat for China. In 1917, in his first published article, he urged his fellow countrymen to take physical education seriously lest China would grow even weaker. 'Our nation is wanting in strength. The military spirit has not been encouraged.'[13] The importance of military power was something that was to remain with Mao for the rest of his life.

Mao always prided himself on his toughness. As students, he and his friends would go on long walks in the winter, wading through icy streams. When he became ruler of China, he made highly publicized swims to demonstrate how fit he was and how self-controlled. In that same early article, he struck what was to become another favourite theme: that physical education helped to bring the emotions under control and strengthen the will. As he told his staff when he was ruler of China, 'Sometimes I am so angry I feel my lungs are bursting. But I know I must control myself and not show anything.' The Soviet premier, Nikita Khrushchev, who had a number of difficult conversations with Mao, compared him to a calm, slow-moving bear. 'He would look at you for a long time, then lower his eyes and begin talking in a relaxed, quiet voice.'[14]

As Mao was to write later in an essay that became compulsory reading for the Chinese, the individual, if his will was strong enough, could move mountains. And for morality, he believed, the individual need refer only to himself. 'Every act in life is for the purpose of fulfilling the individual,' he wrote as a young man, 'and all morality serves [that end].' Although he later proclaimed himself a Marxist, subject therefore to the laws of history, he never gave up that belief, at least where he himself was concerned. He also discovered his own attraction to sheer power. In another article, written in 1917, he talked about the hero whose actions were entirely the expression of his own impulses. 'His force is like that of a powerful wind arising from a deep gorge, like the irresistible sexual desire for one's lover, a force that will not stop, that cannot be stopped.'[15]

By the summer of 1918, Mao had finished at the Normal School and qualified as a teacher. He was not yet ready to settle down, however, and spent much of the next year drifting between Beijing, Shanghai and Changsha. It was an important period both for Mao and for China, a time of radical change and intellectual ferment. Mao shared the disgust that other young Chinese such as Chou En-lai felt when the victorious powers assembled in Paris decided to award what had been German concessions in China to Japan. Chinese nationalists were appalled and deeply angry at what they saw as betrayal by the Western democracies. Some concluded that democracy itself was flawed and wrong for China and that the West would never be China's friend. By now they had an alternative: Marxist ideas were already circulating in intellectual circles in China and, to the north, the Bolsheviks had seized power in Russia and appeared to be putting those ideas into action. When, in the spring of 1920, the new Communist regime in Russia repudiated the old unequal treaties made between China and Russia and made statements (which in the end amounted to little but empty words) about handing back territory seized from China in tsarist days, Chinese nationalists were deeply impressed. Russia was, Mao said at the time, 'the number-one civilised country in the world'.[16] Many Chinese radicals were to move towards Marxism and, after it was established in 1920, the Chinese Communist Party.

Mao was among them, and luck and perhaps his own talents brought him into contact with men who could help him. In Beijing, a young unknown man from the provinces, he found a friend in one of his former professors who helped him get a modest job as an assistant in the library of Beijing University. There his superior was Li Dachao, one of the most prominent of China's early Marxists and the founding co-chairman of the Communist Party. Mao met other Marxists and gradually started to read some of Marx's works which had been translated into Chinese. By 1920, although he had toyed briefly with anarchism, he had decided that he too was a Marxist. By the autumn of that year, he had a job as principal of a primary school in Changsha, but, like Chou, he was spending much of his time and energy on radical politics.

In his personal life, Mao was experiencing much change as well. His much loved mother fell ill and finally died in the autumn of 1919. Although he had sent her medicine, he had not gone near her in the last months. 'I told her', he confided to one of his staff years later, 'I could not bear to see her looking in agony. I wanted to keep a beautiful image of her, and told her I wanted to stay away for a while.' The death of his father a few months afterwards does not seem to have caused him much grief.[17]

At the start of 1921, he got married, this time to a bride of his own choosing. Yang Kaihui was the daughter of his old professor and patron. She was educated and, in the context of the day, something of a radical feminist. The marriage involved love on both sides, but Mao was not an easy husband. Increasingly politics took first place and there were always other women.[18] In the early 1920s, as the fortunes of the Communist Party rose, those of Mao rose with them. Following the advice of the Soviet Union, as Russia had become, the Chinese Communists formed a tactical alliance with the major nationalist party, the Guomindang, to unite China and expel the foreign powers. Mao enthusiastically supported the alliance, a fact ignored in the official biographies, and spent much time away from home working for the United Front.

The alliance led, not as promised by the Chinese Communists' Soviet mentors and paymasters to a Communist revolution, but to a Guomindang supremacy under Chiang Kai-shek. The Guomindang at once turned on its former allies, and by the end of 1927 the Communist Party was largely destroyed in the big cities and Communists were either dead, underground like Chou or, like Mao, on the run in the countryside. Mao made his way into the mountains of south-central China and began, with others, to rebuild Communist strength.

In the next few years, as the Communists gradually developed armed forces and learned how to live among and use the peasants, Mao slowly climbed upwards in the hierarchy. He was helped by an alliance with Zhu De, the Communists' leading military commander, and by the fact that Moscow, which provided so much of the funding and weapons for the Chinese Communists, had spotted him as someone worth promoting. In what are still murky inner-party struggles, Mao picked off his rivals one by one. In 1935, he gained a key ally when Chou En-lai decided to accept his leadership.

By this time, the Communists had been forced to abandon their base in south-central China and were desperately searching for safety from the Guomindang. This, although they did not realize it at the time, was the start of the Long March, that epic event in Communist mythology. Many of the legends that surround the March are just that. Mao for example rarely marched but was carried on a litter, reading. Communist soldiers, according to a recent history, did not swing heroically arm over arm along the chains of a crucial bridge; they strolled over unopposed. Nevertheless, the Long March was key to the rise of Mao and the later success of the Communists. By the time it ended, in the autumn of 1936, the Communists were in the north-west, much closer to Soviet aid and further from the Guomindang, and Mao was firmly entrenched in power.[19]

In 1937, the Japanese, who had already seized Manchuria, swept down into China. Although the Guomindang resisted, it was driven from one big city after another, finally retreating far up the Yangtze river to Chongqing. The invasion, which brought destruction and misery to much of China, weakened the Guomindang – as it turned out, mortally. The Guomindang lost its main tax base and much of its popular support. Its armies rotted from within, and the party and its bureaucracy grew increasingly corrupt. The Communists, by contrast, appeared as dedicated, clean-living patriots. Whether or not that was true, and there are still many questions about what they actually did in the war against the Japanese, the important thing is that outsiders and the Chinese themselves came to believe it. China's war, which had been caught up in the much wider world war, ended with the surrender of Japan in 1945.

The Communists now had an army of over 1,000,000 men and controlled much of the countryside north of the Yangtze. And within the party Mao was now absolute ruler. If his colleagues disagreed, he was to have the final word. In 1945, delegates at a special Party Congress confirmed his special status. A huge sign proclaimed 'March Forward under the Banner of Mao Tse-tung!' Those who had known him for some years found that he was becoming more remote and godlike. Chou En-lai was still a comrade, said an American fellow traveller. 'With Mao, I felt I was sitting next to history.'[20]

In 1945, as he was poised to seize power over the whole of China, Mao was in his prime. Agnes Smedley, an American Communist, who got to know him during the war, was both attracted and disturbed when she met him for the first time in his temporary home of a cave. 'His dark inscrutable face was long, the forehead broad and high, the mouth feminine. Whatever else he might be he was an aesthete. I was repelled by the feminine in him and the gloom of the setting. An instinctive hostility sprang up inside me and I became so occupied with trying to master it that I heard hardly a word of what followed.' His hands, she noted, were 'long and sensitive as a woman's'. She later warmed towards him and decided that what she had seen in him was a deep spiritual aloofness. 'I had the impression that there was a door to his being that had never been opened to anyone.'[21]

Perhaps it had been opened to his wives and to a few old comrades. Possibly, too, he had revealed a little to his children, although Mao's attitude to his two surviving sons, from his first marriage, and his two daughters, from his two later ones, was ambivalent. He saw little of them when they were young, and as adults he found them troublesome. An-ching, his younger son, developed a mental illness, possibly schizophrenia, and both his daughters had severe depressions. His elder son, An-ying, was killed in the Korean War. Mao sat silently for some moments when he heard the news and then said merely, 'In any revolutionary war, you always pay a price. An-ying was one of thou-sands.' According to Mao's daughter-in-law, he was in such agony when he broke the news to her that his hands turned as cold as ice. One of his bodyguards noticed that he lost his appetite for some time afterwards. An-ying was perhaps the last person with whom he had a close affectionate relationship. After his death, said one of the inner circle, 'Mao gradually became ever more reclusive and ever more sus-picious of almost all those around him.'[22]

From his earliest days in power, he subjected the party to repeated purges and inquisitions to hunt out those who were disloyal. And often disloyalty simply meant disagreeing with him. According to Lin Biao's son, Mao preferred to eliminate those he suspected. 'Every time he liquidates someone, he will put them to death before he desists; once he hurts you, he will hurt you all the way.' In the course of his life, Mao lost, pushed away or betrayed many who had once been close to him. He made the Revolution in the name of the peas-ants, yet they suffered more under his rule than they had under the Guomindang as he forced them into collectives and squeezed resources out of the countryside. 'Educate peasants to eat less, and have more thin gruel,' he ordered.[23] He urged intellectuals to lend their talents to building the new China, but when they ventured to express their opinions he had them tortured and jailed, or sent to the countryside for re-education.

Although he wrote one of his most lovely poems about her and in old age described her as the love of his life, Mao abandoned his first wife and their young sons in the turbulent days of the late 1920s without any apparent regret. Yang Kaihui moved back to Changsha to be near her family and Mao made no attempt to keep in touch with her. In a series of letters which miraculously survived, she wrote with increasing desperation of her continuing love for Mao, her misery at being abandoned, and her fears for herself and her children as the Guomindang tightened its grip. In 1930, in retaliation for Communist attacks on Changsha, the local nationalist general had her executed. She was only twenty-nine.[24]

In 1928, while Yang was still alive, Mao got married again, to a young girl from the countryside, He Zizhen, who agreed, rather reluctantly, to become his 'revolutionary companion'. She paid heavily, suffering through the Long March and repeated pregnancies and miscarriages until Mao abandoned her, in turn, for a younger, more glamorous woman. His next and final marriage was to the Shanghai actress Jiang Qing. When that marriage, too, soured, he preferred to avoid a divorce and simply had a series of mistresses, sometimes several at once. It was easy enough for Mao to get them, from among his nurses and assistants or from a special army company of dancers and singers. 'Selecting imperial concubines' was how a senior general described it. Mao preferred young, simple girls who felt deeply honoured to be chosen by the great man, even to the point of taking pride in catching venereal disease from him. When his doctor suggested that the Chairman might want to stop his sexual activities while the disease was treated, Mao refused. 'If it's not hurting me,' he said airily, 'then it doesn't matter.' As far as hygiene was concerned, Mao's solution was more sex, 'I wash myself inside the bodies of my women.'[25]

The long years of struggle and the exercise of supreme power had turned the idealistic young student into someone as indifferent to others as the first great emperor of China himself. (Indeed Mao liked the comparison.) Khrushchev, who got to know Mao over the years, thought he was like Stalin. 'He treated the people around him like pieces of furniture, useful for the time being but expendable. When, in his opinion, a piece of furniture – or a comrade – became worn out and lost its usefulness, he would just throw it away and replace it.' The mature Mao had perhaps been foreshadowed by the young one. In 1915, he had written in his journal, 'You do not have the capacity for tranquillity. You are fickle and excitable. Like a woman preening herself, you know no shame. Your outside looks strong but your inside is truly empty. Your ambitions for fame and fortune are not suppressed, and your sensual desires grow daily.'[26]

According to Chinese astrology, Mao was born in the Year of the Snake. His sign meant that he should have been charming and seductive, which Mao could certainly be. Snakes were also meant to be introverted. As Mao once said of himself, 'I have self-confidence but also some doubt.' Snakes, it was also said, relied on their intuition. It was always wise to be careful of them because they could suddenly bite. Mao preferred other signs in Chinese astrology, and described himself as two-thirds tiger and one-third monkey with the tiger as the dominant force. The tiger, in Chinese popular belief, is fearless and always on the attack, while the monkey is clever, playful, unpredictable and ready to take chances.[27] Tigers are also cruel, and Mao had learned to embrace cruelty.

Like other great dictators, Stalin for example, Mao could also be sentimental at times. He was saddened by the sight of a dead sparrow and he wept regularly at his favourite opera, which told the story of an immortal female snake who fell in love with a human only to be imprisoned for all eternity by a wicked monk. His doctor, however, thought he was incapable of genuine human affection or compassion. Once during a performance in Shanghai, a child acrobat slipped and was badly hurt; Mao kept laughing and talking. He took pain and death, except for his own, lightly, even cheerfully. When widespread famine came with the failure of the Great Leap, Mao was unconcerned. People ate too much, he declared. 'Best halve the basic ration, so if they're hungry they have to try harder.' When the persecutions during the Cultural Revolution drove many Chinese to despair, Mao was unmoved. 'One should never attempt to save people who try to commit suicide. It's they themselves who want to die, so why try to save them? China has such a large population, it is not as if it cannot do without these people.'[28]

Years before, while he was still a student, he had written, 'The birth of this is necessarily the death of that, and the death of that is necessarily the birth of this, so birth is not birth and death is not destruction.' He believed that out of the destruction a new China would come – or a new universe. 'I very much look forward to its destruction, because from the demise of the old universe will come a new universe, and will it not be better than the old universe?' He mused to the Finnish ambassador in 1955 that, even if China or the earth were blown to pieces, 'this might be a big thing for the solar system, but it would still be an insignificant matter as far as the universe as a whole is concerned'.[29]

For Mao, destruction was not only necessary, it was exhilarating. In 1927, he went to observe spontaneous and violent peasant revolts in his own province of Hunan. He wrote admiringly, in a passage that was much quoted during the Cultural Revolution, 'A revolution is not the same as inviting people to dinner or writing an essay or painting a picture or embroidering a flower.' The peasants were turning their world upside down. 'A revolution is an uprising, an act of violence whereby one class overthrows the authority of another.' In 1958, as he prepared to start the Great Leap Forward, Mao described how the remnants of the old China were being cleared away like so much garbage. China, he said, was like a piece of blank paper. 'A clean sheet of paper has no blotches, and so the newest and most beautiful words can be written on it, the newest and most beautiful pictures can be painted on it.'[30]

What was written was not beautiful but hideous for China, but it was very difficult for his colleagues, even the bravest, to stand up to Mao. Chen Yi, a tough and experienced general who had been with Mao from very early days, once burst out as Mao made yet another arbitrary decision, 'I don't understand what's going on! Mao does whatever he wants to do.'[31] After 1949, when the People's Republic was established, the atmosphere around Mao became, in some respects, eerily similar to that of the old imperial court. He was increasingly inaccessible to the general public. When he travelled it was on private trains or aircraft. His houses, and there were many, were usually built especially for him, with his beloved swimming pools, his auditoriums for watching operas and his bomb shelters. Local inhabitants were cleared away and tight security was imposed.

Within his small circle, his underlings, secretaries, security guards and the ever present pretty nurses were utterly dependent on him and vied for his favour. 'I had not worked long for Mao', said his doctor, 'before realizing that he was the center around which everything else revolved, a precious treasure that had to be protected and coddled and wooed.' His staff watched his every mood and waited for his every command. They listened for the bell from his large bed where he lay with his books and, frequently, with his women. Mao hated new clothes so they patched his old ones carefully and made sure that the patches were always the same colour. His bodyguards broke in new shoes for him. If he wanted to eat (and he rarely ate at regular meal-times), they had his favourite foods ready for him. They rubbed him down with hot towels when he wanted to be cleaned. If he was ready to sleep, they massaged his feet and waited for his increasingly strong doses of sleeping pills to take effect. When he got more than thirty hours of sleep per week or when he had a regular bowel movement, they noted it in their logs and rejoiced.[32]

In some respects, Mao remained the peasant he had been so many years before. He still spoke in a thick Hunanese accent and his speech was larded with coarse country expressions. True to the customs of his youth, he slept naked at night and preferred rinsing his mouth with green tea to brushing his teeth. He never really got accustomed to indoor lavatories. When he moved into the Zhongnanhai after 1949, an orderly followed him around the grounds with a shovel until Chou En-lai finally arranged for a special toilet by his bedroom where he could squat.[33]

His colleagues came and went at his command; since he liked to work in the middle of the night, they learned to go without sleep. And they tried, as Mao became ever more capricious, to adjust themselves to his thinking. 'We were terrified', said one, 'of saying something wrong in case he took it as an error.' Chou En-lai, so admired for his subtle intellect and his extraordinary capacity for work, worked like a lackey for Mao. He always, even when he was prime minister of China, acted as Mao's majordomo. He arranged his houses and looked after his family, even leaving Politburo meetings to go off and deal with Jiang Qing's endless medical crises. In Mao's presence, he was, as Lin Biao once said, 'the obedient servant', attentive to the point of subservience and rarely showing emotion, even in response to his master's most outrageous actions. Yet, when Mao lapsed into unconsciousness shortly before Nixon's visit, Chou was so upset, according to the Chairman's doctor, that he completely lost control of his bladder and bowels.[34]

Perhaps over the years Mao become a bit mad. Being in a position where every whim is law, virtually every wish can be fulfilled and every dream is apparently realizable cuts the ropes, of family, society or morality, that tie us all to reality. Think of other dictators: of Hitler raving to the last in his bunker under Berlin that he had a secret weapon; or of Stalin in his final paranoid days preparing yet another purge of his supposed enemies. Mao's own immediate family had a history of mental troubles and, throughout his life, particularly at difficult moments, he had periods when he took to his bed in depression. By the late 1950s, according to his doctor, he was increasingly paranoid. He refused to swim in a new pool because he thought it had been poisoned; he abandoned a newly built house because he felt there was something wrong with its air; and he became convinced that he was surrounded by spies.[35] His dependence on sleeping pills, always heavy, intensified to the point where, by the mid-1960s, he was taking ten times the normal dose.

Zhang Hanzhi, one of Chou En-lai's interpreters, who had known Mao for most of her life, thought that, until that time, he was still a normal human being. 'In the 1970s he changed psychologically and physically. He was put into a role where everything he said was a law. Yours was to obey. He became more and more prejudiced.'[36] The Mao that Nixon and Kissinger met had not been born a heartless tyrant, but untrammelled power had turned him into one. He had, when he chose, complete authority over Chinese policies, whether domestic or foreign. He remained, ill as he was, the final arbiter of any changes to the relations between China and the United States.

Though the night of Nixon's first day in Beijing, the lead item on the Chinese television news was about a group of heroic women workers, and Nixon's arrival was dropped in at the end, almost as an afterthought, when it became official that the US President had been granted an audience with Mao, the news coverage changed overnight. The next day, the front page of the *People's Daily* had large photographs of Mao greeting Nixon, a group shot of Mao, Nixon, Chou and Kissinger, and Chou welcoming Nixon at the airport. Inside there were more photographs and several stories as well as texts of the toasts that Chou and Nixon had exchanged at the previous evening's banquet.[37]

7

The Long Freeze

A FTER HIS MEETING with Mao, Nixon and his advisers, including William Rogers this time, went off in the late afternoon to a
formal session with Chou and his colleagues. Now that Mao had given
his audience, the Chinese were genial and friendly. Chou praised the
Americans' pioneer spirit. And how nice, he said, that the Americans
had so many young people in their delegation. 'We have too many
elderly people in our leadership.' He apologized for the fact that the
meeting with Mao had come so quickly that the American press had
not been able to cover it. He promised, though, that the announcement
and photographs of the meeting would be given to the Americans so
that they could release the story first. Nixon was ecstatic: 'That is
unprecedented. No other nation we have ever dealt with has been so
generous.' As far as briefing the press went, Chou said, he regretted that
he was not as skilled as Mr Kissinger. Nixon disagreed: 'Having read the
transcripts of conversations the Prime Minister had with Dr Kissinger, I
think the Prime Minister can handle himself with anyone in the world.'
It was so refreshing, the President commented, to deal with Chairman
Mao and Chou, who talked 'directly, and honestly, and candidly.'[1]

None of the other Chinese talked in the plenary session. On the
American side, William Rogers made a couple of brief comments,
while Kissinger remained silent. There was no need for the latter to
say anything because it had already been arranged that he would sit in
on the meetings between Nixon and Chou where substantive issues
would be discussed. Rogers and his State Department entourage were
relegated to dealing with the Chinese Foreign Minister and his officials and discussing, as Kissinger put it contemptuously in his
memoirs, 'the obsessions of our East Asian Bureau; the promotion of
more trade and exchanges of persons'.[2]

Nixon talked, as he had with Mao, about how neither China nor the United States was a threat to the other, and how, if they worked together, the world could be a more peaceful place. 'Yes,' said Chou, 'we hope so.' The following day, the two men agreed, they would start in on the difficult issues dividing them. Chou singled out one in particular, 'the Taiwan situation'. Nixon agreed but pointed out that there were many other issues, from Korea to the Soviet Union. It was unlikely that they would be able to solve everything in these first meetings, but they were setting in motion a process. 'Yes, indeed,' said Chou, 'in spite of the fact that there exist now such great differences between us and in the future there will still be differences.' Nixon expressed optimism: 'we will have a chance to know each other as peoples and also to communicate as governments'.[3]

Though in 1972 Americans and Chinese knew each other only second hand and through the distorting lenses of fear and suspicion, it had not always been like that. Before 1949, Americans and Chinese had come to know quite a lot about each other. In the nineteenth century considerable numbers of Americans had come to China to do business or to do good. Americans were fascinated by China, whether it was the China of the 'yellow hordes' and the ancient wisdom and arcane powers of Dr Fu Manchu or the heartbreakingly simple and noble peasants of Pearl S. Buck in the 1930s. American businessmen down the decades dreamed of the markets that lay waiting there, whether for Yankee steel in the nineteenth century or Pepsi-Cola in the 1970s. Missionaries dreamed rather of souls and an immense field in which to do good. From the nineteenth century on, Americans made up one of the largest groups of foreign missionaries in China. They built churches, founded schools and started printing presses. Many of China's great universities of today started out as branches of, for example, the Yale Medical School. Missionary letters home, their books and magazines and their illustrated talks to their home congregations helped to create a China for Americans that was weak and helpless and in need of American assistance. Americans found something intriguing too in the idea of a relationship between the old civilization and their new one.

Over the years, thousands of Chinese went to the United States to acquire Western learning or to make money on the 'Golden

Mountain'. When they returned home, they brought American attitudes and American learning with them. To Chinese nationalists, a
growing force by the late nineteenth century, the United States
appeared in a variety of lights, sometimes merely as part of a larger
West threatening China, sometimes as a sympathetic power, sometimes even as a model. On the other hand, the United States was a
new society, founded on revolutionary principles, and that appealed to
Chinese radicals who blamed their own civilization for their country's
woes. As a young man, Mao urged his fellow students to study
Americans such as George Washington and Abraham Lincoln because
the Chinese needed similar, progressive leaders. 'China is very weak;
she will grow strong, rich and independent only after many years; but
the important thing is that we must learn these things.'[4]

The signals sent by the United States itself were contradictory. In
1900, American soldiers were part of the expeditionary force which
invaded Beijing in the wake of the Boxer Rebellion and forced yet
another humiliating treaty with exorbitant indemnity payments on
China. Along with other foreign troops, American soldiers stayed on
to protect their nationals. Yet at the same time the American government sent notes to the other powers advocating an open-door policy
in China, where all powers had equal rights rather than staking out
exclusive areas, even colonies, for trade and investment. (Even though
the notes were really more about keeping access in China for
American businessmen, they at least assumed that China would continue as a sovereign state.) Moreover, although the American
government had taken its share of the indemnities levelled on China
after the Boxer Rebellion, it remitted most of them to China in 1908
and converted the remainder into a scholarship fund for Chinese students who wanted to study in the United States. In 1972, if they had
been allowed to talk to them, the American visitors would have found
elderly intellectuals who had gone to Princeton or Columbia or
Berkeley on these scholarships.

In the early days of the republic, many Chinese looked to the
United States as a model, of government, but also of society. President
Woodrow Wilson's promises of a new world order founded on justice
and peace, his talk of national self-determination and his evident
antipathy to Japanese attempts to dominate China and the rapid

expansion of Japanese forces into Siberia in the wake of the Russian Revolution made him, briefly, a hero to nationalistic Chinese. That came to an abrupt end in 1919 when Wilson took a prominent role in the gift of former German possessions in China to Japan. The Americans, so many Chinese concluded, were simply imperialists in republican clothing.

As Chiang Kai-shek and his Guomindang moved to unite China in the 1920s, the United States, like most other foreign powers except the Soviet Union, was initially hostile. Chiang, or so it was widely held in the West, was a dangerous radical who was out to expropriate foreign businesses. When Chiang made it clear that, although he was a nationalist, he was no radical, the United States moved cautiously to recognize his regime. In 1928 it signed a treaty with China which for the first time in decades allowed China to set its own tariffs on imports. On the other hand, at the start of the 1930s, when Japan seized Manchuria, the United States merely protested and did nothing more than adopt a policy not to recognize the puppet state of Manchukuo which the Japanese hastily set up there. Now the United States seemed neither a strong friend nor an enemy.

That was gradually to change in the late 1930s as Japan's intentions for China became increasingly clear. The seizure of Manchuria was, for the militarists who now dominated the Japanese government, only a first step to making China part of a greater Japanese empire. The United States, reluctantly, shook itself out of its isolation and moved to counter Japan in the Pacific and on the mainland of Asia. The Japanese invasion of China, with its bombing of Chinese cities and brutal treatment of civilians, enraged American public opinion and led to President Roosevelt's famous 'quarantine speech' where he argued that aggressor nations should be treated as part of a dangerous epidemic. From the end of 1938 onwards, the United States lent money to Chiang's government. By 1941 the Flying Tigers, American pilots under the leadership of General Claire Chennault, were helping to build him an air force.

When Japan attacked the United States at Pearl Harbor on 7 December 1941, the United States and China became allies, even if not necessarily friends. American soldiers, advisers, arms and money poured into the inland provinces which made up free China. Chiang was grateful but not excessively so. As a nationalist, he was prepared to take American assistance but not American advice. And he was not about to risk what remained of his armed forces in all-out attacks on the Japanese; he had done his share of fighting and now it was the turn of his new allies. The Americans found this frustrating. Those on the spot also became increasingly pessimistic about the ability of a creaky, corrupt and inefficient Guomindang to hold China together. The trouble was that the alternative, the relatively small Chinese Communist Party, was hard to imagine as a government for China. Moreover, its ideology ran counter to everything that most Americans believed.

Nevertheless, the American government, acting on the same principle that made it an ally of the Soviet Union against Germany, sent a military mission in 1944 to the Communist headquarters at Yan'an in north-west China. This was the first time many of the Communist leaders had met Americans, other than sympathizers such as Edgar Snow, but, although the Americans demonstrated the conga line at the weekly dances, the contact did little to bring greater understanding.[5] If anything, Mao got the wrong ideas from chatting to the Americans and from watching the Hollywood movies they sometimes showed on an outdoor screen: for example, that Americans did not know how to fight properly.

A small amount of US military aid made its way to the Communist armies, although most American support continued to go to the Guomindang. After the defeat of Japan in 1945, that support continued, sliding into outright American backing for the Guomindang against the Communists in the growing post-war tension between the two camps in China. At first Mao seems to have hoped that he could use the Americans against the Guomindang. He expected, too, that American capitalism would be eager to invest in China, even a Communist one.[6]

Although President Truman sent the eminent General George Marshall on a prolonged visit to China at the end of 1945, in a last-ditch effort to broker a compromise between the Guomindang and the Communist Party, his efforts succeeded only in irritating the former and convincing the latter that the United States was its enemy. By the summer of 1946, China was plunged into civil war. The

United States was clearly in the Guomindang's camp, although it limited its help to equipment, money and international recognition. (Offering American military support was out of the question, given the other demands on US forces.) Mao was bitter, and perhaps embarrassed, by what he saw as American betrayal. In a 1947 speech, he admitted that the Communists had made mistakes. 'It was the first time for us to deal with the U.S. imperialists. We didn't have much experience. As a result we were taken in. With this experience we won't be cheated again.'[7]

In August 1946, Mao gave an interview to the fellow-travelling journalist Anna Louise Strong. Striking what was a favourite theme, he distinguished between the peace-loving and progressive American people and their reactionary leaders. American reactionaries and capitalists (virtually the same thing) were waging war on their own people and looking to dominate the world. Only the Soviet Union stood in their way. 'That is why the U.S. reactionaries rabidly hate the Soviet Union and actually dream of destroying this socialist state.' Fortunately, he went on, 'All reactionaries are paper tigers.' The progressive forces of the world were bound to sweep them all away.[8]

By the summer of 1949, the Communists had swept the Guomindang away, but the Truman administration looked as strong as ever. Although there were some feelers put out by both the Communists and the Americans, neither side was really prepared to deal with the other. It was not so much that an opportunity was missed as that it did not exist in the first place. The Cold War was now an established fact, dividing up much of the world into two camps. The Americans were already deeply concerned about the Soviet grip on Eastern Europe and were moving into, for them, an unprecedented state of military preparedness in peacetime. The Chinese Communists were perceived, with some truth, as heavily dependent on and much under the influence of the Soviets. For their part, the Chinese Communists saw no alternative but to join forces with the Soviet Union. In a major policy statement, Mao wrote that China's critics were accusing it of 'leaning to one side'. Quite right, he went on. 'All Chinese without exception must lean either to the side of imperialism or to the side of socialism. Sitting on the fence will not do, nor is there a third road.' In any case, or so he claimed, Mao expected that revolution would break out in the poorer areas of the world, and perhaps in the United States itself. In a decade or two, China would be much stronger and the US much weaker. 'Why can't we live without the United States?'[9]

Mao was at once a revolutionary and a nationalist and it was never easy to separate the two. He wanted and needed help from the Soviet Union and he confidently expected that, in building socialism, China would make rapid progress. 'We have stood up,' he said in a famous speech in September 1949. 'The Chinese have always been a great, courageous, and industrious nation; it is only in modern times that they have fallen behind. And it was due entirely to oppression and exploitation by foreign imperialism and domestic reactionary govern-ments.' That era, when China could be insulted and humiliated, when its people were regarded as uncivilized, was now over. 'We shall emerge in the world as a nation with an advanced culture.' And with power. 'No imperialists will ever again be allowed to invade our land.'[10]

Yet he also assumed that they would try, especially the leading ones. With the confidence of a civilization that had seen itself for cen-turies as the Middle Kingdom, Mao took it for granted that, out of all the world, China was the centre of the Americans' attention. 'By seiz-ing China, the United States would possess all of Asia. With its Asian front consolidated, U.S. imperialism could concentrate its forces on attacking Europe.' The United States, or rather the reactionaries and capitalists who ran it, was determined to destroy the Chinese people's great revolution: 'they will smuggle their agents into China to sow dis-sension and make trouble'.[11] (Branding opponents of the new regime as the dupes and collaborators of the Americans was of course also a convenient way to eliminate them.)

The foreigners still in China, among them American diplomats, journalists, businessmen and missionaries, must leave. They were probably spies in any case. As Mao put it, the house must be cleaned before guests could be invited in. In its foreign relations, China was starting over, turning its back on the old shameful pattern of unequal treaties, punitive fines and foreign meddling. China, he said, in another of those folksy metaphors he liked so much, was building a new cooking oven. Even though other Western nations, Great Britain for example, were prepared to extend recognition to the new government in China, even at the risk of serious disagreement with the United States, the Chinese Communists were in no hurry to establish relations with the enemy camp.[12]

On the American side, as it became clear in the late 1940s that the Communists were bound to win, there was a debate over how to deal with the new reality in China. Even the diehard supporters of Chiang Kai-shek and the Guomindang were disheartened as he prepared to move his government and his remaining forces to Taiwan. Nevertheless, what was to become known as the China lobby insisted that the United States should not recognize the Communist seizure of power in China. Their opponents, some within the Truman administration, argued that it was important for the United States to establish ties with Communist China. Given the past tensions between China and Russia, it was possible that, at some point in the future, the two Communist regimes would fall out. By 1948, they could point to the encouraging case of Tito's Yugoslavia and the Soviet Union, which had broken off relations. The Soviet leader had ordered other Communist countries in Eastern Europe to follow the Soviet lead and cut diplomatic and economic ties. Stalin was also doing his best to remove Tito permanently by sending teams of assassins into Yugoslavia. Marshal Tito's offence was that, although he was a Communist, he was not Stalin's Communist. He and his comrades had made their own way to power, like Mao, and perhaps as a result Stalin had never been able to trust him. Was it not likely that Mao would one day be an Asian Tito? And that China and the Soviet Union would also find themselves enemies?[13]

These were sensible questions, but few Americans cared to hear them in those early days of the Cold War. In early 1950, Senator Joe McCarthy discovered that accusing the Truman administration of being riddled with Communist traitors was a marvellous way to revive a failing political career. He found a ready-made audience and his attacks helped to harden American attitudes towards the Chinese Communists. Anti-Communists in the United States were already talking about the red tide rising in Asia, of which the Soviet 'puppet regime' in Beijing was only the first wave. Although US allies such as the British thought such American reactions absurd and still hoped to establish relations with the People's Republic of China, Truman and his administration found themselves being pushed in the direction of a harder line. Dean Acheson, the American Secretary of State, who had been trying to make up his mind about the best long-term policy towards the Communist regime in China, publicly denounced the Sino-Soviet treaty in March 1950 as 'an evil omen of imperialistic domination' and warned the Chinese people that they were abandoning their loyal old American friends for the voracious Soviets. In Congress, Walter Judd, a leading Republican supporter of Taiwan, voiced his approval: Acheson had finally recognized the extent of the Communist conspiracy for domination of the world – 'Asia, then of Europe, then of ourselves.'[14] Talk of reaching out to the Chinese Communists, of trying to detach them from the Soviets, became difficult, even dangerous for careers.

By June 1950, it became impossible. With the outbreak of the Korean War, when a Soviet-backed Communist North attacked the South, the Cold War reached a new, acute stage and the battle lines between the Eastern Bloc and the West appeared to be firmly fixed. Although new evidence shows that Mao and the Chinese were unenthusiastic about the attack, they had no choice but to side with the Soviets and the North Koreans. From the American perspective, one in which nuances no longer seemed to make much sense, world Communism was on the move. 'There can be little doubt', Acheson wrote to the British Foreign Secretary, 'but that Communism, with Chi[na] as one spear-head, has now embarked upon an assault against Asia with immediate objectives in Korea, Indo-China, Burma, the Philippines and Malaya and with medium-range objectives in Hong Kong, Indonesia, Siam, India and Japan.'[15] American public opinion, already concerned by the ease with which the Soviet Union had taken over so much of the centre of Europe and by revelations of Soviet spies stealing American atomic secrets, became firmly anti-Communist. Congress moved further to the right as Republican gains whittled away the Democrats' majority. The Truman administration, unfairly castigated for being soft on Communism, was already upping defence spending and moving the United States on to a war footing. When the news came in from Korea of the outbreak of war, Truman responded immediately. Even before the United States had got a mandate from the United Nations to assemble a force to defend South Korea, he had ordered American forces to go there and had sent the Seventh Fleet to protect the straits between mainland China and Taiwan, just in case the Chinese Communists were planning to invade.

Mao had perhaps been thinking of doing just that. Certainly the Communists had concentrated some of their best forces just across from Taiwan. They had few troops in the north near the border with North Korea. The Chinese Communists also had a huge task ahead of them at home, both to consolidate the Communist victory and to begin the long process of setting a war-torn country on the path to recovery. A war with the United States was the last thing they wanted at that point. Events left them little choice. The United Nations forces, predominantly American and under the command of the American general Douglas MacArthur, landed in South Korea and pushed the North Koreans back towards the border with China. American planes flew increasingly close to Chinese airspace and American hawks, including MacArthur himself, made no secret of the fact that they saw an opportunity to get rid of the Communists (or, as they preferred to see it, to retrieve the loss of China), possibly by using atomic bombs on Chinese industrial sites. In late November 1950, Chinese Communist 'volunteers' poured down over the border and it was the turn of UN forces to retreat. The fighting dragged on for another three years as both sides continued to hope for victory. Even when talks started, the mutual suspicions between Communist China and the United States meant that every issue, from the withdrawal of forces to either side of the 38th parallel to the exchange of prisoners of war, took months to settle.

The Korean War finally ended in a truce, with a divided Korea and a deep gulf between the People's Republic of China and the United States. The strategic map of Asia was also altered. Japan, its economy starting to revive partly thanks to spending from the Korean War, was independent again and firmly in the American camp; the United States was committed to the defence of Taiwan; and the Cold War had spread to French Indochina, on China's southern borders, where the French, with copious American aid, were fighting a Communist-led nationalist movement.

In Washington, a Republican administration had taken office at the start of 1953 amid charges that the Democrats had not been tough enough on Communism. Senator McCarthy was revelling in his newly acquired fame as the scourge of Communists and other subversives. President Eisenhower's Secretary of State, John Foster Dulles, talked, perhaps too much, about rolling back Communism. At the Geneva conference of 1954, Dulles was in the bath when a State Department official rushed in to say that the Chinese Communists were prepared to release their remaining American prisoners of war and move towards normalizing relations. While his subordinate perched on the toilet seat, Dulles lay back in the tub and said firmly, 'No, we will not do it.'[16] Dulles tried to build an anti-Communist alliance in Asia to contain China, just as NATO was containing the Soviets in Europe. The CIA tried, in vain, to stir up trouble within China by supporting Tibetan nationalists. At the United Nations, the Americans used their dominance to block China's entry. Taiwan kept the China seat and China's membership in a whole range of international organizations.

The People's Republic, for its part, sent aid to anti-Western and left-wing movements throughout Asia, for example in Vietnam, Indonesia and the Philippines. It also involved itself in the attempt among what were called Third World countries – a growing number as the old Western empires folded – to create a non-aligned movement which would steer a middle course between the two great antagonistic blocs in the Cold War. This of course was regarded with the deepest suspicion by Dulles, who felt that neutrality was a cover for Communist sympathies.

Dulles' hard line was echoed at senior levels in the State Department where Walter Robertson headed the bureau of Far Eastern Affairs. According to a junior colleague, 'There was no question in Robertson's mind that we should be 100 percent pro-Nationalist government on Taiwan and 100 percent anti-Communist government in Peking.' Recognition of the new regime in Beijing was quite simply out of the question. 'As far as I could make out, the Communists would have had to have ceased being Communists to make him shift.'[17]

From 1949 to the start of the 1970s, China and the United States had virtually no diplomatic relations, no summits, no joint meetings, no exchanges of tourists, business leaders or academics. Chinese and American athletes did not compete against each other. Chinese and American journalists did not report from each other's countries. China and the United States did not trade directly with each other and their planes and ships did not visit each other's airfields and ports. American officials would not use the term 'People's Republic of China' and insisted on calling the capital 'Beiping', as the Guomindang still did. Indeed young diplomats were warned that they could damage their careers by the careless use of 'Beijing', which is what the Communists had chosen.[18]

The United States set up an enormous consulate in Hong Kong, still a British colony, partly to ensure that there was no leakage, that goods from the mainland did not move on to the American market under the British flag. The American owners of the new Hong Kong Hilton had to get rid of the expensive Chinese antiques they had just bought because these came from the mainland. The effort to keep goods from Communist China away from Americans produced much work and increasingly arcane debates. If an egg came from Communist China but hatched in Hong Kong, was the chicken Communist or not? Was an egg laid in Hong Kong by a hen from the mainland a Communist one? The Americans were also concerned that important strategic goods did not move into China through Hong Kong. A junior American consular officer once had to spend considerable time on condoms. 'I had to go all around Hong Kong, talking to importers of prophylactic rubbers and asking: How many do you think Hong Kong uses? And how many are reexported to China?' His lengthy report was received with commendations in Washington and he was then sent an urgent follow-up question. 'Please update this carefully. We have heard that the Chinese Communists are using prophylactic rubbers to protect the muzzles of their guns from moisture.' The brief panic ended when the Pentagon got in on the act and a final message came from Washington. 'Our experts have said that if you do try to protect your gun muzzles that way, it will simply rust and pit-out the muzzles themselves because moisture will collect, there is no air in the muzzle. So any prophylactic rubbers that want to go to Communist China, okay.'[19]

The other mission of the American establishment in Hong Kong was to try gaze over the border into China. The China-watchers interviewed refugees and those foreigners and Chinese who were able to travel into China. They pored over Chinese Communist publications when they could get them. They gathered scraps of information in whatever ways they could. Herbert Levin, who later worked for Kissinger on the National Security Council, used to monitor shipments of live pigs from China into Hong Kong. 'When there were suggestions that there were food shortages and crop failures and so forth in China, you could see what provinces the carloads of pigs were coming from, whether they were coming like previous years, whether they were thinner or fatter, and all that kind of thing.'[20] The Americans gained general impressions of what was going on inside China. They knew something about the catastrophe of the Great Leap Forward because streams of desperate refugees forced their way into Hong Kong. They learned about the Cultural Revolution first hand when Red Guards tried to stir up trouble for the British authorities. But the Americans had almost no idea of who was really in power and what the great internal debates were. (Of course, neither did the Chinese people.)

Although the Chinese Communists had far more access to material on American society, it is not clear that they were able to benefit from it, given their own ideological blinkers. None of the top party leadership had ever been to the United States and even a man as knowledgeable and sophisticated as Chou En-lai had naive views of Americans. 'If American troops really invade China,' he said in a 1949 speech, 'we will surround them from the countryside, forcing them to ship all military supplies, including toilet paper and ice cream, from the United States.' Zhang Wenjin, one of the foreign ministry officials involved in planning Nixon's trip, later told an interviewer, 'Chairman Mao and Premier Chou actually knew very little about the United States; they had to rely upon us.'[21]

American society, so the Chinese people were told for years, was deeply corrupt. In 1950, a Chinese pamphlet entitled *Look, So This is the American Way of Life!*, painted a lurid picture of the United States: 'It is a nation that is thoroughly reactionary, thoroughly black, thoroughly corrupt, and thoroughly cruel. It is heaven for a handful of millionaires and hell for countless millions of poor people. It is a paradise for gangsters, swindlers, hooligans, special agents, fascist vermin, profiteers, debauchers, and so on and so forth – all the dregs of humanity.' Chinese propaganda showed Uncle Sam as an avaricious millionaire, his teeth and hands dripping with blood. Chinese newspapers played up American racial tensions and American crime.[22]

The American public and indeed many policymakers back in Washington had an equally simplistic view. The China lobby and publications such as *Time* and *Life* (owned by Henry Luce, a child of American missionaries in China) enthusiastically painted a picture of a sterile and dreadful world behind the Bamboo Curtain with the Chinese people turned into a horde of red ants. The entry of China into the Korean War was taken as more evidence of Communist treachery and the appearance of brainwashed American prisoners of war in Beijing caused a thrill of horror back in the United States. On the right, Senator McCarthy and his supporters, who included a young Richard Nixon, made much of the fact that many American diplomats in China had predicted the collapse of the Guomindang, evidence enough for conspiracy theorists that such men had actively worked for the Communist victory. The diplomats were summoned to Congressional hearings where their motives and loyalty were freely impugned.

The impact on the State Department and on the capacity of the United States to understand what was going on in Asia was devastating. Seasoned and knowledgeable experts were driven out or resigned in disgust. Those who survived were kept away from anything to do with Asia; one of the Department's leading China specialists ended up as ambassador in Iceland. The Department as a whole was shellshocked and became increasingly timid in offering unpalatable advice to its political masters. A young man who started out as a junior diplomat in Hong Kong in the late 1950s remembered older colleagues who were careful about what they sent back to Washington. 'I don't think it meant not reporting facts, it's just that one was cautious.'[23]

On the other hand, the experience of being in Hong Kong tended to make the American China-watchers more pragmatic than their superiors back in Washington. The lack of relations between two such big countries seemed absurd, an anomaly which must be temporary.

'Well, you know,' said an American diplomat, 'what the hell, China's there, we're going to have to recognize it. I mean, it was a fact of life. It wasn't through admiration, it was just, well, let's get on with it.'[24]

Nor were the Chinese Communists yet ready to look for friends among the enemies of the Soviets. In China, no one dared openly suggest that one day relations might be re-established with the United States. Except for one man. 'If there is no war,' Mao told a party conference in 1956, 'the capitalist countries will face economic difficulties. Our door is open. In 12 years, Britain, America, West Germany and Japan will all want to do business with us.'[25]

The door remained open, just a crack. In the aftermath of the Geneva conference, representatives of China and the United States had to talk to each other from time to time, about the exit visas for Americans still in China or the exchange of prisoners of war, for example. The main contacts were through Warsaw, where Chinese and American diplomats met quietly over the years right up until 1970. The Communist Polish government obligingly provided a magnificent old palace for the talks, which it equally obligingly bugged for its Soviet masters. The Americans found the bugging useful, both as a way of communicating with the Soviets and because they were able to tap into the bug, which saved them from making extensive notes.[26]

Occasionally, when there was a crisis, one side or another would break off, but the talks always resumed. Although the issue of Taiwan remained, for the time being, insoluble, both sides saw an advantage in keeping some sort of contact if only as 'a kind of mailbox', as one American put it. 'Even then,' recalled John Holdridge, who was to return to China with Nixon, 'we always had this feeling in the back of our minds – through the Geneva talks, the ambassadorial-level talks, and in various ways – that we didn't want to foreclose any opportunities which might open in the future. We wanted some kind of a relationship.' The Chinese had much the same view. In 1958, after one hiatus, the Foreign Minister, Chen Yi, told his ambassador in Warsaw that the talks might produce some useful results: 'You may shake hands with, say hello to, and chat with the American ambassador. You may have a dinner with him.' China was not begging for negotiations nor refusing them. 'The manner of a great country should be neither haughty nor humble.'[27]

For the most part, the conversations were stilted and formal as both sides presented prepared statements. During the Cultural Revolution, an American remarked casually on an attractive view to a Chinese diplomat who promptly answered, 'Yes it is but not as beautiful as it is in Beijing where the glorious sun of Chairman Mao Tse-tung shines upon the Chinese people twenty-four hours a day.' Years later, after Mao's death, the two men met again in Tanzania. The Chinese looked at the American and said, 'It is a beautiful day, but not as beautiful as it is in Beijing where the glorious sun of—', and started to laugh. 'I look back often on that conversation,' he said. 'By god, how stupid it was.'[28]

8

Breaking the Pattern

IN HIS CONVERSATION with Nixon that February afternoon in Beijing, Chou En-lai returned, yet again, to the famous snub at the Geneva conference in 1954. 'As you said to Chairman Mao this afternoon, today we shook hands, but John Foster Dulles didn't want to do that.' Nixon extended his hand and he and Chou solemnly shook hands again. 'We couldn't blame you,' Chou said, 'because the international viewpoint was that the socialist countries were a monolithic bloc, and the Western countries were a monolithic bloc.' The Chinese knew better now. Nixon agreed: 'We have broken out of the old pattern.'[1]

Nixon would not have been in Beijing if both sides had not been prepared, for their own reasons, to break out of the old patterns. The timing had never been quite right before. In 1949, when the Truman administration considered trying to establish relations with the new Communist regime, the Chinese Communists were not prepared to negotiate. In the mid-1950s, when Chou En-lai offered a settlement of outstanding issues, especially Taiwan, in talks at Geneva, it was the turn of the Americans to be intransigent.

The start of the 1960s brought the best chance in over a decade to end the impasse between the two powers. In China, the failure of the Great Leap Forward temporarily sidelined Mao and brought more pragmatic leaders such as Liu Shaoqi to the fore. In the United States, the inauguration of the new young Democratic President Kennedy promised a fresh approach to the foreign policy and to the troubling China question. Adlai Stevenson, the respected ambassador to the United Nations, published an article in *Foreign Affairs* at the end of 1960 in which he argued that the People's Republic of China should be admitted to the UN. The Secretary of State, Dean Rusk, who was later to become more hardline, agreed that existing US policy on the admission of China to the UN was 'unrealistic'. Reaction from the China lobby and the right was surprisingly muted.[2]

China seemed ready to shift its policies as well. Although the situation in Indochina, particularly in Laos, was deteriorating by 1961, Chou En-lai indirectly let the Americans know that his government hoped to find a way of keeping Laos neutral. In 1962, the United States responded in kind when it used indirect channels to inform China that it was discouraging Taiwan from attacking the mainland.[3] As China-watchers in Hong Kong scrambled to translate the scatological terms the Chinese Communists were using about the Soviets, the split between China and the Soviet Union also promised new opportunities for ending the long freeze between the United States and China.

Inside the State Department, retirements removed some of the older Cold Warriors and brought younger, more open-minded Asian specialists to responsible positions. At the end of 1961, the existence of two Chinas was accepted when what were called Mainland China Affairs began to be dealt with separately from those of Taiwan. Shortly after, a new office of Asian Communist Affairs was created. 'There was a feeling in the air', remembered one of the specialists appointed to it, 'that Kennedy would like to do something about China, but they hadn't really focused on it, so it was a wonderful time, in a way, the sense that people wanted something done, but didn't know quite what they wanted.'[4]

Kennedy himself talked of change and his defenders have claimed that, had he lived, he would have made the sort of breakthrough that only came with Nixon. We will never know. In his tragically short term in office, though, Kennedy seems to have regarded the People's Republic of China with as much mistrust as John Foster Dulles himself. The deepening conflict in Indochina and the growth of Communist influence in Indonesia helped to harden his attitudes towards the Chinese Communists, whom he saw, not entirely incorrectly, as behind much of what was happening. It did not help that China attacked India in the autumn of 1962. The Americans frequently found the Indians infuriating, but they did not like, as they saw it, unprovoked aggression by a Communist power against a

Nixon spent much of his time aboard Air Force One on the long flight to the Far East conferring with Henry Kissinger

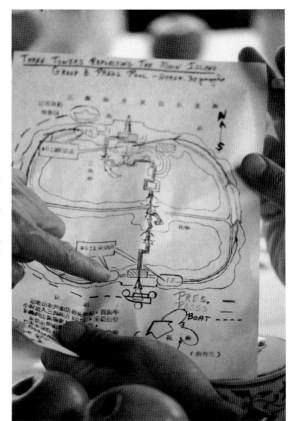

A sketch of the famous West Lake in Hangzhou, showing possible photo-opportunities for when the Nixons toured it. The White House advance team made meticulous preparations for every aspect of the trip

Soldiers from the People's Liberation Army forming a well-disciplined crowd at a sports and gymnastics exhibition staged for the Americans on 23 February

As Chou En-lai waits to greet him, Nixon descends the steps from Air Force One alone.
He is the first American president ever to visit China

The crucial first handshake between Nixon and Chou

Nixon and Chou review Chinese troops as they prepare to leave Beijing for Hangzhou. Pat Nixon follows behind

China was dotted with pictures of Mao. This giant one on the wall of the Forbidden City gazes out over Tiananmen Square in the heart of Beijing

Nixon's first and, on this trip, only meeting with Mao. From left to right, Chou En-lai, Tang Wensheng (Nancy), Mao's interpreter, Mao, Nixon and Kissinger. Winston Lord has been cropped out of the right-hand side of the picture

Another handshake for the cameras. Both the Americans and the Chinese were anxious to overcome the memory of the infamous snub when John Foster Dulles refused to shake Chou En-lai's hand in Geneva in 1954

democracy. In a speech in the summer of 1963, Kennedy talked of the dangers posed by a warlike China which might shortly get its own nuclear weapons: 'a more dangerous situation than any we have faced since the end of the Second World War'.[5] China tested its first bomb in 1964.

After 1964, when Kennedy's successor, President Johnson, made the decision to send greatly increased numbers of American troops to South Vietnam and to start bombing the North, there was little hope that Chinese–American relations were going to thaw. The war brought American forces perilously close to China's borders and awakened American memories of how Chinese troops had attacked in Korea. Would they do the same in Vietnam? Allen Whiting, a senior China specialist in the State Department, kept warning his superiors, 'The Chinese are coming. The Chinese are coming.' And he found a receptive audience right up to Dean Rusk, the Secretary of State.[6]

From China Mao issued a series of pronouncements to the Chinese people and to the world. Returning to an idea he had formulated a decade before, he talked about 'intermediate zones', those parts of the world between China and the great powers. China had an obligation to the oppressed, whether in the intermediate zones of Europe or in those of Asia, to encourage them to take up revolutionary war against their oppressors, in particular the United States. 'The raging tide of the people of the world against the U.S. aggressors is irresistible,' he told journalists from the *People's Daily* at the start of 1964. In 1965, Lin Biao, his handpicked lieutenant and China's Defence Minister, issued a major policy statement, which must have had Mao's approval. 'Long Live the Victory of People's War' talked with relish about the coming destruction of American imperialism, 'the most ferocious common enemy of the people of the world'.[7]

Although the Chinese urged the peoples of Indochina, including the North Vietnamese, to stand on their own feet, China continued to ship significant amounts of aid southwards and Chinese military advisers continued to assist the North Vietnamese war effort. And, of course, such revolutionary wars like the one raging in Vietnam could also help to protect China by tying down the United States. It was a gamble, though, because it also brought American forces on to China's doorstep. Mao perhaps tried to signal to the United States that

China hoped to avoid a repeat of the confrontation in Korea. In January 1965, he had a long chat with his American biographer and old friend Edgar Snow. 'We shall not make war beyond China, and we shall fight in defense only if the U.S. comes and attacks us.' China, he told Snow, was obliged to show its support for revolutions but it preferred to do so by issuing statements and holding meetings. 'We are fond of prattle and empty talk, but send no troops.'[8]

By 1966 Mao was less inclined to make reassuring noises. American escalation in Vietnam coincided with his vengeful return to full power. He was bent on destroying his enemies, a very large and eclectic group, on rooting out 'bad ideas', including foreign ones, and on transforming Chinese society. The Cultural Revolution made chauvinism, always a strand in Chinese thinking, respectable, even essential, for good Maoists. As the Red Guards set about enthusiastically destroying traditional Chinese culture, they also turned on foreign influence and foreign powers. They burned books in foreign languages and tried to ban all foreign music. In 1967 a mob set fire to the British mission in Beijing and beat up British diplomats. Screaming crowds surrounded the Soviet embassy for days on end. It was at this time that the Soviet women and children who were being sent home for safety had to crawl under an arch at the airport while Red Guards spat at them.

Abroad Chinese students and those representatives who had not yet been called back to China to be reformed denounced the authorities in their host countries and did their best to spread the thought of Chairman Mao. In one African country, workers at the Chinese embassy recited Mao's sayings on local buses and tried to present bewildered locals with copies of the Little Red Book and Mao buttons. When some photographs of Mao were vandalized outside the Chinese embassy in Paris, the reaction in Beijing was hysterical, with a massive demonstration against the French embassy. The People's Republic had diplomatic relations with about forty nations in 1966; within a year after the start of the Cultural Revolution, it had disputes with thirty of them. As the leading capitalist power in the world, the United States was of course not only China's mortal enemy but the leading source of foreign poison. Unfortunately for the radicals during the Cultural Revolution, they could only get at it indirectly. Chinese who had worked for Americans or American-owned companies in the past and the handful of American fellow travellers who had stayed on in China after 1949 were all attacked as imperialist spies.[9]

In 1969, Marshall Green, one of the State Department's leading China experts, toured Asian capitals and reported back that the general feeling was that 'China had never been in such a negative, truculent mood as it was at that time. Asian leaders felt that any hope of progress in establishing a constructive dialogue with China was out of the question until the Cultural Revolution subsided.' (On the report Nixon noted, 'this is great'.)[10] In fact that is precisely what was happening.

Even Mao, living amid his layers of protection, surrounded by courtiers eager to please him, was now realizing how dangerously isolated China was in the world and how weakened by the Cultural Revolution. When he addressed a meeting of the Communist Party's Central Committee in the spring of 1969, he called for an end to the violent stage of the Cultural Revolution: 'is this endless quarreling necessary?' Some people, he said, had gone too far: 'It is not good to be crude and careless, which often leads to mistakes.'[11] By that point, virtually all universities and many schools were closed. Factories repeatedly shut down while workers debated arcane political points. Hospitals ran with skeleton, barely educated staff, while trained doctors and nurses languished in the countryside to 'learn from the peasants'. Much of the army was scattered about China's cities and towns keeping peace between angry factions, all claiming the blessing of Chairman Mao. Yet China still had many external enemies. It was barely on speaking terms with India since the two had fought a war in 1962. Even the peaceful post-1945 Japan could not be trusted. Taiwan was still run by a government which claimed authority over the whole of China. The United States was present in force in Vietnam just to the south. Might it not be tempted to take advantage of China's turmoil either to finish off China's ally North Vietnam once and for all or to do something worse? And along China's northern and western borders, Soviet troops were massing.

The United States was a much stronger power, but its confidence, too, had been shaken by recent events. The 1960s had been turbulent, not as turbulent as in China, but in terms of American history an extraordinarily troubling decade with turmoil at home and the loss of prestige abroad. A wave of assassinations – President Kennedy, Martin Luther King, Robert Kennedy – shook Americans' confidence in their own society. President Johnson's War on Poverty did much good, but it also exposed the dreadful slums in some of the United States' richest cities. Many young people and sometimes their elders talked of the need for radical change. Had the United States become Amerika, out of a Kafka novel, or worse, a fascist state? Cities grew used to demonstrations, against poverty, injustice and, of course, the war in Vietnam. University campuses saw teach-ins and sit-ins and protests.

In the South, a black civil rights movement, supported by white liberals, exposed to Americans and to the world the underside of American society. It became clear that Southern blacks lived under a system not that different from apartheid, barred, as they were, from using restaurants or white-only water fountains. Moreover they were denied the most basic of rights, such as that to vote. By the 1960s, Southern blacks and their supporters from the North challenged the system at all points. Freedom riders sat in the white sections of buses. Blacks sat at white-only lunch counters. In the spring of 1963 Martin Luther King called for civil disobedience against unjust laws. That summer he addressed a massive demonstration in Washington. 'I have a dream that one day this nation will rise up and live out the true mean-ing of its creed: "We hold these truths to be self-evident: that all men are created equal."' The next year, during Freedom Summer, an enormous drive started to register black voters in the South. In Washington, President Johnson pushed a Civil Rights Act through Congress.

Southern whites resisted any changes with ferocity. School inte-gration was marked by riots and tear gas. The first black student at the University of Mississippi had to be escorted there by troops with guns. A police chief in Birmingham, Alabama, used fire hoses and dogs on black demonstrators. In 1963 a bomb placed in a church killed four young black girls. A civil rights worker was murdered in Mississippi. (It took thirty years to bring his killers to justice.) The fol-lowing year three civil rights workers were murdered by the Ku Klux Klan. In 1968, Martin Luther King was assassinated in Memphis, Tennessee. Violence in the South touched off violence in the North as blacks rioted in their ghettos. Watts, in Los Angeles, went up in flames in 1965, Newark and parts of Detroit in 1967. After King's shooting, riots broke out in more than 120 cities. In the centre of Washington, the police lost control of the streets and watched helplessly while rioters looted and burned. The army had to be called in to restore order and patrol the city.

While he had some sympathy for the civil rights movement, Nixon disliked much of what he witnessed in the 1960s. He saw in the turmoil a toxic intolerance and contempt for old values and for established ways of doing things. 'I had no patience with the mindless rioters and professional malcontents,' he wrote in his memoirs, 'and I was appalled by the response of most of the nation's political and academic leaders to them.' In private, he called protesters 'rabble' and 'scum' and expressed his suspicion that Communists were behind their demonstrations. He longed for a return to what he saw as basic American values: 'A strong United States patriotism, strong moral and spiritual values.'[12]

The post-war baby boom, which came of age in the early 1960s, had spawned not only a powerful youth culture but a willingness on the part of the young, at least many of them, to challenge existing mores and institutions at a time when many of their elders were also questioning them. Much of the resulting turmoil was froth: sex, drugs and rock and roll. There were massive concerts, at Woodstock, for example, where people sat in the mud and talked of love and peace – young women with flowers in their hair and men with beards, in wild shirts and beads and bell-bottomed trousers. On the extremes, a few, and it was hard at the time to tell how many there were, rejected American democracy altogether and talked of violent revolution or going back to the land to set up their own societies. The movie *Easy Rider* whose biker heroes soared across America high on speed and drugs, pausing every so often to cast an approving eye on struggling communes or score some more drugs, expressed for a generation an incoherent longing for freedom, but from what? Suitably the heroes die before they can grow old and suburban.

Nixon watched the cultural changes with dismay. Look, he told Haldeman in 1971, at that new television show 'that glorified the homosexuals'. In his opinion, 'homosexuality, dope and immorality are the basic enemies of a strong society, and that's why the Russians are pushing it here, in order to destroy us'. The United States, he feared, had suffered irreparable damage from 'the new morality where the individual determines what is moral and what is right', blaming 'the establishment'.[13] The establishment took the blame for it all – poverty, violence, injustice, but above all for Vietnam.

For many Americans at the time, that one word summed up all that had gone wrong with the United States in the 1960s. Vietnam meant loss, of 60,000 American lives, of their country's prestige and influence, and of innocence. Stories of their soldiers taking drugs, reports of casual brutalities – the massacre of civilians at My Lai, for example – shook people back home. Before Vietnam, American soldiers had been our boys and American wars had been righteous – for independence, for a better world in the First World War, to save that world from Fascism in the Second, and, in Korea, to stop the spread of international Communism. Vietnam was, or so many Americans had come to think, not righteous at all. Indeed it was very wrong. The United States was interfering in the affairs of a far-off country whose people wanted their independence. It was backing the corrupt regime of South Vietnam against, or so it was sometimes naively believed, a broadly based nationalist movement in the South and the benevolent socialist state of North Vietnam. Even those who had few illusions about the Communist regime in the North wondered, with the leading American diplomat and thinker George Kennan, what vital American interest was at stake in a small and backward part of South-east Asia; and conservatives worried about what an unpopular and unsuccessful war was doing to the American military and to American society itself.

On paper, the United States should have been able to handle the insurgent forces in South Vietnam and the simple little country of North Vietnam easily – a country of 205,000,000 against one of 20,000,000; the most developed economy and technology in the world against one which was still primarily agricultural; and the most up-to-date weapons against simpler Soviet or Chinese ones. A sour joke which circulated in Washington in 1968 had experts feeding all available statistics from both sides into a computer. The computer was asked, Will the US win the war? The answer: You won in 1966.

The Kennedy and then the Johnson administrations and their

generals had promised victory year after year. The United States had poured money and hardware and young men into Vietnam and the prospect of victory had kept receding. Even for a rich country, the financial burden was proving heavy; from 1962 onwards, the United States ran a budget deficit which ultimately contributed to growing inflation and an increasing indebtedness. It was also, although few people realized it until the crisis of 1973, growing dependent on foreign oil. In 1968, the Tet offensive launched by North Vietnam and its southern collaborators had shaken the faith of the American public in all the promises of victory. Tet in fact was a military victory for the American forces and their South Vietnamese allies, but it did not appear so to public opinion. When Communists could seize Hué, the old capital of Vietnam, with impunity or occupy the outer compound of the American embassy itself in Saigon, it seemed to many Americans that the war was unwinnable. In the United States, in Congress, on Wall Street, in the churches, the universities and the streets, Americans demanded an end to it.

Nixon and Kissinger knew the damage Vietnam had done to the United States internationally as well as at home. The Soviet Union and its allies had watched with pleasure as American power failed to crush North Vietnam. American allies had watched uneasily as their superpower showed its weakness. Their publics had increasingly turned sour on the United States; in Canada and Western Europe, mass demonstrations demanded that the US get out of Vietnam. Much of the criticism, and not just from the left, was disturbingly anti-American. The United States was portrayed as an international bully in which the forces of capitalism ran uncontrolled. In the Third World, American imperialism was routinely condemned, while little was said of the Soviet empire.

Nixon wanted to reverse the decline: 'Power of the United States', he told Haldeman in his first year in office, 'must be used more effectively, at home and abroad, or we go down the drain as a great power. Have already lost the leadership position we held at the end of WW II, but we can regain it, if fast!' To do that, he had to get the United States out of Vietnam but in a way that did not look like a scuttle. 'Peace with honor' was the promise he made to the American public during the election campaign, a slogan that appeased both liberals who simply wanted the United States out of Vietnam and the right who thought that Nixon would show firmness. He was not entirely disingenuous. He loathed the North Vietnamese and would have defeated them if he could. He did not simply want to abandon the South (as in the end he did). Unfortunately he had no real plan for getting the United States out of Vietnam, merely a hope that the negotiations with the North Vietnamese which had started in the Johnson administration could be made to work, perhaps through the application of judicious amounts of force and the right sorts of promises.

His main interest was in the big issues facing the United States, its relations with the Soviet Union above all. The Soviets were pushing ahead with the development of advanced nuclear weapons and were expanding their navy. Under Brezhnev's leadership, they were showing an aggressive determination to hang on to what they had and to spread their influence in fresh parts of the world. Brezhnev not only justified the Soviet invasion of Czechoslovakia in 1968 as necessary to save socialism there but said, in what came to be known as the Brezhnev Doctrine, that he would do the same thing in other socialist countries when the Soviet Union deemed it necessary. In the Middle East, the Soviets were supplying huge amounts of weaponry and sending thousands of advisers to radical Arab states such as Egypt and Syria.

Even apart from what the Soviets were up to, the world had dangerous pockets of instability, in the Middle East of course where the Arab–Israeli conflict showed every sign of heating up again, in Latin America where military regimes often combined a contempt for democracy with anti-Americanism, in South Asia where India and Pakistan remained in a state of armed tension, and of course in Southeast Asia itself where the war in Vietnam was spilling over into Laos and Cambodia. The United States also had problems in Europe, with France, for example, as it asserted its independence in often irritating ways. The key Cold War alliance of NATO was, as Kissinger put it, in 'a state of malaise'. One of the reasons that Nixon took a trip to Europe a month after his inauguration was to show that the United States was ready to consult with its allies and that it was no longer completely preoccupied with Vietnam.[14]

Vietnam, though, kept intruding itself. The North Vietnamese, sure that victory was at hand, were not prepared to negotiate seriously and so the war dragged on, with more Americans dying and more American resources being used up. 'No matter what facet of the Nixon presidency you're considering,' Haldeman told an audience in the late 1980s, 'don't ever lose sight of Vietnam as the over-riding factor in the first Nixon term. It overshadowed everything else, all the time, in every discussion, in every opportunity, in every problem.' In his first November in office, Nixon and his staff watched from a barricaded White House as hundreds of thousands of anti-war protesters filled the centre of Washington. As a radical fringe turned violent, government offices filled with tear gas. 'Very strange emotional impact', reported Haldeman, 'as they took down American flag and ran up Viet Cong.'[15]

Nixon feared, among much else, the effects that Vietnam would have on American thinking about the world. Would the United States in its bitterness become extremely nationalistic or take refuge, as it had done after the First World War, in passive isolationism? For a president who had spent much of his career on foreign policy and who believed that the United States was a force for good in the world, either alternative was abhorrent. Nixon also recognized that, like it or not, the United States was no longer the dominant power it had once been in the world. It now had to deal with its own relative decline and the rise of confident newer powers. Early on in Nixon's administration, his Under-Secretary of State, Elliot Richardson, wrote a memorandum which accurately captured the President's thinking:

> The Nixon foreign policy, as I understand it, is built first of all on a realistic awareness of changes in the world that have taken place over the past decade. For purposes of the role of the United States, the most important of these are: (a) the increasing capacity and determination of individual nations to maintain their own independence and integrity; (b) the subordination of ideologies to these over-riding national objectives; and (c) the recognition that United States economic and military resources, in light of competing domestic demands, are not as unlimited as they may once have seemed.[16]

It was a point of view echoed a few days later, on 18 December 1969, by Nixon's National Security Adviser, Henry Kissinger, who told a press briefing that the days when the United States was the richest and most stable country in the world, 'the country without whose leadership and physical contribution nothing was possible', were over. Other countries were now playing a much greater role in the world. There were new nations to deal with as well as the fact that Communism was no longer a monolith. 'We, therefore, face the problem of helping to build international relations on a basis which may be less unilaterally American.'[17]

Both Nixon and Kissinger also believed that, as Nixon put it in a letter to Melvin Laird, his Secretary of Defense, 'the great issues are fundamentally interrelated'. He did not want, he said, to establish artificial links. 'But I do believe that crisis or confrontation in one place and real cooperation in another cannot long be sustained simultaneously.' The Soviets should realize that, if they wanted to enjoy the benefits of trade with the United States, for example, they ought to be ready to talk arms control – or be helpful over Vietnam. In one of his early meetings with Dobrynin, in October 1969, Nixon told him: 'if the Soviet Union found it possible to do something in Vietnam, and the Vietnam war ended, the U.S. might do something dramatic to improve Soviet–U.S. relations, indeed something more dramatic than they could now imagine'. Linkage, as the tactic came to be known, was also, in Kissinger's words, 'an overall strategic and geopolitical view'. Ignoring the fact that events were connected made coherent policies difficult if not impossible. The difficulty, he complained, was that Americans were not used to seeing the world in this way. 'American pragmatism produces a penchant for examining issues separately; to solve problems on their own merits, without a sense of time or context or of the seamless web of reality.'[18]

In that seamless web of reality, China was increasingly coming to figure. Nixon had always been, and remained, firmly opposed to Communism, but by the time he was president some of the passion had gone out of him, as it had out of many of his contemporaries. The Soviet Union, they all knew, had an evil system and was the enemy of the United States, but they had become accustomed to dealing with it. If they could deal with one Communist power, why not another? American dealings with the Soviet Union were an example of what might be possible. The Cold War was a conflict, but it was also a relationship. Statesmen on both sides had gradually come to the realization that nuclear weapons meant they could not afford a hot war between the United States and the Soviet Union. The two sides had been obliged to talk to each other. Like individuals in an intense relationship, they had got to know each other's ways and what to expect. They had continued to fight each other, but indirectly. And sometimes they had collaborated – to limit the spread of nuclear weapons to other powers, for example, or to ease tensions in the Middle East.

By the end of 1969, Kissinger had come round to Nixon's point of view, that an opening to China was worth trying for. 'We moved to China,' he wrote later, 'not to expiate liberal guilt over our China policy of the late 1940s but to shape a global equilibrium.' The United States, if all went well, could end up holding a balance between China and the Soviet Union for, of course, 'constructive ends – to give each Communist power a stake in better relations with us'. Or, as he said to Nixon in 1973, referring to the national drinks, 'With conscientious attention to both capitals, we should be able to continue to have our mao tai and drink our vodka too.'[19]

In the autumn of 1969, Kissinger began to prepare the press for a shift in policy. As he told a briefing in December, 'We have always made it clear that we have no permanent enemies and that we will judge other countries, and specifically countries like Communist China, on the basis of their actions and not on the basis of their domestic ideology.' If China could be brought in as a player, the existing bilateral relationship between the United States and the Soviet Union could become a triangle to the benefit, so Kissinger and Nixon assumed, of the United States. 'The hostility between China and the Soviet Union', wrote Kissinger in his memoirs, 'served our purposes best if we maintained closer relations with each side than they did with each other.' The United States would be in the middle, keeping the balance or, as Kissinger preferred to call it, the equilibrium between the two. Both the Soviet Union and China would then have a strong incentive to deal with the United States 'constructively'. This, he always said firmly, was not a crude attempt to play a China card against the Soviet Union, or vice versa, but not everyone, alas, understood the subtle distinction.[20]

9

The Polar Bear

IN THEIR TALKS with the Americans, both during Kissinger's pre-liminary visit and now during Nixon's, the Chinese did not lay great stress on the Soviet Union. Occasionally they referred to 'our northern neighbour' or 'another big power' or made jokes about polar bears. During his conversation with Nixon, Mao refused to be drawn on the subject at all. In fact, as the Americans were well aware, the Chinese were locked in a dispute with the Soviets which had all the bitterness and hurt feelings of a family fight. They were also deeply concerned about what the Soviet Union might be planning. If the Americans were hoping to play the China card against the Soviets, the Chinese saw an America card for precisely the same purpose.

In December 1971, Chou En-lai explained to his colleagues that improved relations between the People's Republic and the United States would act as a brake on Soviet expansionism. 'The US got stuck in Vietnam; the Soviet revisionists caught the opportunity to expand their sphere of influence in Europe and the Middle East. The US imperialists have no choice but to improve their relations with China in order to counteract the Soviet imperialists.' Nixon was under pressure from his own people to mend fences with China, but China was going to make sure it got something in return. 'When he comes, he has to bring something in his pocket.' With Nixon's visit, China now had a chance to make use 'of the contradictions between the US and the USSR and to magnify them'.[1] China also, although Chou seems not to have spelled it out, possessed the means with which to deter the Soviet Union.

The relationship between the two great Communist powers, and, before that, between China and Russia, dated back several centuries. In one of the first exchanges after the Nixon visit, a visiting Chinese scholar gave a lecture on China's foreign policy, which, he said, was about undoing the wrongs and humiliations of the recent past. The first question from his audience was to ask him what period he was talking about. Charles Freeman, of the State Department, was interpreting. 'And he said, "Well, some people would argue that this means everything since the Yuan Dynasty," which was the Mongols in the twelfth century. He said, "I don't agree with that. I think it's everything since the Treaty of Nerchinsk," which was in 1689.'[2] For many Chinese, recent history began with the treaty that acknowledged the Russian presence to the north and which set the boundary, much the same as it is today, between Russia and China. By the eighteenth century, there was a small Russian community in Beijing with its own Orthodox church.

The relationship between the two peoples, the Chinese and the Russians, was never an easy one. Part of the tension was cultural. The Chinese, who regarded most other peoples as uncivilized, found the Russians particularly impulsive and lacking in self-control. Russian sweat, so folklore had it, was stronger than that of other Westerners. Russians had their own stereotypes. Even Russian Communists were not immune to the old fears of the Yellow Peril, fed by memories of the Mongol hordes (when relations soured in the 1960s the Soviet press took to comparing Mao to Genghis Khan) or of the Boxer Rebellion at the end of the nineteenth century, when foreigners were indiscriminately attacked. The atmosphere in Beijing was 'typically Oriental', Nikita Khrushchev found on his first visit in 1954. 'Everyone was unbelievably courteous and ingratiating, but I saw through their hypocrisy.' Even Chinese hospitality was suspect. 'I remember, for instance, that the Chinese served tea every time we turned around – tea, tea, tea.' The Chinese were basically immoral, a 'remarkably unattractive' Soviet diplomat remarked during the Cultural Revolution to the urbane Belgian sinologist Simon Leys. 'Moral individual conscience is the treasure and unique legacy of our Western Christian civilization!'[3]

The mutual mistrust was about much more than culture alone. From the Chinese side, it was about national humiliation. Russia had been one of the powers imposing the unequal treaties and threatening to carve up China. When the Russians had expanded eastwards to the

Pacific in the nineteenth century, they had seized territory the Chinese regarded as theirs. At the turn of the century, there had been Russian moves into Manchuria with Russian-built railways and a Russian port at Manchuria's southern tip. When Japan challenged Russian control there, a weak China had been obliged to sit on the sidelines as the Russo-Japanese War of 1904–5 was fought to decide which outside power ran one of China's richest provinces. After the Bolshevik Revolution of 1917, the new Soviet rulers had made that notorious promise to hand back to China the territory seized in the old tsarist days but, somehow, the moment for doing so never arrived. In fact, in 1924, the Soviet Union blocked China's hope of re-establishing control over territory the Chinese had long argued was theirs by recognizing the independence of Outer Mongolia. As the Second World War drew to a close, Stalin shocked the Chinese Communists by signing a treaty with their enemy, Chiang Kai-shek. Not only did the treaty give the Nationalists recognition as the legitimate government of China but it granted the Soviet Union extensive concessions including the use of the southern port of Dairen in Manchuria. The Soviets were also active in China's western province of Xinjiang, hoping, with the aid of local Communists, to turn it into another Outer Mongolia.

Although representatives from the Soviet Union helped to bring the Chinese Communist Party into existence and provided much essential funding, the Chinese Communists acquired much to reproach their mentors with over the years. Soviet advice to work with the Guomindang in the 1920s in the hopes of overthrowing it later had produced instead the triumph of Chiang Kai-shek and the near annihilation of the Communist Party. That had led in turn to the long years when Mao and his colleagues stumbled about the countryside trying to find a safe haven.

Even when Chinese Communist fortunes improved after Japan invaded China, Stalin continued to put his faith in Chiang Kai-shek and the Guomindang as the natural rulers of China and to urge caution on the Chinese Communists. When the Second World War ended, the Soviet leader urged Mao to go to China's wartime capital of Chongqing and have talks with Chiang Kai-shek rather than trying to fight the Guomindang. In the spring of 1949, when Chinese

Communist forces stood on the banks of the Yangtze, ready to continue their advance southwards, Stalin told Mao he should be content to control the northern part of China. In 1950, when the Communist victory was complete, Stalin told Liu Shaoqi, 'We feel that perhaps we hampered you in the past.' And he made what was, for Stalin, a highly uncharacteristic statement: 'We did not know a lot about you, so it's possible that we made mistakes.'[4]

What the Soviets did know, they did not much like. In 1941 and 1942, while the Soviet Union was fighting for its survival against Nazi Germany, Stalin had begged Mao in vain to attack Japanese forces in China in order to prevent them from attacking the Soviet Union itself. In the event, Japan had respected its non-aggression pact with the Soviet Union and the Chinese Communists had launched a half-hearted attack only in 1943. In any case, Stalin always had trouble with foreign Communists who were too independent. In China, Stalin would have preferred someone educated in Moscow. The Soviets, as keepers of the revolutionary flame, also regarded the Chinese Communists as ideologically primitive. Mao, in Stalin's words, was a 'margarine Marxist'.[5] It was particularly irritating, then, when the Chinese Communists lauded the greatness of Mao's thought and held his ideas up as a model for the rest of the world.

The years after 1949 saw much public rhetoric about the undying friendship between the Soviet and the Chinese peoples, and friendship associations sprang up in both countries, acquiring millions of members overnight. Underneath the surface, however, the mutual suspicions and old grievances festered. Stalin feared either that the Chinese Communists would make their peace with the Americans or that they would recklessly provoke a military confrontation over, especially, Taiwan. In either case, from Stalin's point of view, the Soviet Union would find an aggressive United States on its eastern doorstep. Although Mao made it clear that he was leaning to the Soviet side in world affairs, he was also determined to get Taiwan back. For that, however, he needed substantial Soviet military assistance. China as a whole needed whatever aid the Soviets could supply to start the long work of rebuilding and developing its economy. Mao knew that Stalin hoped to keep the People's Republic as a junior partner in the Communist bloc and he knew that the Soviets had allies within his own party. In Manchuria, the local Communist leader Gao Gang prominently displayed portraits of Stalin. There were none of Mao to be seen. (An emergency meeting in Beijing condemned Gao for shaming China in this way and most of Stalin's portraits came down.)[6]

In December 1949, Mao went off to Moscow by train to negotiate a new treaty between China and the Soviet Union and to obtain much-needed Soviet aid. This was at a time when the Chinese Communists were confronting the daunting problems of establishing their new regime in a China badly damaged by years of war. The first meeting, when Mao's train pulled into Moscow, gave a hint of what was to come. The Soviet welcome was formal but disdainful. Two senior Soviet officials, Molotov and Bulganin, greeted Mao but refused to have any of the elaborate lunch that the Chinese had prepared, not even a drink. That evening, when Mao finally met Stalin, the two Communist statesmen chatted politely but with reserve. Both circled around the issue of what sort of agreement should be made between their two countries, whether, as the Soviets wished, their existing treaty with the vanished Guomindang government should simply be updated, or, as Mao wanted, a new treaty, more favourable for China, should be drawn up. Stalin simply stonewalled, keeping Mao hanging about for two months in comfortable seclusion at the Soviet leader's own dacha outside Moscow. When Stalin abruptly cancelled a day of talks, Mao shouted in a rage to his Soviet attendants that he was left with only three things to do: 'The first is to eat, the second is to sleep, and the third is to shit.'[7]

The two sides finally hammered out a new treaty of Friendship, Alliance and Mutual Assistance by the middle of February 1950. At the banquet to celebrate, both Mao and Stalin appeared to be in bad moods. It did not help that Stalin chose the occasion to make a speech denouncing Tito of Yugoslavia. The treaty, as the Chinese Communists had wished, was a new one but it contained several of the same provisions as the previous treaty with the Nationalists. Xinjiang province and Manchuria were both effectively Soviet spheres of influence, with Soviet companies working there on very favourable terms. China and the Soviet Union would defend each other against Japan and its allies, which now included the United States. Stalin had made some minor concessions: Soviet control of two key Manchurian cities and a railway, for example, would end sooner than before. He had also promised financial aid, though less, as it turned out, than the Soviet Union was to provide to its satellite East Germany. In addition, the two sides had reached a tacit understanding that the Soviet Union would leave spreading revolution in Asia to the People's Republic of China. From the United States' perspective, the Sino-Soviet friendship and the alliance looked solid, and were deeply worrying in the context of the loss of Eastern Europe to the Soviet Union, the explosion in August 1949 of the first Soviet atomic bomb, the discovery of extensive Soviet spy rings in the West, and then of course the Korean War.[8]

Stalin may have hoped that the United States would not become involved in that war and that a victorious North would provide him with a united Korea firmly under his sway. Or, in the spirit of the gambler he was, he may also have seen an advantage in the United States entering the conflict because that would put pressure on the People's Republic and force it closer to the Soviet Union. In either case, the needs of China were clearly of secondary importance to him. Although he encouraged the Chinese Communists to enter the war against the American-led forces, he proved surprisingly reluctant to provide them with adequate military assistance. He would not, he said, be able to send units of the Soviet air force right away to give the Chinese air cover. In the end, the Soviet Union sent a significant number of planes (the Soviet pilots wore Chinese uniforms in case they were captured) and other military hardware. What we now know, of course, is that the war also added fresh strains to the relationship between the Chinese and the Soviets. The Chinese had to pay for everything they received, and China did not finally settle the last of its debt until 1965.[9] When relations between the two great Communist powers soured in later years, Chinese officials complained about the inferior guns and ammunition sent by the Soviet 'merchants of death'.

Stalin's death at the beginning of 1953 did not improve matters. The Chinese were annoyed by the Soviet assumption that the Soviet Union would continue to lead world Communism. Mao, it could be argued, was now the senior Communist statesman. Within China and throughout the Third World, Mao's thought and the Chinese way of making a revolution based on the peasantry were held up as examples to emulate. By implication, the Bolshevik Revolution and the Soviet pattern of development were being downgraded as proper models. The Soviets did not like what they saw as Chinese pretensions. Khrushchev, who had emerged by 1956 as Stalin's successor, felt that Mao was always putting the Soviets down.[10]

By the mid-1950s, both sides were increasingly prone to look for offence. When Khrushchev made his sensational secret speech in 1956 to denounce Stalin's mistakes, even using the word 'crimes', the Chinese were annoyed, more because they had not been told in advance than because they cared about Stalin's reputation. And Mao, whose own personality cult was already formidable, did not care for the idea of toppling great leaders from their pedestals. When the Chinese offered to send labourers to Siberia, Khrushchev, so he said, smelled a rat: 'they wanted to take over Siberia without war'. Then, in the late 1950s, when Khrushchev suggested that the Soviet Union and China establish a combined submarine fleet which would operate in the Pacific out of Chinese bases, it was the turn of the Chinese to be suspicious. 'Better take the whole sea-coast of China,' said Mao sarcastically. He himself would go up to the hills and fight a guerrilla war again. If, he told Khrushchev, the Soviet Union 'insisted on stopping China's nostrils, what else could be done?'[11] What particularly annoyed the Chinese was that the Soviet Union gave only lukewarm backing to the longstanding Chinese Communist goal of reuniting Taiwan with the mainland. In the late summer of 1958, when the People's Republic suddenly started shelling Taiwan's islands of Quemoy and Matsu off the Chinese coast, the Russians were alarmed that this might lead to a full-scale confrontation with the United States which could drag the Soviet Union into a major war. Although Moscow eventually produced a statement of support for the People's Republic, it was not as enthusiastic as Mao and his colleagues would have wished. In 1959, as China and India moved towards a confrontation over their borderlands, the Soviet Union tried to make peace and, if anything, showed itself to be sympathetic to the Indians.

By this point, the Chinese Communists were coming to the conclusion that the Soviets were generally rather indifferent allies and even worse revolutionaries. Within the Soviet Union, a new privileged class seemed to be emerging and when China, under Mao's prodding, embarked on the Great Leap Forward in 1958, the Soviets did not show the proper admiration for this utopian programme of rapid development towards socialism. Indeed, Khrushchev described the Great Leap as 'reactionary', and, to make his remarks even more insulting, did so to an American politician. Moreover Khrushchev was talking of 'peaceful coexistence' with capitalist countries, arguing that the threat of nuclear annihilation meant that the struggle between Communism and capitalism would have to be carried on by other means than all-out war. Mao reacted with scorn. He had long believed that change in society, whether domestic or international, occurred only when there was struggle, violent struggle, between different classes. For the Soviet Union to advocate change through peaceful means meant that the Soviet leaders were prepared to accept an unfinished and imperfect revolution.[12]

Mao's motive behind the shelling of Taiwan's two little offshore islands, Quemoy and Matsu, in 1958 may have been in part to disrupt the growing thaw between the Soviet Union and the United States. Soviet leaders found him curiously unconcerned about the possibility of an escalation: 'Russia will drop its atomic bombs on America and America will drop its atomic bombs on the Soviet Union. You may both be wiped out. China too will suffer, but will have four hundred million people left over.' When the Soviet Foreign Minister, Andrei Gromyko, dashed to Beijing to try to defuse the crisis, Mao talked airily of how the Chinese could retreat inland after an American nuclear attack. That would lure the Americans in and then the Soviets could counterattack with their full force, including their nuclear weapons. Gromyko was 'flabbergasted'.[13]

Mao's attitude to nuclear war was a mixture of bravado and fear. On the one hand he described the bomb as a paper tiger and, in his more philosophic moods, downplayed its importance in the grand scheme of things. 'If the worst came to the worst,' he told the Indian Prime Minister, Jawaharlal Nehru, 'and half of mankind died, the other half would remain while imperialism would be razed to the ground and the whole world would become socialist; in a number of years there would be 2,700 million people again and definitely more.' As he told his nonplussed comrades at an international Communist meeting in

Moscow in 1957, nuclear war would speed up the transition to socialism.[14]

Meanwhile, Mao and his colleagues in the People's Republic wanted their own bomb, partly for its symbolism as a marker of China's newly regained independence. As his Foreign Minister Chen Yi said, 'Even if it meant becoming destitute, we had to develop China's own high-tech weaponry.' China saw the American–Soviet test ban treaty of 1963 as 'nuclear blackmail' and an attempt by the two superpowers to deny China its rightful place in the world. Here was yet another in the long list of humiliations that China was suffering at the hands of outside powers. As the Chinese government said in reply to a Soviet memorandum in 1963, 'the Chinese people will never recognize the monopoly of nuclear forces by several powerful countries and their claim to be able to order other countries about'. Indeed one of the grievances which led to the final, very public rupture between China and the Soviet Union was Khrushchev's reluctance to hand over a sample bomb to China's nuclear scientists and then, in the early 1960s, the ending of all Soviet assistance, including nuclear. When the Chinese successfully exploded their first bomb in the autumn of 1964, Mao celebrated with a massive dance performance in the Great Hall of the People and wrote a brief poem. 'Atom bomb goes off when it is told / Ah, what boundless joy!'[15]

Later, Mao denied that he had ever made light of nuclear war. 'We have no atomic bomb,' he assured Edgar Snow, untruthfully, in 1965. 'If some other country plans to launch a nuclear war, the whole world may suffer disaster.' By that time, he was starting to realize that the nuclear stalemate meant that war between the Soviet Union and the United States was unlikely. Indeed, if the Soviet Union was as reactionary as he suspected, it might join forces with the US to attack China. 'These two superpowers', he told a visiting Australian Communist in 1968, 'are nuclear powers. Our country, in a sense, is still a non-nuclear power.' He was also disappointed in the failure of revolutions around the world, in Latin America and, closer to home, in Asia, in Indonesia, for example, because he had counted on such movements to weaken and eventually topple the great powers.[16]

In his new mood of pessimism, Mao started to prepare China for a possible attack. In 1964, he ordered a vast movement of crucial industry inland to the mountains and high plateaux of the west of China. The Third Front, as it was called, involved dismantling hundreds of factories and uprooting thousands of workers. It harked back to the heroic early days of the Japanese invasion in 1937 when the Guomindang retreated away from the coast, but it made little sense in the era of long-range bombers and rockets. The cost to China, and to the unfortunate workers and managers who found themselves in remote valleys and mountains, was crushing. Mao's Third Front ate up funds otherwise available for development, at one point perhaps as much as two-thirds of the total invested in China. It has left factories absurdly far from their supplies and their markets. Many have been quietly abandoned or moved.[17]

Towards the end of the 1960s, Mao made another of his sweeping decisions: China must prepare for invasion. Gigantic mounds of earth were thrown up outside major cities and military sites. In the cities themselves, the Chinese constructed a whole underground world. An American diplomat was given a tour after Nixon's visit: 'They had air purifiers and everything. They had flour mills down there, hospitals, dormitories, workshops, all sorts of things. They were really quite large. Of course, it would not have stood up against nuclear warfare of the kind they had in mind, but it shows you how much labor was involved in all these places. Digging so many underground cities was unbelievable. They did it for fear of the Soviet Union.'[18]

By the end of the 1960s, Mao and what was left of the foreign policy establishment in Beijing were convinced that the chief threat to China, greater even than the United States, was the Soviet Union. In August 1968, Soviet forces had rolled into Czechoslovakia to crush the moderate reform movement and to keep that country firmly under Soviet control. The reaction from Beijing was furious: 'The most barefaced and typical specimen of fascist power politics played by the Soviet revisionist clique against its so-called allies.'[19] The Chinese Communists had no sympathy for the reformers but they were highly alarmed by the Soviet Union's justification for its invasion. If Soviet forces could intervene in Czechoslovakia, why not in China?

It was a question that occurred not only to the Chinese but to the Soviet leaders as well. The Soviet Union had been highly critical of Mao since the early 1960s and, when he started the Cultural

Revolution in 1966, saw this as final proof that he was not a proper Marxist at all but a fanatical adventurer who was destroying the Chinese Communist Party and weakening the cause of socialism worldwide. Soviet opinion was outraged by the activities of radical Maoist students in the Soviet Union and by the treatment of Soviet diplomats in China. Soviet radio called on the Chinese people to rise up and, in 1967, a leading Soviet military newspaper said that the Soviet Union stood ready to help the Chinese free themselves from Mao's rule.[20]

As relations between the two great Communist powers worsened, the 4,000-mile border between them, which had never been entirely settled, became increasingly tense. That the border, established over several centuries, was seen by the Chinese as a product of that long period of national humiliation when outside powers had stripped China of its territory and ignored its sovereignty only added to the tension. The tsars had dictated unequal treaties and the Soviet 'imperialists' had continued the tradition. In 1951, at a time when the People's Republic was heavily dependent on the Soviet Union, the Chinese had signed an agreement with the Soviets covering the rivers which formed much of the border. The Chinese were also obliged to accept Soviet military control of disputed areas; along the edge of Xinjiang province in the west, for example, Chinese herdsmen had to get Soviet permission to use their traditional grazing lands. An even more sensitive area was in the north-east, where Manchuria met Soviet Siberia. The border here was formed by rivers, the Amur which ran across the top of Manchuria and the Ussuri which marked off the long strip of Soviet territory running down the eastern border of Manchuria to the great Soviet port of Vladivostok. Much to the resentment of the Chinese, the Soviet Union remained in control of more than 600 out of 700 river islands. Chinese fishermen had to get Soviet permission to use the rivers and the islands. In the late 1950s, the Chinese government repeatedly asked for the 'unequal' border arrangements to be renegotiated, but the Soviets refused, partly because they did not want to admit that the old agreements were unequal. As relations between the two sides worsened, the number of incidents along the borders increased. In 1964, Khrushchev reluctantly agreed to open discussions. When the Chinese claimed huge tracts of Siberia and control of most of the islands, he suspended the talks.[21]

The Cultural Revolution brought a heating up in the rhetoric, and both sides also stepped up their patrols. The Chinese became increasingly aggressive: Chinese soldiers and fishermen demanded access to Soviet-controlled islands as a right. According to Chinese estimates, there were over 4,000 incidents between 1964 and 1969. These seem to have been at a fairly low level, though, with patrols spraying each other with water or hitting out with sticks. The confrontations tended to follow a ritual: one side would send out a patrol; the other would protest the border violation; and, after some exchanges, both sides would withdraw. In late 1968, however, Soviet armoured vehicles ran over and killed four Chinese on an island in the Ussuri river.[22]

In response to what they saw as Chinese provocations in the period, the Soviets had been increasing their forces in the Far East. Between 1965 and 1969, Soviet divisions in the area increased from about seventeen to twenty-seven. A new treaty with Outer Mongolia allowed the Soviet Union to station a couple of divisions in that country as well. The Soviets also kept some 225 bombers in the Far East and deployed medium- and short-range rockets capable of carrying nuclear warheads. With a range of 2,000 kilometres, their SS4s could reach major cities in northern China. Although the People's Republic did not yet have a comparable nuclear force, it probably had twice as many soldiers as the Soviet Union in the region by 1969. And Mao, or so he said, had great faith in the determination and will of the Chinese to fight even if it meant going back to guerrilla warfare. In reality, both sides seem to have felt apprehensive. The Soviets felt outnumbered and unprepared to fight a conventional war, while the Chinese, with reason, were concerned about the impact of the Cultural Revolution on the training and discipline of the People's Liberation Army.[23]

The danger with wars of nerves is that they can lead to mistakes and, in early 1969, it looked as though the Soviet Union and China might find themselves in a major conflict. Trouble started over a mud-flat called Zhenbao (or Damansky) Island in the Ussuri river. (It had been the scene of fighting many years earlier in the Russo-Japanese

War of 1904–5.) In late December 1968, Soviet and Chinese soldiers fought with sticks. In the new year, the fighting went on, with growing casualties. Then on 2 March 1969 the Chinese sent armed guards on to the island who refused to withdraw in the expected fashion when the Soviets challenged them. Instead the Chinese opened fire. According to the Chinese, more than fifty Soviets were killed. (Soviet sources said thirty.) Two weeks later, the two sides fought on Zhenbao a second time, now with heavy artillery and tanks, and there were even more dead, according to one source sixty Soviets and twelve Chinese. Another source says there were over 800 dead Chinese. Both sides claimed victory. The Chinese scornfully described the Soviet soldiers as 'politically degenerated and morally decadent'. Their own soldiers, they said, 'armed with Mao Tse-tung Thought', had easily dealt with even the Soviet tanks. The Americans, though, got intelligence that the Soviets had plastered the island with heavy artillery fire, leaving nothing but a pock-marked surface. The Chinese tried to deliver a note of protest to the Soviet ambassador in Beijing. He refused to receive it. The Chinese threw the note over the Soviet embassy wall; the Soviets threw it back out. The propaganda from both sides became highly emotional with much reference to heroic deaths and bloodstained last letters filled with patriotic sentiments. Soviet commentators now described Maoism as 'a criminal racist theory' and the Chinese responded with talk of wild beasts.[24]

Much about the events of 1969 remains obscure, although both Chinese and Soviet scholars seem to agree that the Chinese did the most to provoke the exchanges. There has been much speculation since about what motives China might have had. Was Mao sending a signal to the Americans that the rupture between the People's Republic and the Soviet Union was permanent? Perhaps the signal was rather a 'bitter lesson' to the Soviet Union, to show it that the Chinese would resist any aggression or an invasion like the recent one of Czechoslovakia. China had done something similar before when it had attacked India in 1962 and then withdrawn after savaging Indian forces, and it was to do it again with Vietnam in 1978. Or, and this is a possibility given his preoccupation with making the Chinese properly revolutionary in their outlook, Mao wanted to create a situation which would rally the Chinese in resistance to the Soviets. As he told

Chou En-lai after the second Zhenbao battle, 'we should let them come in, which will help us in our mobilization'.[25]

Whatever the causes of the clashes (and they continued throughout the next months), both sides were left in a highly agitated state, each wondering what the other was up to. The Soviets feared that the new Chinese aggressiveness might be a foretaste of something even worse. Members of the Politburo, said a high-ranking official who later defected to the West, were panicking. 'A nightmare vision of invasion by millions of Chinese made the Soviet leaders almost frantic.' Soviet hardliners, including the Defence Minister, disagreed: the time had come to deal with China once and for all. 'Those squint-eyed bastards,' the Soviet ambassador at the United Nations complained to American diplomats. 'We'll kill those yellow sons-of-bitches.' Others, among them Alexei Kosygin, the Soviet Premier, urged that the Soviet Union should try and defuse a dangerous situation. Kosygin used a hotline for the first time in years to telephone Beijing, asking to speak to either Mao or Chou En-lai, but the Chinese operator refused to put through a call from a 'scoundrel revisionist'. The next day, the Chinese Ministry of Foreign Affairs sent a cool note to say that 'in view of the present relations between China and the Soviet Union, it is unsuitable to communicate by telephone'. If the Soviet Union had anything to say, it could do so in writing. Yet, when the Soviets tried to initiate discussions through an exchange of memorandums, the Chinese at first refused to reply and then sent a patronizing admonition: 'Please calm down, don't get excited.'[26]

To persuade the Chinese into a more accommodating frame of mind, Soviet hardliners gained government permission to carry out a limited military action in August on the borders of the Soviet Union and Xinjiang province in China's far west. If their attack on Chinese positions resulted in full-scale war, so be it. Although Kosygin and the other moderates continued to hope for discussions with the Chinese, they also explored other options. The Soviet Union sent out a score of delegations to Asian countries to see about establishing an Asian Collective Security system which would clearly be directed against the People's Republic. In June 1969, American intelligence picked up reports that Soviet bomber units had been sent to Outer Mongolia and were carrying out what looked like mock attacks on Chinese targets. In August, a Soviet diplomat in Washington had lunch with an official from the State Department. What, the diplomat asked, would be the US reaction if the Soviet Union were to bomb a Chinese nuclear facility? The Americans picked up reports of similar queries to Warsaw Pact countries in Eastern Europe. Late that month, Nixon and Kissinger were both briefed by Allen Whiting, a China specialist, who warned that the Soviet Union was getting itself into a position where it could successfully attack. (This may have been the moment that Kissinger finally accepted that Nixon was right, that the time was favourable for an American move towards China.)[27]

The Nixon administration was seriously concerned: it did not want either a general war or to see China defeated. It sent out signals to both sides. In late August Richard Helms, Director of the CIA, gave diplomatic correspondents a confidential briefing which inevitably leaked into the press. He warned of a possible Soviet strike on China. A week later Elliot Richardson, the Under-Secretary of State, told a political science conference in New York that the United States had no intention of exploiting the hostility between the Soviet Union and the People's Republic. 'We could not fail to be deeply concerned, however, with an escalation of this quarrel into a massive breach of international peace and security.'[28]

Opinion among the Chinese leadership after the March clashes had also been divided. A group led by Mao's chosen successor Lin Biao believed that the Soviet Union was ready to take serious action against China, while men such as the former Foreign Minister Chen Yi argued for diplomacy to resolve the tensions. Mao himself, who was the final arbiter of China's policy, seems to have had trouble making up his mind. He told Chou En-lai to stop the fighting after the second clash on Zhenbao Island in March, but he also gave orders that China should prepare to fight a war. Nothing much was actually done. Mao perhaps thought that the Soviet Union had been taught its lesson. In any case, he assumed that its main interests lay in Europe, not the Far East.[29]

By the late summer of 1969, however, Mao could not ignore the evidence that the Soviets were up to something. The Soviet attack on 13 August apparently shocked him considerably and, when he learned that the Soviet Union might be planning a sudden nuclear strike on

China, he became, in the words of a Chinese expert, 'extremely nervous'. On 28 August, the Central Committee of the Chinese Communist Party issued new orders to the Chinese to prepare for war. The party also used the opportunity to order an end to the often violent struggles between different factions of Red Guards. When Ho Chi Minh, the leader of North Vietnam, died in Hanoi on 3 September, Chou En-lai dashed down to pay his respects but did not stay for the funeral, partly because the situation was so serious but also because he did not want to meet Kosygin, who was representing the Soviet Union.[30]

On 6 September, a member of the Soviet party asked the North Vietnamese to let the Chinese know that Kosygin was prepared to stop in Beijing for talks on his way home. When he got the news, Mao dithered for several days, and Kosygin was already in Tashkent, on his way home to Moscow, when word came that Chou En-lai would meet him at Beijing airport. Kosygin, who had already landed in Tashkent, took to the air again and landed in Beijing early on the morning of 11 September. On Mao's orders, to show their displeasure, the Chinese kept the Soviets at the airport. Kosygin and Chou En-lai, with their aides, met for three and a half hours in the VIP lounge. Both sides denied that they intended to make war on the other. Kosygin may have offered to withdraw Soviet troops from the disputed territories. Both sides certainly agreed that they should try to sort out their border issues, although Chou continued to complain about the unequal nature of the existing agreements. The Soviets talked optimistically about restoring normal trade and diplomatic relations. Chou agreed that their proposals would be shown to Mao but warned that the People's Republic would continue its polemics against fellow Communist parties when they went wrong. The Soviets replied primly that they had nothing against reasonable polemics. 'Lies and curses do not add persuasiveness and authority to a polemic, and only humiliate the feelings of the other people and aggravate the relations.'[31]

The relations unfortunately remained aggravated and indeed highly dangerous for the next several months. Each side mistrusted the other too much for one meeting to help. When Kosygin flew on to Moscow, the Chinese noticed that none of his senior colleagues came out to meet him at the airport. Did that mean that the rest of the Soviet leadership did not want peace with China? Had Kosygin promised that the Soviet Union would not launch a nuclear strike on China? The Chinese record of the talks was not clear. (The Soviet record has the Soviets saying that rumours of such a strike were 'contrived imperialistic propaganda'.) And perhaps the Chinese were right to be suspicious. In what was apparently a move to put more pressure on the People's Republic, Victor Louis, a Moscow-based journalist who acted as a conduit for Soviet views, published an article in a London newspaper saying how easy it would be for the Soviet Union to launch a surprise attack on China, perhaps against China's own nuclear facilities in Xinjiang province. Louis also talked about how the Chinese people were starting to rise against Mao. The Soviet Union, he said, was ready to offer 'fraternal help'. These and other signs led the Chinese leadership, notably Mao and Lin Biao, to the conclusion that Kosygin's visit was a smokescreen to conceal the true Soviet intentions. Perhaps to send the Soviet Union a warning, China tested two nuclear devices that September, the first in almost a year.[32]

There was something close to panic in Beijing that autumn. On 22 September, Chou En-lai told a People's Liberation Army conference, 'The international situation is extremely tense. We should be prepared for fighting a war.'[33] The armed forces were put on high alert, and proper training, so disrupted by the Cultural Revolution, was resumed. Immense tunnels were constructed to link Zhongnanhai to the Great Hall of the People and a special hospital. Thousands of key personnel and their files as well as universities and colleges were moved out of the cities, and Chinese forces were sent to forward positions ready to repel an invasion. Ordinary citizens were given shovels and told to start digging.

The Chinese waited anxiously. Perhaps the attack would come on 1 October, China's National Day. Lin Biao ordered all planes in the Beijing area to be flown away and obstacles were placed on the runways. When 1 October came and went, the Chinese decided that 20 October, when a Soviet delegation was due to arrive to start talking about the borders, might be the day. What if the Soviet plane carried nuclear bombs rather than negotiators? Mao and Lin Biao hastily left Beijing for the south. The remaining leadership moved into underground shelters in Beijing's Western Hills. Chou did not reappear in his office for several months and moved back only in February 1970 when the worst of the panic was over. Throughout 1970, though, the Chinese continued to anticipate a Soviet invasion. To this day, those years are remembered in China as a time of great danger.[34]

There is an old Chinese saying that 'When the extreme is reached, the reverse will set in,' and indeed Mao was now starting to think seriously about doing something about China's isolation in the world. In February 1969, to help him clarify his thoughts, he set up a special four-man group to study the international situation. All its members were hardened revolutionaries who had led the Communist armies in the long struggle for power. After 1949, all had become marshals in the People's Liberation Army. In 1969, all had plenty of time on their hands because each had been attacked and disgraced during the Cultural Revolution amid mad accusations that they were counter-revolutionaries. (In fact their crime was to have suggested that the Cultural Revolution was going too far.) They were among the luckier of the top leadership, though, because Mao did not feel particularly vindictive towards them. Chou En-lai was able to provide them with a certain amount of protection and had sent them to live in secure factories in Beijing where their duties were minimal and their real job was to read materials on international affairs and discuss them with each other. Chou instructed, 'You should not be confined to the established views and conclusions, which need to be altered partly or totally.' With the thoughtfulness that made so many love him, he urged the four elderly men not to work too hard: 'Take care of your health.'[35]

The group's leader, the former Foreign Minister Chen Yi, was chosen by Mao himself. Marshal Chen, who had been a Communist for almost as long as Mao himself and was also a poet, was one of the Revolution's outstanding generals and one of the few men Mao called friend. He was brave and outspoken, qualities which had got him into trouble during the Cultural Revolution when, for example, he told a meeting of radical students that they were acting senselessly. What, he demanded, was the point of parading the older generation – the very people who had made the Revolution – in dunces' caps and accusing them of all sorts of improbable crimes? He refused to believe that the party was riddled with traitors as the Red Guards claimed. 'Pick on me,' he shouted defiantly, 'and expose me to the public! A member of the Communist Party, he's worth nothing if he dare not stand up and speak the truth.' They had responded to his challenge with a series of meetings to denounce him. At one point, in the summer of 1967, Chen was trapped in the Foreign Ministry for several hours until Chou managed to rescue him and send him out of harm's way.[36]

In December 1968, in spite of his own precarious position, Chen had bravely written a report, in contradiction of official propaganda, arguing that the United States was focused on the Americas and Europe rather than on the Far East, and that the tension between the Soviet Union and the United States suggested, although he did not say so explicitly, an opening for China. Between the two superpowers, Chen probably favoured the US. 'If the US could change its current hostile attitude towards us,' he had commented in the late 1950s, 'there would be a future for the bilateral relationship.' Chen was a devout Communist but also a strong Chinese nationalist and he found it difficult to forgive the Soviet Union for an abrupt cancellation of all its aid agreements in 1960. 'What kind of Marxist–Leninism is this? Even capitalist countries would not do something like this!'[37]

The four old marshals were allowed to read virtually anything they wanted, including translations from foreign newspapers. They were also given unlimited green tea and a couple of younger colleagues, 'strong labourers' as Chen described them, to help with their researches. In their discussions, they cautiously started to question one of the main assumptions of China's foreign policy: that the Soviet Union and the United States were equally hostile to China. Perhaps China could manoeuvre between them. Chen Yi, as always, was the boldest. 'Due to strategic necessity, Stalin signed the non-aggression treaty with Hitler. Why can't we play the America card?' American policy, he pointed out, had been changing subtly. He wanted to suggest to the leadership that China resume the Warsaw talks with the United States which had been temporarily broken off the previous year.[38]

In July, the Four Marshals submitted their first report. While it contained the standard abuse of American capitalists and Soviet revisionists and the usual praise for the 'invincible Mao Tse-tung Thought', they daringly pointed out the conflicts between the United States and the Soviet Union. They also argued that a major attack on China was not imminent. The United States had been too badly burned in Vietnam, and the Soviet Union was deterred by fear of what the US might do.[39]

In September, with the fear of Soviet attack building, they sent Chou En-lai a second report which underlined their earlier conclusions. 'The last thing the US imperialists are willing to see is a victory by the Soviet revisionists in a Sino-Soviet war, as this would [allow the Soviets] to build up a big empire more powerful than the American empire in resources and manpower.' Although in the long term China was struggling against both powers, its strategy should be to use the one against the other. In some 'further thoughts', Chen Yi spelled out what this could mean. 'It is necessary for us to utilize the contradiction between the United States and the Soviet Union in a strategic sense and to pursue a breakthrough in Sino-American relations.' He had some 'wild' ideas about how to do this. China should use the Warsaw talks to propose to the Americans that their two sides hold meetings 'at the ministerial or even higher levels' to discuss the major issues. When Foreign Ministry officials quailed at passing on such heresy to Chou and Mao, Chen insisted.[40]

Apparently Mao said nothing at all when he saw the reports. He was in the process of working out his own thoughts on the correct strategy for China. It was clear that China could not continue to sustain the enmity of the two superpowers as well as of most of its neighbours. Chou, as always, waited for direction from the Chairman. When the Swedish ambassador asked him that June whether the Soviet Union or the United States was the greater threat to China, Chou was curiously vague: 'Now the situation is changing; we should wait and see.'[41] Could the fences with the Soviet Union be mended? Was it in China's interest to seek that solution? Or was there an alternative? Chinese history, which still held the Communist leaders in its thrall, offered an instructive lesson. In the third century AD, during a period of disunity, one of China's greatest strategists had allied his kingdom with a second to defeat a third.

That autumn, Mao asked his doctor to consider a problem. 'We have the Soviet Union to the north and the west, India to the south, and Japan to the east. If all our enemies were to unite, attacking us from the north, south, east, and west, what do you think we should do?' Dr Li confessed that he was at a loss. 'Think again,' Mao said. 'Beyond Japan is the United States. Didn't our ancestors counsel negotiating with faraway countries while fighting with those that are near?' The doctor, not surprisingly, was dumbfounded. How, he asked Mao, could China negotiate with the United States? It was easy, Mao replied. Unlike the Soviet Union, the United States had never occupied Chinese territory. And its new President, Richard Nixon, was a right-winger. 'I like to deal with rightists. They say what they really think – not like the leftists, who say one thing and mean another.' (Although Mao could not know it, Nixon had just startled his cabinet in Washington by saying that it was not necessarily in the best interests of the United States to see the Soviet Union crush China.) Another Chinese statesman was also watching and waiting. 'Once China and the Soviet Union have any contact,' said Chen Yi, 'the US will get impatient just like an ant on top of a hot pot. Nixon will not be satisfied at being left behind and will try to catch up.' The world had been surprised when Kosygin and Chou had met in Beijing that autumn. 'If a Sino-US summit meeting could be held, it would shock the world even more!'[42]

10

The Banquet

THE RIGHTIST WAS now in Beijing. The first night of the visit,
Chou En-lai invited Nixon, as the Chinese always did special
guests, to a banquet given in his honour at the Great Hall of the
People, that monstrous Stalinist structure which ran along one side of
Tiananmen Square. Banquets, toasts, the exchange of gifts, all have
been part of diplomacy throughout recorded Chinese history. The
Chinese Communists took such protocols as seriously as their predecessors had done 'Their whole idea', said Winston Lord, Kissinger's
assistant who in 1985 would come back to China as the American
ambassador, 'is to inculcate in outsiders coming to the Middle
Kingdom a sense of obligation for their hospitality and friendship. In
effect, they seek to create ties of alleged friendship. They want us to
feel that friends do favors for other friends.'[1]

The Americans – the entire party, from the President and Mrs
Nixon to the crew of their aircraft – gathered in the foyer of Nixon's
villa at the Diaoyutai along with Chinese protocol people and trans-
lators for the motorcade into the centre of the city. At the Great Hall,
they walked into an enormous lobby two storeys high with polished
floors and massive chandeliers, where Chou En-lai and his colleagues
waited to greet them. The guests made their way up the grand staircase for a series of photographs, carefully posed according to rank, and
were then ushered into the massive, sombre hall filled with round
tables and decorated with Chinese and American flags. It could hold
up to three thousand people for a banquet; that evening there were
perhaps a thousand. As the Americans entered, a Chinese military
band started playing a medley of American folk songs. (In imperial
China, officials had always believed in using music to soothe visiting
barbarians.)

Mao himself had apparently approved the guests on the Chinese side. While there were representatives from the Beijing revolutionary committee, one of the new organs created during the Cultural Revolution, none of the leading radicals was present, not even Mao's wife Jiang Qing. (She later told the Nixons that she had been too ill to come.)[2] The Chinese who were present were largely officials, from the government, the Communist Party or the People's Liberation Army. Ye Jianying, one of the Four Marshals who had written the bold reports in the summer of 1969 urging China to rethink its views on the world, was there, as was Ji Pengfei, the ineffectual Foreign Minister, and his much more competent deputy, Qiao Guanhua.

On the other side of the world, Americans watched on their morning television shows as the band played the Chinese and American national anthems and the banquet began. The Nixons and the top-ranking Americans sat with Chou En-lai at a large table for twenty, while everyone else was at smaller tables of ten. Each person had an embossed ivory place-card in English and Chinese in gold lettering and chopsticks inscribed with his or her name. The Americans had all been briefed on how to behave at Chinese banquets. Everyone had been issued with chopsticks and urged to practise ahead of time. Nixon had managed to become reasonably adept, but Kissinger remained hopelessly clumsy. The distinguished television reporter Walter Cronkite shot an olive high into the air. 'The Chinese take great pride in their food,' said a White House memo, 'and to compliment the various courses and dishes is also recommended.'[3]

As the band played on – 'Oh, Susanna', 'Turkey in the Straw' and that Cultural Revolution favourite, 'Sailing the Seas Depends on the Helmsman' – teams of waiters brought dish after dish. Nixon, who had once ordered a banquet at the White House timed by stopwatch and who had been delighted when it came in under an hour, had no complaints this evening as the two former enemies celebrated a new relationship and the American networks covered it live for four hours. Large turntables rotated on each table, laden with duck slices garnished with pineapple, vegetarian ham (according to the English menu), three-coloured eggs, carp, chicken, prawns, shark fin, dumplings, sweet rice cake, fried rice and, in a nod towards Western tastes, bread and butter.

Some of the Americans, including John Holdridge from the State Department, spoke Chinese well and a few of the Chinese spoke English. Otherwise conversation was through interpreters. At the head table, Nixon and Chou En-lai exchanged desultory remarks through Mao's interpreter Tang Wensheng. Rogers told long stories about his hero, the great golfer Sam Snead, to the Chinese Foreign Minister, a tough old revolutionary who had no idea what golf was. Mrs Nixon chatted away politely, asking her Chinese hosts such questions as how many children they had.[4]

Chou En-lai, who was smoking Chinese cigarettes, turned to Mrs Nixon and gestured to the picture of two pandas on the package. 'We will give you two,' he said. According to Chinese sources, Mrs Nixon screamed with joy. Although the Americans had dropped some hints, the Chinese had been noncommittal on the pandas. Like banquets, the exchange of presents has always been important in diplomacy and giving the right presents, not too lavish and not too simple, has been an art, one which the Chinese had traditionally excelled at. In imperial China, the emperors had despatched gifts – silks, brocades or porcelain, for example – to other rulers as a mark of imperial favour and, often, to keep them quiescent. Communist China had continued to send gifts abroad, often as before porcelain or cloth, but now, as an indication of its revolutionary nature, to peoples and not rulers. In special cases, it also offered pandas, just as its predecessors had done. Placid bears which spend most of their time eating or sleeping perhaps signal a placid relationship. The famous Empress Wu presented a pair to the Emperor of Japan in the seventh century and Chiang Kai-shek another pair to the United States during the Second World War. After 1949, the Communist gave pandas to the Soviet Union and North Korea as marks of friendship. Ling-ling and Hsing-hsing were now destined for the National Zoo in Washington.[5]

The presents issue had caused much anxiety in the White House – what to expect from the Chinese and what to give them. On Kissinger's secret trip in July 1971, he had taken along a piece of rock brought back by American astronauts from the moon. The Chinese had received it much as the Qianlong Emperor had received British woollens brought by Lord Macartney – with a certain amount of disdain. Medals in lucite were considered and dropped and finally ceramic models of American birds were made for senior officials while more junior ones got silver bowls, cigarette lighters or cufflinks with the presidential seal. Nixon also presented a pair of musk oxen and two giant redwood trees from California. The trees, in particular, proved awkward to transport; once in China, one of them promptly got worms and languished, though the other flourished. (The Canadians, when they cemented their new relationship with China, chose to send their national animal. A pair of beavers were loaded into a washroom on an Air Canada plane to splash about on their way to China.)[6]

At their places at the banquet, each person had three glasses, one for water or orange juice, one for wine, and one for China's famous maotai, 'white lightning' to the American journalists, or, as Dan Rather put it, 'liquid razor blades'. At their table, Chou En-lai said proudly to Nixon that maotai, with its alcohol level of more than 50 per cent, had been world famous since the San Francisco World's Fair of 1915. He took a match to his cup. 'Mr Nixon, please take a look. It can indeed catch fire.' (Back in the United States, when the President tried a similar demonstration by setting a bowlful on fire, he nearly burned down the White House.) He understood, Nixon said, that Red Army soldiers had once drained dry the town where maotai was produced. 'During the Long March, maotai was used by us to cure all kinds of diseases and wounds,' Chou answered primly. 'Let me make a toast with this panacea,' said Nixon. (Alexander Haig, who had experienced maotai on his advance trip to Beijing in January, had worried about its effect on the notoriously weak-headed Nixon. 'UNDER NO REPEAT NO CIRCUMSTANCES', he had cabled, 'SHOULD THE PRESIDENT ACTUALLY DRINK FROM HIS GLASS IN RESPONSE TO BANQUET TOASTS.')[7]

'At banquets,' the White House had warned, 'the wine and Mao Tai are for toasting only. These glasses should not be raised without toasting one of your Chinese friends.' With Chinese sitting at each table, the toasting started early on. Haldeman, who was a teetotaller, tried repeatedly to explain to his incredulous hosts that he could not drink alcohol. John Holdridge found himself playing an old drinking game of counting fingers with the Minister of Electric Power. The loser had to drain his glass to a shout of *ganbei*. 'Aided only in part by

148

the *mao tai*,' Holdridge remembered, 'the atmosphere in the Great Hall was electric. Surely everyone there, and every TV watcher, must have sensed that something new and great was being created in the U.S.–China relationship.'[8]

From their tables at the far end of the hall, the journalists, most of them American, stood on their chairs and used field glasses to watch the historic scene. Nixon wanted them there, just as he wanted the live television coverage, because he understood their power so well. He always read the thick daily summaries of press coverage and covered their margins with comments and orders. He wanted their attention but not too much; as he told Haldeman, his image should be 'more aloof, inaccessible, mysterious'. Yet he also delighted in showing the press his boorish side; as he once told an aide, 'So much for their fucking sophistication.'[9]

Nixon despised most journalists as 'clowns' who were irredeemably liberal in their bias. And he was convinced that they hated him in return 'because I have beaten them so often'. They had been wrong and he had been right on a whole range of issues, from Alger Hiss to what the American people wanted. (Early on in his presidency, he ordered his senior staff to prepare lists of friends and foes among the press; the latter was much the longer list.) He intended to circumvent what he saw as the liberal establishment in the media and reach out directly to middle America, where his support lay. With the powers of the presidency he could make news, whether by creating photo-opportunities or going on the networks with major policy statements. (He could also, and did, place wiretaps on reporters to see where they were getting their stories.) The camera, Nixon believed, was more effective for him than print. As Kissinger said unkindly, 'television in front of the President is like alcohol in front of an alcoholic'.[10]

In Haldeman, he found the man he needed. With his background in advertising, Haldeman was quick to see the possibilities of television. As he told Nixon in the run-up to the presidential election, the time had come 'to move out of the dark ages and into the brave new world of the omnipresent eye'. With Haldeman's help, Nixon created a new office of communications and a separate office for television. The White House generated a stream of material. A presidential photographer and a navy film crew stood by to catch Nixon being presidential or playing with his dog, Prince Timahoe. Staff writers composed editorials and news releases which went not just to the major papers but to thousands of small-town papers across the United States. Washington reporters complained that they no longer had access to the President and no way of finding out what that remote and isolated figure was thinking. That was the way Nixon and Haldeman wanted it. When the press criticized the President, over his failure to bring the Vietnam War to an end for example, the administration fought back. In late 1969, Vice-President Spiro Agnew was unleashed; in a series of speeches, overseen by Nixon himself, he excoriated the media as 'a tiny, enclosed fraternity of privileged men elected by no one'. Journalists seen as particularly hostile found they were no longer included on presidential trips or given background briefings. In some of the worst cases, the tax people or the FBI turned up to investigate them.[11]

When Chou En-lai had suggested to Kissinger, in their discussions on the President's visit, that ten journalists might be about the right number to accompany Nixon, the Americans had negotiated the number upwards until they got permission to bring approximately ninety. When some 2,000 applications from journalists came into the White House press office, the President's staff announced criteria for selection. In fact, Nixon himself picked the reporters, making sure that the television networks got far more spaces than print media. He also took great pleasure in refusing places to papers like the *New York Times*. (On his first trip to China, Kissinger managed to warn Chou En-lai obliquely about talking to James Reston from the *Times* who was about to arrive in Beijing.) A reporter from the New York paper *Newsday*, who had just written a series investigating the complicated financial relations between Nixon and Bebe Rebozo, and who apparently met the criteria for going to Beijing, was told simply 'no room'.[12] Several of the top network brass managed to get themselves accredited as technical staff, much to the annoyance of the beleaguered print journalists. Few of them, apart from the writer Theodore White, had ever been to China or had any particular knowledge of it.

Nixon, for all his distrust of the press, understood how important it was that his visit received favourable coverage. American public opinion, for so long hostile to Communist China, still had to be persuaded that the President was doing the right thing in opening up relations. Nixon, as always, was also conscious of his own place in history. When Kissinger made his second, public trip to China in the autumn of 1971, part of his mission was to discuss press coverage. Staff from the White House whose job it was to prepare for presidential visits reviewed the schedule and checked out possible sites for photo-opportunities. At the beginning of 1972 Alexander Haig, Kissinger's assistant, spent a week in China working on the final arrangements with a party of technical experts. Then, on 1 February, an advance party of nearly a hundred arrived in China to prepare for Nixon's visit. One of their most pressing tasks was to set up the communications that would make live television coverage possible.

The Chinese expected to work with the advance team on the trip but they were amazed by the detailed planning it undertook to make sure, among other things, that the President would get maximum media coverage. At Beijing airport, for example, the Americans carefully worked out the best place for the President's plane to land so that it would stop in the right place and at the right angle for good shots of Nixon's descent towards the waiting reception party. The runway was carefully measured and marked up with paint.[13]

Because of China's relative isolation, the Chinese had not kept up with the sort of technology the Americans took for granted. When Kissinger flew in on the President's own plane on his October 1971 visit, Chinese assumed the controls for the flight from Shanghai to Beijing. The Chinese pilots took one look at the inertial navigation systems in the cockpit and then ignored them completely, flying visually, with one making hand signals to the other. The Chinese had never seen a Xerox copier and were fascinated by the one the American advance party brought. (When the Americans realized that the Chinese were copying all their documents out by hand, they arranged to leave their copier behind.) China did not have the facilities to transmit to satellites or to ship film rapidly out of the country. Nor were the Chinese media expected to get stories out quickly. The senior Chinese journalist (one of only a handful) who was assigned to cover the Nixon visit remembered being struck by how fast American journalists worked, how they used newsflashes for a breaking story or how one would write a lead paragraph and others finish up a story.

'We will have to compete in speed,' she told herself, 'we will have to make some reforms in the way we do things.' She also looked longingly at their equipment, the portable telephones or the microphones on long sticks.[14]

While the Americans were prepared to bring in whatever they needed, they found that they had to be careful of Chinese sensitivities. On his October 1971 visit, Kissinger raised the issue of a ground station for satellite transmissions. Perhaps, he suggested, the necessary equipment could be flown in on a Boeing 747 which could then act as a self-contained unit. Chou offered to buy the plane, equipment and all. 'If we cannot buy it, we will rent it from you.' The compromise reached was that the Chinese would put up a suitable building (which they did in record time) and rent it to the Americans. The Americans would provide the equipment which the Chinese in turn would rent. (The negotiations proved difficult because the Chinese became convinced that the Americans were undercharging them and they insisted, to the confusion of American officials, on paying more than the asking price.) Chou also expressed a certain scepticism about the American hope that the visit would enhance Nixon's image as a world leader. 'This we find difficult to understand,' he told Haig. 'The image of a man depends on his own deeds and not on any other factors. We do not believe that any world leader can be self styled.'[15]

In the three weeks before Nixon arrived, the advance party worked around the clock to set up press facilities, work out camera angles at all the places the President and Mrs Nixon might visit, and make sure that the Chinese knew what they needed. Could they get a telex going? Were there going to be phone lines at the Great Wall? Were there forklifts in China capable of unloading heavy equipment? The Chinese were bewildered but co-operative. Their technical experts fell on unfamiliar new technology with enthusiasm and asked to copy all the manuals into Chinese. Giant US Air Force planes flew into Shanghai to disgorge tons of equipment including gallons of chemicals for developing film. As the first plane landed and the first big network control truck rolled out, Tim Elbourne, the White House staffer responsible, stood with his astonished Chinese colleagues, and wept with pride.[16]

Back in the United States, the administration continued to try to add names to the list of journalists who would be arriving with the President. The lucky ones received special briefings. Beijing was cold in the winter, they were warned; many journalists rushed off to buy special fur coats and long underwear. They should look after their health; if they went into a Chinese hospital, they might never come out. They must expect to work very long hours because they would have far fewer staff than they were used to.[17]

Two chartered planes carried the reporters, camera crews and their support staff along with their briefing books and equipment to China just ahead of Nixon. The journalists, who included television stars such as Walter Cronkite and Eric Sevareid, the writer James Michener and William Buckley, a conservative the White House was wooing, travelled together on one plane. A young Barbara Walters, one of only three women in the group, was annoyed to find herself relegated to what was nicknamed the Zoo Plane with the photographers and technicians.[18]

On the way out to China, the journalists practised, just as the official party was doing, using chopsticks on the airline food. They also played cards for the Chinese currency with which they had all been issued. According to Helen Thomas, a reporter, some of her colleagues even gave up drink and immersed themselves in their books and papers on China and their guidebooks. As she said, in what was a common metaphor used by most Americans from Nixon down, visiting China was like going to the moon. Even the most experienced and worldly-wise old hands rushed to their windows to take their first pictures of China as the planes crossed into Chinese airspace.[19]

In Beijing, the press corps were housed near Tiananmen Square in the cavernous Soviet-style Minzu Hotel (Nationalities, in English). In the rooms, plainer than most of the journalists were used to, boxes of sweets, fresh fruit, tea and stamps had been thoughtfully laid out. In the bathrooms the wooden toilet seats had been freshly lacquered; unfortunately the extract of sumac in the lacquer brought out painful boils on those who were allergic to it. (The advance party had already encountered what they nicknamed 'Baboon bottom'.)[20] Next door was a new building with a basketball court and bowling alley, thrown up in a matter of weeks after one of the Americans in the advance party had mentioned that the journalists might like to exercise.

Chinese, many of them journalists themselves, were assigned to each American, as interpreters, guides and minders. A young student, brought in from a local university, was deeply impressed by the Americans' dedication to their work; he decided then to become a journalist. Many of the Chinese, although the Americans never knew it, had been brought back from the countryside where, as intellectuals, they had been undergoing thought reform. The Chinese were invariably polite and openly curious about American ways of doing such things as filing stories, or about exposures and film speeds. Sometimes the Chinese had to admit that they were baffled. 'I understand almost everything you are saying,' said one to a television producer. 'The feed, the uplink, the standup, but there is one thing you keep saying that I don't understand. Please explain what is "the Fucking Audio?"'[21]

Partway through the banquet, Chou En-lai got up on to the stage on one side of the hall. Speaking through his personal interpreter, he welcomed Nixon and Mrs Nixon on behalf of Chairman Mao and the Chinese government. The President, Chou went on, was visiting China 'at the invitation of the Chinese Government'. This innocuous phrase had caused much difficulty on Kissinger's first, secret trip when the Chinese wanted to make it look as though Nixon had asked to come to China.

The banquet, like Nixon's trip itself, was about symbols, about handshakes and about the exchange of toasts between leaders whose countries had for decades treated each other with suspicion. It was about status, about fears of being snubbed as Dulles had once snubbed Chou, and about losing or maintaining prestige in the eyes of the world, or, equally important, in the eyes of the Chinese and American peoples. It also carried echoes of the long and sometimes difficult relationship between the Chinese and foreigners. No matter whether or not China really was the kingdom at the centre of the world, Chinese governments down the centuries had used rituals that implied that their emperor was chosen by heaven to rule the world and that all other rulers were his inferiors. Presents sent to the Chinese emperor and trade with China were both described as tribute. It may not have been a realistic view of the actual relationships between China and foreign nations, but it was a very powerful one. Inferior rulers, in other words all those outside China, had to ask for permission to enter the emperor's lands; they were not invited by the emperor because that would have implied a relationship of equals.[22]

Continuing his toast, Chou En-lai sounded a more modern note. In a reflection of the Chinese Communist view that the masses of the world would one day unite, he said that the Chinese people sent cordial greetings to the American people. Both peoples wanted a normalization of their relationship. 'The people, and the people alone, are the motive force in the making of world history.' All present there knew why there had been a twenty-year freeze between their two nations. Thanks to efforts on both sides contact had been re-established. Of course, it was not going to be easy. 'The social systems of China and the United States are fundamentally different, and there exist great differences between the Chinese Government and the United States Government.' Neither side wanted war, though, and both were willing to work together on a basis of mutual respect. 'We hope', Chou concluded, 'that, through a frank exchange of views between our two sides to gain a clearer notion of our differences and make efforts to find common ground, a new start can be made in the relations between our two countries.' And he lifted his glass in a toast to the Americans and Chinese in the room and to friendship between the Chinese and American peoples. Coming down from the stage, Chou circled the tables of the official party, toasting each person in turn. One of the Americans noticed that he only touched his lips to his glass each time.[23]

After a few more courses, it was Nixon's turn to reply. He wanted his toast to appear spontaneous even though he and his staff had been working on it for weeks. This had led to an awkward scene with Charles Freeman, his young interpreter from the State Department, just before the banquet. Freeman, who came from an old New England family, was an immensely civilized, cultivated and witty man with, among other abilities, a great gift for languages. He had learned Chinese in the US and in Taiwan and spoke an elegant fluent Chinese studded with allusions to classical literature. Although both Nixon and Kissinger did not like to use State Department interpreters for fear they might leak information, Freeman was told earlier that evening that he would be interpreting for Nixon. When he asked for the prepared text of the toast, Chapin, the appointments secretary, had said that there wasn't one. Freeman pointed out that he worked on earlier drafts and that he also knew that Nixon was planning to quote some of Chairman Mao's poetry. 'And if you think I'm going to get up in front of the entire Chinese politburo and ad lib Chairman Mao's poetry back into Chinese, you're nuts.' Fortunately Ji Chaozhu, who was Chou En-lai's interpreter, agreed to fill in and Mao's poetry was translated back into Chinese correctly. Nixon glowered at the unfortunate Freeman throughout the dinner, making him so nervous that he took up smoking again. Two days later, after Freeman had shown his usefulness in interpreting, Nixon offered a tearful apology and said fulsomely to Chou En-lai that Freeman might well be the first American ambassador to China. 'It was odd,' thought an embarrassed Freeman as Chou muttered something that sounded like 'That'll be the day.'[24]

Nixon's reply to Chou started with compliments to his hosts for their hospitality. The food was 'magnificent', as was the army band. 'Never have I heard American music played better in a foreign land.' Like Chou, he admitted that there were many differences between China and the United States. Nevertheless, together both peoples could build a peaceful world, in which the young, like his own daughters, could be free from the fear of war. 'So, let us, in these next five days, start a long march together, not in lockstep, but on different roads leading to the same goal, the goal of building a world structure of peace and justice in which all may stand together with equal dignity and in which each nation, large or small, has a right to determine its own form of government, free of outside interference or domination.' Coming to the passage that Freeman had so dreaded, he quoted Mao: 'Chairman Mao has written, "So many deeds cry out to be done, and always urgently. The world rolls on. Time passes. Ten thousand years are too long. Seize the day, seize the hour."'[25]

Nixon raised his glass in a toast to the absent Mao, to Chou En-lai and to the friendship of the Chinese and American peoples. The band struck up 'America the Beautiful'. Nixon was delighted to learn that Chou had chosen the tune himself because it had been played at the President's inauguration, and when Chou raised his glass to his guest's next inauguration, Nixon thought it 'very significant'. To the sound of music, the President did his round of toasts at the important tables. 'It was really quite spectacular,' thought Haldeman, who watched Nixon with the pride of a good stage manager. 'He moved very forcefully, took a firm stand in front of the individual, looked him squarely in the eye, raised his glass and clinked the other person's, took a quick sip, then he raised his glass again and gave a little staccato bow to the individual, and then he turned, marched to the next individual, and repeated the performance.'[26]

Not everyone shared Haldeman's pleasure. 'The effect', according to William Buckley, the conservative journalist, 'was as if Sir Hartley Shawcross had suddenly risen from the prosecutor's stand at Nuremberg and descended to embrace Goering and Goebbels and Doenitz and Hess, begging them to join with him in the making of a better world.' On the other side of the world, Enver Hoxha, the Albanian dictator whose country had been one of China's few friends in the dark days of the 1960s, wrote in his diary: 'The orchestra at the banquet played "America the Beautiful"! The beautiful America of millionaires and multimillionaires! America, the centre of fascism and barbarous imperialism!'[27]

According to Chinese custom, the banquet ended abruptly with the last course. The guests headed for the cars and the journalists rushed to file their stories. A famous American television reporter ran after a bewildered Qiao Guanhua, the Deputy Foreign Minister, trying in vain to get an exclusive interview. 'I'm Eric Sevareid,' he announced to a man who had probably never heard of him. John Burns, a Canadian journalist, took Nixon's chopsticks as a souvenir. Although a New York dealer sent a cable with an offer of $10,000, Burns kept them.[28]

Back at his guesthouse, an euphoric Nixon called Haldeman and Kissinger into his bedroom for an hour to go over the events of the first day in China, from the arrival to the meeting with Mao and finally the banquet. To Nixon's pleasure, Haldeman was able to report that the press coverage so far had been very good. 'P. finally decided to fold up for the day after we reviewed the schedule for the week again, and that's the end of a very memorable day in American history.'[29]

II

Opening Moves

GIVING HIS TOAST at the banquet, Chou had said: 'The peoples of our two countries have always been friendly to each other. But owing to reasons known to all, contacts between the two peoples were suspended for over twenty years. Now, through the common efforts of China and the United States, the gate to friendly contacts has finally been opened.' Opening that gate had been a tricky and difficult process and there had been many times when it looked as though it would never occur.

Kissinger later described the steps by which the United States and China overcame their own prejudices to open up relations as an intricate minuet, 'so delicately arranged that both sides could always maintain that they were not in contact, so stylized that neither side needed to bear the onus of an initiative, so elliptical that existing relationships on both sides were not jeopardized'.[1] The setting was right; both sides had their own reasons for wanting to talk. Yet, without the right individuals to push the process ahead, it could have failed any number of times. Given his supreme authority in China, Mao, once he was convinced of the need to deal with the United States, could direct that his officials work with the Americans. He could also ensure that no word came out in China of Kissinger's first visit and the painstaking negotiations leading up to it. He could not, though, guarantee how the Americans would behave or prevent the American press from jumping on the story. Fortunately Nixon, with Kissinger in a crucial supporting role, was determined to carry off the opening to China and do so before public opinion could form.

If every message back and forth, each step in the negotiations to arrange Kissinger's secret visit and then Nixon's had been conducted publicly, the Americans would have found themselves with a very public controversy. As General Alexander Haig put it: 'the sensitivity of opening up a dialogue with the People's Republic of China could not be over-estimated and was very likely to have caused such a brouhaha in our legislature that the whole initiative could have been squashed before it was even born'.[2] And American allies such as Japan and of course Taiwan would have certainly made their views known. The Chinese Communists, who had little understanding of how an open society worked, would have concluded that the American government was not sincere in wanting an opening and would have pulled back.

It is true that Nixon and Kissinger were able to take advantage of a powerful current that was already flowing in favour of a Sino-American relationship, but without their skilful and, yes, secretive handling of the opening it might well not have happened. Both men had a natural bent towards secrecy which some of their colleagues have characterized as obsessive, and it did not always serve them well when they failed to keep their own experts informed or when, in Nixon's case, he tried to cover up the Watergate break-in. While secrecy is not always necessary in human affairs, in negotiations of this delicacy, with such huge potential for misunderstandings, it was essential. Nixon and Kissinger claimed, perhaps unfairly, that the State Department always leaked, but they were probably right to keep knowledge of their first contacts with China restricted to a very small number. As it was, a *New York Times* correspondent managed to figure out that something was up in the autumn of 1970 by merely picking up hints on the diplomatic circuit.

In later years both Nixon and Kissinger also made much of their own courage and determination in creating the opening to China in defiance of a timid bureaucracy and the enormously powerful pro-Taiwan China lobby whose tentacles stretched everywhere, into Congress and throughout the media. In an interview he did in 1998, Kissinger claimed that the State Department thought that any rapprochement with the People's Republic was 'extremely dangerous'. Soviet specialists warned of the dire effects on Soviet–American relations if the United States tried to play at triangular diplomacy. 'Of course,' wrote Kissinger in his memoirs, 'we envisaged nothing so crude as "using" the People's Republic against the Soviet Union.'

The bureaucracy, he claimed, not only leaked like a sieve but refused to accept Nixon as its legitimate leader. 'Here was a President who didn't follow the *New York Times* editorial direction. And that was considered against nature.'[3]

Although he constantly complained about liberal eggheads, Nixon could actually count on considerable support from the academic community, and from within the State Department. By 1968, the old hardliners who had shaped policy towards China had pretty much retired. The younger generation felt, as one of them said, 'we should be moving in the direction of rapprochement with Peking'.[4]

In the months before Nixon took office, both China and the United States continued, as they had done over the years, to send out the equivalents of messages in a bottle, and sometimes an answer came back. The Voice of America had moderated the language it used in its Chinese broadcasts directed at the People's Republic. And so the Guomindang's Beiping became the Communists' Beijing. Although the Americans did not know until later, this change in language was remarked upon in China, where there was much speculation about what it meant.[5] Just after the Soviet invasion of Czechoslovakia in August 1968, the State Department sent a message to the Chinese suggesting that both sides resume the talks which had gone on between the American and Chinese ambassadors in Warsaw since the mid-1950s. The Chinese, who were alarmed by the Soviet interference in the affairs of a fellow Communist state, agreed with unusual speed.

John Holdridge, who was in China as part of the Nixon trip, remembered the excitement in Washington, especially when the Chinese reply said, 'It has always been the policy of the People's Republic of China to maintain friendly relations with all states, regardless of social systems, on the basis of the five principles of peaceful coexistence.' The Five Principles – Chou mentioned them in his toast at Nixon's welcoming banquet – had been sacrosanct in Chinese foreign relations ever since Chou had brought them up with Prime Minister Nehru of India in the early 1950s. Although they had not prevented India and China from going to war some years later, they expressed high-minded sentiments about equality, non-aggression, mutual respect for sovereignty and territorial integrity, non-interference in each other's internal affairs, and, curiously, peaceful coexistence, the phrase that had so infuriated the Chinese when Khrushchev used it about Soviet relations with the United States. 'Boy,' said Holdridge, 'bells bonged all over.'[6]

Both sides agreed that they would restart the Warsaw talks. The first of the new round was scheduled for 20 February 1969, but before this could take place a Chinese diplomat jumped out of a window of his embassy in the Hague and asked for, and was granted, asylum in the United States. (He turned out to be mentally disturbed and proved to be no use to the Americans.) The Chinese immediately accused the CIA of arranging to abduct him. 'All this once again', said their note, 'reveals the vicious features of the new U.S. Government which has inherited the mantle of the preceding U.S. Governments in flagrantly making itself the enemy of the Chinese people.'[7] The meeting was postponed indefinitely. The Americans did not move at once to reopen contacts with the People's Republic. And it is doubtful, given their continued preoccupation with the Cultural Revolution and their longstanding suspicions of the Americans, that the Chinese would have responded. Mao's change of heart towards the United States, furthermore, did not take place until the autumn, after the fighting with the Soviet Union.

Throughout the year, nevertheless, the Americans sent out strong hints that the United States hoped to mend fences with the People's Republic. In a major foreign policy speech in New York that spring, Rogers declared, 'we shall take initiatives to reestablish more normal relations with Communist China and we shall remain responsive to any indications of less hostile attitudes from their side'.[8] Nixon had ordered an end to the provocative sweeps by high-speed US Navy patrol boats near the coast of China in the Taiwan Strait in his first month in office and that autumn he ended the regular patrols through the Strait by the Seventh Fleet. Although his press conference in Guam in late July 1969 referred to the People's Republic of China as having a 'very belligerent' foreign policy, he also announced, in what became the Nixon Doctrine, that the United States was going to learn from its mistakes in Vietnam and not get militarily involved in supporting its allies.

In July, Kissinger's revamped National Security Council recommended that the United States should take steps to improve the relationship with China without waiting for any Chinese response. The administration eased up its restrictions on trade and travel between the United States and China. American passport holders from certain professions – scholars and doctors, for example – were now allowed to travel to China and bring back whatever they bought there to the United States. (At first only a handful of Americans were able to take advantage of this.) American companies would no longer get into trouble if their foreign subsidiaries sold goods to China. Small changes, perhaps, but they signalled that a major rethinking of American foreign policy was under way.

The Americans also used roundabout channels to send a quiet message to the Chinese. American diplomats suggested to the Poles, the Cambodians and the French that they let Beijing know that the United States wanted to start talking again with a view to improving relations. In Paris, the American military attaché was told to stand by for a visit – which never came – by Donald Rumsfeld, in those days a minor member of the administration, who would be bringing a letter for the Chinese. On the plane carrying him on from Guam on his Asian tour, Nixon ordered Holdridge to draft a letter with the same message to the People's Republic. During a brief stay in Pakistan, which had cordial relations with China, Nixon urged General Yahya Khan to be his intermediary with the Chinese. He may have asked the same of another dictator, President Nicolae Ceaucescu of Rumania, whom he visited next. In late August, the Americans tried to reactivate their Warsaw contacts. When American diplomats called on the Chinese embassy, they were received cordially, but the Chinese declined to discuss resuming the talks. (The Chinese ambassador himself was back in China for re-education.)[9]

Nixon, who liked leaks when they were his own, was also working quietly at home to prepare the way for a shift in American policy towards China. At the beginning of February, he directed the NSC to undertake a study of current US policies towards both Chinas, of possible Communist Chinese intentions in Asia, and of 'alternative U.S. approaches on China and their costs and risks'. He also told Kissinger to let it be known quietly in government and political circles that the administration was exploring the possibilities of a rapprochement with China. 'I would continue to plant this idea.' Nixon himself

planted it with key figures such as Mike Mansfield, the Senate majority leader, when he told him that the time had come to involve China
in 'global responsibility'. Later that June, Mansfield used Prince
Sihanouk of Cambodia to contact Chou En-lai to ask whether he
could visit China, a move the Chinese noted with interest although
they did not send a reply.[10]

That autumn Nixon suggested to Kissinger that he bring up the
possibility of a 'subtle' American move towards China with two old
hardliners, Walter Judd, a Congressman from Minnesota, and Senator
Karl Mundt. Where the China lobby, that collection of Cold Warriors
who steadfastly opposed recognition of the People's Republic, had
once thrown its weight about to effect, it had run out of steam by the
late 1960s. Many of its initial supporters, such as Henry Luce, had disappeared from the scene, though his widow Claire Boothe Luce was
still active; others like Nixon himself were thinking that it was time to
move on. American public opinion, always difficult to gauge, seemed
torn between fear and suspicion of Red China and a willingness to
accept its membership of the United Nations. By the late 1960s, academics were increasingly calling for opening up contacts with their
counterparts in China. Perhaps more importantly, people in business
were calling for trade relations.[11]

For most of Nixon's first year in office, the People's Republic of
China showed no signs of being aware that anything had changed in
American attitudes. In June, in response to an American query, the
Chinese chargé in Warsaw said that his government had no immediate plans for resuming the suspended talks. In fact, the Chinese
government, and in the end that meant Mao, was paying attention to
the American signals. The Chinese also had a spy in Washington, in
the CIA. Mao, moreover, was already inclined to think that Nixon
was someone he could deal with. He had apparently read Nixon's
1967 article in *Foreign Affairs* and recommended it to Chou En-lai.
When Nixon became president, Mao approved the publication of his
address in the *People's Daily*. True, it appeared under the headline 'A
Desperate Confession', but it disseminated Nixon's message about
wanting an open world, where no people lived in 'angry isolation'. At
some point Chou En-lai ordered all government departments with
any interest in the United States to watch American policies closely. In

July, when an American yacht sailed into Chinese waters near Hong Kong and the local security forces arrested the two American crew, Chou dealt with the case personally. He ordered that there be no publicity and none of the usual rhetoric about CIA agents.[12] The two Americans were later quietly released.

As 1969 wore on and the threat from the Soviet Union reached its most acute phase, China's need to break out from its isolation became apparent. The Four Marshals produced their reports on China's grand strategy and Mao pondered them. Gradually China began to send ambassadors abroad again. A number of American allies were no longer prepared to wait, and China for its part was clearly receptive to increasing contacts with the world in general, if not the United States in particular. Between 1970 and 1971, China re-established diplomatic relations with a number of countries, from Italy to Iceland.

Most significant of all, it opened talks with the United States' neighbour, Canada. The Canadians, while they shared Western concerns about the Soviet Union in the early decades of the Cold War and had fought in the Korean War, had never felt as strongly about the Communist Chinese threat. Canadian missionaries, who had been active in China for decades, were generally sympathetic to China, whatever government was in power. Most of the China experts in Canada's foreign service were missionary children who had grown up in China. Canadians by and large did not share the United States' hard line towards Communist China and, like other American allies, were alarmed by the insistence of the Americans on prolonging the Korean War and by loose talk about using the atomic bomb to dislodge the new regime. The Department of External Affairs, as it was then known, advocated establishing diplomatic recognition in the 1950s, and the Liberal government of Louis St Laurent concurred. The Canadians, however, had to try to balance a number of factors.

Canada still looked to Britain for leadership, and the British had established their relations with China. In addition, an increasing number of Commonwealth countries were recognizing the People's Republic in the 1950s and Canada cared about Commonwealth solidarity. Then there was the United States, always a factor in Canadian thinking. If Canada moved too far away from American policy, it might damage both the North Atlantic Treaty alliance and the bilateral relationship. American administrations tended to be easily irritated if they felt their allies were getting soft on Chinese Communism. In the early 1960s, when a Chinese classical opera company came to Toronto, the American authorities announced that any American citizens who bought tickets were violating American law. When a few determined Americans came anyway, they were welcomed by Canadians who were irritated, as so often before and since, by the American government's attempt to enforce American laws outside the United States.[13] On the other hand, Canada had much more at stake in its relationship with the United States than in that with China, and, so the Canadian government, whatever it thought and sometimes said, did not move on the issue.

At the end of the 1950s, the Canadians suddenly found themselves being courted by the Chinese Communists, not for recognition but for Canadian wheat. Reports were coming out of China of severe shortages (an understatement). The Canadian government briefly contemplated a gift but decided that the Chinese might see charity as an insult. In any case the Chinese were prepared to pay hard currency at first and seemed eager to take a lot more Canadian wheat if some credit arrangement could be worked out. Canadian wheat farmers were delighted and Canadian public opinion in general was quiescent, so, although the Americans raised objections, Canadian governments in the 1960s continued to allow trade between Canada and China. In Hong Kong, a Canadian trade commissioner travelled back and forth to China on a diplomatic passport and behaved much like a Canadian diplomat. In Ottawa, the Department of External Affairs discussed recognition of the People's Republic year after year, but nothing happened until the end of the decade.

In 1968, things began to move when Canada got a new prime minister. Although he had a reputation as a radical free thinker, Pierre Trudeau was essentially a pragmatist. He himself was not particularly interested in American culture or in the United States, but he knew that Canada had little choice but to get along with its giant neighbour. On the other hand, he thought Canadian foreign policy was stuck in a rut, and understood that Canadians were increasingly willing to distance themselves from the United States. Canadians had just celebrated their centenary as a nation and, perhaps to their own surprise, were enjoying a burst of cultural activity and of Canadian nationalism. And an influx of American draft dodgers and deserters was persuading Canadians not only that the Americans were very wrong but that Canadians were very right over Vietnam. (Canada had not become a combatant largely because its role on the International Control Commission set up in 1954 to monitor the agreements governing Indochina precluded it from doing so.) And it seemed to Trudeau, who had actually visited China twice as a private citizen, illogical for nations not to recognize its government.

Shortly after he took office, Trudeau ordered a complete review of Canada's foreign policy. As far as Asia was concerned, the experts were to take into account the separate government in Taiwan. As the Canadians moved cautiously towards a change in their policy towards China, the Americans were not pleased. The Secretary of State, William Rogers, reportedly told his Canadian counterpart, 'We hate like hell what you are doing but you are still our best friends.' In January 1969, the Canadian cabinet authorized its representatives in Stockholm to contact the Chinese embassy. (Sweden was good neutral territory and had excellent communications.) The Canadian third secretary duly invited a Chinese acquaintance to attend dinner at his house and watch a new film on Dr Norman Bethune, the Canadian doctor seen by the Communists as a saintly figure who gave his life for the Revolution. The Chinese diplomat had to refer the invitation back to Beijing and two weeks later, on the afternoon of the dinner, an urgent telegram came back with authorization, possibly from Mao himself. The Canadian-made film, which also depicted Bethune's lively and varied romantic career, may have left the Chinese bewildered but they did recognize the friendly intent. Permission was received from Beijing to start talks about establishing diplomatic relations Although Chinese knowledge of the outside world was limited at this time thanks to the Cultural Revolution, Canada was seen as a relatively friendly power within the American camp; Canadian interest in talks was perhaps a sign of changes in American thinking.[14]

The talks, highly formalistic and drawn out with the necessary references back to the respective capitals, took place alternately at the Chinese embassy, which was in an elegant old Stockholm house, and its Canadian counterpart, which was in a nondescript office building in the red-light district. By the autumn of 1970 an agreement was ready and after some last-minute discussions over whether Chinese or Canadian paper should be used (Swedish was the compromise), Canada and the People's Republic of China agreed in October to establish diplomatic relations. The first Canadian diplomat arrived in Beijing in November to look for accommodation. In February 1971, the Chinese opened their embassy in Ottawa.

By this point, the United States had secretly made its own contact with the People's Republic of China. Since no answer had come from the Chinese to the roundabout messages that the Americans had been sending, in the late autumn of 1969 Nixon and Kissinger decided on a direct approach. Walter Stoessel, the American ambassador in Warsaw, was told to make contact with local Chinese diplomats. On 3 December, he and a colleague who spoke some Chinese went to a gala fashion show being put on by the Yugoslavians to which the whole diplomatic corps had been invited. As the chief Chinese representative was leaving, the Chinese-speaking American bumped into him. 'I introduced myself. And he was, you know, being very Chinese and bowing with hands clasped. I said, "I want you to meet my ambassador."' Stoessel passed on the message from the US government suggesting talks and asked if they could meet again. The Chinese diplomat hastily said in Chinese, 'Okay. Okay,' and fled to his waiting car. 'If you want Chinese diplomats to suffer a heart attack,' Chou En-lai later said to the Americans, 'you just have to speak to them on diplomatic occasions.'[15]

The Chinese embassy immediately reported this 'unusual behaviour' back to Beijing and Chou En-lai went straight to Mao. 'The opportunity is now coming,' he told the Chairman. 'We now have a brick in our hands to bang on the door with.' Four days after the fashion show, Lei Yang, the Chinese chargé, quietly called on the American embassy to announce that the Chinese government had decided to release another pair of American yachtsmen who had been in Chinese custody since February. On 11 December, Stoessel returned the call at the invitation of the Chinese. The press started to notice the black limousines with their national flags going back and forth and the State Department, following standard procedure, also informed its own departments and selected embassies abroad. Nixon, according to Kissinger, worried that news of the initiative was leaking too soon; 'We'll kill this child before it is born.' Kissinger saw this as yet another example of the rigidity and incompetence of the State Department and yet another good reason why the White House should deal with China policy. On 8 January 1970 China and the United States announced that the Warsaw talks were resuming. Nixon, in the foreign policy report he sent to Congress a month later, said, 'it is certainly in our interest, and in the interest of peace and stability in Asia and the world, that we take what steps we can toward improved practical relations with Peking'.[16]

Stoessel, under instructions from Washington, told Lei Yang at an informal meeting on 20 January that the United States was prepared to send a high-level representative to Beijing if necessary for discussions. At their first formal meeting on 20 February, Lei, who had received his instructions from China, replied that the Chinese would be pleased to receive a high-level envoy 'to explore further solutions to the fundamental questions in Sino–American relations'. He mentioned what was for the Chinese the most fundamental of all and that was the future status of Taiwan. The United States wanted to improve relations with China but it continued to support 'the Chiang Kai-shek clique' which had long since been repudiated by the Chinese people. 'Is this not self-contradictory?' Nevertheless, the meeting ended with an agreement to meet again. The Chinese politely declined the offer of a cup of tea and left. In the event, that was to be the last of the formal Warsaw meetings.[17]

In the United States, a debate broke out between the White House and the State Department about whether it was wise to think of sending an emissary to China before relations had improved significantly. Would such a move, the State Department asked, cause problems with America's allies in Asia such as Japan and Taiwan? Would the Chinese use the evidence of American interest to put pressure on the Soviet Union to mend fences? Kissinger was infuriated by what he saw as bureaucratic rigidity of the worst kind. Of course the diplomats wanted to continue the old-style talks, 'without result, true, but also without debacle or controversy'. As the Americans argued among themselves, they kept postponing the date of the next meeting. In the spring, the long-running conflict in Indochina upset the delicate negotiations through Warsaw. In March, the situation in Cambodia suddenly deteriorated when Lon Nol, an American-backed general, overthrew the neutralist government of Prince Sihanouk. By the beginning of May, Sihanouk had established a government in exile in Beijing and South Vietnamese and American forces were invading Cambodia to prop up Lon Nol. The Chinese put out a statement condemning the 'brazen' invasion and said that it was not 'suitable' for the meeting scheduled for 20 May to be held. Tiananmen Square filled with an enormous protest rally and Mao called on the people of the world to defeat 'the U.S. aggressors and all their running dogs'.[18]

It looked as though Chinese–American relations were going back into the deep freeze. Nixon in any case was preoccupied with Indochina and with the widespread protests in the United States as a result of Cambodia. Mao, as became apparent later, was brooding over the loyalty of his chosen successor, his Defence Minister Lin Biao. Nevertheless, there were some encouraging signs that the will to improve relations remained on both sides. In the second week of May, as Washington and the rest of the country were rocked by demonstrations against the Cambodian invasion and bombings, Nixon, to the dismay of his security and staff, impulsively decided to go out and talk to the demonstrators. In a strange late-night conversation by the Lincoln Memorial, he tried to explain himself and his ideals to a group of students. In rambling but widely reported remarks, he urged them to travel, to know not just their own country but the world. One of the overriding hopes he had for his administration was that 'the great mainland of China be opened up so that we could know the seven hundred million people who live in China and who are one of the most remarkable people on earth'. In an interview with *Time* later that autumn, he said, 'If there is anything I want to do before I die, it is to go to China. If I don't, I want my children to.'[19]

Although the Cambodian invasion in May 1970 disrupted the gradual opening of contacts between China and the United States, the two sides did not pull back completely to their old stance. In July, after American troops had withdrawn from Cambodia, the Chinese suddenly released an unfortunate clergyman who had languished in a Chinese jail for two decades. (He was carried across the border on a stretcher to Hong Kong and died soon afterwards.) The Chinese also announced that another imprisoned American had committed suicide several years earlier. The United States, for its part, dropped its longstanding opposition to Italy's exporting heavy trucks to China. The Italians profited by getting frozen pork as an exchange. That autumn, at a state banquet for Ceaucescu of Rumania, Nixon used the words 'People's Republic of China' for the first time.

Nixon and Kissinger, partly because they did not trust the State Department to manage the contacts through Warsaw, by this point had decided to establish their own, highly secret channels of communication. One, they hoped, would be through Paris. Vernon Walters, the military attaché, who had been standing by for over a year, got orders in the summer of 1970 to pass on word from Nixon to the Chinese embassy that the United States was prepared to hold secret talks and that Nixon would send a high-level official to Paris if necessary. At some point, and it is not clear from his memoirs exactly when, Walters found himself standing alone with his Chinese opposite number, Fang Wen, as they waited for their cars after a reception at the Polish embassy. He took the opportunity to say in French that he had a message from the President for the Chinese government. Fang's jaw dropped and he hastily said, 'I'll tell them; I'll tell them; I'll tell them.' He jumped into his Mercedes limousine and drove off before Walters could hand over his letter.[20] Walters finally delivered it a few days later. The Chinese greeted him cautiously but courteously.

The channel did not immediately produce results. It took until the following summer, and only after he had made his secret trip to Beijing, for Kissinger to be able to talk to the Chinese ambassador in Paris. For some reason, perhaps because secrecy had become second nature, he flew in and out of Paris incognito and had himself smuggled in and out of Walters' apartment and the Chinese embassy. Over time Walters himself became very friendly with Fang, also a retired general. They conducted much detailed business about the arrangements for Nixon's trip and compared notes about the Soviets – a menace – and about how they would deal with drug dealers – execution. The Chinese invariably gave Walters a present of preserved apricots as he left; he could not bear their taste and, for fear of compromising security, filled up his safe with them.[21]

The other secret channel Nixon and Kissinger opened up was

through Pakistan, and this is the one that finally produced the dramatic breakthrough they were looking for. Nixon had been using Yahya Khan to send indirect messages to Beijing since 1969. In the autumn of that year, for example, the Americans asked Yahya to let the Chinese know that they were cancelling the Seventh Fleet's patrols in the Taiwan Strait. According to Chinese sources, the direct channel was opened in the early spring of 1970 but did not become really active until late in the year. Modern technology was bypassed as the two sides used only trusted emissaries in a way that would have been familiar to the ancient Greeks or the great Venetian diplomats of the Renaissance. If Nixon wanted to contact Beijing, he or Kissinger passed a message, typed on ordinary paper and unsigned, to Agha Hilaly, the ambassador of Pakistan in Washington, who in turn took it himself to Yahya. In Pakistan, Yahya then called in the Chinese ambassador and read the message to him. The two men then carefully checked the Chinese diplomat's handwritten notes, and the contents of the American message went on to Chou and Mao in Beijing. Eventually a reply would come back through the same circuitous route. Hilaly would arrive at the White House with a handwritten note from Yahya and would dictate its contents to Kissinger and then carefully carry the paper away again. The messages sometimes took several days and, in one case, three weeks to reach the other side. The Chinese never entirely understood why Nixon insisted on such secrecy. It was all a bit mysterious, Mao told his old friend Edgar Snow, that Nixon wanted to keep all contacts with China secret even from the State Department. Nixon and Kissinger tried to explain that if word of the negotiations leaked out the resulting political uproar in the United States would make it difficult to carry on.[22]

On 1 October, the Chinese sent what they considered a very public message to the Americans when Mao invited Snow to accompany him on the reviewing stand in Tiananmen Square on China's National Day. A picture of the two was published in the *People's Daily*. Snow, who had first met Mao when the Communists were holed up in Yan'an in the late 1930s, stayed on in China for a couple of months more and had a long conversation with Mao. He was glad, the Chairman said, that Nixon had won the election. 'If he wishes to come to Beijing, please tell him he should do it secretly, not openly –

just get on a plane and come.' Nixon had made it clear that he wanted to talk directly to the Chinese and not through the Warsaw discussions. 'Therefore I say I am ready to hold talks with him if he is willing to come. It doesn't matter if the negotiations succeed or fail, if we quarrel or not, if he comes in the capacity of a tourist or the President.' Taiwan was clearly an issue between them but what did it really have to do with Nixon? The situation had been created by earlier administrations. Ten million people in Taiwan were nothing compared to the billion in the rest of Asia. 'Will China and the U.S. remain for 100 years without establishing relations? After all, we haven't occupied your Long Island!' Unfortunately the United States missed the significance of Snow's visit, partly because he himself took several months to find a publisher for the story of his visit and partly because official Washington tended to write him off as a fellow traveller so that no one went to see him at his home in Switzerland. Snow, who was old and ailing, seems not to have made any attempt to brief the government. Nixon claims in his memoirs that the Americans knew about the interview a few days after it took place. Kissinger, on the other hand, says the Chinese over-estimated American subtlety and intelligence-gathering and that Washington did not know about the interview for several months, by which time the channel through Pakistan was producing results.[23]

Although Yahya was increasingly preoccupied with the growing threat of secession by East Pakistan and the resulting tensions with India, he continued to act as intermediary. In October 1970, while he was in the United States for the twenty-fifth-anniversary celebrations of the United Nations, he paid a visit to Nixon and Kissinger in Washington. Nixon asked Yahya to carry word to the Chinese that the United States was anxious to normalize relations. Yahya flew to China on a state visit in November and duly conveyed his message to Chou En-lai. 'This is the first time', the Chinese Prime Minister remarked, 'that a proposal has come from a Head through a Head, to a Head! The United States knows that Pakistan is a great friend to China and therefore we attach great importance to it.' Chou also made it clear, however, that the Chinese would only accept a special envoy in order to discuss the withdrawal of American forces from Taiwan.[24]

Yahya, possibly because he was trying to cope with cyclone damage in East Pakistan and coming elections in both halves of his country, took several weeks to deliver Chou's reply, which the Americans finally received on 8 December. Kissinger found it encouraging and downplayed the Chinese linking of the Taiwan issue to a visit by an American representative. In fact, the Chinese demand for American withdrawal from Taiwan was an obstacle and the American message that went back on 16 December said firmly that 'The meeting in Peking would not be limited only to the Taiwan question but would encompass other steps designed to improve relations and reduce tensions.' As for the American presence on Taiwan, it was the general policy of the United States to 'reduce its military presence in the region of East Asia and the Pacific as tensions in this region diminish'. The Americans apparently sent a copy through their Rumanian channel as well which the Soviets in time picked up. At some point, Nixon and Kissinger also considered, but rejected, establishing another channel through Ottawa where the Chinese opened an embassy in February 1971. But the danger of the contacts being noticed were thought too great; in addition, Nixon could not bear Trudeau. The State Department remained unaware of all these developing contacts.[25]

The Chinese duly received the American reply and the channel then went silent for several months. Nixon gave his second foreign policy report to Congress in February and said that the United States wanted to remove the obstacles on its side to greater contacts between the Chinese and American peoples. 'We hope for, but will not be deterred by a lack of, reciprocity.' On 15 March, the United States ended all restrictions on travel by Americans to China. Still Beijing remained silent. Kissinger said in his memoirs that he took the time to educate himself, partly by meetings with academic experts. 'It would be satisfying to report that my former colleagues conveyed to me flashes of illuminating insight.' The academics proved incapable of providing advice on strategies for the next few years or on immediate issues. 'I listened politely,' Kissinger claimed, 'chastening any impatience with the recognition that I could hardly have been more relevant when I served as an academic consultant to two previous administrations.'[26]

On 6 April, 1971, the Chinese government suddenly invited an American table-tennis team, which was competing in the World Table

Tennis Championship in Japan, to visit China. The decision to initiate what became known as 'ping-pong' diplomacy had been made at the highest levels, indeed by Mao himself, after chance encounters brought Chinese and American table-tennis players together. Chinese teams, which had been condemned during the wildest days of the Cultural Revolution as 'sprouts of revisionism', were only just starting to take part in international events again. The tournament in Japan was the first to have seen a Chinese team for several years. Mao had agreed that the Chinese could take part, but the team was sent off with orders to report back to Beijing three times a day and with strict instructions on how to behave. 'During the contest, if we meet with officials of the US delegation, we do not take the initiative to talk or exchange greetings. If we compete with the US team, we do not exchange team flags with them beforehand, but we can shake hands and greet each other.' Early on in the tournament, when an American player casually said at a banquet, 'Hi, Chinese, long time no see. You guys played well,' the incident was immediately reported. And when the Americans asked jokingly about why they had not been invited to play in China along with Mexico and Canada, the lights burned late in Beijing as the Chinese tried to work out what this meant. Chou En-lai submitted a cautious report to Mao which reflected the views of both the Foreign Ministry and the State Sports Commission that the time was not yet ripe to invite an American team to China, although there might well be opportunities in the future. The Americans could leave their addresses, said Chou, but it must be made clear to them that the Chinese people were firmly opposed to 'the conspiracy of "Two Chinas"'. (The People's Republic always insisted that there was only one China and that Taiwan was part of it.)[27]

On 4 April, as the tournament was winding down, a pair of players, one American, the other Chinese, caused a fresh incident to perturb Beijing. The American team were generally clean-cut athletes, 'the kinds of Americans that you pray to be involved in something like this', an American diplomat remembered. Glenn Cowan, though, the US junior champion, came from California and liked to consider himself part of the counter-culture. 'He's apt to wear a purple passion shirt with tie-dye leopard-like pants,' a long-suffering team official recalled, 'he has long Dartagnanian locks, he's a floppy hat that he wears and he's sort of a hippy.' By chance, Cowan found himself out at the practice centre without a ride back to the main tournament hall. A Chinese player beckoned him towards a bus in which he found most of the Chinese team, all smiling at him. Cowan was babbling cheerfully on to the uncomprehending Chinese about how they were all oppressed when Zhuang Zedong, a world champion and one of the Chinese stars, came forward and presented him with a silk brocade scarf. When the head of the Chinese team tried to stop his player, Zhuang brushed him aside. 'Take it easy. As head of the delegation you have many concerns, but I am just a player.' As the players got off the bus, a crowd of journalists recorded the scene. To his embarrassment, Cowan did not have anything to give in return. He managed to find a red, white and blue shirt with a peace emblem and the words of the Beatles' song 'Let It Be', and he presented this the following day with maximum publicity to the Chinese athlete. 'Hippy opportunist,' said the American official.[28]

Mao, who had been following the events in Japan with intense interest, sat chain-smoking for the next two days in Beijing while Chou's report lay on his desk. The tournament in Japan would be over on 7 April and he still had not made up his mind on whether or not to invite the Americans to China. On the 6th, he approved Chou's recommendation that they do nothing. That night, as usual, his nurse read him the news-stories about the tournament. Mao said approvingly, 'Zhuang Zedong not only plays good Ping-Pong but knows how to conduct diplomacy as well.' At midnight, after he had already taken his customary heavy dose of sleeping pills, he suddenly sat up and ordered his nurse to contact the Foreign Ministry at once with orders to invite the American team. It was only when she had made the call that he allowed himself to fall asleep. As Mao subsequently put it, the small ping-pong ball could be used to move the large ball of the earth.[29]

The invitation which reached the Americans the next day had more than a ring of the Middle Kingdom about it. Since the Americans had requested an invitation 'so many times', China had agreed to accede to their request. 'If they are short of travelling expenses, we can render them assistance.' The first American diplomat to hear on the ground in Japan replied simply that, if the team decided to go, it would not be against current American policy. He then dashed to his records and found with relief several of Nixon's statements expressing hope that contacts would be resumed between China and the United States. In Washington, the desk officer at the State Department had the same reaction. 'Go for it, do it.' He then went home and told his wife that he would be out of a job if he were wrong.[30]

Neither man lost his job. Nixon and Kissinger were surprised but delighted by the invitation. A rather bewildered group of ping-pong players and officials from the US Table Tennis Association headed for China, filled with last-minute advice from American diplomats and laden with cameras and tape recorders that reporters had pressed on them as well as all the American pens the embassy in Tokyo could find to give as presents. The team, who were the first American delegation into China since 1949, arrived in Canton by train and then flew north to Beijing and later Shanghai. Everywhere they saw the giant portraits of Mao, the cartoons with a pygmy Nixon and a giant Chinese, and the slogans which said 'Down with the US imperialists'. On the streets the locals stared at them with amazement, especially at Glenn Cowan with his long hair and at a teenage girl player in her mini-skirt, and the Americans stared back. One young American girl spent much of the time in tears because she would not eat Chinese food; finally the Chinese made her a hamburger and French fries.[31]

Chou oversaw all the detailed arrangements for their reception and even had the Forbidden City, which he had closed to save it from the Red Guards, reopened for sightseeing. The trip, 'an international sensation' in Kissinger's words, received extensive publicity in the world's press. The handful of foreign journalists stationed in Beijing were joined, and this was another breakthrough, by reporters from the big American news services. In China itself, all the matches were broadcast live on television and radio. Chou ordered the Chinese players to let the Americans win some of them.[32]

On 14 April, Chou held a lavish reception in the Great Hall of the People for the visiting teams. In alphabetical order, the teams from Canada, Colombia, Great Britain, Nigeria and the United States climbed up the impressive staircase that Nixon was going to climb a year later. Chou was a charming host, chatting with all the players, posing patiently for photographs, and deprecating his own ability at ping-pong. He made jokes about the weather with the British and talked to the Canadians about his admiration for Dr Norman Bethune. His most significant words were of course directed at the Americans. To the president of the US Table Tennis Association, he quoted a Chinese proverb about the joy of having friends from afar. 'Your visit', he said as he toasted the Americans, 'has opened a new chapter in the history of the relations between Chinese and American peoples.' And he went on: 'With you having made the start the people of the United States and China in the future will be able to have constant contacts.'[33]

As the reception came to an end, Chou asked if there were any more questions. Glenn Cowan popped up. 'What do you think of the hippy movement?' He did not know much about it, Chou said, so his views might be rather superficial. Perhaps young people around the world were dissatisfied and wanted change, but they had not yet found the ways to bring that about. 'When we were young,' the old revolutionary said, 'it was the same thing too. Therefore, I understand the ideas of youth, they are very curious.' Cowan replied that the hippy movement was really very deep: 'It is a whole new way of thinking.' Chou suggested that more was needed: 'spirit must be transformed into material force before the world can move forward'. (Cowan's mother apparently sent Chou flowers with thanks for educating her son.) Chou concluded by commending Cowan for not playing too badly against the Chinese team and wished him progress. 'I could talk for hours,' Cowan told reporters. He became, temporarily, a great sinophile, talking about staying on in China, which in his view was so much less conformist than the United States. That desire vanished when he found himself ill in a Chinese hospital.[34]

The whole visit was 'vintage Chou En-lai', in Kissinger's opinion. 'It was a signal to the White House that our initiatives had been noticed.' The Americans were careful to respond. On 14 April, Nixon ended most of the remaining restrictions on trade between the United States and China. Two days later, he spoke to the American Society of Newspaper Editors and, while he was careful to warn them not to get their hopes up about an immediate breakthrough with China, he added that he had told his daughter Tricia that he had a suggestion for her honeymoon. 'I hope sometime in your life, sooner rather than later, you will be able to go to China to see the great cities, and the people, and all of that, there.' He was noncommittal about his own chances of getting there, but at the end of April he told a press conference, without any prodding, 'I hope and, as a matter of fact, I expect to visit Mainland China sometime in some capacity.'[35]

Because Nixon and Kissinger had kept the secret of their contacts with Chou En-lai so well, the United States also sent out some contradictory signals. Spiro Agnew, the Vice-President, in a rambling impromptu press conference late one night, complained vociferously about the favourable press coverage of China during the ping-pong team's visit and the whole policy of removing obstacles to contacts. Nixon sent orders to Agnew to keep quiet about China and to the White House press office to say that Agnew completely supported the President's China policy. At the end of April, a State Department spokesman said rightly that the United States' position on Taiwan was 'an unsettled question'. In London, Rogers, who knew nothing of the secret channels to China, said that Mao's comments to Edgar Snow did not constitute a 'serious invitation' to Nixon to visit China. He added some pointed remarks about Chinese foreign policy being 'expansionist' and 'rather paranoid'. Kissinger was unreasonably outraged at these 'bureaucratic shenanigans' which he saw as a power grab by the State Department.[36]

On 27 April, fortunately, Hilaly, Pakistan's ambassador in Washington, finally brought the long-awaited reply from Chou En-lai to Nixon's secret message of the previous December. The Chinese repeated their insistence that the US must withdraw its forces from Taiwan before relations could be restored but, and this was a softening of their previous position, suggested that the matter be discussed in Beijing by a special envoy from Nixon or even by Nixon himself. Kissinger was, he later wrote, elated: 'every once in a while a fortunate few can participate in an event that they *know* will make a difference'. As he sat in his study that night, he recalled, he experienced a rare moment of peace and hope. 'The message from Peking told us above all that despite Indochina we had a chance to raise the sights of the American people to a future of opportunity.'[37]

Through the good offices of Hilaly, Nixon sent a swift reply to

Chou. The Chinese message was 'constructive, positive and forth-coming' and the United States intended to send one back in the same spirit. With an eye on his domestic politics, Nixon also asked that the Chinese not give visas to any American politicians for the time being. On 10 May, Kissinger called Hilaly in and handed him the formal American reply for transmission to the Chinese. Nixon accepted Chou's suggestion that he visit Beijing himself for conver-sations to deal with the important issues dividing their two countries. In order to arrange that, he proposed a secret visit by Kissinger to exchange preliminary views on 'all subjects of mutual interest' and to work out the details of the visit and its agenda. '*It is also understood that this first meeting between Dr. Kissinger and high offi-cials of the People's Republic of China be strictly secret.*' The Chinese again were mystified by this insistence on secrecy. 'If they want to come,' said Mao, 'they should come in the open light. Why should they hide their head and pull in their tail?' Kissinger has always made a good case for the need for secrecy before his first visit. He also points out that the Americans proposed a second, public one, for him, once the ice had been broken. When the only contact the United States had with China was through Pakistan and when American and Chinese statesmen had no idea of the others' think-ing, it would have been very dangerous to allow several weeks of public and potentially damaging speculation before the visit took place. Such open comment, whether from enthusiasts or opponents, might have spooked the Chinese, worried American allies, and made the trip a domestic liability in the United States. American oppo-nents of an opening to China would have had time to rally and other nations might have intervened. 'The tender shoot so painstakingly nurtured for more than two years might well have been killed.'[38] 'Looking back,' said Bill Brown, who was deputy director of the State Department office which dealt with the People's Republic of China, 'I don't feel that the American people were such sheep or that it was so delicate in Congress and in the American body politic.' It has never been clear, though, why the fact of Kissinger's trip to Beijing had to remain secret until it was over. Kissinger's own, unconvincing explanation was that the Chinese insisted. The trip did, of course, make a wonderful adventure and a wonderful announcement and that in itself may have appealed to both Kissinger and Nixon with their great awareness of history.

The Chinese received the American message on 17 May and, a few days later, an assurance that a recent advance in arms-limitation talks between the Soviet Union and the United States was not directed against China. 'President Nixon wishes to emphasize', the message transmitted through Pakistan said, 'that it is his policy to conclude no agreement which would be directed against the People's Republic of China.' In Beijing, Mao ordered Chou to call together the Politburo, the inner circle of the Chinese Communist Party, to prepare a reply. In his opening speech, Chou talked about how American power was declining and how the United States was now anxious to get out of Vietnam. That gave China an opportunity to improve relations with its former enemy, a move that would help China in several ways such as furthering the peaceful reunification of its territory and providing support against its enemies. (The Soviet Union was not mentioned specifically.) If the opening succeeded, it would make the rivalry between the United States and the Soviet Union even fiercer; if it failed, well, it would show the Chinese people the reactionary face of American imperialism.[39]

Mao approved the report and Chou despatched a reply. The Pakistanis alerted Kissinger that they were sending a highly important message by special courier. At 8 p.m. on 2 June, Hilaly, his hands shaking, handed over two sheets of paper to Kissinger who read them with relief and then elation. Chou extended a warm invitation to Kissinger to come to Beijing in June to prepare the way for Nixon's visit. 'It goes without saying', Chou added, 'that the first question to be settled is the crucial issue between China and the United States which is the question of the concrete way of the withdrawal of all the U.S. Armed Forces from Taiwan and Taiwan Straits area.' As Kissinger recognized, this was a considerable modification of the original Chinese position that the forces must be withdrawn before talks could take place. Kissinger rushed over to the White House, where Nixon was hosting a state dinner for the unlovely dictator of Nicaragua, Anastasio Somoza. As Nixon read the message Kissinger said solemnly, 'This is the most important communication that has come to an American President since the end of World War II.' He later pushed the date back to the Civil War.[40]

The two men talked until nearly midnight about what lay ahead. As Kissinger was leaving, Nixon decided that they ought to celebrate, so he hunted out a bottle of very good brandy. The two men raised their glasses and Nixon, according to his memoirs, proposed a toast. 'Henry, we are drinking a toast not to ourselves personally or to our success, or to our administration's policies which have made this message and made tonight possible. Let us drink to generations to come who may have a better chance to live in peace because of what we have done.'[41]

12

The Secret Visit

Nixon's toast in the White House when he and Kissinger received Chou's invitation was, he admitted, rather formal, but it was after all 'a moment of historical significance'.[1] It was also merely a beginning. So much had to be arranged before Nixon could go to China, from technical details about landing his plane safely to the sorts of subjects he would discuss while he was there. Presidential visits always required detailed advance work and China was unknown territory. Moreover, until all the details were worked out, there was always the danger that one side or the other would pull back. The choice, therefore, of the emissary was crucial.

In their message which reached Washington on 27 April 1971 the Chinese had suggested that Kissinger himself might be Nixon's special envoy. Kissinger, understandably, was longing to go. He had already sent a message through Hilaly telling the Chinese that it was 'essential' that he be the first to meet Chou: 'No one except Kissinger is best qualified to have these discussions as he is the *only* person (repeat only) who knows President Nixon's thinking and his mind and can take decisions on the spot without having to refer back to Washington for advice & instructions.' Kissinger was right: he was the obvious choice, but it was one that Nixon shrank from making. He was already envious of the press coverage Kissinger was getting and of Kissinger's growing reputation as a smooth man about town. And so Nixon, much as Eisenhower had once done with him, refused to commit himself. Kissinger could not go, so he said initially, 'because that would break all the china with State'. Kissinger had to sit by as Nixon wondered out loud about going himself. That would be too dangerous, Kissinger argued. What about Rogers? Kissinger rolled his eyes. 'Henry wasn't too enthusiastic,' Nixon recalled later. 'Let me put it that way.' Perhaps those experienced and distinguished diplomats David Bruce or Henry Cabot Lodge? Nixon ruled them out because they were both too much identified with the American presence in Vietnam. Or Kissinger's old patron, Nelson Rockefeller? 'Intriguing,' said Kissinger, but Rockefeller would not obey his instructions. Or George Bush, the US ambassador to the UN? 'Too soft and not sophisticated enough.' Thomas Dewey, the distinguished Republican elder statesman? Unfortunately, said Kissinger, he had been dead for several months.[2]

'Henry', said Nixon, 'I think you will have to do it.' The decision was hard to avoid. Kissinger knew Nixon's mind and had been involved at every stage of the secret negotiations. Moreover, said Kissinger, who understood his President well, 'of all the potential emissaries I was the most subject to his control'. As a still relatively obscure National Security Adviser, he did not have his own con-stituency or his own power base. Nixon still hoped to downplay the significance of what was clearly an extraordinary trip. Perhaps Kissinger could meet Chou somewhere other than Beijing. Kissinger made sure that all other sites were ruled out. Surely, Nixon also sug-gested, there was no need to have Kissinger's name appear on any joint communiqué announcing that a representative of the American government had visited China. 'Reality', said Kissinger, 'took care of this problem.'[3] He set his staff to preparing briefing books while he and Nixon waited for the final confirmation from the Chinese.

In Pakistan, the American ambassador, Joseph Farland, received a mysterious message ordering him to meet Kissinger somewhere in California. He was to travel to a private airport and ask for a certain aircraft. He was not to tell the State Department about his trip. An irritated Farland followed orders and found himself on a patio in Palm Springs with Kissinger. 'Henry, I've come halfway around this damn earth and I don't know why.' He said, 'I want you to put me into China.' I said, 'I don't think that's very funny, Henry.' Once Farland was persuaded that Kissinger was serious, the two men concocted a plan. Kissinger was due to make a tour of Asia which he intended to make as boring as possible in order to shake off the press. His sched-ule would include a weekend in Pakistan where the embassy would put out word that he had come down with a bug he had picked up in

India. As a result all his appointments would be cancelled and, so everyone would be told, he would retreat to the hill station of Muree to recuperate. While his aircraft remained conspicuously parked on the runway, he would fly into China on a civilian plane provided by the government of Pakistan.[4]

Pakistan was an obvious jumping-off place to go into China. Its government had shown its discretion and its loyalty to the Americans in setting up the channel and its national airline had regular flights to Beijing. Yahya Khan, who promised Washington that he would make 'absolute fool-proof arrangements' at his end, entered into the plans with enthusiasm, checking off all the details himself. Farland did his part before Kissinger arrived by insisting that a couple of his more observant staff in the embassy take their annual leave. He despatched the embassy doctor to East Pakistan. The Chinese sent in an aircrew in readiness.[5]

In Beijing, Chou En-lai set up a special high-level group and himself took personal charge of the preparations for Kissinger's visit. Under Mao's orders, he also called together an extraordinary meeting of the Politburo to prepare for the negotiations. Chou started out the deliberations explaining that the United States was no longer as powerful as it had been at the end of the Second World War. It had lost ground economically, and its involvement in Indochina in particular had done its position in the world much damage. The Americans' anxiety to extricate themselves from a hopeless struggle had prompted the need for contact with China, and this was China's opportunity to promote its own security and achieve the reunification of the country 'by peaceful means'. The Politburo sent on its recommendations to Mao, who approved them. To prepare the Chinese people for the shock that a country which had been treated as its main enemy for twenty years was now becoming something else, Chou spoke to a meeting of party officials from around the country to outline the new policy. Mao also ordered that the transcript of his chat with Edgar Snow, in which he invited Nixon to come to China, be released in the Chinese press.

The recommendations demonstrated the importance that Taiwan had in Chinese thinking. The United States must indicate that it was going to withdraw its troops from the island and must recognize that

Taiwan was Chinese territory and that the government in Beijing was the only one representing China. On the other hand, China would undertake to liberate Taiwan peacefully. This was significant because up to this point the government in Beijing had always refused to rule out the use of force. If the Americans brought up the issue of the United Nations, the Chinese must make it clear that they would not accept two Chinas being represented there, a solution being suggested by the United States and other nations. The Chinese should also let the Americans know that they should withdraw their troops from the rest of Asia, from Indochina to Japan. If all went well, the two sides might be able to talk about permanent diplomatic representation in each other's capitals. There was nothing in the recommendations about any sort of concerted policy towards the Soviet Union.[6]

In Washington, the Americans were also getting ready. Winston Lord, Kissinger's assistant, prepared separate sets of briefing books, for those who were going on the public Asian tour and for those who knew about the secret detour, now christened Polo One, to Beijing. (Somehow, as the Kissinger party made its way from one Asian capital to another, he managed to keep the different briefing notes and itineraries in the right hands.) Kissinger's own notes for Polo One ran to eighty pages of careful statements of America's position on areas it considered important: Indochina, Taiwan and relations with the Soviet Union, of course. His briefing book also included the American positions on Korea and on South Asia, where relations between India and Pakistan were fast deteriorating, as well as drafts of the toasts which Kissinger intended to give. The Chinese, he argued, were likely to be tough negotiators. They might well ask that the United States pull its troops out of Taiwan, but the United States had some bargaining chips on its side. China very much wanted to be recognized as a great power, and a summit meeting with Nixon would be 'spectacular proof'. The Chinese might also suggest some form of alliance directed against the Soviet Union.[7]

On 1 July, the day Kissinger left for Asia, Nixon gave him last-minute instructions with, as Kissinger put it, 'his invariable hard-line rhetoric with which he sent me off on every mission'. Nixon warned him against being too forthcoming. Kissinger should be 'somewhat enigmatic' on Taiwan and not suggest that the United States was abandoning its support for Taiwan 'until it was necessary to do so'. He should raise three spectres with the Chinese: what he, Nixon, might do if the stalemate in South Vietnam continued, and the threats to China from Japan and the Soviet Union. If the Chinese wanted a summit with him they would have to release all the American POWs shot down on aerial spying missions whom they still held, be helpful on Vietnam, and – this was to appeal to American farmers – accept some grain shipments from the United States. In return, Kissinger could suggest that, once the summit had been held, the United States would be happy to set up a hotline between Beijing and Washington and perhaps make an agreement on avoiding an accidental nuclear war. Nixon's advice was mostly 'boilerplate', Kissinger said dismissively in his memoirs.[8]

Although Kissinger had co-opted some foreign service officers to serve at the National Security Council, he had not shared the news of his upcoming trip to China with the State Department, even with Rogers himself. The State Department was understandably puzzled by why the National Security Adviser needed to go off on a fact-finding mission to Asia. It was also concerned that, by going to India and Pakistan, he might be giving the impression that the United States was interfering in their already tense relationship. The secrecy also caused difficulties with Vice-President Agnew, who had to be talked out of a long-planned visit to Chiang Kai-shek which would have placed him in Taiwan just as Kissinger was arriving in Beijing. Although Nixon and Kissinger did not know it until later, one part of the government had ferreted out the secret. The Joint Chiefs of Staff, exasperated by the secrecy around American foreign policy, had set their own spy to work. Charles Radford was assigned from the navy to work as a stenographer and clerk at the National Security Council. He simply made extra copies of all documents that came his way and passed them on to his military superiors.[9]

Fortunately for Nixon and Kissinger, their initiative remained secret. Both men of course were taking a considerable risk. Kissinger was going off into the unknown. According to Yahya, he was apprehensive, even frightened, and asked the President of Pakistan to accompany him on that first trip. 'I told him', said Yahya, 'that I'd send one of my generals along, if he wanted moral support, but I personally could not go. Chou En-lai had given me his word that he would look after him.'[10] Kissinger was taking a political risk too. If he did not bring back concrete results from his meetings with Chou, his own position in Washington would be weakened and that of the State Department, which had warned all along about rushing too precipitously into negotiations, would be enhanced.

In 1971, Nixon needed successes, particularly in foreign policy, which he had always claimed as his own. He was already looking ahead to the next presidential election, but his record so far was mixed: the war in Vietnam was grinding on and negotiations with the North Vietnamese were stalemated; Laos and Cambodia were slipping further under Communist influence; and the Soviet Union was being difficult. 'We're playing for very high stakes now,' Nixon had said to Kissinger that April as the Americans waited to hear from the Chinese, 'we have very little time left, and we cannot diddle around.'[11]

Kissinger and his party left Washington on the evening of 1 July. Because all the presidential planes were in use ferrying Nixon to the West Coast or Agnew off to the Middle East and Africa (his compensation for not going to Taiwan), Kissinger was given a converted air force tanker, so old that it needed extra-long runways. 'On takeoff,' remarked Kissinger, 'one had the feeling that the plane really preferred to reach its destination overland.' While Kissinger had a large, comfortable cabin, the rest of his group which included Winston Lord, John Holdridge and some others from the NSC and two Secret Service men, were jammed in together along with their typewriters and briefcases. Every so often Kissinger would emerge in his dressing gown to go over his messages. 'The scene was reminiscent of a Roman galley,' said Holdridge, 'with the captain directing imperiously from the stern and the rowers laboring uncomfortably in banks of two along the hull!' The plane lumbered on to Saigon, Bangkok and then India, where Kissinger had dinner with an intensely suspicious Prime Minister Indira Gandhi. She was covertly supporting the forces in East Pakistan that were rebelling against Yahya's government and may have suspected that the United States was planning to offer Pakistan assistance.[12]

On 8 July, Kissinger reached Rawalpindi in West Pakistan. He was suffering, so his aides said, from an attack of Delhi belly. A sharp-eyed

American diplomat was impressed at how much he nevertheless managed to eat at Ambassador Farland's buffet lunch. That evening Yahya gave a small private dinner and, as Kissinger continued to complain about his stomach, insisted that his guest must go with his aides into the hills to Yahya's own bungalow where the cool air would revive him. One of the Secret Service agents with brisk efficiency sent a colleague to check out the presidential quarters; the Pakistan government was forced to keep him there until Kissinger had gone and returned.

At 3.30 in the morning, Kissinger, disguised in a floppy hat and dark glasses, was whisked off through deserted streets to the Rawalpindi airport in a small blue car driven by Pakistan's Foreign Minister. The other Americans followed with the luggage. The Pakistan International Airlines plane waited, its engines already running. At the top of the stairs, a party of Chinese officials, among them Nancy Tang, Mao's personal interpreter, waited to greet the Americans, much to the shock of the Secret Service agents, who had no idea what was going on or where they were off to. One started to reach for his gun. A stringer for a London newspaper who happened to be at the airport seeing his mother off noticed the unusual activity and asked a policeman what was up. 'It's Henry Kissinger; he's going to China.' The reporter rushed off to send the story to London, where it was spiked because his editor assumed he must have had too much to drink. In the American embassy the next day rumours went round that something was not quite right about the story of Kissinger's illness.[13]

Nixon himself nearly let the secret out when he gave a speech in Kansas City on 6 July. He talked in a statesmanlike way of a new world order where the five main powers would be the United States, the Soviet Union, Western Europe, Japan and China. It was essential, he said, that his administration take the first steps towards ending the isolation of China. The comments were overlooked by the American press but picked up by alert British and Asian journalists. The White House managed to persuade them to keep quiet.[14]

The plane took off into the darkness. Kissinger disappeared into the special VIP cabin and the rest of the Americans without thinking arranged themselves on the right-hand side of the aisle and the Chinese took the left. Dawn came up to reveal the Hindu Kush, the

great range of mountains that helps to divide China from its neighbours. As the plane crossed into Chinese airspace, Winston Lord,
perhaps by design, found himself at the front, the first American official in twenty-two years to reach China. The Chinese and Americans
chatted politely among themselves. Holdridge, who had visited China
as a child before the Second World War, noticed that one of the
Chinese aircrew quietly pocketed all the packages of cigarettes the
steward brought round. 'This seemed a hopeful sign that he was
human, and that China was still China.' Kissinger, who spent much of
the time poring over his notes, had a brief flash of anger when he realized that his assistant had forgotten to pack a change of shirts for him.
He borrowed a couple (as luck would have it, with labels saying
'Made in Taiwan') from the much taller Holdridge. Kissinger managed
to hold the sleeves up with elastic bands but spent his time in China
looking, said Lord, rather like a penguin.[15]

On the other side of the world, Nixon had just broken the news of
Kissinger's trip to Rogers, whom he had invited to San Clemente
partly to keep an eye on him. It had not been a good few weeks for
Rogers. In May, he had been deeply hurt and distressed when he was
informed, shortly before it was announced, that Nixon and Kissinger
had negotiated a major arms deal, SALT 1, with the Soviet Union and
that Kissinger had been having regular secret meetings with Anatoly
Dobrynin, the Soviet ambassador to Washington. Now he was given
a feeble story about how Kissinger had been in Pakistan when the
Chinese had unexpectedly invited him to Beijing to meet Chou.[16]

The PIA plane flew on, across the vast desert which the silk route
had once crossed, and landed at a military airport outside Beijing
around lunchtime. On the ground, a small party, headed by Ye
Jianying, one of the Four Marshals whose reports had started Mao and
China down a new path in international relations, waited to escort
them to the Diaoyutai. Holdridge found himself in a car with Huang
Hua, an experienced diplomat who had just been appointed ambassador to Canada. 'You know,' said Huang as he opened the
conversation, 'in 1954 at Geneva, your Secretary of State refused to
shake the hand of our premier, Premier Chou En-lai.' Holdridge hastened to assure him that there would be nothing similar this time.
When Chou arrived at the Diaoyutai that afternoon, he climbed out

of his limousine with his arm outstretched. Holdridge remembered the scene years later: 'Kissinger strode out to greet him. Kissinger extends his hand, handshake, and boom, boom, boom, boom – flash-bulbs all over the place, videotape, etc. This was an historic handshake.' Chinese who were present thought that Kissinger was nervous and tense.[17]

The Chinese kept the news of Kissinger's visit secret until after he had left, but word began to spread in the inner circles of government. Zhang Hanzhi was a young official in the Foreign Ministry. She and her colleagues sensed that something was happening. Government ministers looked excited. Two of the top interpreters had disappeared. At lunchtime they reappeared and broke the news. 'It was like a bomb exploding in the Foreign Ministry.'[18]

That first day, Kissinger and Chou talked until nearly midnight. Chou began the discussions by inviting Kissinger to make an opening statement. 'Besides, you have already prepared a thick book.' Kissinger hastily explained that he rarely used written notes but that he wanted Nixon to know what he was going to say. After he had gone through his summary of American concerns, it was Chou's turn.[19] The two men and their colleagues settled down for what were to be seventeen hours of conversations. They had only two days to get to know each other and develop the necessary level of trust to enable the contact which had been established with such difficulty to produce fruit.

Chou was experienced, his diplomatic skills sharpened after years of negotiating with the Communists' enemies such as the Guomindang, and their one-time friends such as the Soviet Union. He also had the self-control and patience that surviving through the long years of war and inner-party struggle had brought. Kissinger was much younger but he had an equal talent for diplomacy. If he was not as seasoned as Chou, he was learning quickly. The two statesmen, the old hand and the novice, laid themselves out to charm each other. Kissinger lavished praise on China, 'this beautiful and, to us, mysterious land'. Oh, said Chou, 'When you have become familiar with it, it will not be as mysterious as before.' Kissinger also took every opportunity to flatter Chou himself: 'It is hard to believe that the Prime Minister could be anything but cool-headed.' When the question of taping their conversations came up, Kissinger demurred: 'you will be so much more

precise and better organized than I, that I would be shown up at a dis-
advantage'. That was probably untrue, replied Chou. 'You are younger
and have more energy than I.'[20]

In those first encounters, Chou and Kissinger discovered the main
areas where they agreed and disagreed. For China, Taiwan was the
most important issue, while for the United States getting out of
Vietnam was of equal importance. The Chinese made it clear that,
although they did not intend to use force to reunite Taiwan with
China, they were not prepared to see two Chinas in the world or in
international bodies such as the United Nations. They wanted the
United States to recognize that Taiwan was part of China and to set a
timetable for withdrawing American forces. The United States,
Kissinger hinted, expected that one day there would be only one
China, though it could not say so right away for political reasons. In
any case, it intended to withdraw its troops, but that was linked partly
to what happened in Indochina. Once the United States was safely
out of its wars there, it could dismantle many of its bases in Asia. Chou
refused to be drawn into making any promises on Indochina. The
peoples there must decide their own fates.[21] Kissinger also devoted
considerable effort to reassuring the Chinese that the United States
had no intention of colluding with other powers (neither the Soviet
Union nor Japan was mentioned specifically) against China. Indeed
Nixon promised that the United States would not take any major steps
affecting China without discussing them with the Chinese first. Chou
would not be drawn into discussions of a common front between
China and the United States.

Late on the night of Kissinger's first day in China, Chou En-lai
made his report to Mao. The Chairman was pleased to learn that the
United States intended to start withdrawing troops and support from
Taiwan. As for Vietnam, said Mao in an altruistic fashion, it was
important that the United States settle it because people were getting
killed there. 'We should not invite Nixon to come just for our own
interests.' Mao also ordered Chou to make a statement the following
morning on the big issues, pointing out that 'all under the heaven is
in great chaos'. The theme was a favourite one of Mao's, who believed
that historic changes – the victory of Communism, for example –
occurred when the world was in turmoil. In a fit of bravado, perhaps

because he did not like the idea of Kissinger reassuring China that the United States would not collude with others against it, Mao added that Chou could tell the Americans that China was quite ready to be divided up among the United States, the Soviet Union and Japan if they chose to invade. In fact, according to Chinese sources, Mao was relieved to hear that the United States had no aggressive intentions towards China. If that were true, the Chinese military could move even more troops north to the border with the Soviet Union.[22]

The next morning, Chou arranged for the Americans to have a tour of the Forbidden City. They were taken first to a small museum to see an exhibit of artefacts dug up during the Cultural Revolution. It was a sad display, although the American visitors could not know it, in light of the widescale destruction of China's cultural heritage during the Cultural Revolution. The Forbidden City was closed off to keep any Chinese from seeing the extraordinary visitors. The Americans wandered through the great imperial courtyards and some of the halls where the emperors had once maintained harmony between heaven and earth. 'We absorbed', Kissinger told Nixon, 'the magnificently simple and proportionate sweeps of the red and gold buildings.' His unfortunate assistants, Lord remembers, sweated in the summer heat under the burden of their briefcases, which they dared not leave behind.[23]

The meetings resumed at noon, in the Great Hall of the People. The Chinese had pointedly selected the Fujian Room, named after the province that faced Taiwan. Chou duly made a strongly worded statement which faithfully echoed Mao's views. And perhaps he shared them; it was after all a difficult change of direction for an old Communist to find himself talking to a representative of the biggest capitalist power in the world. 'There is chaos under heaven,' he told the Americans, who were taken aback by the change in his tone. 'In the past 25 years,' he went on, 'there has been a process of great upheaval, great division, and great reorganization.' The two super-powers were vying to control neutral countries and the territories that lay between them. 'The Soviet Union is following your suit, in stretching its hands all over the world.' China, Chou said, was still a weak country, but it did not fear a combined attack from its three main enemies. Already it was preparing for a people's war. 'This would take some time and, of course, we would have to sacrifice lives.'[24]

All over the world, the people were mobilizing. 'Such resistance is stimulated by your oppression, your subversion, and your intervention.' The United States was enmeshed in Taiwan and Indochina; it was encouraging Japanese militarism; and it was conniving with the Soviets to keep a monopoly of nuclear weapons. Perhaps it was not worth Nixon's coming to China at all if the differences between their two countries remained so serious, especially over Taiwan, which was a small matter for the Americans but not for China. 'Taiwan is not an isolated issue, but is related to recognition of the People's Republic of China, and it is also related to the relations of all other countries to China.' If Nixon wanted to come to China, he would have to discuss Taiwan.[25]

Kissinger rallied and was equally firm back. He wanted to make it clear, he said, that the Chinese had been the first to suggest that Nixon came to Beijing and they must decide when the time was right. On the other hand, a visit by Nixon would take China and the United States a long way to solving the issues between them. 'It also has tremendous symbolic significance because it would make clear that normal relations are inevitable.' On Taiwan, Kissinger said, he had already explained that the United States intended to withdraw its forces and that the other issues the Chinese worried about – the recognition, for example, that Taiwan was part of China – would settle themselves in due course. In time, too, relations between the United States and China would move on to a normal, peaceful footing.[26]

Once Chou had said his piece, he reverted to his usual courteous self. He noted that he had followed American wishes in keeping the visit a secret. The *New York Times* reporter James Reston, who was on his way to Beijing, had found himself on such a slow train that he would not arrive until Kissinger had left. As for the American politicians who wanted to visit China, 'I have a great pile of letters from them on my desk asking for invitations, which I have not answered.' Nixon would very much appreciate that, Kissinger said. 'This is done', Chou replied, 'under the instructions and wisdom of Chairman Mao.'[27]

By this point it was after 2 p.m. Their Peking duck was getting cold, Chou said, and the Americans might like a break. The summer heat and the tension of the morning were too much for one of the Americans, who fainted just as they moved into lunch. Over their duck, Chou asked Kissinger whether he had heard of the Cultural Revolution. It had been a difficult period, Chou said, and at one point he had been locked in his office by Red Guards. Mao, of course, was right to have launched it. Even the violence, while it got out of hand at times, was necessary to keep the revolutionary spirit alive. 'China was now firmly guided by the thought of Mao Tse-tung.' Perhaps, Chou remarked later that afternoon, Mao would talk more about the Cultural Revolution when Nixon visited. 'We sometimes wonder whether we can talk about such things. But Chairman Mao speaks completely at his will.' At the end of lunch, Chou, the thoughtful and gracious host, took the Americans off to the kitchens to show them how their meal had been prepared.[28]

After the friendly interlude, the two sides resumed their tough debate. They touched on Indochina and the American presence there, Japan, Korea, the Soviet Union, the tension between India and Pakistan in South Asia, subjects that were to become staples of their discussions over the next years. Of more immediate concern was the question of Nixon's visit. The Chinese, Chou said, were prepared to issue a formal invitation but they had a concern about the timing. Would it not be better for Nixon to meet the Soviet leaders first? China did not want to create any more tension with the Soviet Union. 'You saw, just throwing a ping-pong ball has thrown the Soviet Union into such consternation.' Kissinger said that the United States expected to have a summit with the Soviet Union, possibly in the next six months. In fact he had learned in Bangkok that the Soviets had postponed the summit indefinitely, so he decided to push for an early Nixon visit, partly as a way of putting more pressure on the Soviet Union. Kissinger suggested that Nixon should visit China in March or April of the following year. Chou agreed that he would take the matter to Mao.[29]

He regretted, Chou said, that he had to leave for an appointment which would last until 10 p.m. (It was with a delegation from North Korea.) He and Huang Hua would come later that evening to continue their discussions and to work on a common announcement, about both Kissinger's trip and the forthcoming Nixon one. The Americans went back to their villa at the Diaoyutai for dinner. They drafted an announcement and waited for the Chinese officials to re-appear. Ten o'clock came and went with no Huang and no Chou. The Americans walked in the gardens to avoid eavesdroppers and wondered what the delay meant. 'For all we knew,' wrote Kissinger in his memoirs, 'the Chinese had had second thoughts.' At the very least, he suspected, the Chinese were trying to unsettle them.[30] In fact, Huang was waiting for Mao to give him instructions. Some time after eleven, Chou appeared, full of apologies. Huang Hua would come shortly with a Chinese draft and they could compare its word-ing with the American version. Kissinger and Chou chatted for a short time and then Chou took his leave.

Huang finally arrived around midnight with wording which had Nixon asking for an invitation to China so that he could settle the issue of Taiwan, as a necessary first step towards normalizing relations. 'I rejected both propositions,' Kissinger said later. 'We would not appear in Peking as supplicants. We would not come for the sole pur-pose of discussing Taiwan or even simply to seek "normalization of relations".'[31] The wrangling went on until 1.40 in the morning, when Huang suggested that they take a short break. He disappeared and the Americans waited until nearly 3 a.m. before they learned that he would not be back until 9 a.m. The Americans were puzzled and disturbed. Their plane had to leave by 1 p.m. if Kissinger was to make his schedule in Pakistan and they needed that announcement.

Although they could not know it, Huang had rushed back to Mao's house only to find that the Chairman had gone to bed. When he finally managed to see him the next morning, Mao had dealt briskly with the issue of who wanted the invitation: 'none took the initiative, both sides took the initiative'. The wording was now sorted out easily. Chou En-lai, 'knowing of President Nixon's expressed desire to visit the People's Republic of China', had duly invited him. Nixon would come some time before May 1972. The meeting between the American and Chinese leaders was to seek the normalization of rela-tions and to exchange views on matters of concern to both sides. 'President Nixon has accepted the invitation with pleasure.' Kissinger, who was so deeply impressed by Chou En-lai and his 'extraordinary personal graciousness', might have been taken aback if he had heard Chou's speech to his colleagues later that year. Nixon, said Chou, had 'eagerly' asked to be invited to China, like a whore who would 'dress up elaborately and present herself at the door'.[32]

The Chinese agreed that the announcement would be issued on the evening of Thursday 15 July so that the Americans could get good coverage in the weeklies such as *Time* and *Newsweek* and in the weekend papers. As the Americans prepared to leave for their flight, Kissinger expressed his hopes that his visit had laid the ground for a new friendly relationship between the Americans and the Chinese. Chou said they had taken the first step. He had, said Kissinger, been deeply moved 'by the idealism and spiritual qualities of yourself and your colleagues'. Chou replied, 'I suggest that we have a quick lunch.'[33]

The last meal was a cheerful one with even dour Chinese officials smiling. Chou presented the Americans with Chinese tea, 'a little token', and when they boarded the PIA plane the Americans found sets of Mao's works in English and photograph albums of their visit. On the way to the airport, Marshal Ye talked to Kissinger about his early days fighting for the Communists. None of them on the Long March had thought that they would live to see victory. 'Yet here we are and here you are.'[34]

'Those forty-eight hours, and my extensive discussions with Chou in particular,' Kissinger wrote in his subsequent memorandum for Nixon, 'had all the flavor, texture, variety and delicacy of a Chinese banquet. Prepared from the long sweep of tradition and culture, meticulously cooked by the hands of experience, and served in splendidly simple surroundings, our feast consisted of many courses, some sweet and some sour, all interrelated and forming a coherent whole.' Kissinger found in Chou not only an intellectual equal but an extraordinary and subtle negotiator who never bothered with petty detail or with scoring points. The Chinese, he felt, were generally good to negotiate with; they laid out the main things they felt strongly about right at the start. It was such a pleasant change, Kissinger told Nixon, after the Soviets with their pettiness, their bullying and their bluster. Chou for his part thought Kissinger 'very intelligent', and, as he said on a later occasion to visiting American newsmen, 'He can talk for an hour without giving one substantive answer.'[35]

As the American party headed back towards Pakistan, their secret, amazingly, was still safe. In Rawalpindi, Farland, the American ambassador, put on a convincing display of annoyance to explain why Kissinger was late in coming down from his rest in the hills. 'That stupid ass is up there in the Murree bazaar arguing about some horrible piece of rug or something, looking for bargains.' On the other side of the world in Washington, a small group in the State Department inadvertently learned the truth when Marshall Green, the Assistant Secretary of State for Asia and the Pacific, joked to his colleagues that Kissinger probably did not have Delhi belly at all but had gone off to China. As he spoke, Green realized what he had just said. He dashed up to see Rogers, who went pale and made him swear that he and his staff would not say another word.[36]

The Kissinger party finally landed in Pakistan and piled into cars to drive up to meet the road coming down from Muree and then back to the airport. Kissinger stopped briefly to see an excited Yahya and to talk to American officials. Farland managed to get Kissinger to one side: 'I got everything I wanted,' Kissinger said. 'It was a total success on my part. I did a beautiful job.' At six o'clock that evening, the Americans, back on their own uncomfortable plane, took off for Teheran, where Kissinger had a brief meeting with the Iranian Foreign Minister and sent off a telegram. In California, Haig read its one word – 'Eureka!' – and went at once to see the President. Nixon said, 'Al, I told you so. I told you so.' Forgetting all his earlier instructions about keeping communications to a minimum, he ordered Kissinger to send an immediate report. 'Conversations', wrote back Kissinger, 'were the most intense, important, and far-reaching of my White House experience.' He urged Nixon not to talk to anyone, not even Rogers, until he, Kissinger, was back in the United States.[37]

Early on the morning of 13 July, Kissinger arrived in California. He and Nixon and Haldeman, with some help from Rogers, went over the trip and discussed how to deal with the news over the next few days. What had it meant when Chou wished Kissinger well in his negotiations with the North Vietnamese? How would the Soviet Union react to the announcement that Nixon was going to China?

Should Nixon make a dramatic or low-key speech on his television appearance scheduled for 15 July? Haldeman worried about press coverage. Kissinger was exhausted and perhaps a bit let down after all the excitement of the previous days. Rogers was gentlemanly and generous in congratulating him. The President was thrilled and excited and longing to spill the news. On 14 July, he took the distinguished British journalist Henry Brandon and his wife around the garden at San Clemente. He hinted that he was about to make a major statement and stopped to pick a white Peace rose for Mrs Brandon. By the time he had finished struggling with the stem, it had almost no petals left.[38]

At 5.45 the next evening, Nixon went to a studio in Burbank for his speech. He spoke briefly, revealing that Kissinger had held talks with Chou En-lai in Beijing. He then read out the announcement that Kissinger and Chou had agreed on. He was taking this step, Nixon said, because of his conviction that all nations would benefit from a better relationship between the United States and China. 'It is in this spirit that I will undertake what I deeply hope will become a journey for peace, peace not just for our generation but for future generations on this earth we share together.' He reassured old friends, and, without mentioning it by name, the Soviet Union, that the United States did not intend to harm any nation with its new relationship. As he left, a handful of protesters shouted, 'Get out of Vietnam.' Nixon, who rarely took his staff out to dinner, carried them off to the faded splendour of what had once been a leading Los Angeles restaurant and ordered an exceptionally expensive bottle of wine. (Ehrlichman later bargained the price down from $600 to $300.)[39]

Although Nixon had been braced for loud criticism from the right, his announcement was greeted with general approval and even enthusiasm in the United States. The Senate Democrat leader Mike Mansfield said, 'I am astounded, delighted and happy.' Enthusiastic entrepreneurs dreamed, as their predecessors had done a century earlier, of huge untapped markets. The State Department heard from a casket-maker in Texas who wanted to be the first to sign up Chinese for American coffins for their ancestors. The agent for a nightclub singer tried to get Kissinger to help arrange a tour of China's nightclubs.[40]

A few conservatives, and inevitably the China lobby, grumbled about surrendering to Communism, but Nixon did his best to reassure them. They should realize, he told Haldeman, that the opening to China was useful against the Soviets and would help in Vietnam. It also helped Nixon. The Vietnam War dragged on and the negotiations in Paris with the North Vietnamese were not producing significant results. He was struggling domestically. The economy was in trouble with inflation running at over 7 per cent. Thanks largely to Vietnam, massive holdings of American dollars were now in foreign hands, and the booming economies of countries such as Japan and West Germany were producing goods to challenge American exports. Nixon was under pressure to impose wage and price controls and to devalue the American dollar. By late August, thanks in part to the way in which his move towards China showed him as a master of foreign policy, the polls were indicating that he had taken a significant lead over Senator Ed Muskie, his Democratic challenger in the presidential race of 1972. Nixon let the Chinese know that he would prefer that they did not allow in American politicians before his own trip.[41]

American allies were divided. The British, who already had diplomatic relations with the Chinese, approved of the change in American policy, but their Prime Minister Edward Heath was deeply hurt by not being taken into Nixon's confidence. The Western Europeans were generally pleased; leaders such as Willy Brandt in West Germany hoped that the Soviet Union might now become more amenable to better relations between East and West in Europe. The Japanese were insulted by being told only at the last moment and the Taiwanese were furious and very worried. The Soviet leadership was, according to an adviser to Brezhnev, 'in a state of confusion, if not shock'. Many feared that China was moving into the American camp and might even form a common front against the Soviet Union. The Soviets told the United States that the summit, which they had postponed, could now take place. While there was no way of gauging Chinese public opinion, one person at least was happy. 'With this move by the Chairman,' exclaimed the old Marshal Chen Yi, 'the whole game is enlivened.'[42]

Two days after Kissinger left Beijing, Chou En-lai flew to Hanoi to reassure the North Vietnamese that China was not abandoning them.

Indeed, he argued, better relations between China and the United States would eventually convince the Americans that they need not worry about Asia but should concentrate on Europe and the Soviet challenge there. That in turn would help North Vietnam bargain with the United States. The North Vietnamese were not persuaded. China, in their view, was 'throwing a life buoy to Nixon who had been drowning'. When the North Vietnamese Prime Minister visited Mao later that year he tried unsuccessfully to persuade the Chairman not to receive Nixon. The busts of Mao and copies of his Little Red Book started to vanish from the Hanoi shops as the Chinese move became yet another in the litany of grievances Hanoi had against Beijing.[43]

Chou then flew on to North Korea to deliver a similar message. Back in Beijing, he met with Prince Sihanouk of Cambodia, who had been exiled from his own country by an American-backed general, and with the Albanian ambassador. Sihanouk had little choice but to accept the news. In Tirana, Enver Hoxha, the Albanian dictator, was shocked. 'The Chinese', he wrote in his diary, 'have made a major opportunist mistake, have shown themselves to be rightists and their action is revisionist and to be condemned.' He was also furious that he, such a loyal ally to the Chinese, had been kept in the dark. 'What shamelessness on the part of the Chinese!' he complained. 'We, naturally, were to be informed after the Prince of Cambodia!'[44]

In the months after Kissinger's visit, the Chinese also faced a major political crisis at home. It is still not clear whether this arose from Mao's paranoid fantasies or from a real plot against him. By the summer of 1971, he had become convinced that his Defence Minister and chosen successor, Lin Biao, was leading a move to supplant him. (Kissinger, who of course could not know this, had brought a present for Lin.) In a typically indirect move, Mao ordered several generals close to Lin to make self-criticisms. On the night of Kissinger's first day in Beijing, when Chou was briefing Mao on his opening encounter with the Americans, the Chairman had spent an hour on the issue of whether or not the generals were really sincere. They were not, he concluded. Moreover, behind them, 'someone' was plotting.[45]

Being close to the Chairman had always been dangerous, as Lin well knew, and he had done his best to avoid doing anything that might make Mao see him as a rival. During the Cultural Revolution he had turned the People's Liberation Army into Mao's tool. He energetically held up Mao and Mao Tse-tung Thought as the infallible guides for China and for revolution. His standard response, even to the most outlandish of Mao's decrees, was 'If the Chairman has expressed his approval, then I approve.' He had asked Mao not to name a successor at all and, when Mao had insisted, reacted by doing his best to avoid any decisions. Lin may not have been entirely sane. He had been in ill health ever since he was badly wounded in the war against Japan in 1938. There were stories that he had become a morphine addict, cured only after a trip to the Soviet Union, and later reports that he restored himself by inhaling fumes from a motorcycle he kept in his house. He panicked at the sound of water and hated going outside. He had to have shots of what was said to be Vitamin C before he went out in public or received foreign dignitaries. During the Cultural Revolution, he stayed in seclusion at his house, working as little as possible.[46]

While he had occasionally intervened to protect the People's Liberation Army from being seriously disrupted by the Cultural Revolution, Lin's advice to a subordinate who faced attack was, 'You should be passive, passive, and passive again.' It had not worked and now Mao was attacking Lin's closest associates and muttering darkly that Lin had said things that were not 'particularly proper'. Lin's son, an ambitious air force officer, had gathered a group of like-minded young men about him who were concerned about the continuing chaos of the Cultural Revolution and who feared for China's future. He was also rightly worried that his father was about suffer the same fate as other eminent Communists such as the disgraced former President Liu Shaoqi. The group may have simply talked or may have actually started plotting a seizure of power.

By the second week of September 1971, it was clear that Mao was assembling a case against Lin. On the evening of 12 September, Lin's son apparently persuaded his parents, who were resting in the resort town of Beidaihe, to board a plane he had standing by. They would run either south to Guangdong or north to the Soviet Union, as far from Mao as possible. Lin's daughter, an unhappy and troubled young woman who deeply resented her mother for pushing her into a marriage she did not want, informed the authorities. For some reason, and we may never know what it was, the plane with the elder Lins and their son was allowed to take off. It crossed out of China over Outer Mongolia and apparently ran out of fuel. None of those on board survived.[47]

The incident led to a major crisis within the top leadership of the People's Republic. For several days all planes were grounded and staff worked late in government buildings in Beijing as the limousines came and went. Party officials and gradually the Chinese public were fed a string of improbable stories about how Lin had been a traitor for years and how Mao, out of the goodness of his heart, had kept hoping to redeem him. Mao himself, according to his doctor, was extremely depressed at Lin's apparent betrayal.

Increasingly access to Mao was controlled by his bodyguards and his young women. As his health failed and his slurred speech and thick Hunanese accent became increasingly difficult to make out, his close companion Zhang Yufeng became more and more important as one of the few people who understood him. When he met foreign visitors, he was invariably accompanied by one or more of what people in the Foreign Ministry called 'the five golden flowers'. The two most important were nicknamed the mesdemoiselles Wang-Tang. Nancy Tang was Mao's personal interpreter, Wang Hairong his grandniece. Both had risen to prominence and to high office during the Cultural Revolution by attacking their seniors in the Foreign Ministry. Both enjoyed their new power and became increasingly arrogant and self-righteous. Wang, of course, had the added advantage of being related to Mao and could stop all argument by claiming that she was relaying the sacred words of the Chairman himself.[48]

When what came to be known as the Lin Biao affair finally leaked out in the autumn of 1971, the Americans assumed that part of the trouble, perhaps the major issue, between Lin and Mao was over Mao's shift towards the United States. Lin, after all, had always been vociferously anti-American in his public statements. But that was true of all the Chinese leaders, including Mao himself. Lin may well have disliked the idea of a rapprochement with the United States but there is little firm evidence to date that he told Mao so. In a speech to party officials that December, it is true, Chou said, 'That US–China relations are a betrayal of principle, of revolution, of Vietnam, as Lin Biao said, is nonsense and an insult to the Party.' By this point, the dead Lin was being accused of all sorts of crimes. In his first conversation with Nixon, Mao also dropped hints: 'In our country also, there is a reactionary group which is opposed to our contact with you. The result was that they got on an airplane and fled abroad.'[49] On the other hand, Lin had survived over the years by subordinating himself to Mao, not by disagreeing with him.

From the American perspective, whatever its causes, Lin's disappearance removed a possible focus of opposition to Mao's shift in policy. It also made the violently anti-American radicals such as Mao's own wife, Jiang Qing, draw back, while Chou En-lai, who was known to agree with Mao, gained in authority. Word went out to party officials to prepare for Nixon's visit by studying Mao's negotiations with the Guomindang after the Second World War. 'Why shouldn't we negotiate with President Nixon?' Chou asked a visiting British journalist. 'For instance, in the past we talked with Chiang Kai-shek.' American and Chinese diplomats had talked for sixteen years in Warsaw, but, Chou went on, the Communists had learned during their civil war with the Guomindang that big problems could be solved only by talking to the man at the top. To get ready for Nixon, the top Communist leaders watched American movies and American-made television shows on technology. Chou, who had taken personal charge of the planning for the visit, ordered that all officials under the age of fifty who were going to be involved with the visit should learn English. (It was optional for the rest.) He also prepared himself by reading parts of Nixon's *Six Crises* and watching that Nixon favourite, *Patton*.[50]

13

Getting Ready

I N FEBRUARY 1972, Ron Walker, head of the White House advance team, arrived in China with his party of nearly a hundred technicians and specialists to prepare for Nixon's visit. They took with them tons of equipment and emergency supplies, from American toilet paper to whisky to a world where there were, in those days, no ice cubes, no telexes and no hamburgers. They found the Chinese hospitable, polite and very concerned to make the Nixon trip a success. What exactly did the President eat for lunch? What temperature would he like his villa to be?

Both sides found their new relationship challenging, occasionally difficult and frequently bewildering. What, asked a young interpreter, who had heard the Americans' favourite song, 'American Pie', did the line about the Father, Son and Holy Ghost mean? An American who tried to explain was startled when the interpreter said she had never heard of Jesus. From time to time, the Chinese joined the Americans to watch the movies brought out from the United States, such as *Butch Cassidy and the Sundance Kid*. One day, to much embarrassment, a Chinese official walked in on a showing of *The Graduate*, just as Mrs Robinson was undressing. There were potentially more serious incidents, like the evening a homesick technician smoked too much of the marijuana and drank too much of the vodka he had brought with him and set his hotel room on fire.[1]

Walker, codenamed Road Runner after the hyperactive cartoon character, was used to dropping in on cities and towns around the world and bullying and cajoling the locals to make sure that every detail for a presidential visit, including thorough press coverage, was in place. This time, he complained to Washington that he was finding it hard to get clear answers to all his demands and questions. When the

Chinese head of protocol demurred over a particular arrangement, Walker snapped back, 'I don't give a rat's ass what you say, we're going to do it this way. We always do it this way.' The Chinese was puzzled: 'What's a rat's ass?' When it gradually dawned on him, there was a major crisis and a senior official had to fly out from Washington to smooth everything over.[2] The agreement that Nixon would visit China was the first, most important step, but there were many times in the next few months when it looked as though the visit might never take place. The minuet, in Kissinger's description, was performed on the edge of a cliff, by dancers who were never quite sure what moves others were about to make.

After Kissinger's first secret visit, the Chinese and the Americans used the Paris channel to talk about everything from refuelling the American aircraft to relations with the Soviet Union. In October, Kissinger travelled back to Beijing, this time openly, as the Chinese had requested, to start drafting the joint communiqué which was to be issued by both sides at the conclusion of the President's visit and to continue work on the arrangements for Nixon's trip. 'China,' Kissinger told Chou, 'despite its long experience in handling outsiders, has never undergone anything like the phenomenon of a visit by an American President.' Kissinger flew in Air Force One so that the Chinese could get used to dealing with the President's aircraft. He also brought a much larger party which included communications and security experts as well as Dwight Chapin, Nixon's appointments secretary, who was heading the White House advance team. This time, too, there was an official representative from the State Department, an experienced China hand called Al Jenkins. 'My task', said Kissinger in his memoirs, 'was to give him a sense of participation without letting him in on any key geopolitical discussions, especially the drafting of the communiqué.'[3]

Kissinger took off from the United States this time and landed in China at Shanghai on 20 October. From there two Chinese pilots took over the controls, just as they would when Nixon arrived. In their conversations in Beijing, the Chinese also insisted that Nixon should travel in a Chinese plane for part of his trip within China. It was not usual, Kissinger said, for American presidents to travel on any planes but their own. 'It's on our territory,' Chou said simply, and pointed out that he himself would accompany Nixon. 'We will be responsible, and your Secret Service men can also have a look in our plane because everything will be all right.'[4]

In Beijing, although the American party had no way of knowing it, the repercussions from Lin Biao's flight were still causing trouble in the upper echelons of the party. Chou En-lai was much preoccupied with trying to clean up the mess and in fending off attacks from the radicals. At the Diaoyutai where the Americans were again housed, a ripple from off-stage reached them when they discovered copies in their rooms of an English-language news release condemning American imperialists and calling on the people of the world to overthrow them. Kissinger gathered all the releases up and handed them over to a Chinese official with the comment that some previous guests must have left them behind. Chou was furious and embarrassed at what may have been an attempt by radicals in the official Chinese news agency to derail the delicate process of opening up relations with the Americans. He immediately reported to Mao, who made light of it: 'Tell the Americans, these are nothing but empty words.' The next day as Kissinger drove to the Great Hall of the People, the Chinese Deputy Foreign Minister tried to explain that, just as the Americans communicated with each other through newspapers, so did the Chinese through slogans. He showed Kissinger a wall where a poster denouncing the United States had been freshly covered up with a welcome for the Afro-Asian Ping-Pong Tournament.[5]

The American party stayed in Beijing for a week trying to work out the details, both small and large, of Nixon's visit. (To guard against Chinese listening devices, they played a tape of Johnny Cash country and western songs; whenever they wanted anything like a cup of tea from the Chinese, they turned the music off and spoke loudly.) The Americans toured some of the sights Nixon would see: the Great Wall, the Ming Tombs and the Summer Palace. Jiang Qing, Mao's wife, put on one of her famous revolutionary operas for them. Interestingly, the programme also contained a performance of a Beethoven symphony by the Beijing Philharmonic which was appearing for the first time since the Cultural Revolution had started. The communications experts met together trying to reconcile the colossal demands of the Americans for rapid communications with the antiquated state of the Chinese telephone system and to make arrangements for satellite transmission. The Americans wanted to bring the President's special armoured limousine; the Chinese insisted that he would be perfectly safe in one of their cars. The issue was finally settled when Nixon said he did not care which car he used. The American chief of security bewildered the Chinese when he asked them to round up all the usual trouble-makers before Nixon arrived. His Chinese counterpart complained about the American's arrogant manner.[6]

The Americans, Kissinger told Chou, would bring their own interpreters: 'but in private meetings between the Chairman and the President we may want to rely on your interpreters in order to guarantee security'. He could not, Kissinger claimed, trust American interpreters not to talk to the newspapers. The Chinese agreed with understandable alacrity. Using their interpreters would give them greater control over the record of Nixon's conversations. Finding enough English speakers was something of a problem, however; the Chinese brought them in from all over the country, often from the farms where they had been sent during the Cultural Revolution.[7]

On the whole Kissinger and Chou concentrated on the big political issues: the Soviet Union, the tension in South Asia, Japan, Korea and the United Nations. Taiwan was at the top of China's list, Vietnam on the Americans'. Kissinger was usually accompanied only by Winston Lord. He did not want, he told Chou, to share the discussions of major issues 'with colleagues not in my own office'. Jenkins from the State Department was therefore sent off to talk to one of Chou's subordinates about issues Kissinger considered less important, such as trade, or was kept occupied with trips to see an oil refinery and a chemical plant. With Chou, Kissinger said, it was as though the two of them were resuming a seamless conversation. 'Everything ever said to me by any Chinese of any station was part of an intricate design – even when with my slower Occidental mind it took me a while to catch on.'[8]

In their twenty-five hours of conversations, Kissinger and Chou covered much of the world and much past history, but they kept coming back to Taiwan. And it was to be Taiwan that caused them the most trouble when they came to drafting the communiqué for the conclusion of Nixon's trip. Kissinger had come prepared with a detailed draft which he handed over to the Chinese on 22 October. 'It is such a long one,' commented Chou. The draft contained much fine language about how the Chinese and Americans recognized each other's differences but how they wanted to work together for international peace and security. Neither side was seeking hegemony, a favourite word used by the Chinese to attack the superpowers. The draft also skated over the key areas of dispute such as Taiwan, expressing the hope that the issue could be settled peacefully. It was the sort of standard communiqué issued when nations still had important matters to work out. Mao disliked it intensely, perhaps because as an old revolutionary who still dreamed of leading a world revolution he did not care for the idea of subscribing to something so bland and conventional. The United States, he told Chou later that night, was talking about peace and security. 'We have to emphasize revolution, liberating the oppressed nations and peoples in the world.' It was all empty talk, Mao went on, when the Americans said they would not interfere in other countries' internal affairs and swore that they were not seeking to dominate the world. 'If they did not seek hegemony, how could America expand from 13 states to 50 states?' Chou should tell the Americans that it was better for everyone to speak frankly. Anything short of that would be 'improper'.[9]

Chou duly complied with his instructions. On the morning of 24 October, he told Kissinger that they must face the fact that there were significant differences between the positions of their respective countries. To do otherwise would be dishonest, the sort of thing the Soviet Union might do. The Americans, Chou lectured Kissinger, were behaving like Metternich had after the Napoleonic Wars: trying to suppress revolution and maintain order by relying on old friends. Metternich had failed in the end because he could not hold off revolution for ever. The Americans were facing something similar in the present. 'This awakening consciousness of the people is promoting changes in the world, or we might call it turmoil.' Look at Vietnam, at the rest of Asia, at Africa, at Latin America, even at Europe. The Americans should understand the power of revolution; after all they had once been revolutionary themselves when they fought for their independence. Both the United States and China wanted peace; but,

Chou demanded, 'shall this generation of peace be based on hopes for the future or on old friends?' That was a fundamental difference between their two countries. If the United States preferred to behave as Metternich once had, it would find itself facing revolutionary challenges after a few years. 'Of course,' Chou concluded blandly, 'perhaps limited by your system, you are unable to make any greater changes, while we, due to our philosophy, foresee such a thing.'[10]

The Chinese prepared their own draft, which set out their general approach and their views on major issues, and left a space for the Americans to do the same. The Chinese also added the requisite revolutionary sentiments, about oppression breeding resistance, for example, and peoples making revolution. Mao was pleased. The communiqué, he said, now had a 'voice'. On the evening of 24 October Chou read out the new draft. 'I had wanted to escape from it today,' he told Kissinger, 'but it appears not possible.' Kissinger was taken aback, but, as he said in his memoirs, gradually came round. 'I began to see that the very novelty of the approach might resolve our perplexities.' On Taiwan, the Chinese insisted that the Americans set a timetable for withdrawing all their troops and to recognize China's sovereignty over the island. Kissinger could not go that far, although he stressed that the American military forces would gradually be withdrawn once the United States had extricated itself from Vietnam. He hinted, too, at greater concessions in the future once Nixon had been re-elected in the autumn of 1972: 'I have told the Prime Minister two things: first, it's possible for us to do more than we can say, and secondly, it's possible for us to take more measures after next year than during next year.' Nixon, he promised, would reaffirm that when he came to China. Kissinger told Chou, though, that the Chinese would have to tone down their criticisms of the United States: 'it will be said that the President came 12,000 miles in order to be asked to sign a document containing the sharpest possible formulations against United States policy'.[11]

Kissinger delayed his flight back to the United States and he and Winston Lord worked late into the night of 24 October on the Chinese draft, seeking, said Kissinger, 'a tone of firmness without belligerence'. All the next day and night, the two sides went back and forth. 'I pointed out with melancholy', Kissinger later reported to

Nixon, 'that the Chinese draft still accentuated our differences in provocative fashion.' The two sides gradually inched closer together on the wording of the communiqué. The language became calmer, although the differences remained. And Taiwan remained intractable. Finally, on the morning of 26 October, as Air Force One stood ready at Beijing airport, Kissinger came up with language on Taiwan that seemed acceptable to both sides. 'The United States acknowledges that all Chinese on either side of the Taiwan Straits maintain there is but one China. The United States Government does not challenge that position.' Chou accepted it, later remarking to his colleagues, 'After all, a Dr is indeed useful as a Dr.' By eight o'clock on the morning of the 26th, the two sides had agreed on a draft. As he stood at the door of the Diaoyutai guesthouse to see Kissinger off, Chou spoke in English for the first time: 'Come back soon for the joy of talking.'[12]

'The one thing that Doctor Kissinger had not worked out yet', according to Chapin, 'was how he was going to be able to keep Secretary of State Rogers from attending various meetings, but for the most part it was all coming together in a way that pleased Doctor Kissinger.'[13] As Air Force One taxied down the runway, a coded message came in from Washington. The United States had lost its battle at the United Nations to keep Taiwan as a member. Ever since 1949, the Americans had insisted that Chiang Kai-shek's Republic of China in Taiwan was the true representative for China and so Taiwan and not the People's Republic had occupied the China seat on the Security Council, in the General Assembly and in the UN's agencies. At home, the well-organized and well-funded China lobby had made sure that there was no weakening of resolve. At the start of the 1960s, when the Kennedy administration looked at the possibility of having both Chinas in the UN, Nixon, at the time out of office, led the campaign to make sure that the United States continued to support Taiwan as the only true China. It was getting increasingly difficult, however, to hold the line at the UN itself. In the 1950s, determined lobbying by American diplomats and emergency measures such as sending a US Navy aircraft to collect the delegate from the Maldive islands had kept the status quo intact. By the close of the decade, however, the end of the big European empires was producing new nations by the dozens and most Third World countries and, of course, the

Communist ones voted year after year for an Albanian resolution to admit the People's Republic. In the 1960s the Americans had been able to hold off the inevitable only by getting the vote classified as 'important', which meant that a majority of two-thirds was required – but even on that, time was running out.

In his first couple of years in office, when Nixon was questioned about American policy on the China representation issue, he merely said he had no plans to change that policy 'at this time'. In fact, he was gradually modifying his longstanding opposition to having the People's Republic in the United Nations. This was largely because of his moves towards the People's Republic but also because it had become clear that the United States was about to lose the vote at the UN. In 1970 the General Assembly voted by a slim majority for the Albanian resolution to expel Taiwan and give its seat to mainland China. A compromise solution, floated briefly by the United States and others, that the People's Republic take the seat on the Security Council but that Taiwan remain in the General Assembly went nowhere when both Chinas refused to accept the presence of the other in the United Nations. When Kissinger raised the issue of dual representation in his conversations with Chou during his first, secret, trip to China, Chou made it clear that China intended to reclaim what was rightfully its own, not share it with an illegitimate government. When Mao heard the proposal, he said firmly, 'We will never board their "two China" pirate ship.' That same summer, Washington sent a special envoy to sound out Chiang Kai-shek. The old leader was also firm; 'he would rather be a piece of broken jade lying smashed on the floor than a whole tile on a roof'.[14]

At the start of 1971, a high-level study group in Washington concluded that the United States was likely to lose the annual important-question vote and therefore the requirement for a two-thirds majority on the Albanian resolution. American allies such as the United Kingdom and Canada were indicating that they were no longer prepared to vote with the United States. Taiwan, the study concluded, might be expelled as early as that year. While the study merely laid out American options, increasingly the thinking in official Washington was that the United States should be seen to put up a good fight for Taiwan but that the admission of the People's Republic to the UN was in reality a good thing. On his secret trip to China that summer, Kissinger tried one last face-saving move for the United States when he promised Chou that the American government would allow China's admission by a mere majority but that it would still insist that expelling a member required two-thirds. The People's Republic would be in right away and Taiwan would be out soon. Chou was not interested: 'we do not consider the matter of reclaiming our seat in the U.N. as such an urgent matter. We have gone through this for 21 years, and we have lived through it.'[15]

The sensational news of Kissinger's visit to China served to undermine the American position, but the American delegation at the UN, led by its ambassador, George H.W. Bush, fought on during the summer and early autumn. They were handicapped because Washington delayed sending them clear directives about what American policy was, whether to keep to the old line or try to get some sort of compromise, until September. That autumn, when the General Assembly met, the Americans spent the days lobbying to keep the admission of the People's Republic of China as an important question requiring a two-thirds majority Each night the Americans met to go over their lists as their old friends slipped away. Then, as the crucial vote in the General Assembly approached in October, Kissinger made news headlines with his second trip to China. 'So', said one of the American diplomats, 'that was the coup de grâce. If there was any lingering possibility that we could hold a line, that pretty well ended.'[16]

Kissinger, who has been criticized at the time and since for the timing of his trip, may well have chosen his dates deliberately. In a conversation with Rogers and Nixon on 30 September, he said he had been told that the week between 19 and 28 October was the tricky one. Rogers complained strenuously that Kissinger was almost certain to be in Beijing when the vote took place: 'everybody would think we were deliberately undercutting our own effort'. Kissinger agreed to see if he could change his trip, but later that day he and Nixon talked alone and agreed that it was not worth it. 'I think', said Kissinger, 'the votes are set now.' Nixon agreed.[17]

On the morning of 26 October, as Kissinger and Chou En-lai were conducting their last-minute discussions on the draft communiqué in

Beijing, it was still the evening of the 25th in New York and the crucial vote was approaching in the General Assembly. Suddenly, to the dismay of the Americans, the Saudi ambassador proposed a break for dinner. The delegates poured out of the hall and, although the Americans searched the cafeteria and nearby restaurants, many simply vanished into the night. When the General Assembly reconvened, two votes took place: one to have the admission of the People's Republic determined by a simple majority, the second to expel Taiwan. When the result was announced, many delegates, from African countries for example, danced in the aisles, while the delegation from Taiwan slowly filed out. Nixon told the press that he was 'outraged' by the display but privately he was relieved that the issue had finally been resolved. He detailed Kissinger and Haldeman to tell conservatives such as Ronald Reagan and Barry Goldwater that the administration had fought as hard as it could to keep Taiwan in the UN.[18]

In New York, Bush told the American delegation that their job was now to meet the representatives of the People's Republic and treat them courteously. There must be no regrets. He could not resist a moment of irritation, though, when Kissinger said how disappointed he was. 'So was I. But given the fact that we were saying one thing in New York and doing another in Washington, the outcome was inevitable.'[19]

In Beijing the news caused something close to consternation. The Foreign Ministry was still painfully rebuilding itself after the Cultural Revolution and China had very few experienced diplomats available. And Mao himself had said that whatever happened China would not join the United Nations that year. Chou hastily called his top officials together to discuss China's response. The radicals took a hard line. China should not belong to a bourgeois and bureaucratic institution, 'where people drank coffee, chatted and fought each other orally, which could not speak truly for the oppressed nations and peoples'. The moderates argued that China needed at least a year to study the UN and prepare for participation. As Chou was agreeing, a messenger arrived to summon them to Mao's house. They found a smiling Mao, who brushed aside all objections. China must send a delegation right away. He had enjoyed two major victories that year, Mao said, first when Lin Biao's plot against him had been uncovered, and now

China's victory at the UN. The United States had lost the votes of even its old allies such as Canada and the United Kingdom, who had behaved like good rebellious Red Guards. China's first speech at the UN must throw down the gauntlet to the imperialist superpowers and encourage the peoples of the world to make revolution. If China's spokesmen needed ideas, Mao advised, they could use the notes prepared for the discussions with Kissinger.[20]

China's ambassador to Canada, the relatively experienced Huang Hua, was hurriedly sent to New York and an official party flew into LaGuardia on a Chinese plane. Mao spoke to them before they left: 'One cannot capture the tiger cubs unless one risks going into the tiger's den.' The Chinese representatives had little idea of what to expect in the United States, a Chinese diplomat later recalled, beyond the stories of poverty and oppression which were standard fare in the Chinese press. There were inevitably awkward moments, when a small band of pro-Taiwan supporters demonstrated outside the Chinese headquarters, and a potentially serious incident when one of the Chinese delegation unexpectedly died of what turned out to be food poisoning. On the whole, though, the Chinese were pleasantly surprised to find the Americans friendly. The Americans, for their part, were impressed by the serious and low-key way in which the Chinese set about learning the ropes.[21]

Kissinger and Nixon found the presence of Chinese diplomats at the UN useful, too, as yet another private channel to Beijing. Outside a small circle in the White House, only Bush, under strict instructions not to tell the State Department, knew that Kissinger was meeting Huang Hua and his colleagues in a safe apartment in New York. Kissinger suggested that the Chinese limit their contacts with their American opposite numbers at the UN itself. 'We do not want to overwhelm you with every bright idea of our bureaucracy.' Huang could call him at the White House on a special line. It would not cause any comment, said Kissinger, if he gave a woman's name. The only one he should not use was 'Nancy'.[22]

The channel was useful for working on Nixon's trip and very helpful when a major crisis blew up in South Asia. It had been brewing for decades. The relationship between India and Pakistan had been an uneasy one ever since 1947 when the subcontinent was partitioned to leave a predominantly Hindu India and an overwhelmingly Muslim Pakistan. Partition had seen the mass killings of minorities caught on the wrong side of the divide and had given rise to prolonged disputes over the distribution of resources, over water and over territory, notably the mountainous state of Kashmir. In 1965 a major war broke out which ended with an uneasy ceasefire brokered by the Soviet Union. Both sides looked for allies; Pakistan placed itself firmly in the Western camp in the Cold War and drew closer to the United States, while India positioned itself as a leader of the non-aligned nations but tilted towards the Soviet Union. The emergence of China as a major player in Asia after the Communist victory in 1949 added another factor. The Chinese Communists initially built good relations with India but those soured in the late 1950s as both the powers vied for leadership in Asia and the Third World. India infuriated China by giving shelter to Tibetan refugees including the Dalai Lama himself and the two sides clashed over disputed territory along their common borders. In 1962, the two countries went to war. The result was a Chinese victory. Pakistan, despite the fact that it was pro-West and was firmly opposed to Communism, understandably supported China. It was rewarded by Chinese arms shipments and diplomatic support against India.

In the early 1970s, Pakistan, to the concern of both China and the United States, started to fall to pieces. Partition had left an awkward and probably unworkable country, its two wings separated by almost a thousand miles of an unfriendly India. Only Islam held East and West Pakistan together and that was never enough to overcome linguistic and cultural differences. The army, with officers largely from the West, developed the habit of intervening in politics on the grounds that no one else could hold the country together, and from 1958 to 1969 Pakistan was ruled by a general, Ayub Khan. When he stepped down, he handed over power to Yahya Khan, like Ayub another Westerner. The inhabitants of East Pakistan increasingly resented what they saw as the political dominance of West Pakistanis. In the summer of 1970, a series of cyclones devastated much of the East, but aid was slow to arrive from the central government. In December, when Yahya reluctantly held general elections, the separatist Awami League took almost every seat in the East. 'Mr President,' said Kissinger when they met in the summer of 1971, 'for an elected dictator you ran a lousy election.'[23]

The Awami League held enough seats to form the government of Pakistan, but Yahya simply refused to call the Assembly together. During 1971, the two halves of Pakistan moved towards an open confrontation. In March, the Awami League called a general strike and declared East Pakistan independent. The army cracked down harshly, arresting Mujibur Rahman, the leader of the Awami League, and using American-supplied tanks and planes to crush opposition. Thousands, then millions, of refugees fled across the border into India. The crisis proved both a burden and an enormous temptation for India to break up its enemy. It was an open secret that Indira Gandhi's government was supporting East Pakistan's resistance with arms and money. Much of the world condemned the brutality of Yahya's regime, and senior State and Defense Department officials in Washington as well as virtually all foreign service officers in East Pakistan urged the American government to take a stand and rein in Yahya's government. In addition, most senior officials in Washington argued that, because India was bigger, richer and more stable than Pakistan, it made more sense for the United States to remain on friendly terms with it than to do so with Pakistan. Kissinger, though, talked obliquely about Yahya's special relationship with Nixon. What none of his listeners knew until the summer, because of the extreme secrecy surrounding the contacts with China, was that Nixon and Kissinger saw protecting the channel through Pakistan to Beijing as a matter of paramount importance. Even when the contacts between China and the United States came out into the open, both men felt a sense of gratitude towards Pakistan. 'Why is it our business how they govern themselves?' Kissinger complained to a high-level inter-agency group in Washington that summer. 'The President always says to tilt toward Pakistan, but every proposal I get is in the opposite direction. Sometimes I think I am in a nut house.'[24]

Nixon and Kissinger also preferred Pakistan to India. 'The Indians are no goddam good,' said Nixon as he and Kissinger discussed the crisis. 'Those sons-of-bitches', Kissinger agreed, 'have never lifted a finger for us.' And they found Yahya, the helpful, brisk soldier, much easier than the Indian Prime Minister, Indira Gandhi, whom they saw, among other things, as moody, snobbish and devious. In their private conversations, where admittedly they tended to let off steam, they called her an old witch and a bitch. As the subcontinent drifted towards war in the summer of 1971, however, it was the soldier who made matters worse, not the bitch. Yahya refused to make any serious concessions to the people of East Pakistan and talked of trying Rahman for treason. Mrs Gandhi, on the other hand, was apparently trying to find a political and not a military solution to the crisis throughout the spring and summer of 1971.[25]

Kissinger, however, was convinced after his visit to New Delhi in July that war was likely and when, on 9 August, India signed a friendship treaty with the Soviet Union, he concluded that it was inevitable. He also assumed that, in helping India, the Soviets were sending a contemptuous signal to China: if it did nothing to help Pakistan, China would stand revealed as weak; yet, if it did intervene, the Soviets could use the excuse to attack it. And if Pakistan lost a war with India, as was almost certain, a good friend of both the United States and China would be humiliated.[26]

The signals from China, though, were far from clear. On Kissinger's first visit in July, Chou said that China would not stand idly by if Pakistan were attacked, although he did not say what form China's assistance might take. Chou was also probably trying to put over a lesson, Kissinger later assured Nixon; 'those who stand by China and keep their word will be treated in kind'. During Kissinger's second, October visit, Chou not only was reluctant to spend much time on South Asia but he sounded more cautious when it came to support for Pakistan. 'I believe', Kissinger wrote in his summary of their talks, 'the PRC [People's Republic of China] does not want hostilities to break out, is afraid of giving Moscow a pretext for attack, and would find itself in an awkward situation if this were to happen.'[27]

Hostilities did break out. Indian troops were making minor incursions into Pakistan by late November and, on 3 December, Pakistan attacked India in force in the west. Both Nixon and Kissinger saw the conflict as a Cold War confrontation, with the Soviet Union backing India and the United States therefore obliged to keep the balance in the subcontinent by backing Pakistan. If Pakistan broke up, Kissinger argued, it would be a triumph for the Soviet Union. That in turn would have a catastrophic impact on the American position in the Middle East, where Arab states backed by the Soviets would be emboldened, and on American relations with China. Moreover, the Chinese, Kissinger insisted, needed to be shown that the Americans were reliable friends.[28]

Nixon and Kissinger had been working hard behind the scenes to help Pakistan. 'We are trying desperately', Nixon told Pakistan's Foreign Minister in November 1971, 'not to allow this terrible tragedy, this agony that you're going through, to be the pretext to start a war.'[29] In the second week of December, as the war raged, Kissinger got a message to the Shah of Iran, who agreed to send ammunition into West Pakistan. Following Nixon's instructions, Kissinger also ordered an American naval task force to sail towards the coast of East Pakistan, or Bangladesh as it was starting to be known. This was to put pressure on the Indians and warn the Soviets off, although the reason given out publicly was that the aircraft carrier and its escort ships were needed to save the handful of American citizens left in Bangladesh. For all their sympathy for Pakistan, once the war had actually started Nixon and Kissinger also worked with the Soviet Union to get cease-fire proposals acceptable to both sides.

On 12 December, Nixon and Kissinger had a panicky conversation about the situation in the subcontinent and its ramifications for the larger global scene. They feared that India, which was already occupying most of East Pakistan, was going to invade West Pakistan and turn it into a satellite state. And behind India, so they assumed, was its patron, the Soviet Union. The time had come, they agreed, to stand up against India's naked aggression and force the Soviet Union to decide between continuing to back India and working with the United States for a ceasefire. 'A typical Nixon plan,' said Kissinger. 'You're putting your chips into the pot again. But my view is that if we do nothing, there's a certainty of a disaster.'[30]

At that point, Haig entered to say that the Chinese mission in New York urgently wanted a meeting. Kissinger, who had talked to Huang Hua, the Chinese ambassador to the UN, two days before, was already extremely nervous about China's intentions. Huang had talked about how the Soviet Union and India were trying to encircle China and expressed his country's support for Pakistan. At Haig's news,

Kissinger exploded: 'They're going to move. No question, they're going to move.' If China came in to protect its friend Pakistan, then it was likely that the Soviets would also intervene. The United States, Kissinger argued, could not simply stand by. If it did, China might be defeated or humiliated. At best, the American initiative to open relations with China would be finished. So what, Nixon asked, should they do? 'Start lobbing nuclear weapons in, is that what you mean?' Kissinger did not answer directly but painted an apocalyptic picture. 'If the Russians get away with facing down the Chinese, and if the Indians get away with licking the Pakistanis, what we are having now is the final, we may be looking right down the gun barrel.' Even if the United States managed to stay out of the widening conflict, it would be damaged, perhaps irrevocably. 'It will be a change in the balance of power in the world of such magnitude.' Nixon was less pessimistic; 'Russia and China aren't going to war.' He was right. When Haig dashed off to see Huang Hua he discovered that China intended to support ceasefire proposals already before the United Nations.[31]

By 16 December, India and Pakistan had agreed to ceasefires in both the east and the west, Yahya Khan had left office in disgrace, and Bangladesh was an independent state. India was stronger and what was left of Pakistan much weaker, a factor that was going to drive the latter in the search for its own nuclear weapons. On the other hand, the new American relationship with China remained good. Chou En-lai, so Kissinger heard through Zulfikar Bhutto, the new Prime Minister of Pakistan, thought that the United States had saved West Pakistan. Kissinger himself suffered a temporary eclipse. Nixon was already annoyed at his increasing public prominence. Moreover Kissinger's behaviour during the crisis, when, for example, he leaked a threat to cancel the forthcoming summit with the Soviets, made Nixon wonder about his judgement. When the columnist Jack Anderson ran sensational and accurate stories about how Nixon and Kissinger had tilted towards Pakistan, Nixon blamed Kissinger's office, unfairly, for that as well. For a couple of weeks, Kissinger found that the President did not have time to meet with him or return his phone calls. He threatened to resign but, in the end, so he told Haldeman, decided that Nixon and the country needed him, especially with the trip to China coming up and then the Moscow summit. The freeze ended and the two men resumed their relationship, 'close on substance, aloof personally', as Kissinger put it.[32]

There were now only a few weeks left before Nixon's trip to China. The State Department and the National Security Council were working hard on briefing books for Nixon and Rogers. In the State Department itself, a special three-man team, under orders of the strictest secrecy, was writing a series of position papers and opinions for Kissinger. Because none of their colleagues was supposed to know what they were doing, the unfortunate trio had to do their regular work and then sneak away for much of the night to do Kissinger's. At the NSC, Charles Freeman, who had been moved over from State, was also churning out material. He worked round the clock, often getting only two or three hours of sleep a night and forgetting to eat. At the last moment, someone decided that Pat Nixon should have her own briefing book. Freeman had twenty-four hours to produce a summary of Chinese arts and culture with brief descriptions of every place she would be seeing. 'For me', he recalled, 'that period of a couple of months, I guess, six weeks, felt like a year.' All over Washington, under orders from Kissinger, different departments of the government were doing specialized studies. The reports would disappear into the National Security Council, where Kissinger's own team would use what they wanted. Sometimes the NSC staff would simply take the first page of a briefing off and substitute their own. The State Department fought back with a special letterhead which made it more difficult for the NSC staff to pass off State papers as their own.[33]

The Chinese were also making their preparations. The policy for receiving the Nixon party, the government decided, should be 'treat guests with politeness and respect; not an arrogant attitude, nor a servile one; not too warm treatment, nor too cold'. Chou set up a special team at the Diaoyutai which included Ye Jianying, one of the Four Marshals, Zhang Wenjin, an experienced diplomat who had been one of the first victims of the Cultural Revolution in the foreign ministry, and Xiong Xianghui, a protégé of Chou's who had worked closely with the Four Marshals. Chou himself frequently chaired their meetings. The team prepared analyses of the international situation and American domestic politics and gathered whatever information they could about Nixon and Kissinger, from their thinking to their personalities. Although Mao had approved the visit, Chou still had to deal with the radicals who quibbled over details. The Ministry of Culture objected to a Chinese band playing 'America the Beautiful' at the welcome banquet. Mao's wife, Jiang Qing, did not want American television crews 'doing propaganda for Nixon on Chinese soil'.[34]

In January 1972, when Kissinger sent his deputy Alexander Haig out to China to make the final preparations for the Nixon trip, the radicals continued to cause difficulties. Haig, who was checking out the places Nixon would see, spent an evening in Shanghai, a radical stronghold. At the banquet, something went badly wrong. According to the Chinese, Haig sat silently through the meal and refused to return a toast from one of his hosts. Haig's version is that the toast was offensively anti-American and that he decided not to reply. Moreover, according to Haig, at the end of the banquet, Wang Hongwen, a leading radical and later to be tried as a member of the Gang of Four, came up to him and rudely announced that the banquet was over. Haig's party continued on to Hangzhou, where they received a cool greeting from the local officials. Although it was bitterly cold, they were all taken out on the famous West Lake, as Nixon would be. There was nothing on the boat to eat, just cups of tea. Zhang Hanzhi, one of the interpreters accompanying the Americans, asked the locals what was going on. All sorts of delicacies had been prepared, she was told, but they had received a phone call from Shanghai instructing them to be unfriendly. 'Everyone is scared of the Shanghai radicals so we withdrew all the food.' Zhang and the others who had come with the Americans had an emergency meeting and reported the situation back to Chou, who in turn called Mao. 'Chou En-lai really criticized us very, very seriously. And he said, what happened in Shanghai and Hangzhou almost upset the whole strategy of Mao Tse-tung's plan of breaking the ice between the U.S. and China.'[35]

Haig had been sent out to do more than sightseeing. He had a delicate mission. He had to reassure the Chinese that the United States was firmly on their side against the Soviet threat and he also had to downplay the bombing campaign that the United States was carrying on against North Vietnam. In addition, he was to see if he could get some modification in the wording in the communiqué on Taiwan. 'I have complete confidence in him,' Kissinger had told Chou in October, although Haig was, he took care to point out, more of a soldier than a negotiator. It was an impression that Haig, who was both clever and devious, liked to play up.[36]

On their arrival in Beijing, Haig and his party were given the obligatory banquet with the repeated toasts in maotai. Just as Haig was collapsing into bed, he was summoned back to the Great Hall to meet Chou. He found the Prime Minister surrounded by senior officials and a host of journalists and cameras. When he saw Haig, Chou began a strident denunciation of American imperialism. At the end, Haig said firmly that he was not prepared to have his country insulted. If necessary, he and his party would leave. Chou at once dismissed most of the officials and the journalists and his tone changed to a more friendly one. How was Kissinger? Chou had heard that he had the flu. And was this Haig's first trip to China?[37]

The two men talked until early in the morning. The Soviets, Haig said, offering what he called a blunt soldier's assessment, had tried, unsuccessfully of course, to divide the United States from the People's Republic in the recent conflict on the subcontinent. The Soviet Union was bent on encircling China. That was why they were supporting India, why their Foreign Minister had just visited Japan, and why they were encouraging Hanoi to step up its activities in Laos and Cambodia. What was more, the North Vietnamese were unwilling to talk to the United States about ending the war in Indochina; indeed they seemed determined to humiliate the Americans. Haig did his best to portray the American bombing campaign against the North as a way of countering the Soviet Union. 'We feel strongly that Moscow is urging Hanoi in the direction of continued military action and as such, they are forging another link in the chain which is designed to constrain the People's Republic.' Chou was not impressed by the reasoning: 'the U.S. bombing has increased the Soviet influence in this area'. Nor was Mao impressed when Chou made his report. So the United States was worried about China? 'Its concerns for us are just like a cat feeling sad for a mouse!'[38]

In an indication of just how sensitive the Chinese remained in their dealings with foreigners, Mao and Chou were both annoyed by Haig's attempt to be reassuring. The United States, Haig said in his late-night conversation with Chou, thought that the 'viability' of China should be maintained. After the meeting, Chou turned to the interpreter, Zhang Hanzhi. What does 'viability' mean, he asked her? He sent away for English dictionaries and they pored over them together. It struck them both as patronizing and insulting to suggest that China was not a viable country. When he met Haig next, Chou was stiff. Yes, he said, China was not yet a strong country but it was quite capable of looking after itself, just like North Vietnam. Socialist China had been born and had survived in the midst of struggle against foreign aggression and it remained ready to meet enemies from all sides. 'Facts have proved and will continue to prove that all schemes to isolate, encircle, contain and subvert China will only end up in ignominious defeat.' Haig apologized for having used the simple language of a soldier, which, he feared, might have been misunderstood.[39]

During his conversations in China, Haig also tried, somewhat to Chinese bewilderment, to stress how important it was that Nixon's trip be a visible success. Within the United States, Haig said, striking a theme which Kissinger had emphasized on his own earlier visits, there was an unholy alliance opposed to the President. The American left, dominated by Moscow, the conservatives who supported Taiwan and unnamed forces in the bureaucracy all wanted Nixon's trip to fail because it would slow up the rapprochement between the United States and China. (It would also hurt Nixon's re-election chances, although Haig did not mention that.) Nixon and Kissinger, Haig went on, thought it essential that nothing, no public embarrassment, mar the President's time in China. 'It is in our mutual interest', he assured Chou, 'that the visit reinforce President Nixon's image as a world leader.' As part of that effort, Haig hoped that they might take a look at the draft again. It would be nice, for example, if it could include something positive about opening up trade, for example, between their two countries. More importantly, it would be helpful for Nixon domestically, particularly in appeasing the conservatives, if they could water down the part on Taiwan in the communiqué and find a formulation 'somewhat less truthful and somewhat less precise than the language which Dr. Kissinger carried away with him during his visit'.[40]

'How can Nixon talk about being a world leader?' Mao asked

Chou when they discussed the American requests. Nixon could not even lead the United States: 'He admits that the so-called pro-Soviet, pro-Taiwan and bureaucratic forces all oppose him domestically.' As for changing their joint communiqué, Mao said, they should give the Americans a scare by adding something about the people of the world wanting revolution. Chou dutifully conveyed the Chairman's sentiments back to Haig. 'The image of a man', he said severely, 'depends on his own deeds and not on any other factors.' As far as the wording on Taiwan was concerned, the Americans should realize how much the Chinese had already conceded to find an acceptable formula. And so the Taiwan question and the communiqué itself remained to be settled during Nixon's visit.[41]

It is not surprising that there were times, as Haig admitted, when he felt that the whole Nixon trip might not come off. Both sides, though, had too much at stake to back out lightly and so Haig's trip ended on a friendly note. When the Americans passed through Shanghai again to pick up their plane, they found a completely different atmosphere. On Mao's orders, the top officials responsible for Shanghai had flown down from Beijing to host a lunchtime banquet at the airport. The room was lavishly decorated and everyone was smiling broadly. This time Haig made his toast. As the Americans boarded their plane, each was presented with a giant box covered in pink brocade and filled with sweets. Mao had heard reports of how the Americans had pocketed the sweets left in their hotel rooms and so had ordered a farewell present. Factory workers had worked through the night and the paste was still wet on the boxes. Haig, who had casually expressed an admiration for miniature trees, was given a tiny exquisite evergreen as well.[42]

Three weeks before Nixon was due to arrive in Beijing, the White House advance party, under Ron Walker, left Washington. Haig spoke solemnly to them about their great responsibility to make sure Nixon's visit went well. 'The whole tone of our relationships with China are going to evolve from the atmospherics, if you will.' They would find the advance work more difficult and more sensitive than on any other presidential trip. The Chinese would be watching them closely. 'So be very, very careful.'[43]

14

Down to Business

THE 22ND OF FEBRUARY is George Washington's birthday. That day, a Tuesday in 1972, Nixon spent the morning at the Diaoyutai, working, according to the official news release, on White House business. He had hoped to create a newsworthy item by signing a bill to end a dock strike back in the United States and then present the pen to Chou En-lai, but this had foundered in the face of Chou's careful lack of comprehension. Accepting the pen, Chou told Kissinger by way of excuse, might seem like Chinese interference in American internal affairs. The Americans eventually gave up on the idea.[1]

Nixon called Haldeman in to go over the previous day's events. It was very significant, Nixon thought, that at one point Chou had raised his glass in a toast to the President's next inauguration. As for the coverage in the American media, it was all that Nixon and Haldeman could have hoped for. While press reports of the arrival at the airport had been low key, the ones of the meeting with Mao and the banquet were highly enthusiastic. Nixon was delighted that they had noted his handling of his chopsticks and his clinking glasses with Chou. Kissinger, when he joined them, was in equally good spirits. With the meeting with Mao and Chou's friendly attitude, the Americans agreed, they were off to a very good start.[2]

Kissinger was on his way to see Qiao Guanhua, the Deputy Foreign Minister, and that afternoon he would join Nixon for the first of the President's private conversations with Chou En-lai to explore the issues which divided the United States and China and to look at the big strategic picture. (Having the Secretary of State for these high-level talks was apparently not considered.) Kissinger was very busy that week in 1972. His National Security Adviser did not, said Nixon complacently, get much sleep between the meetings with

Chou, another set, usually late at night, with Qiao Guanhua on the final version of the communiqué, and briefings for Nixon.[3]

While Nixon and Kissinger met with Chou for the rest of the week, another set of meetings went on in parallel between Rogers, the Secretary of State, and Ji Pengfei, China's Foreign Minister. They talked, Kissinger wrote dismissively in his memoirs, about those obsessions of the State Department's East Asian bureau, trade and exchanges. Kissinger had in fact taken considerable pains to ensure that this happened. He had made it clear in his first visits to China that the State Department was not to be trusted. Now, when he met Chou En-lai and Qiao Guanhua on the first day of the Nixon visit to discuss the agenda for the week, he stressed that the subjects to be discussed in the conversations between Rogers and his counterpart should be limited to those of lesser importance. He was outlining who knew what among the American delegation to ensure 'that by inadvertence your people do not say anything in the private meetings with the State Department that will be a surprise to them'. They had a complicated system in the United States, Kissinger said wryly; the Chinese did things in so much simpler a way.

No one outside Nixon's immediate circle, Kissinger told the Chinese, knew how much information he had passed on to them about American relations with the Soviet Union or about the way he and the President had worked with the Chinese during the crisis between India and Pakistan. No one knew about the assurances he, Kissinger, had already given on Taiwan. Nixon would be repeating those. In a plenary session, asked Chou? No, replied Kissinger, privately. The Americans, though, would give the State Department fuller details once they were all back in the United States. Furthermore, Kissinger went on, no one had seen the draft communiqué, although Rogers had been shown the two paragraphs dealing with Taiwan. There was no need, Kissinger thought, for Rogers in his meetings to discuss the communiqué at all, but it might be useful for the Chinese to outline their position on Taiwan so that the State Department records showed it.[4]

When Rogers tried to raise the subject of Taiwan, the Chinese firmly told him they could not discuss it with him because the issue was being dealt with by Kissinger and Chou. Ji in any case had no particular expertise in foreign affairs and showed little aptitude for diplomacy. As Mao once memorably said of him, 'Sitting here with me till his stool sank into a hole, he did not even break a fart.' Chou En-lai and Mao tolerated Ji but relied far more on his deputy, Qiao.[5]

Charles Freeman, who acted as interpreter in the Rogers–Ji talks, had taught himself to read Chinese characters upside down. He noticed that Ji relied as heavily on his briefing books as did Rogers. When the Chinese, as they tended to do in all their discussions with foreigners, rehashed past grievances, Rogers, whose grasp of history was shaky, found himself debating the origins of the Korean War and whether or not the United States wanted to dominate the world. 'So', Freeman recalled, 'it was a lively, but rather inconsequential, venting of views.'[6]

The important issues were being discussed elsewhere. The meetings with Mao and Chou on the day of Nixon's arrival had set the tone for Nixon's and Chou's discussions. Both men touched on the reasons that it had taken so long for their two governments to talk directly to each other. Each offered assurances that his country had no designs on the other. Each spoke for his own nation; both also were speaking for the benefit of the absent Mao, Nixon to reassure him of the peaceful intentions of the United States towards China, and Chou of his loyalty. It was only possible for China to move towards the United States, Chou remarked, because of the great trust that the people had in Chairman Mao. Nixon agreed eagerly: 'Chairman Mao takes the long view, as I do.'[7] While Chou and Nixon frequently disagreed, they did so in a polite and even friendly spirit.

There were no clear agendas for the talks, perhaps because so much ground had already been covered by Kissinger and Chou the year before, partly because the fact of the talks themselves was as important as the content. Both men wanted to discuss their common enemy, the Soviet Union, and both had an interest in other issues, from the balance of power in Asia and the Pacific to the Middle East. The Chinese, however, focused on one issue in particular: Taiwan. The position of the People's Republic was then and has remained ever since that the island is part of China, its status purely a domestic matter. Outsiders, the United States above all, had no business involving themselves. The existence of a separate government and another China was an affront to the Chinese nation and to Chinese nationalism.

It was impossible to deal with each issue in isolation. When the Chinese talked about Taiwan, they brought in their relations with Japan which they claimed to fear had designs to move troops on to the island. While the Americans were prepared to make concessions on Taiwan and cut back on their support for it, they hoped that, in return, the Chinese would put pressure on North Vietnam to negotiate in good faith with the United States. And both sides had to keep the larger international context in mind. As Nixon said that in that late-afternoon plenary on his first day in Beijing, 'we cannot discuss a critical area like South Asia, and India, without evaluating the policy of the Soviet Union toward that area'.[8]

For his first private meeting with Chou that Tuesday afternoon, Nixon went to the Great Hall of the People. They met, not by coincidence, in the Fujian Room, where Kissinger had held his first talk in the summer of 1971. Chou politely asked Nixon to present his views first. The Chinese always insisted on this, on the grounds that it was their custom with guests. It was also, of course, a useful negotiating tactic and one which they used even when they were guests themselves. As Qiao once said to Kissinger, 'We have two sayings: one is that when we are the host, we should let the guest begin; and the other is that when we are guests we should defer to the host.'[9]

Nixon had prepared for this moment with his usual care, talking for hours to Kissinger and reading widely. Freeman lent him several books on China (which he never managed to get back). In the detailed briefing books which the National Security Council and the State Department prepared, almost every page is marked up with Nixon's underlinings and scribbled comments. A couple of days before he left Washington, Nixon jotted down his key ideas on one of his favourite yellow legal pads.

What they want:
1. Build up their world credentials
2. Taiwan
3. Get U.S. out of Asia

What we want:
1. Indo China (?)
2. Communication – To restrain Chinese expansion in Asia
3. In Future – Reduce threat of confrontation by China Super Power

What we both want:
1. Reduce danger of confrontation & conflict
2. A more stable Asia
3. A restraint on U.S.S.R.[10]

Kissinger gave Nixon much advice beforehand on what to expect when he met the Chinese leaders for the first time. He would find them extraordinarily civilized, at once charming and efficient (so unlike the Russians). Indeed, the Americans would find it hard to resist being seduced by the famous Chinese hospitality. In a memorandum he wrote a couple of weeks before Nixon's departure, he waxed eloquent: 'The drama and color of this state visit will surpass all your others.' And, added Kissinger, who knew his President well, 'The conversations will be at a far greater intensity and length than any previous diplomatic talks you have conducted.' Nixon should start out each discussion with the 'broad philosophic touch' to show the Chinese that he was master of the big strategic picture. The Chinese wanted to know, as Chou had recently told Zulfikar Bhutto, the new Prime Minister of Pakistan, what principles the Americans based their thinking on. For the Chinese themselves, principles were crucial; they would be firm on those, flexible on tactics.[11]

In another memorandum he sent Nixon a couple of days before the flight to China, Kissinger reminded him that the Chinese were fanatics, committed to revolution, yet also highly pragmatic. They needed the Americans because China was faced with threats from the Soviet Union and a resurgent Japan, as well as with the possibility that Taiwan might abandon all claims to the mainland and declare its independence. Nixon, Kissinger said, would find Chou the practitioner and Mao more the philosopher. He would enjoy dealing with the charming and articulate Chou, who would be, in Kissinger's opinion, at once ambiguous, evasive, oblique and frank. Chou was tough and sometimes it would be necessary for Nixon to stand up to him. 'Chou's firmness, however, is not the kind of brutalizing toughness which we have come to expect from the Russians, but rather a hardness and consistency of purpose derived from fifty years of revolutionary experiences.' The most important thing Nixon could achieve would be to assure the Chinese that the Americans were serious and reliable. 'If in our formal and informal talks we can impress the Chinese with these intangibles, we will have truly made your visit an historic success. If we fail to do so, we can expect the Chinese to be an increasingly thorny adversary, and history could record your visit as a gallant but stillborn venture.'[12]

In his opening remarks, Nixon did his best to follow this advice. He intended, he told Chou, to speak frankly and to keep the record of their talks secret: 'I'm determined where the fate of our two countries, and possibly the world, is involved, that we can talk in confidence.' He also wanted Chou, he said, to convey a very important message to Chairman Mao: 'When I give my word – I don't give it very often – I want him to know that I will keep it.' What the United States desired, in the long run, was the complete normalization of relations with the People's Republic. The issue of Taiwan, he recognized, was a problem, but he was prepared to work with the Chinese for a peaceful resolution which would remove an irritant in their relationship.[13]

Nixon took care to remind the Chinese that he had taken a considerable risk in coming to China. His own bureaucracy, particularly in the State Department, opposed him. Back in the United States, an unholy alliance across the political spectrum wanted him to fail to establish a new and productive relationship with the People's Republic. The left, according to him, were pro-Soviet while the right backed Taiwan. Then there were those who were pro-Indian or pro-Japanese. Another source of danger were the isolationists, who wanted the United States to cut its military budget in half and withdraw its forces from Europe and Asia.

He was, Nixon assured Chou, anything but a militarist; indeed he was a Quaker. He was convinced, however, that the world would become dangerously unstable without a strong United States as a counterweight to aggressive nations such as India and, of course and above all, the Soviet Union. China, in his view, clearly benefited from the American presence in Asia. The Soviet Union had to think twice before it embarked on adventures, for example on the subcontinent. In addition, the United States acted as a brake on another enemy of China's: Japan. The Americans hoped that Japanese militarism was a thing of the past, but who could tell? If the United States, which currently gave Japan its military protection, were to withdraw its forces, the Japanese might well rearm and, given their strong economy and their past, that would not be a good thing for China or indeed the rest of Asia. Moreover, the United States did not want to see Japanese forces moving into Taiwan or South Korea if American forces had to move out. As long as the United States remained in Asia, it could keep Japan under control. 'But,' Nixon warned Chou gravely, 'if the U.S. is gone from Asia, gone from Japan, our protests, no matter how loud, would be like – to use the Prime Minister's phrase – firing an empty cannon; we would have no rallying effect because fifteen thousand miles away is just too far to be heard.'[14]

In his response, Chou paid little attention to the suggestion that having American troops in Asia helped China. Indeed, he pointed out, their presence in Indochina was only helping the Soviets increase their influence there. He also refused to be drawn into discussions of a common front against the Soviet Union. When Nixon suggested that a stronger China alongside the United States could balance the power of the Soviet Union in Asia and, incidentally, allow the US to cut back its own military spending, Chou was firm: 'You have too much confidence in us. We don't want to.' Both the superpowers, he said sternly, were spending far too much on their military. Their arms race, sooner or later, would result in war. It could be a good thing for the world if the two of them could get on better terms and start to limit their armaments. The Chinese, he said, had made it clear that they had no objection to Nixon having a summit with the Soviets before he visited China. As it was, he had chosen to visit China first. 'Moscow is carrying on like anything,' Chou said. 'But let them go on. We don't care.'[15]

As he had done in his earlier conversations with Kissinger, Chou dwelled on the past, in particular on the injustices done to China and the sufferings of the Chinese people. China's past contained much more, of course, than a sorry tale of weakness and humiliation at the hands of outsiders. In the great Tang dynasty, for example, China had been confident and strong and had reached out to the world. For the Communists, however, it was the Century of Humiliation that mattered. Their history of China was one of survival in the face of oppression; the victory of Communism had finally allowed China to 'stand up' and face off the imperialists.

In that story, the United States played a key role. (This was a standard Chinese negotiating technique, to stress the faults of the other side.)[16] The United States, Chou reminded Nixon, had sided with Chiang Kai-shek against the Communists during the Civil War and had then protected him in Taiwan ever since President Truman had sent the Seventh Fleet to defend the island; and later, in the 1950s, the despised Dulles had signed a defence treaty with Taiwan which remained in effect. In the Korean War, Truman's armies had driven towards the Yalu river border in North Korea and the Chinese Communists had been obliged to intervene. When the two sides signed a truce in 1953, the Americans had allowed Chiang Kai-shek to entice prisoners of war from the People's Republic to settle in Taiwan. (The fact that several thousand of their soldiers had chosen not to go home still rankled with the Chinese Communists.) In 1956, the United States had failed to live up to its promises at the Geneva conference of 1954 to hold elections in Vietnam. It had backed successive illegitimate regimes in South Vietnam, Cambodia and Laos and sent its soldiers to fight the peoples of Indochina.

In Chou's remarks then and on subsequent days, he singled out three other countries which had been troublesome to China. India, for one. If you read the book *Discovery of India* by Indira Gandhi's father, Jawaharlal Nehru, Chou told Nixon, its real meaning was all too clear. 'He was thinking of a great Indian empire – Malaysia, Ceylon, etc. It would probably also include our Tibet.' From 1959 onwards India had unfairly mounted attacks on China along their common border. The Chinese had complained several times to Nehru, by then Indian Prime Minister. 'He was so discourteous; he wouldn't even do us the courtesy of replying, so we had no choice but to drive him out.' So China had gone to war, justifiably, in 1962 to teach India a lesson. It was a pity, Chou thought, and Nixon agreed with him, that Pakistan had lost the recent war with India. They had both let Bhutto know that he must protect Yahya Khan. Yahya had not been a good general or a good leader, Chou said, but he had done both the United States and China a service in getting Kissinger to Beijing for his first, crucial talks. 'One doesn't burn down a bridge', said Nixon, 'which has proved useful.' Nixon and Chou also agreed that India must be pressured to withdraw its remaining troops from Bangladesh and West Pakistan. They promised to keep in touch through their secret Paris channel on the matter of recognizing the new state of Bangladesh.[17]

Chou also expressed a surprising amount of concern about Japan. The Chinese could not forget what Japan had been like in the past and the suffering it had caused China. This was a theme he had raised repeatedly with Kissinger as well in their talks in 1971.[18] The Japanese economy was developing with ominous rapidity. Japan needed both raw materials and markets abroad. 'Expanding in such a great way as they are towards foreign lands, the inevitable result will be military expansion.' Perhaps, Chou suggested to Nixon, they could share anything they learned about what Japan was up to.

The Americans, Chou charged, had been careless in helping Japan to rebuild after the Second World War. 'You helped Japan fatten herself, and now she is a very heavy burden on you.' It had also been a mistake to receive the Japanese Emperor in the United States; as Chou had said earlier to Kissinger, he remained the basis on which a renewed Japanese militarism could be built. Kissinger's view, as he told Nixon, was that the Chinese were deeply ambivalent about how to prevent this. While they blamed the United States for Japan's resurgence, they also recognized that the United States could act as a brake on its rearmament and expansion. Although the Chinese wanted the United States to reduce its forces in Asia, Chou in his talks both with Kissinger and now with Nixon repeatedly expressed concern that Japan would move its troops into countries such as Taiwan and South Korea to fill the vacuum.[19]

Although Korea had been a battlefield between China and the United States in the 1950s and had played a major role in the long chill in their relations, it was now relegated to the sidelines. China had a close but occasionally tense relationship with the North, which like North Vietnam showed an unwanted independence and a tendency to drift into the Soviet camp, and the United States was allied to South

Korea. As Kissinger put it in his summary for Nixon of his conversations with Chou in October 1971, both powers would stick with their friends but neither wanted another war between the two Koreas. What is important, Nixon told Chou when they briefly discussed Korea, is for both of their countries to restrain their small, impulsive allies. 'It would be silly, and unreasonable, to have the Korean peninsula be the scene of a conflict between our two governments.' It would be good, Chou said, if the two Koreas might one day be peacefully reunited. It would, however, take a long time.[20]

Apart from Japan, the other main threat to China, from Chou's perspective, was the Soviet Union. The Soviets, he told Nixon, were socialists in word only; in reality they were imperialists and troublemakers. Soviet leaders, from Stalin onwards, had been false to China. They had talked of handing back the territory Russia had taken in the time of the tsars; of course, they had not done so. After the Second World War, the Soviet Union had signed a treaty with Chiang Kaishek and left the Chinese Communists on their own. In the conflict between China and India at the start of the 1960s, the Soviets had encouraged India to attack China and when the Chinese had remonstrated with Khrushchev, he had answered them rudely. And, of course, in 1969 the Soviets had threatened a major war with China itself. China had been the innocent party in the fighting that had broken out in March of that year and had always been willing to negotiate.[21]

The Soviets, Chou complained, hated China, but at the same time they sometimes wanted to relax the state of tension 'to a certain extent'. The difficulty in dealing with the Soviets, was that they negotiated only when it suited them and they did not negotiate in good faith. They repeatedly raised new issues or tried to get the Chinese to accept their draft agreements. Of the top Soviet leaders, Kosygin was reasonable if unimaginative, but Leonid Brezhnev, who was more ambitious and aggressive, unfortunately had more power. Nixon offered reassurance in his talks with Chou on 23 February. The United States certainly did not want war between China and the Soviet Union and it was prepared to back China. The US had been ready to do so during the crisis between India and Pakistan the previous December and it would continue to oppose any aggression against China. 'This we do', Nixon said solemnly, 'because we believe that it is in our interest, and in the interest of preserving peace as well, world peace.' He assured Chou, however, that the United States remained firmly committed to improving relations with the Soviet Union and getting agreements which would lower tension in the world. Nixon may have intended a subtle hint that China should not take American friendship for granted. Kissinger had indirectly conveyed the same message during his visits. 'We are making some progress with the Soviets,' was the way Winston Lord put it, 'and you Chinese should be sure that you keep up with us and improve relations with us, so that we don't get ahead of you in relations with the Russians.' In the new triangular diplomacy, of course, Nixon and Kissinger intended that the United States should hold the balance between the other two powers.[22]

Chou also made much of China's comparative weakness. 'We are still backward,' he said to Nixon in their first private exchange of views that Tuesday in Beijing, 'and we admit our backwardness.' China, Chou insisted, had no ambitions to become a superpower. 'We can only say', he had told a visiting American journalist in 1971, 'that China is comparatively important, not so very important.' Foreign visitors invariably found this self-deprecation charming. Look, Chou once said to an American diplomat, as he showed where his long winter underwear had stretched below his trousers: 'We cannot expect to export if we have this kind of quality.'[23]

Chou may well have had in mind the ancient Chinese adage, 'Feign weakness', as a way of deceiving one's enemies. He was also taking the high moral ground for China. Superpowers, to the Chinese Communists, meant the United States and the Soviet Union, both of which wanted domination of the world, or, in Chinese Communist terminology, hegemony. China was not only renouncing such imperialist ambitions, but was also placing itself at the head of all those nations and peoples who resisted such dominance. Chairman Mao taught them, Chou said, 'that once one thinks one is number one under heaven one is bound to suffer defeat'. Vietnam, he added pointedly, was only a small country but with a great people. The world, he said, in another faithful echo of Mao, was in a state of turbulence. The Chinese knew the risks they were taking in not seeking to be powerful, and were aware of the danger that the United States and the

Soviet Union might collude with their other enemies such as Japan to invade their country.[24]

Nixon and Kissinger went to extraordinary lengths to convince the Chinese that the United States had no intention of colluding with the Soviet Union or indeed any other nation to harm China. While neither man went into much detail in his memoirs, the picture has become clearer over the years of the extent to which they provided the Chinese with information, much of it highly secret. On his first, secret, visit, Kissinger told Chou that he was prepared to give him anything the Chinese might want to know about American discussions with the Soviet Union, including the very delicate and important Strategic Arms Limitation Talks (SALT), 'so as to alleviate any concerns you should have in this regard'. In any talks with the Soviets, the Americans would also consult the Chinese when there were clauses that might apply to third countries. Kissinger was true to his word. On his second visit in 1971, he brought copies of various agreements between the United States and the Soviet Union, including one on methods for preventing an accidental nuclear war. That December, when he met Huang Hua in New York to discuss the war between India and Pakistan, Kissinger told him, 'Incidentally, just so everyone knows exactly what we do, we tell you about our conversations with the Soviets: we do not tell the Soviets about our conversations with you. In fact, we don't tell our own colleagues that I see you.'[25]

Now, in February 1972, while the press got details about Milton and Mathilda, the pair of musk oxen Nixon was presenting to China, Kissinger was quietly giving the Chinese the fruits of American intelligence-gathering about the Soviet Union and top-secret information about the state of discussions between the United States and the Soviet Union. Much of what he gave the Chinese was not known even at the highest levels of the State Department because Nixon and Kissinger preferred to use their own secret channels in dealing with Moscow.

In a long meeting on Wednesday 23 February with Qiao Guanhua and Ye Jianying, the Vice-Chairman of China's Military Commission, Kissinger handed over classified material on Soviet military capabilities and a list of the main issues between the United States and the Soviet Union. The Chinese must have been delighted as Kissinger displayed lists of Soviet hardware, from bombers to missiles, and pulled out maps showing Soviet military dispositions along their common border. Ye exclaimed in English at a photograph, 'Rocket!' He wanted details: two-stage or one-stage? And how many kilotons were the nuclear warheads? Kissinger provided them and much more: numbers, speeds, ranges, sites.

Kissinger was careful to underline that, while Soviet strategic forces – the long-range bombers, and the land- and submarine-based missiles – were targeted on the United States, they could easily be used against China. While no one in the American government, not even the intelligence people themselves, he said, knew that he was handing over this information, he wanted the Chinese to have the same information as he and Nixon when they all faced future crises.[26]

At the same meeting, Kissinger also gave the Chinese a full briefing on the state of American negotiations with the Soviet Union. A number of things were happening in Europe to ease tensions between the Soviet Bloc and the West: there would probably be treaties on Berlin, whose status had remained in limbo since the end of the Second World War; there might be a conference on European security and possibly some talks to reduce the level of forces all round in Europe. Both sides also had an interest in the Middle East, particularly in the possibility of negotiations between Israel and Egypt, as well as in arms control in the Indian Ocean, and would probably discuss those issues at the forthcoming Moscow summit.

The two superpowers were also negotiating on a whole series of measures from a treaty on the moon (too far away for us, said Qiao) to civil aviation. Most of them were unimportant except for SALT. He thought, Kissinger said, that the Soviets and the Americans would probably get an agreement soon on strategic weapons, which in nuclear-war terminology meant the long-range missiles and bombers that could deliver nuclear warheads to the other's territory. A few matters had still to be settled – the number of missiles and submarines each side could retain, for example – but the United States would keep China informed of the progress of the negotiations. Of course, Kissinger added, the United States would avoid doing anything that might be used against China.[27]

Qiao and Marshal Ye were grateful: the information was very useful and an important sign of the sincere desire of the United States to improve relations with China. When the Chinese wanted anything more, Kissinger said, they had only to ask. Before he left China, they should all see if there were some way to set up a secure, secret channel. The Chinese should not believe anything they read in the press: 'If I have not told you, it isn't true.'[28]

Over the next few years, Kissinger continued to provide the Chinese with secret information. In 1974, shortly before the Vladivostok summit between President Ford and Brezhnev, he visited China with his assistant Robert McFarlane (later President Reagan's National Security Adviser), who found himself handing over hundreds of pages of classified material. McFarlane defended the practice. The Chinese repaid the favour by giving the Americans access to sites in China for gathering intelligence on the Soviet Union. More importantly, the Americans were indirectly putting pressure on the Soviets, who probably knew about the exchange of information between their enemies, perhaps even from the Chinese themselves, and ought to have been dismayed at such evidence of a close working relationship between them. Of course, the other possibility, which McFarlane does not mention, is that the Soviet Union might well have concluded that the United States was not to be trusted and might therefore have tried to mend its own fences with China or, and perhaps in addition, step up its own military preparations.[29]

As Kissinger had been when he first met him, Nixon was very impressed by Chou's elegance, his mental agility – and his stamina. In their four-hour session that Tuesday afternoon, Nixon noticed, the younger men, both American and Chinese, grew dozy but Chou remained alert throughout. After his trip to China, Nixon liked to compare himself to Chou. 'Nixon is a card player,' he said of himself in a written comment on a newspaper article, 'as smooth as that inveterate sharpster, Chou.' For a time, he kept his unfortunate staff up later than usual; after all, Chou stayed up all night, he told Haldeman.[30]

15

The Irritant: Taiwan

ARLY ON THE morning of Wednesday 23 February 1972 Nixon
wrote one of his memorandums to himself in preparation for his
second private meeting with Chou that afternoon.

> Taiwan–Vietnam = tradeoff
> 1. Your people expect action on Taiwan
> 2. Our people expect action on V. Nam
> Neither can act immediately – But both are inevitable.
> Let us not embarrass each other.

Both Nixon and Kissinger assumed that there was a rough parity
between the two main irritants that stood in the way of a better relationship between the United States and China – and that the Chinese
were making a similar assumption. The American presence in
Vietnam made it difficult for the Chinese to move towards a full
normalization of relations; the Communist Chinese insistence on
regaining Taiwan was a problem for the Americans. Eventually, the
Americans were going to withdraw from Vietnam; in the long run,
Taiwan was going to become part of China again. The China experts
in the United States had got it completely wrong, Kissinger wrote in
his memoirs, when they told him that the most important issues
for the Chinese were Vietnam and Taiwan rather than the balance
of power in the world.[1]

The main challenge, for both sides, so the Americans assumed,
was to manage and improve the relationship between the United
States and the People's Republic, within the context, of course, of
their mutual fears of the Soviet Union. The United States was deeply
concerned about the marked increase in Soviet arms spending which,
or so analysts feared, was bringing Soviet forces up to equality with

American ones. Unless the arms race and indeed the whole competition between the Soviet Union and the United States were brought under control, the future of the world was grim indeed. For all that they denied trying to play a China card, Nixon and Kissinger were convinced that the Soviet Union had become more amenable to negotiations after the first word of the American opening to China. For their part, the Chinese, so the Americans believed, wanted the United States as a counterweight to the Soviet Union in Asia. While this was clearly true, the Chinese had reservations about American reliability. Talk of détente between the Soviet Union and the United States made them uneasy. Would the lowering of armaments and tensions in Europe, for example, simply give the Soviets a freer hand against China? Were the Americans foolishly appeasing the Soviets? 'Take care!' Mao warned the Americans in 1973. 'The Polar Bear is going to punish you.'[2]

To Nixon and Kissinger, Vietnam was an obstacle to the better relationship between the United States and China, but one which, so they fervently hoped, was in the process of being removed. What they perhaps never entirely realized was that the Chinese Communists did not see Taiwan as merely one of several irritants in the relationship between China and the United States. Taiwan, in the Communist view, belonged to China and that was as important to them as their troubles with the Soviet Union itself. 'That place is no great use for you,' Chou said to Kissinger in July 1971, 'but a great wound for us.' In their very first conversation, Kissinger assured Chou that the United States did not back the permanent separation of Taiwan from China. 'As a student of history,' Kissinger said, choosing his words with care, 'one's prediction would have to be that the political evolution is likely to be in the direction which Prime Minister Chou En-lai indicated to me.' Chou replied at once: 'The prospect for a solution and the establishment of diplomatic relations between our two countries is hopeful.' John Holdridge, who was present as one of Kissinger's aides, was convinced that without that statement from Kissinger the talks could not have continued.[3]

Taiwan, the *People's Daily* claimed during Kissinger's second visit, 'has been China's sacred territory since ancient times'.[4] In fact, for much of its history Taiwan, or Formosa as generations of Europeans had known it, had gone its own way, free from outside interference. Almost a hundred miles off China's coast, it had been too far away and too wild to be subdued. It was only in the late seventeenth century that the Qing dynasty had managed to incorporate Taiwan into its empire. The historical claim was dubious, but that was beside the point. For the Chinese Communists, and indeed for most Chinese nationalists, the separation of Taiwan from the mainland was a legacy of the past, yet another example of the way in which outside imperialists had humiliated and exploited China.

In 1895, following a devastating loss in a war with Japan, China had surrendered the island, which then became part of the growing Japanese empire. The Taiwanese, a mix of the indigenous inhabitants and Chinese immigrants, learned Japanese at school and were encouraged to adopt Japanese customs. In the twentieth century, another war brought a change of masters. At the Cairo conference of 1943, Allied leaders decided to return Taiwan to the government of China, still in those days that of Chiang Kai-shek. In 1945, after Japan's surrender, Chiang's forces moved in to claim it. The Guomindang officials were both corrupt and brutal and, in 1947, the Taiwanese rose up in opposition. Chiang cracked down; the island was increasingly important to him as a possible refuge.

As the Civil War in China went in the Communists' favour, hundreds of thousands of Guomindang troops and officials, along with many private citizens, abandoned the mainland for Taiwan. By 1949, Chiang had shipped China's remaining silver and gold reserves, a large part of the national archives and the pick of the treasures from the old imperial palaces to Taiwan. (The National Palace Museum in Taipei remains one of the great depositories of Chinese art and artefacts to this day.) At the start of December 1949, as the Communists closed in on Chengdu, one of the last cities to hold out, Chiang climbed aboard a plane and took off in heavy fog for Taiwan.

He fully intended to come back in triumph to the mainland. 'I should become aware', he wrote in his diary on Christmas Day, 'that the new undertaking and history should begin from today.' Chiang, after all, had known both setbacks and triumphs before, and he remained firmly convinced that destiny had singled him out. An elder in his village described him as 'stubborn, jealous, tactless, bad-tempered and egotistical'. A boy from a modest merchant family, he had made his way upwards in the turbulent China in the years before the First World War. Like his contemporaries Mao and Chou, he was a great nationalist; unlike them, he never moved to the left. He remained deeply conservative in his social and political attitudes. His second wife, the beautiful Meiling Soong, encouraged his increasingly dictatorial and chauvinist tendencies. 'Direct, forceful, energetic, loves power,' Roosevelt's wartime military emissary, General Joe Stilwell, described her in his diary. 'No concession to the Western viewpoint in all China's foreign relations. The Chinese were always right; the foreigners were always wrong.'[5]

As a young man, Chiang had become a soldier and had fought in the Revolution of 1911. In the 1920s, he had moved into the leadership of the new nationalist party, the Guomindang, and in 1927 had successfully led the Northern Expedition which had brought unity to China for the first time in a decade. He also turned on his Communist allies and did his best to exterminate them. In 1937, he had become a hero to millions of Chinese when he agreed to lead a new coalition of the Guomindang and the Communists, this time in opposition to Japan. When the Japanese had responded by invading China, he and his armies had retreated inland to their wartime capital of Chongqing. He had returned in triumph in 1945 to the great coastal cities of China and become head of China's government. In the next three years, in the opinion of many of his own generals and of American observers, he did much to throw it all away through bad military decisions and policies which alienated his supporters and so eased the way of the Communists into power.

After their victory, the Chinese Communists made it clear that Taiwan was unfinished business in the work of reclaiming what they regarded as China's proper territory. They had tried unsuccessfully, in October 1949, to capture the offshore islands of Quemoy and Matsu from Chiang's forces. In 1950, they took Hainan island, off China's south coast, and occupied Tibet. That summer they also moved significant numbers of troops into Fujian province, on the Chinese side of the Taiwan Strait. In Washington, as Chiang brooded in Taiwan, his wife did her best to rally American policymakers and American public opinion to come to his and the island's defence.

The Truman administration had no stomach for what most of its members regarded as a futile cause. 'The Nationalist armies did not have to be defeated,' said Dean Acheson, the Secretary of State, 'they disintegrated.' The US military chiefs recommended only that the United States send some military supplies but they opposed sending any American troops. President Truman concurred and said publicly in January 1950 that the United States had no intention of giving help to Guomindang forces on Taiwan. Acheson, in what later became a notorious statement, defined the defensive perimeter of the United States in the Pacific as including Japan and the Philippines; significantly, he did not mention Taiwan. The State Department prepared a draft of the statement to be issued when the Communists finally took the island.

What changed Truman's mind and that of many Americans was the Korean War, which broke out in June 1950. The United States hastily assembled a coalition of forces for Korea and Truman ordered the Seventh Fleet into the Taiwan Strait to protect Taiwan, now suddenly seen as a vital strategic asset for the United States in the face of world-wide Communist aggression. (The fleet was also, although it was not admitted openly, to prevent Chiang from attacking the mainland.) Shortly afterwards, the United States made a significant shift in its views on the status of Taiwan; it was no longer part of China, but what it was remained to be decided. (Chiang Kai-shek's view, not surprisingly, was that it was the only legitimate China, the Republic of China; until the 1990s ageing deputies in Taiwan's parliament still claimed to represent provinces of the mainland.) Chou described the patrols by the Seventh Fleet as 'armed aggression against the territory of China', but the Chinese Communists reluctantly accepted that they would have to abandon hope of invading Taiwan for the time being. One of the first things Chou did when he and Kissinger met in the summer of 1971 was to remind the Americans that Truman had prevented Taiwan from being reunited with the Motherland and that, to add insult to injury, Dulles had signed an 'illegal' defence treaty with Chiang Kai-shek. It also rankled with the Chinese that the Americans maintained a military mission on the island, which, at the height of the Vietnam War, reached some 10,000 men.[6]

In the 1950s and 1960s, the Taiwan issue not only contributed to keeping the United States and the People's Republic apart, it also threatened to engage them in conflict. Chiang continued to dream of his triumphant return, and he got considerable support and encouragement from the US military, the CIA and parts of the State Department – as well, of course, from the China lobby. By the mid-1950s, the United States was giving Taiwan $200 million a year in aid, much of it for military purposes. American and Taiwan intelligence bases in Taiwan worked together to eavesdrop on Communist radio transmissions, and American planes with Taiwanese pilots flew over the mainland on spying missions. Radio transmitters on Taiwan beamed rousing calls to the mainland Chinese to rise up against their Communist masters and balloons drifted across the Taiwan Strait bearing leaflets with similar messages. Guomindang raiding parties blew up railway lines and harbours on the mainland. Chiang's naval forces harassed Chinese Communist shipping and occasionally captured fishermen from the mainland, who would be given lavish meals and then escorted back. Another remnant of Guomindang power, a body of troops, survived the Communist victory for years in the north of Burma, by the border with China. They had backing from the United States and Taiwan. Although the Americans eventually concluded that the exercise was pointless, Chiang continued to support these forces throughout the 1960s. Whether he gained anything beyond irritating the Americans is doubtful; the Guomindang forces, who found themselves in one of the great opium-growing areas of the world, developed an increasingly successful and absorbing occupation as drug dealers.[7]

The Chinese Communists complained loudly, and from time to time the Americans themselves tried to rein in Chiang and the Guomindang. 'We tried to discourage the use of force,' said Marshall Green, 'making them realize that, if they could live a life of virtue, this would radiate out and, in time, would have a favourable impact on all of China.'[8] In a way, that is what happened. The move to Taiwan was good for the Guomindang. Some of its most conservative and corrupt supporters had been thoroughly discredited and Chiang himself recognized the need for reform. The Guomindang had failed to provide effective government for the whole of China, but in a smaller Taiwan it proved over the years to be reasonably competent. It helped of course that Taiwan received American aid and American investment. An island which had a grand total of four paved roads in 1950, by the 1960s was one of Asia's success stories.

The United States found, as great powers frequently do, that their client would not listen when they urged him to concentrate on building up Taiwan and leave the Communist regime on the mainland to its fate. In the late 1950s, Dulles and American diplomats were seriously concerned by Chiang's nonchalance about the prospect of using nuclear weapons; they would have been even more worried if they had known that Chiang guessed, rightly, that the United States could not afford to abandon him once it had made its commitment in the early 1950s.[9] Any American government which had done so would have faced uproar at home and run the risk internationally of showing weakness in the face of the Communist threat. As a result, the United States repeatedly faced crises over Taiwan which threatened to drag it into a major war with China and, at least until the Sino-Soviet split in the early 1960s, with the Soviet Union too.

A string of little islands, some of them no more than large rocks, just off the coast of China, which Guomindang troops had seized and fortified, were, like Berlin in Europe, particular flashpoints. At the south end, Quemoy was at the entrance to the important port of Xiamen (Amoy) (for the People's Republic, as one American diplomat said, it was like having Manhattan held by an enemy force),[10] and at the north, Matsu sat a few miles off another major port, Fuzhou. From time to time, tensions would flare up, either because of Guomindang activities or because of Communist attacks, whether in the form of commando raids or shelling from their shore batteries.

The worst crisis came in August 1958, when Mao suddenly decided on a serious and sustained bombardment, possibly because the Americans were preoccupied with a crisis in the Middle East, more likely because he needed something to rally the Chinese people as the Great Leap Forward lurched into its most radical phase. In two rousing and widely publicized speeches to the Supreme State Council, he called on the Chinese people and the peoples of the world to resist American imperialism. The Eisenhower administration felt itself obliged to respond. Although its treaty with Taiwan did not include protecting the islands, Congress had subsequently passed a resolution authorizing the President to use armed force in their defence. Eisenhower sent a huge flotilla to reinforce American forces in the Taiwan Strait and American ships started escorting the ships from Taiwan resupplying the beleaguered island garrisons. The supplies included American guns capable of firing nuclear warheads. 'Such a few shots,' said Mao. 'I did not expect the world to get so stirred up over it.' The possibility of a major war between the United States and the People's Republic of China was very real during those tense weeks of late August and September. The Soviet Union, which privately was dismayed by Mao's belligerence and apparent willingness to risk nuclear war, issued a public warning that it could not stand by if its ally were attacked. Chiang Kai-shek urged the Americans to take a strong stand and threatened to send his own planes in to bomb the Communists' shore batteries.[11]

Fortunately, the Americans had no intention of being drawn into a major war by Chiang or by Mao. American naval vessels were careful to stand well away from the islands, out of range of Communist shells. Dulles told a press conference that the question of the Guomindang returning to the mainland was 'highly hypothetical', and he and Chiang issued a joint statement that had been carefully crafted in Washington to the effect that the United States supported the Guomindang's desire to restore freedom to the mainland but that this would be done mainly through political means. Mao, for all his talk about not fearing a nuclear war, was similarly cautious, sending impossible orders to his local commanders to fire their shells so that they hit only Guomindang military and ships and not American. The American and Chinese representatives in Warsaw resumed their talks and the shelling from the mainland petered out. Both sides claimed victory. The United States, though, had made it clear that it did not want Taiwan to precipitate it into a war with the People's Republic. Mao later boasted to Edgar Snow that he had forced the Americans to send in their troops, and then, by ending the shelling, left them with nothing to do. 'Therefore the American troops are subject to transfer at our mere beckoning, a bit like Chiang Kai-shek's troops.' Behind the scenes, the Soviet and Chinese Communists had taken another big step towards their eventual split.[12]

After 1958, the Communists did not try seriously to retake the islands. They contented themselves with bombarding their garrisons with loud propaganda and issuing 'serious' warnings, about a thousand over the years, to the United States about its naval vessels coming too close to the Chinese shoreline. When Nixon visited China, the warnings suddenly stopped. Mao claimed it suited the Chinese Communists to leave the islands in Guomindang hands. 'We will let them hang there, neither dead nor alive, using them as a means to deal with the Americans.' And the Guomindang presence there kept open a possible link to the Guomindang itself and Taiwan. If Chiang were to abandon the islands, the gap between the mainland and Taiwan would suddenly lengthen physically, from a few to a hundred miles, and perhaps in thought as well.[13]

When he talked to Nixon in February 1972, Chou claimed that the Communists had let Chiang know this. 'We advised him not to withdraw by firing artillery shells at them – that is, on odd days we would shell them, and not shell them on even days, and on holidays we would not shell them. So they understood our intentions and didn't withdraw.'[14] The Chinese Communists, with their insistence that Taiwan was and always had been part of China, did not want to encourage any thought that there might be a China on the mainland and a separate state out in the Pacific called Taiwan or simply two Chinas. For years the People's Republic had refused to join organizations where Taiwan was represented or have full diplomatic relations with any country that recognized the government of what the Guomindang insisted was the Republic of China.

The Communists also watched Taiwan apprehensively for signs of an independence movement, something that was not unlikely given Taiwan's history and the fact that many of its inhabitants had no ties to the mainland. In his talks with Kissinger and then with Nixon, Chou demanded that the Americans promise not to support the independence movement in Taiwan. In his meeting with Nixon on 24 February he noted with some asperity that Professor Peng Mengmin, a leading figure in the movement, had received some support in the United States and had fled from Taiwan with American help. (By coincidence, Peng had once been a student of Kissinger's.) Chiang Kai-shek, Chou added approvingly, knew how to deal with talk of independence; he would suppress any such movement in Taiwan.

Nixon and Kissinger did their best to reassure Chou. 'I told the Prime Minister,' Kissinger said, 'that no American personnel, directly or indirectly, nor any American agency, directly or indirectly, will give any encouragement or support in any way to the Taiwan Independence Movement.' If Chou had any information, Kissinger asked, he should send it on through their secret channel and the Americans would take action against the movement. 'I endorse that commitment at this meeting today,' Nixon added.[15]

It was perhaps a curious position for the leader of a nation which had done so much in the past to support national self-determination, but Nixon was determined that Taiwan should not stand in the way of his rapprochement with the People's Republic of China. When they had first contemplated their opening, Nixon and Kissinger had prepared to abandon Taiwan, slowly, quietly and, if they could, without enraging the right. Kissinger, as someone who was primarily concerned with Europe, had never taken much interest in it. As he told Chou the first time they met, he had never been there. Nixon, by contrast, knew Taiwan well. In his heyday as an anti-Communist he had been one of its prominent supporters. In the 1950s he had been all for allowing Chiang to attack the mainland, and he apparently shared Chiang's faith that the Communist regime would crumble. By the 1960s, however, when he had time to travel and reflect, he was reconsidering many of his former views. 'Chiang was a friend,' he told an interviewer much later, 'and unquestionably one of the giants of the twentieth century. I wondered whether he might be right, but my pragmatic analysis told me he was wrong.'[16]

Nevertheless, in his first years as president, even while he was rethinking his China policy, Nixon continued to reassure Chiang of his support. 'I will never sell you down the river,' he told Chiang's son in the spring of 1970. As the secret channel to Beijing began to produce results, Nixon had to face doing just that. In April 1971, as they waited anxiously for Chou's reply to one of Nixon's messages, Nixon told Kissinger: 'Well, Henry, the thing is the story change is going to take place, it has to take place, it better take place when they got a friend here rather than when they've got an enemy here.' Kissinger agreed: 'No, it's a tragedy that it has to happen to Chiang at the end of his life, but we have to be cold about it.' In the end, said Nixon,

'We have to do what's best for us.' As Kissinger prepared to leave for his secret trip to China, Nixon reminded him one last time: 'he wished him not to indicate a willingness to abandon much of our support for Taiwan until it was necessary to do so'.[17]

In his briefing notes for that first trip, Kissinger expected, he said, that the Chinese would want some agreement on reducing American forces in Taiwan and in the Strait (although he found it encouraging that they used the word 'eventually' when they talked of the prospect). He thought, though, that the Chinese might well be prepared to accept a continuation of the existing political relationship between the United States and Taiwan. In the account of his meetings with Chou that he wrote for Nixon, he noted the Chinese 'preoccupation' with Taiwan, but he may not have taken it all that seriously. Certainly in his memoirs, he gives the impression that Taiwan only came up briefly during that first visit.[18]

That is not what the record of the talks shows and not how the Chinese viewed them. Huang Hua, who was present, told the Canadian Foreign Minister shortly afterwards that they had focused almost entirely on Taiwan. While this was an exaggeration, Kissinger and Chou spent much of their time on the subject. The Chinese, from the first tentative contacts, hoped to make their recovery of Taiwan a precondition for any improvement of relations between the United States and China. Taiwan came at the top of the list of the instructions to Chou worked out by the Politburo and approved by Mao before Kissinger's secret trip: 'All U.S. armed forces and military installations should be withdrawn from Taiwan and the Taiwan Strait in a given period. This is the key to restoring relations between China and the United States. If no agreement can be reached on this principle in advance, it is possible that Nixon's visit would be deferred.'[19]

In the very first message that Chou sent to Nixon in December 1970 through the Pakistan government, he said, 'in order to discuss the subject of the vacation of Chinese territories called Taiwan, a special envoy of President Nixon's will be most welcome in Peking'. The Americans did not want, and indeed could not allow, their withdrawing of support from Taiwan to be a precondition to either Kissinger's visit or Nixon's or that the agenda for their discussions with the Chinese be confined to that one subject. In his replies to Chou,

Nixon insisted on a broad agenda, which dealt with all the important issues between their two countries. The Chinese accepted this. Taiwan remained at the top of their list but they focused on getting American troops out rather than on their end goal of reuniting it with China. Nixon did not make a concrete commitment on the withdrawal from Taiwan but pointed out that, as tensions in Asia diminished, the United States would be cutting back on the forces it had there. Both sides had so much at stake in improved relations that they were prepared to compromise. Both had to do so, however, in a way that did not look as though they were showing weakness.[20]

During Kissinger's two trips in 1971, he worked out the basis for an agreement on Taiwan. He has since been criticized for too readily abandoning an old American ally and for exceeding his instructions by promising more than he should have. Yet the Chinese Communists had made it amply clear that, without American concessions on Taiwan, they were not prepared to move forward to put Sino-American relations on to a more normal footing. Moreover, as Chou, a master at diplomacy himself, well knew, negotiations proceed by a combination of clear statements, hints and suggestions. Kissinger, when it was necessary, gave firm commitments to the Chinese but he also hinted at more to come once Nixon had been re-elected as president in the autumn of 1972. The United States, he said categorically, did not support the idea of two Chinas or of a mainland China and a Taiwan. The United States accepted the Chinese claim that Taiwan was a part of China, although here he expressed himself cautiously, saying that the United States would like to see a solution of the issue 'within the framework of one China'. As he said to Chou: 'There's no possibility in the next one and a half years for us to recognize the PRC as the sole government of China in a formal way.' Once Nixon had made a successful visit to China, Kissinger promised, and once he had been re-elected for a second term, the United States would be able to move ahead rapidly to establish full and normal diplomatic relations with the People's Republic of China. 'Other political leaders', he told Chou in what was a familiar theme, 'might use more honeyed words, but would be destroyed by what is called the China lobby in the U.S. if they ever tried to move even partially in the direction which I have described to you.'[21]

Kissinger also indicated that the United States was going to end its support for Chiang Kai-shek, although he was vague about the fate of the United States' defence treaty with Taiwan. The Americans, Kissinger said, realized that China did not recognize the legitimacy of the treaty; 'maybe history can take care of events'. (History did not take care of them and the continued existence of the treaty was going to cause considerable trouble with the People's Republic later on.) The United States, Kissinger also promised, would not support any attempt by the Taiwanese to become independent. The Chinese Communists, who did not fully understand how a democracy worked, were puzzled and disturbed by apparent American contradictions, when, for example, Senator Jacob Javits called, just after Kissinger's October 1971 visit, for a plebiscite where the people of Taiwan might express their views: 'This rabid nonsense', said the Hsinhua news agency, 'fully demonstrates that, even after its defeat in the General Assembly, US imperialism is still pushing the scheme to create "one China, one Taiwan".' When Chou expressed repeated fears about Japanese expansionism, Kissinger reassured him that the United States would oppose any Japanese military presence on Taiwan. (In their darker moments, the Chinese worried, or said they did, that Japan was plotting with leaders of the Taiwanese independence movement.) On the other hand, Kissinger promised, once the United States had found a way to make peace in Vietnam, it would set a firm timetable to remove the two-thirds of its forces in Taiwan which were only there because of the war. The remaining American forces would be withdrawn as relations between the United States and China improved.[22]

Not all the concessions by any means came from the American side. The Chinese accepted that the United States could not turn away from Taiwan overnight. Mao was particularly pleased, however, when Kissinger, on his first visit, promised that part at least of the American troops would be pulled out. The United States, Mao exclaimed to Chou, was evolving. Like an ape moving towards becoming a human being, its tail – its forces in Taiwan in this case – was growing shorter. Armed with Mao's approval, Chou talked in a friendly and positive way about the gradual lowering of tension over Taiwan and the normalization of relations between China and the United States. Although American troops were clearly going to remain in Taiwan for some time, he conceded that normalization of relations could proceed in parallel rather than, as the Chinese had first insisted, with the troop withdrawal as a precondition. In a chat that autumn of 1971 with Jack Service, a former American diplomat whom he had known during the Second World War, Chou made it clear that he understood that American policy on Taiwan would have to evolve over time.[23]

When Kissinger said that the United States hoped that the fate of Taiwan could be resolved peacefully, Chou replied, 'We are doing our best to do so.' Although Kissinger tried repeatedly on both his visits in 1971 to get Chou to say explicitly that China had given up the option to reunite Taiwan with the mainland by force, he in turn had to be content with strong hints. China, said Chou, was showing great restraint on the Taiwan issue: 'for the sake of normalization of relations between the two countries, we are not demanding an immediate solution of this in all aspects, but that it be solved step by step'. And Chou accepted the American wording for the draft communiqué for the Nixon visit, which said that the Americans would encourage the Chinese people to settle the matter 'through peaceful negotiations'.[24]

When Nixon set out for Beijing, the final wording on Taiwan had still not been settled. 'The trouble', as Kissinger had said to Chou in a moment of frankness, 'is that we disagree, not that we don't understand each other.' The Chinese wanted Taiwan to be part of China, if not right away, at a firm date in the future; the Americans could not openly accept that. 'The Prime Minister', said Kissinger, 'seeks clarity, and I am trying to achieve ambiguity.' Before he started his discussions with Chou, Nixon seems to have wanted to take the high moral ground and be completely frank with the Chinese. As he reviewed the references to Taiwan in his opening statement to Chou, he scribbled in the margin, 'won't play games – tell you what we will do – what we cannot do'. One thing the United States could not do was break its treaty with Taiwan. Echoing what he had already said to Chou, Kissinger advised Nixon, 'We could allow history to take care of this problem.' By the time all American troops had withdrawn from Taiwan and full relations had been established between the People's Republic and the United States, the treaty would probably lapse anyway.[25]

Because much of the record on the Chinese side is still restricted, it is not yet possible to know in detail how Chou planned to deal with Taiwan in his talks with Nixon, but he can only have been pleased at the way in which Nixon opened with the issue at their first private meeting on 22 February. 'There is one China,' the President started, 'and Taiwan is part of China.' Nixon then reiterated the other undertakings made by Kissinger: no support for any Taiwan independence movements; the use of American influence to keep Japan out of Taiwan, and to stop Taiwan from attacking the mainland; and the gradual reduction of American forces on the island. The United States, he said, was committed to both a peaceful resolution of the issue and the normalization of relations with China.

Nixon had been scornful, before his trip, when Kissinger suggested, as he had already said to Chou, that the Americans could agree to do more than they could say publicly: '1. too dangerous 2. sounds tricky,' he wrote in one of his notes to himself. Now, however, he said to Chou: 'my record shows I always do more than I can say, once I have made the direction of our policy'. Chou offered the Americans tea and snacks but made no immediate comment. Much later in the meeting, after he had spend considerable time rehearsing past American misdeeds, Chou said airily that the Taiwan question was really rather easy to discuss. 'We have already waited over twenty years – I am very frank here – and can wait a few more years.' And he threw in a promise: when Taiwan came back to the Motherland, China would not put any nuclear bases there. In their discussion two days later, Chou also assured Nixon that the People's Republic would not use its armed forces against Taiwan as long as American forces were there. As in his talks with Kissinger, however, Chou was not prepared to renounce the use of force against Taiwan. Indeed China has never renounced it.[26]

In the meeting on 24 February, Nixon continued to ignore his own advice to himself about not promising more than he could safely admit in public. He intended to move on normalization in his second term, he told Chou, and he was going to withdraw all American forces from Taiwan. He could not, however, make that explicit in their joint communiqué because it would give his opponents something to attack him on during the campaign. 'I must be able to go back to Washington and say that no secret deals have been made between the Prime Minister and myself on Taiwan.' Once he was safely re-elected, he would have four years 'to move us towards achieving our goal'. The difficulty was to express the issue in language which would reassure the Chinese without alarming the Americans. As Nixon put it, 'Our problem is to be clever enough to find language which will meet your need yet does not stir up the animals so much that they gang up on Taiwan and thereby torpedo our initiative.' That difficult task was left to Kissinger and Qiao Guanhua.[27]

Chou pushed Nixon hard on Taiwan but on the last day of the visit, 28 February, he reminded him that China could wait for some time more to settle the issue. Indochina, he said, was another matter. There had been fighting there since the end of the Second World War. 'People there have been bleeding.' China could not help but be sympathetic. 'We have an obligation to sympathize with them and support them.' If President Nixon and Dr Kissinger were sincere, and Chou believed they were, in wanting to reduce tensions in the Far East, then the question of Vietnam and its neighbours in Indochina was the 'key point'. It was a great pity, though, that the Americans had kept on the attack even while Nixon had been in China: 'You have given the Soviet Union a chance to say that the music played in Peking to welcome President Nixon has been together with the sounds of the bombs exploding in North Vietnam'.[28]

16

Indochina

JUST BEFORE HE left Washington, Nixon made a note to himself: '1. Taiwan – most *crucial* 2. V. Nam – most *urgent*.'[1] When he took office, he had optimistically believed that he could extricate the United States from the war in Vietnam within six months. On the ground, though, the North Vietnamese showed no signs of weakening, and in Paris the peace negotiations, which had started in 1968, dragged on. The war, far from winding down, had expanded, to draw in Cambodia and Laos. The conflict was overshadowing the Nixon presidency much as it had the Johnson; it was hurting American society and harming Nixon's ability to deal with the big issues facing the United States abroad, such as relations with the Soviet Union.

The public Paris talks which involved the governments of the United States and North and South Vietnam, as well as the Communist-backed National Liberation Front for South Vietnam, were stuck in endless wrangles over such matters as the type of table to be used. However, while Kissinger had been dealing with the opening to China, he had simultaneously been conducting highly delicate and secret talks, also in Paris, with the North Vietnamese representatives in an effort to get the peace process moving ahead. The North Vietnamese were prepared to talk but not to make significant concessions, and the two sides remained apart on a number of issues. The two most important were the insistence by North Vietnam that President Nguyen Van Thieu's government in the South be removed, something the United States dared not do unless it wanted to be charged with betraying an ally, and North Vietnam's refusal to state publicly that it would withdraw its troops from the South as the Americans withdrew theirs. It did not help matters that Nixon, who was convinced that it was always best to negotiate from a position of strength, was trying to bomb the North Vietnamese into a more conciliatory frame of mind. In the spring of 1970, he extended the war into Cambodia, bombing and attacking the Communist bases there, and in February 1971 into Laos. Both escalations of the war caused massive protests in the United States, and the Cambodian incursion led the Chinese Communists ostentatiously (but as it turned out only temporarily) to break off their developing contacts with the Americans.

Both Nixon and Kissinger placed great hopes in using their opening to China to put pressure on North Vietnam to make more substantial compromises in the Paris negotiations. Both men assumed, in spite of much evidence to the contrary, that the Communist world was organized like an army or a successful corporation, with all low-ranking officers following orders from above. North Vietnam, just like North Korea or East Germany, was a subordinate which would surely do what it was told. There was a difficulty, though, in knowing which of its quarrelling senior partners – the Soviet Union or the People's Republic of China – it would obey. At first Nixon and Kissinger hoped that the Soviet Union was the key; in an early meeting with Dobrynin, the Soviet ambassador in Washington, Kissinger painted an attractive picture of better relations between their two countries, with frequent summit meetings. The only condition was that the Soviet Union helped the United States get a settlement in Vietnam. The Soviets, who were having their own troubles with the North Vietnamese, whom they found stubborn and irritatingly independent, made it clear that they were happy to talk about improved relations but that they were not so easily scared into doing the Americans' bidding.[2]

Nixon and Kissinger, who invariably thought in terms of linkages, of trading gains in one area for concessions in another, increasingly placed their hopes on their new relationship with the People's Republic of China. Surely it would make sense for the Chinese Communists to help over Vietnam, indeed over the whole of Indochina, in return for the Americans giving them much of what they wanted on Taiwan? On 27 April 1971, the day Chou's invitation to Nixon to send a high-level emissary arrived in Washington, Kissinger was euphoric about the possibilities opening up: 'Mr

Chou hosts a welcome banquet in the Great Hall of the People the day of Nixon's arrival in Beijing

Nixon and Chou toasting each other in maotai, the formidable Chinese alcoholic drink

The American and Chinese flags fly side by side in the Great Hall of the People
as Nixon addresses the guests at the welcoming banquet

Chou, the urbane host, with the Nixons

Nixon working out his ideas on one of his favourite yellow legal pads

Nixon and Chou in one of their private meetings. Kissinger and Qiao Guanhua also face each other across the table

A scene from *The Red Army Detachment of Women*, one of Jiang Qing's revolutionary opera/ballets, during a special performance for the Americans

Nixon and Jiang Qing at *The Red Army Detachment of Women*

The President and Mrs Nixon and their party on the Great Wall

Pat Nixon had her own itinerary of visits to communes, hospitals and schools. Here she watches a student singing, presumably a revolutionary song

Pat Nixon admiring a panda at the Beijing Zoo. The Chinese have used gifts of pandas for centuries to foster their foreign relations

Nixon held an impromptu press conference outside his villa at Hangzhou
and then posed with the journalists

Air Force One brings Nixon back to Andrews Air Force Base near Washington
for a triumphal homecoming

President, I have not said this before but I think if we get this thing working, we will end Vietnam this year.' After his first two visits to China, Kissinger remained optimistic. He had been cautious, he told Nixon on the eve of the President's trip, not to embarrass Chou by asking too openly for his assistance. 'Nevertheless, from July onward the two key issues in our dialogue have been Taiwan and Indochina, and they contain an inherent *quid pro quo*. Only we can help them concerning Taiwan; and they can help in Indochina. Accordingly, I have indirectly but consistently linked these two in my talks with Chou.' He was sure, Kissinger went on, that the Chinese had already spoken forcefully to the North Vietnamese.[3]

As Nixon went over the briefing notes Kissinger had prepared, he jotted down his own thoughts on how he would stress the importance of the United States getting out of Indochina with the Chinese.

1. Helps on Taiwan troop removal
2. Reduces Soviet hand there
3. Reduces irritant to our relations
4. Gets us out – gives them a fair chance

While the Chinese certainly understood how important ending the Vietnam war was to the Americans (Kissinger and Nixon told them so repeatedly), they denied that it was important to China and firmly refused to be drawn in to helping to settle the conflict. While the Chinese had been made nervous by the American presence in South Vietnam, the fact that, in the early 1970s, the Americans were finding it difficult to withdraw left a bargaining chip on the table for China as it negotiated with them over Taiwan.[4] Furthermore, China – so Mao certainly insisted – was the centre of world revolution. North Vietnam was part of the worldwide struggle against imperialism and had to be supported.

'We have had no military advisers,' said Chou mendaciously, the first time he met Kissinger. 'They were only to build roads.' In fact the Chinese had been supporting the North Vietnamese Communists and then the Viet Cong in South Vietnam ever since the start of the 1950s, first in the war against the French and then against the Americans. The Chinese government itself calculated that its aid amounted to some $20 billion between 1950 and 1975, when the fighting finally ended with the fall of Saigon. China sent hundreds of thousands of guns, millions of bullets and shells, uniforms, boots, even mosquito netting. It also sent military missions and troops, some 320,000 of them in the late 1960s. True, Chinese soldiers did build roads, but they also manned anti-aircraft guns and ground-to-air missiles. The presence of so many Chinese troops also freed up North Vietnamese to fight the South Vietnamese and American forces.[5]

Propaganda from both Hanoi and Beijing talked about the relationship between the Chinese and the North Vietnamese as being that between the rear and the front lines or between the lips and the teeth. The lips, however, did not always cover the teeth properly and the teeth sometimes quietly bit the lips. Communist brotherhood, just as in the case of the relationship between the Soviet Union and the People's Republic of China, was not enough to paper over deep cultural and historical differences. China and Vietnam have had a long and complicated relationship which goes back many centuries. To the Chinese, with their self-centred view of the world, the Vietnamese were younger brothers, the 'half-cooked' as one expression had it, who had not yet become thoroughly civilized. While the Vietnamese absorbed much from Chinese civilization, they also resented their great meddlesome neighbour to the north. In 111 BC, the Chinese conquered the northern part of Vietnam and remained in possession for a thousand years, until a revolution led by two formidable sisters liberated it. Chou's frequent reminders that the new China was not responsible for the imperialist sins of the old dynasties and his gesture of laying wreaths on the sisters' graves was not enough to reassure the Vietnamese.

The Chinese Communists, for all their rhetoric about international revolution, tended to look out for China's interests first. In 1954, because China was apprehensive that the conflict in Vietnam might draw it into a major war with the United States, Chou En-lai pressured the Vietnamese Communists to come to terms with the French and accept the establishment of Laos and Cambodia as neutral countries and the temporary division of Vietnam. The Vietnamese agreed, but it rankled ever after. When the United States, the leading imperialist power, got bogged down in Vietnam in the mid-1960s, the Chinese encouraged the Vietnamese Communists to fight on, partly because Mao needed something to radicalize the Chinese people as he launched the Cultural Revolution, partly because a settlement might leave the Soviet Union, which was becoming the more important patron of North Vietnam, too strong. North Vietnam tried to steer a course between its two difficult patrons but, from time to time, when, for example, it openly backed the Soviet invasion of Czechoslovakia in 1968, it showed which camp it was favouring.[6]

When the North Vietnamese decided in 1968 to start peace talks with the United States, Chou told them that they were being 'too fast and too hurried'. And the criticisms kept coming as the talks moved very slowly ahead. The North Vietnamese were showing the white flag by even agreeing to talk; at the very least, they should have insisted on a full halt to American bombing, not a partial one; and they should never have accepted the 'puppet regime' of South Vietnam as a participant in the talks. At a reception to celebrate the anniversary of Vietnam's independence, Chou took the opportunity to say that the North Vietnamese were bound to win the war, if only they would fight on. Tensions also grew over Laos and Cambodia, where both North Vietnam and China manoeuvred to get hold of the local Communist forces and so extend their own influence.[7]

Chou hinted at the differences in his first conversation with Nixon ('the ideology of Vietnam, too, may not necessarily be completely the same as ours'), but neither Nixon nor Kissinger seems to have been aware of the potential for China and North Vietnam to fall out. Both men preferred to believe that China was capable of bringing the Vietnamese Communists into line if it chose. Shortly before Nixon left for China in 1972, the Americans found out that Le Duc Tho, North Vietnam's chief negotiator at the Paris talks, was going to be in Beijing at the same time. General Walters, who managed the secret channel through Paris to Beijing, sent a message to ask whether the Chinese would arrange a meeting between Nixon and Le Duc Tho. A brusque refusal came back: the Americans and the Vietnamese should settle their own affairs.[8]

This should not have come as a surprise, because Chou had made it amply clear in his discussions with Kissinger in 1971 and later with Haig in January 1972 that China did not want to get involved and that, moreover, it continued to support North Vietnam. At their very first meeting in July 1971, Chou laid out China's position and he never subsequently deviated from it. Like all peoples, the Vietnamese must choose their own political system and, he said pointedly, 'So long as no foreign force interferes in that area, then the issue is solved.' The United States, he went on, must withdraw all its troops and all its military installations. Moreover it should end its support for the Thieu government in South Vietnam and that of Lon Nol in Cambodia. As long as the war continued, China would keep on supporting the heroic people of Vietnam, and those of Cambodia and Laos as well.[9]

Chou could not resist providing his customary history lessons. From Truman onwards, he told the Americans, their presidents had meddled in the affairs of Vietnam and the other countries of Indochina. China, he said blandly and untruthfully, never attempted to influence the internal affairs of its neighbours. The United States had broken many promises along the way, including the one to respect the agreements reached at Geneva in 1954. The infamous Dulles had refused to hold the elections scheduled for 1956. 'This was false, dirty, what Dulles did,' said Chou, striking the table with his hand, in what Kissinger felt was a genuine display of emotion.[10]

Nevertheless, Kissinger drew surprisingly optimistic conclusions: Chou, he told Nixon after his first visit, understood the linkage the Americans were making between Taiwan and Indochina and did not object to it. On his last day in Beijing in July 1971, Kissinger claimed, Chou had talked about Indochina in 'an astonishingly sympathetic and open manner' and hinted that the United States would find North Vietnam more generous than expected. It may have helped that, in their talks, Kissinger had made some significant concessions. 'If there are no negotiations,' he had assured Chou at their first meeting, 'we will eventually withdraw, unilaterally.' He also showed a willingness to jettison the government of South Vietnam. 'Our position is not to maintain any particular government in South Vietnam.' The United States could not, of course, take part in overthrowing its former allies. 'If the government is as unpopular as you seem to think, then the quicker our forces are withdrawn the quicker it will be overthrown.' Once the United States had gone, Kissinger said, it would not intervene whatever happened. This was certainly not the public position of the United States. In an address to the nation a few months before Kissinger's secret trip, Nixon had said that the United States should not announce that it would pull out no matter what North Vietnam did. 'We would have thrown away our principal bargaining counter to win the release of American prisoners of war, we would remove the enemy's strongest incentive to end the war sooner by negotiation, and we will have given enemy commanders the exact information they need to marshal their attacks against our remaining forces at their most vulnerable time.' Moreover the United States had an obligation to the people of South Vietnam. 'Shall we leave in a way that gives the South Vietnamese a reasonable chance to survive as a free people? My plan will end American involvement in a way that would provide that chance.'[11]

Kissinger left Beijing confidently expecting that Chou was going to put some pressure on the North Vietnamese to come to terms with the Americans. In fact, shipments of weapons from China to North Vietnam were already going up sharply (as North Vietnam later said, 'to cover up their betrayal and to appease the Vietnamese people's indignation'). Chou made his trip to Hanoi right after Kissinger left, to brief the North Vietnamese and to reassure them that China's commitment to their struggle was as strong as ever. At some point during the year, he also told a leading North Vietnamese Communist that China intended to press the Americans to withdraw their forces completely and by a fixed date. 'If they do not comply we will fight hard.' If Nixon was not sincere in saying that he wanted to get out of Vietnam, China would be able to expose his 'deceptive schemes'.[12]

China found itself in an awkward position. It could not, for the sake of its revolutionary credentials, openly abandon North Vietnam but it was finding its small, recalcitrant ally an increasing liability. In December 1971, Chou spoke relatively frankly to a Chinese Communist Party meeting. Of course, he said, China remained committed to supporting Vietnam, Laos and Cambodia in their struggle against American imperialism. 'But, for the present, it is not appropriate to praise Vietnam excessively; we should treat her as we do the other two nations.' In the end, the nations of Indochina had to settle their own issues. North Vietnam was nervous about Nixon's visit, Chou went on, even though the Chinese had explained why it was necessary. 'If she cannot figure it out for the moment, just let her watch the development of the truth.'[13]

The North Vietnamese leaders, in shock at the news of the sudden breakthrough in Sino-American relations, were not to be consoled. 'Vietnam is our country, not yours,' one exclaimed to Chou. 'You have no right to say anything about it; you have no right to discuss this issue with the United States!' Kissinger's visit had come at a particularly bad time because their front organization in South Vietnam had shortly before issued a programme which was designed to appeal to American public opinion with a call to end the war and allow democracy and self-determination for the people of Vietnam. In the general enthusiasm with which the announcement of Kissinger's visit was received, the programme's impact was blunted. The Hanoi newspapers did not mention the news that Nixon was going to visit China for months. In Paris, the chief negotiator from North Vietnam complained about Nixon's 'perfidious maneuver' to divide socialist nations from each other.[14]

The day that Nixon arrived in Beijing, the Chinese embassy in Hanoi had its customary spring party. To the surprise of the Chinese officials not a single North Vietnamese came. Another Chinese friend from Indochina also showed his displeasure. Prince Sihanouk of Cambodia, whose government had been overthrown by forces backed by the United States, could not bear to remain in Beijing while Nixon was there. He left his comfortable villa in the Diaoyutai for Hanoi and did not return until Nixon had gone.[15]

Although Nixon barely touched on Vietnam in his opening remarks on 22 February, Chou homed in on the issue at once. Nixon had talked about the whole world; he, Chou, preferred to deal with the areas, close at hand, that mattered most to China. He urged the United States to get out of Indochina and quickly. 'As to how to resolve this issue I can't say, since we do not take part in the negotiations nor do we want to take part.' Nixon tried to persuade Chou that American intentions to withdraw were sincere and honourable but that the obstacle was the North Vietnamese, who were refusing to negotiate in good faith. If Hanoi remained obdurate, Nixon warned Chou, when the subject came up again two days later, the United States might have to step up the war. He would understand, Nixon added, if China had to react. He also tried to put pressure on Chou by pointing out that he and the Republicans would be in trouble if the

Democrats were able to say that the United States had compromised on Taiwan but gained no concessions in return from the Chinese on Vietnam. Nixon urged the Chinese to use their influence with Hanoi.[16]

Chou, as he had with Kissinger, refused to commit himself to helping the United States. China, he repeated, when he and Nixon returned to the subject of Indochina two days later, must support its friends, even, and this was a prescient observation on Chou's part, if the peoples of Indochina embarked on wars among themselves after the Americans had left. Whatever occurred would not be the fault of China, which only wanted peace and tranquillity in the region. If North Vietnam was expanding into Cambodia and Laos, he said, ignoring the long history of Vietnamese expansion into its neighbours' territory, this was only because of its need to counter the United States. Now there was also the danger that 'a certain big power' might try to move in to set up a sphere of influence. (Indeed Alexander Haig firmly maintained after his trip to China in January 1972 that the Chinese had hinted to him that they would prefer the United States to remain in South Vietnam as a counter to the Soviet Union.)[17]

'The channel of negotiations should not be closed,' was the most Chou would say. 'We can only go so far,' he added. 'We cannot meddle into their affairs.' China would not negotiate on behalf of the peoples of Indochina. Nixon was forced to recognize that, as with the Soviet Union, linkage did not always work: 'what the Prime Minister is telling us is that he cannot help us in Vietnam'. Chou underlined the message on 28 February as Nixon was preparing to leave China. 'We have no right to negotiate for them. This I have said repeatedly. This is our very serious stand.'[18]

The mere fact that Nixon went to China, though, did help the United States. The North Vietnamese were obliged to recognize that China placed a high priority on enhancing its new relationship with the United States. When Chou flew to Hanoi in March 1972 to brief the North Vietnamese on the Nixon visit, he told them, 'if the problem of Indochina is not solved, it will be impossible to realize the normalization of China–U.S. relations'. Although he also reassured them that China intended to continue its support for North Vietnam, his North Vietnamese comrades got the message. 'Now that Nixon has talked with you,' said the party secretary, Le Duan, 'they will soon hit us even harder.' The Americans did indeed hit hard that spring; in retaliation for a major North Vietnamese attack in the South, American planes bombed the North and mined Hanoi's harbour of Haiphong. China criticized the United States publicly and continued to send large amounts of aid to North Vietnam but, through one of Kissinger's private channels, made it clear that it still wanted to proceed with normalizing relations. The Chinese also encouraged both the United States and North Vietnam to bring the Paris peace talks to a conclusion. Why not let South Vietnam's President Thieu participate in the provisional coalition government for the South, Mao suggested to the North Vietnamese? Once the American troops had gone, they were unlikely to come back. 'After rest and reorganization, you can fight again to reach the final victory.'[19]

That is in effect what happened. On 27 January 1973, Kissinger and Le Duc Tho, his opposite number in Paris, signed a peace agreement which brought America's Vietnam war to an end. Both men subsequently shared the Nobel Peace Prize, but the peace lasted only until the spring of 1975 when North Vietnam's armies, in violation of the agreements, swept down on the South. Saigon fell in April and Vietnam was finally reunited. In the same month, the Khmer Rouge, now independent of what had once been a Vietnamese-dominated Indochinese Communist Party, swept out of the jungles in Cambodia to seize the capital Phnom Penh. In Beijing, a frail Mao welcomed Pol Pot with maudlin enthusiasm. 'You have achieved in one stroke', he told him, 'what we failed [to achieve] with all our masses.'[20] Pol Pot, who already had his own hideous and utopian plans for Cambodia, needed no encouragement. He restarted Cambodia's calendar at Year Zero and did his best, through mass murder and brutality, to transform Cambodian society into his own bizarre vision of Communism. At the end of 1975, Laos fell to the Pathet Lao, a Communist party backed by the Soviet Union.

The peace and tranquillity that Chou had claimed to wish for Indochina did not come about immediately. Outside powers, this time predominantly the Soviet Union and the People's Republic of China, continued to meddle in its affairs. Vietnam and Laos moved increasingly into the Soviet camp and Cambodia, now renamed Kampuchea, gravitated towards China. Pleading poverty, the Chinese cut their aid to Vietnam back sharply. Yet they managed to find substantial amounts for Kampuchea. Almost immediately Vietnam and Kampuchea clashed over disputed territory, and in 1978 Vietnam invaded Kampuchea and installed its own puppet government. The Vietnamese occupation lasted for ten years, until 1991. Relations between China and Vietnam also went from bad to worse and, in 1979, Chinese troops invaded Vietnam to teach it, so China said, a lesson. History and longstanding cultural differences and more contemporary disputes about such issues as borders all contributed, as they had done in the case of China and the Soviet Union, to the triumph of national interests over Communist internationalism.

17

Haldeman's Masterpiece

'THE CHINA TRIP was Bob Haldeman's masterpiece, his Sistine Chapel,' said a member of the White House staff. The handshakes, the glasses raised in toasts, the American flag flying in Beijing; Nixon with Mao, Nixon on the Great Wall, at the Forbidden City or in the Great Hall of the People; Mrs Nixon at a model farm, in a kitchen, kindergarten or factory. The images flowed back to the United States, targeted for prime-time evening television. It was a presidential election year at home and Haldeman wanted to make sure that Nixon shone out as the great leader and statesman while the Democratic candidates beat each other up in the primaries. The American press corps joked about Nixon's primary being in Beijing. The stage management of the trip was superb, and it was obsessive in its attention to detail. The advance parties had checked out virtually every site Nixon would visit, paced out the steps he might take and planned every camera angle.[1]

In his conversations with Chou, Nixon was loftily dismissive about publicity. 'I do not believe', he said, as he told Chou about the American musk oxen, 'in making a public spectacle of a state gift.' And he was, typically, rude about the American press. As he arrived at Nixon's guesthouse for their talks one morning, Chou asked the waiting crowd of journalists if they were enjoying their time in China. 'Better than they deserve,' said Nixon in a loud whisper. Yet, every morning while he was in China, Nixon pored over the detailed summaries of the press coverage back home – the hours of television and radio and the stories in the big national papers as well as the small local ones. The most important thing, as Nixon knew well, was the image he was projecting; as Haldeman put it in his diary, 'on TV the American President received by a million Chinese is worth a hundred times the effect of a communiqué'. There were bound to be some obliging Chinese masses, he and the President thought. Kissinger, in the preparations for the trip, had urged that Nixon's trip not be a media circus, staged for the American public on the eve of the new presidential campaign. It would, he pointed out, hurt the image of the United States in the wider world. 'Pretty hard to argue it,' wrote Haldeman, 'except that from our viewpoint, and the P. concurs in this, we need maximum coverage in order to get the benefit from it, especially in the short term.'[2]

Nixon had found the perfect stage manager. A tireless worker, Haldeman was about order and control, starting with himself. He did not drink or smoke, and, as a Christian Scientist, did not believe in illness. Although he been a Republican since his college days at Stanford and had worked on Nixon's campaigns in California, he had no political ambitions of his own. He served Nixon with ruthless efficiency. As chief of staff, he kept the President's schedule. The Berlin Wall, his enemies sometimes called him and Ehrlichman, because he was the President's gatekeeper, but he was more of a buffer between the world and a man who was uncomfortable dealing with strangers or with difficult confrontations. (He also knew when not to pay attention to Nixon's wilder orders.) Haldeman's failing, in Kissinger's view, was that he saw everything from a public relations perspective. From his days as a successful advertising man in Los Angeles, where he had looked after, among others, the Sani-flush and the Walt Disney accounts, Haldeman knew how to sell an image. Like Nixon himself, he believed that virtually every political problem could be solved by getting out the story the White House wanted. Like Nixon, too, he despised the press. During that week in China, there were no daily press briefings and virtually no hard news. 'Never before', complained John Chancellor from NBC news, 'had an American President travelled abroad in peacetime under such a cloak of secrecy.'[3]

The Chinese leaders used their own press coverage to accustom their people to the great shift in China's foreign policy. The authorities had already let the news of the Kissinger visits out; once Nixon had met with Mao, the newspapers and Beijing television and radio filled up with stories and pictures. The Chinese also did their best to manage the American coverage. The American journalists had

Chinese helpers (who were also minders) constantly at their sides. The hotel staff went through the waste baskets to make sure that nothing was thrown out by mistake and carefully laid out paperclips, empty toothpaste tubes, used razorblades and carbon paper. At factories, managers made prepared speeches filled with impressive statistics and praise for Chairman Mao's thought but were suddenly shy when it came to answering questions. The same little girl presented flowers to Pat Nixon in each city on the tour. When the Nixon party visited the Ming tombs, they saw carefully staged scenes: children, with touches of rouge on their faces, skipping; families dressed in bright new clothes having picnics and listening to revolutionary songs on their transistor radios; groups of friends playing cards, apparently oblivious to the bitter cold. At the end of the Nixon visit, a sharp-eyed Canadian journalist noticed, a party official marched around with a large bag to collect the radios. 'Your press correspondents have pointed this out to us,' Chou later admitted to the Americans in what amounted to a public self-criticism. 'We admit that this was wrong.'[4]

The Chinese laid on a packed programme, designed to show both the New China with its factories and schools, and the glories of the Old. The American journalists grumbled at the lack of hard news about the conversations between Nixon and Chou, and at the lack of contact with ordinary Chinese. Their reports, especially those by conservatives such as William Buckley, took on a sardonic edge. Nixon worried that his hosts might be upset by criticisms. Haldeman reassured him; it would only show the Chinese authorities what sort of problems his administration faced back home. As the relentless pace of sightseeing went on, the American journalists also grew increasingly tired. The press were working without their usual backup staff; network executives, who had got themselves listed as ordinary reporters, found themselves pressed into service to carry lights. Moreover they were having to stay up late into the night to file their stories back to the United States. Dirck Halstead, a photographer from Associated Press, found he was managing on bourbon and about one hour's sleep a night. His Chinese minder, who had to stay with him, was in despair. 'Please, Mr Dirck, you must get some sleep! You will die if you don't!'[5]

Nixon regarded sightseeing as a waste of time and, as he had done throughout his career, set his wife Pat to work. As he put it bluntly to Haldeman, she could come along as a 'prop' to provide material for the press while he, Nixon, had his conversations with Chou. Mrs Nixon dutifully prepared for the trip. Her briefing book provided her with summaries of the key points of Chinese history and culture, and she read some of Mao's poetry and the selected quotations in the Little Red Book. Pat Buchanan, then a speechwriter in the White House, sent her some sample questions and answers for exchanges with the press. If she was asked about her role, Buchanan suggested, she should say that while she was out meeting the Chinese people, the President was devoting his time to the all-important work of meeting the Chinese leaders – and that she enjoyed being part of the President's team.[6]

Pat Nixon had always been a good team player, from the moment she had to take on responsibility for looking after her brothers. Her mother died when she was fourteen, her father four years later. 'As a youngster life was kind of sad,' she once confided, 'so I had to cheer everybody up. I learned to be that kind of person.' She worked her way through university and took a job teaching in Whittier high school where she met the young lawyer Richard Nixon. Marriage to him gave her much: two daughters whom she adored, position, wealth and finally the White House. Whether she wanted it all is another matter.

In the early years of Nixon's career, she continued to hope that he would throw it all up and return to California to practise law. Occasionally Nixon made her promises that he would, but the pull of politics was always too strong. When he decided, against her wishes, to run for the vice-presidential nomination in 1952, she heard about it first on television. She dutifully campaigned, as she always did and always would. 'I don't know anyone,' said a former teacher of Nixon's, 'who has so disciplined herself to endure a life she does not like.' Pat Nixon never allowed herself to be sick and never complained about the endless days travelling and the nights in hotel rooms. Her husband was a devoted but absent father and she brought their two daughters up largely on her own. She took all her duties, as a Senator's wife, then as a Vice-President's, seriously and sometimes to the point of obsession. When she became the First Lady she insisted, as she had always done, on answering every letter she received with a personal reply. Some of Nixon's staff thought her desperately lonely and admired her stoicism; others, like Haldeman, found her irritating and impossibly stubborn.[7]

Nixon once dictated some notes about his wife to his devoted secretary, Rose Mary Woods. (He was hoping they might be useful for an article in a woman's magazine.) 'She has', he said proudly, 'great character and determination and is not the type of person who makes a fool of herself in public in order to get attention.' Nixon, and it reflects his generation as much as his own reserve, never showed his wife much affection in front of others. Indeed he ignored her much of the time. In the 1968 campaign, Ehrlichman noticed, Nixon sat at the front of their aircraft, while Pat and the girls were at the back, until the next landing. 'Day after day, four, five, or six times a day, the family would be assembled and disassembled, along with the camera tripods and loudspeakers.' By the time he was president, Nixon was spending more and more time apart from his wife; for relaxation, he went off with his male friends such as Bebe Rebozo and Robert Abplanalp. In Washington, there were stories of Pat Nixon's anger with Nixon, hints that she had long since ceased to care for him. The first time Kissinger met Mrs Nixon, he praised her husband immoderately. 'Haven't you seen through him yet?' she asked. Nixon's enemies used his marriage as yet another example of his deformed character. He was, so it was said, incapable of human affection. 'They tried to love each other,' said Harry Truman's daughter Margaret, 'but the gulf remained, a kind of black hole that sucked into it the good feelings that might have made Nixon a more human, more stable President.' She was seeing them from the outside, as most people did. Perhaps, in the end, all that can be said is that they had a working partnership and that it took more of a toll on Pat Nixon than on her husband.[8]

On the China trip, she worked as hard as always. She inspected the kitchens at the Beijing Hotel. The food, she said politely, looked good enough to eat. How do the workers make their glass flowers, she asked at a factory? 'Can they just take a little bit of this and a little bit of this?' The manager explained that they had to follow a design. She watched acupuncture on an elderly patient, hugged children in a hospital. When her guides lauded the leadership of Chairman Mao, she smiled blandly and said, 'Oh, yes, I'm acquainted with his philosophy.'

She shopped for souvenirs, brocade for the girls and white silk pyjamas with green piping for Nixon. The staff in the Friendship Store, assuming that the wife of the American President must be another acquisitive capitalist like Imelda Marcos who had recently been in Beijing, showed her an expensive piece of jewellery. She hastily put it down before she could be photographed. Occasionally another Pat Nixon surfaced. At the Evergreen People's Commune, she wondered what breed of pigs she was seeing. 'Male chauvinist,' snapped back an American woman journalist. Everyone, including Mrs Nixon, laughed.[9]

On Tuesday afternoon, she toured the Summer Palace, the extraordinary collection of pavilions, lakes and gardens, built at the end of the nineteenth century by the tyrannical Dowager Empress who had controlled China in the dying days of the Qing dynasty. That evening, with Nixon, she met China's modern empress when Mao's wife Jiang Qing laid on a performance of one of her new proletarian operas. Chou En-lai had obliquely warned Nixon that morning about what to expect. 'It was difficult to combine classical ballet with revolutionary themes.' Like everyone in China, Chou was very careful about what he said about Jiang Qing. As she targeted first one, then another, of China's top leaders in the factional fights during the Cultural Revolution, he adeptly switched his support to her.[10]

Humourless, self-righteous, capricious and vengeful, Jiang was a dangerous enemy. The Cultural Revolution had brought her out of the shadows into the centre of power. She and her fellow radicals, many of them, like her, from Shanghai, had answered Mao's call to rid China of its old culture and to attack all those counter-revolutionaries who stood in the way. Jiang Qing and her closest associates (they were later tried and condemned as the Gang of Four) enthusiastically spearheaded the purging of the Communist Party and the evisceration of China's cultural and educational institutions. They burned books and banned China's traditional art forms as well as most foreign culture. Mozart and Beethoven were too bourgeois and so were many foreign instruments. (The piano, though, was spared because Jiang Qing had played as a girl.) Chinese film-making came to a halt as directors tried, in vain, to meet the changeable standards laid down by the revolutionaries.

When the Nixons met her, she looked like a severe governess or prison warder, but when she had first caught Mao's eye in the late 1930s in Yan'an she was a beautiful and charming young actress. Jiang Qing's beauty and determination had helped her survive a difficult life. She was born to a small businessman and his concubine in Shandong province, the birthplace of Confucius, on the eve of the First World War. Her mother eventually fled from a household where she was despised and beaten, and eked out a living as a domestic servant and possibly, so Jiang Qing's enemies later said, as a prostitute. The young Jiang frequently went hungry and was often left alone while her mother was out on mysterious errands. At her primary school, where, she said, a few poor children were admitted for show, she was teased by the other children for her poverty. She acquired a lifelong resentment of the upper classes and a contempt for traditional Chinese values.

By the time she was sixteen, at the start of the 1930s, Jiang Qing had discovered the theatre. It was an exciting time as the Chinese grappled with new and revolutionary ideas and she found herself drawn into the world of the left-wing intellectuals in Shanghai and Beijing. As her private life went from one romantic drama to another, her acting career slowly developed. Her most famous role, and one which she remembered fondly, was Nora in Ibsen's *A Doll's House*. At some point, or so she always claimed, she became a secret member of the Communist Party. She was also briefly arrested by the Guomindang police in Shanghai. Stories circulated for years that she had gained her release in return for providing the names of Communists.[11]

By 1937, when the Japanese attacked Shanghai, Jiang's career was stalled and her latest and perhaps most serious relationship had just ended. She had no reason to stay and, as a known left-winger, every reason to flee, so along with many others she decided to head for the Communist enclave in Yan'an. By comparison with the hardened revolutionary women who had survived the Long March, Jiang was fresh and glamorous. She threw herself in Mao's way, sitting enthralled at the front row of his lectures and sending him admiring notes. 'I worshiped Mao,' she told an American academic years later. Mao responded with enthusiasm, inviting her back to his cave in the hillside.

She rapidly became a fixture in his life. Mao was already estranged from his second wife, but even the Chairman could not simply put one wife aside and take another. The private lives of Communists belonged to the party and the party was puritanical. He Zizhen, Mao's wife, had endured much, the Long March, the repeated pregnancies, the forced abandonment of her children as the Communists fled, and she had many supporters, among them the other senior wives such as Chou's. When Mao, who was infatuated with Jiang, insisted, a compromise was reached. He could divorce and remarry, but his new wife had to stay out of politics. Jiang deeply resented the prohibition and those she felt were responsible for it. The Cultural Revolution gave her ample opportunity for revenge.[12]

The marriage was only happy for a few years. The couple fought, among other things, over Jiang's decision to get herself sterilized after she bore Mao a daughter. Her health deteriorated and, in 1956, she was treated in the Soviet Union for cervical cancer. When Mao resumed his womanizing, without bothering to conceal it from her, she was deeply hurt. Mao's doctor once discovered her weeping on a bench outside her husband's quarters in the Zhongnanhai. She begged Li not to say anything. 'Just as no one,' she said, 'Stalin included, could win in a political battle with her husband, so no woman could ever win the battle for his love.' By the end of the 1950s Mao and Jiang lived increasingly separate lives. Understandably, perhaps, she became even more sensitive to slights than before and grew obsessed with her health. Dr Li was constantly called in to examine her for largely imaginary illnesses. When she could not sleep, it was because someone had tampered with her pills and when she found her bath too hot it was a plot by her nurses to harm her. Li thought her main problem was that she was bored and lonely. She was also terrified that Mao would abandon her as he had abandoned his other wives. Mao tried in vain to reassure her. She was useful to him as a secretary and he valued her devotion and her complete dependence on him.[13]

Mao needed someone like Jiang to make his Cultural Revolution and she leaped at the opportunity he offered her. 'I was Chairman Mao's dog,' she famously said when she was on trial after his death. 'When he said "Bite," I bit.' Her health miraculously improved. She revelled in her new power and her moment in the sun, the adoring

crowds, the banners with her sayings, the army generals who obse-
quiously asked for her guidance. She dashed about the country in her
private plane with its silk sheets to stir up revolution and held herself
up as the model of the new proletarian culture. Top officials in Beijing
got urgent calls in the middle of the night to stand by for a gift from
Jiang; a basket of turnips she had grown arrived in a special car. With
an astonishing lack of self-awareness, she invited Roxanne Witke, a
young American academic, to watch her at work in her lavish private
garden in Canton as she solemnly laid out specimens of her orchids.[14]

Those who had slighted her in the past now paid a heavy price.
Jiang turned the Red Guards loose on Liu Shaoqi's wife, Wang
Guangmei, one of the party elders who had relegated her to a minor
role in Yan'an. Wang was accused of the crime of dressing like a
bourgeois by wearing flowered dresses and a necklace on state visits
abroad; she was paraded in front of jeering crowds in an evening dress
and a necklace made of gilded ping-pong balls. Rivals, even colleagues, from Jiang's Shanghai days, were paraded through the streets
in dunces' caps. Shanghai police records were purged and acquaintances from that period who might have kept incriminating material
about her affairs or her dealings with the Guomindang police had
their houses ransacked by people who claimed to be Red Guards;
every scrap of paper, including a child's school notes, was carted off to
Jiang to be destroyed.[15]

Jiang condemned China's film industry as steeped in old-fashioned
and incorrect values. It shut down because she was too busy to
come up with clear guidelines for the sorts of films she wanted. She
did, however, have more success in the field of Chinese opera. The
traditional operas, with their plots revolving around mythical beings
and great historical figures of the past and their classical singing and
dancing, were plainly retrograde. Under her guidance, six model
revolutionary operas were created; they were the only ones performed
all over China until Mao's death. It was one of these that the Nixon
party was to see.

Jiang was determined that the evening would be a success. She sent
off Qiao Guanhua, the Deputy Foreign Minister, to brief the Nixons
on what they were about to see. She also agonized over whether
to wear a dress. In the China of 1972 dresses were frowned upon as

274

bourgeois, while shapeless suits were good proletarian wear. In the end, she was wearing a suit when she welcomed the Nixon party to the special theatre in the Great Hall of the People. Nixon found her 'unpleasantly abrasive and aggressive' as she shot questions at him. Why had Jack London committed suicide? Why hadn't Nixon come to China before now? Nixon had a question of his own: who had written the opera? It was 'created by the masses', said Jiang proudly. As she later told Roxanne Witke, 'one could not have expected him to grasp the magnitude of her personal responsibility for the creation of a new model theater for the nation'.[16]

Perhaps by design, the opera – *The Red Detachment of Women* – was about Hainan Island, which had been reunited, as Taiwan had still not been, with Communist China. Interpreters whispered the plot in the Americans' ears but it was not difficult to follow, because the good characters – peasants, Communists, guerrillas – bounded on looking noble and upright while the villains – landlords and their minions – slunk on with averted faces. In spite of the propaganda, Nixon found it an enjoyable spectacle. 'This is certainly the equal of any ballet that I have seen, in terms of production,' he told American reporters. 'It was', thought Haldeman who had also enjoyed the performance, 'rather an odd sight to see the P. clapping at the end for this kind of thing, which would have been horrifying at home, but it all seems to fit together somehow, here.' Ron Walker, the White House advance man, took some Chinese records home and used to entertain his friends with spirited imitations of the dancing until he fell and had to have knee surgery.[17]

It snowed that night and the next day, a Wednesday. The Americans watched with some amazement as thousands of ordinary citizens came out with shovels and brooms to clean the streets. That evening, the Chinese laid on another entertainment with table tennis and gymnastics, two sports at which they excelled. The crowd was made up largely of military and athletes, all dressed in coloured uniforms and seated in sections. They had been carefully briefed to applaud the Americans loudly as they came in. During the evening, as the lights played on each section, there were more loud cheers for the television cameras. Haldeman was deeply impressed by the organization.

Nixon told reporters the next day that he had never seen such athletes. 'Just superb.' In his diary, he struck a more sombre note: 'not only we but all the people of the world will have to make our very best effort if we are going to match the enormous ability, drive and discipline of the Chinese people'. The United States must take care to build a good relationship with China as it developed. 'Otherwise,' he later wrote, 'we will one day be confronted with the most formidable enemy that has ever existed in the history of the world.' That night, Nixon did not sleep well and got up at 5 a.m. to smoke a Great Wall cigar and jot down his thoughts about the trip.[18]

Nixon had tried to avoid sightseeing, but the Great Wall was too good a photo-opportunity to miss. Early on Thursday morning, when the Americans back home were settling down to their evening television, the Nixon party, accompanied by Chou and Marshal Ye, drove thirty-five miles to where the Wall swoops down north of Beijing. There are many myths about the Great Wall: that it is the only man-made structure that can be seen from the moon; that it was first built, all 4,000 miles of it, by the Qin Emperor in the second century BC; and that it existed down through time to hold off the barbarians who threatened the most sophisticated and advanced civilization in the world. Its mere existence, despite invasions and revolutions, is seen in China as a sign of the will of the Chinese people themselves to endure and triumph. It symbolizes, says a recent Chinese encyclopaedia, 'the great strength of the Chinese nation'. In reality, the Wall, which cannot be seen from the moon, was built piecemeal over the centuries, sometimes to protect China itself, but it was also built by warring kingdoms to defend themselves in the periods when China was not united, or as an aggressive move by Chinese rulers to stake out a claim in barbarian territory. In its early and greatest phase, the Tang dynasty did not bother with walls at all, preferring to reach out to the world and, if necessary, deal with threats through diplomacy or force. The section of the Wall that Nixon saw was built not by the Qin Emperor but a mere four hundred years ago under the Ming dynasty.[19]

The Wall near Beijing is still an extraordinary sight as it coils its way up and down the hills and Nixon had a marvellously clear day for his visit. He went hatless in spite of the cold, and his party, who felt obliged to follow his lead, shivered along as he climbed a short distance upwards. The bolder made snowballs and threw them into the valleys below. The American press corps swarmed around the President. Walter Cronkite hopped along as the electric socks he had brought against the cold gave him a series of shocks. The White House advance party had worked out the best sites for photographs and the live television cameras were already positioned on two of the Wall's towers. Nixon shook hands with all the Chinese present for the cameras. 'Imagine climbing all these mountains carrying stones,' he said to an American journalist. To Marshal Ye, he praised the architecture and said what a pity it was they did not have time to climb all the way up to the summit. 'Haven't we already had our summit meeting in Beijing?' Ye replied and quoted a line from Mao to the effect that you are not a real man until you get to the Great Wall. Ron Ziegler urged the reporters to ask Nixon for his impressions. 'I think that you would have to conclude', the President said solemnly, 'that this is a great wall and that it had to be built by a great people.' And, in words which have been repeated approvingly ever since in China, he added, 'A people who could build a wall like this certainly have a great past to be proud of and a people who have this kind of a past must also have a great future.'[20]

After fifteen minutes at the Wall, he headed off to another of China's architectural glories, the tombs of the Ming emperors with their great avenue of stone guardians and animals. Nixon, who was clearly bored with the whole expedition by this point, managed to summon up a few more thoughts for the journalists. The tombs were not that old in terms of China's thousands of years of history, he pointed out, but they were yet more evidence of the rich history of the Chinese people, 'a reminder that they are very proud in terms of cultural development and the rest'. It had been worth coming all the way from Washington to see the Wall and now the Ming tombs. Would he advise Americans to apply for tourist visas, a reporter asked? Nixon said he would. The journalists, who were desperate for hard news, fell on this titbit. Perhaps there had been some agreement reached on exchanges.[21]

That evening, Nixon who was already annoyed that Chou had suddenly added a Peking-duck dinner to the timetable, asked Haldeman and Kissinger to cut down on the time allocated for the Forbidden City the following morning. Perhaps they could also cut out some of the toasts at the remaining banquets. He was persuaded to back down on the latter when Kissinger pointed out that he would offend his Chinese hosts. On Friday morning, though, Nixon galloped through the Forbidden City on a shortened schedule in an hour and a half. He saw what he needed to, in Haldeman's view, and generated some more pictures and quotations. 'Give me a pair of those,' he said when he was shown earplugs that an emperor had worn to screen out criticisms. When Chou called his attention to a display of ancient eating utensils which included gold spoons, Nixon joked, for the benefit of the reporters, that he thought the Chinese only used chopsticks. 'How do you think we eat soup?' Chou retorted.[22]

By Friday, Nixon, who was still having trouble sleeping, was tired and grumpy. He grumbled to Haldeman about his problems and how nobody in the press understood him. He was also worried about the communiqué, which was still not settled, although Kissinger and his Chinese counterpart Qiao Guanhua had been working long hours on the wording. His own conversations with Chou were running out of steam because the two men had covered the main issues by now. When they met that afternoon for an hour, Nixon told Chou he was through talking. The two men chatted in a desultory way about Africa and the Middle East. Libya was a strange country, they agreed. Why, Chou wondered, was it not possible for Israel to return the occupied territories to the Arabs? It was very difficult, Nixon replied, but he would make sure that Kissinger kept the Chinese informed on the delicate negotiations he was conducting on that very subject.

Chou also took the opportunity to reiterate China's suspicions of the Soviet Union. While he still hoped that Sino-Soviet relations could be mended, he had to say that China would not negotiate under the threat of attack. It was curious, Chou thought, that the Soviets, who were so strong, seemed to have such a fear of China. 'Pathological,' Nixon agreed. When Nixon went to the Soviet Union for his summit meeting in May, Chou advised, he hoped that the President would make it clear that the United States and China were not colluding against the Soviet Union. Nixon assured Chou that he would. He had something to ask Chou. Would the Chinese consider releasing John Downey, a CIA pilot who had been shot down over

China twenty years previously? Downey's mother was old and sick. It might be possible, Chou said; it appeared that Downey had been behaving rather well recently. Downey was freed a year later and resumed his interrupted life, going to Harvard Law School and ending up a judge.[23]

Nixon excused himself as the hour went on. This was the night of his banquet for the Chinese, held in the Great Hall of the People, and he wanted to be present to receive his guests. Many of them were unable to decipher the invitations which the Americans had inadvertently printed in a classical script no longer used on the mainland. The Chinese provided the cooks but all the ingredients – from Florida oranges to California champagne – had been flown out from the United States. At each table there were packages of American cigarettes with the presidential seal and, much to the surprise of the Chinese, the inevitable health warning from the US Surgeon-General. Although a band played a cheerful selection of American tunes such as 'Billy Boy' and 'She'll be Coming Round the Mountain', the mood was subdued. Nixon, who always had trouble with social events even when they were important, sat silently, only rousing himself to talk to Chou when the cameras were on him. As one journalist said, it all seemed rather anti-climactic after the events of the week. Nixon, in his toast, praised the Great Wall and the Chinese people with their great past and their great future and said how, in their talks, he and Chou had begun to remove the wall between their two peoples. Two journalists from North Vietnam refused to raise their glasses. In his reply, Chou agreed with the President but said that there still were important differences in principle between the two sides. Rumours went round among the journalists that there was still trouble over the communiqué.[24]

18

Audience Reactions

WHILE AMERICAN AUDIENCES were watching Haldeman's spectacular from China, so were others, with reactions that ranged from Albania's outrage to Canada's approval. China's allies such as North Korea and North Vietnam, which were already tilting towards the Soviet camp, watched with alarm but muted their criticisms for fear of alienating their giant neighbour. In India Mrs Gandhi publicly warned the United States and China not to think they could collude in South Asia. Asian countries which had defence treaties with the United States – they included South Korea, Japan, Taiwan, Malaysia, Thailand, Singapore, the Philippines, New Zealand and Australia – wondered what the American commitment now meant. The head of Australia's foreign service wrote to his ambassador in the United States: 'the proposition that the United States is Australia's best friend does not any longer command general support'. The British, who had invested much in their 'special relationship' with the United States, were irritated at the way the Americans had kept them in the dark over the opening to China. The British Prime Minister, Edward Heath, felt particular hurt because he had assumed that he and Nixon had a good relationship. 'He never really recovered', said an American diplomat, 'from Nixon's not informing him on such major policy.' Heath from that point on invested more energy in improving Britain's relationship with the European Union.[1]

During Nixon's week in Beijing, Joseph Kraft, an American journalist, went with a Russian acquaintance to a reception at the Soviet embassy for Soviet Armed Forces Day. 'A sadder party there never was.' The Soviets were very apprehensive about the meaning of Nixon's trip. When Kraft told the ambassador that Nixon hoped that his visit to Beijing would improve the atmosphere at his forthcoming

Moscow summit, the ambassador was incredulous. 'We'll have to see about that.'[2]

The Soviets had been concerned ever since they had first got wind of contacts between the United States and the People's Republic after Nixon's election. The KGB, the Soviet secret police, had planned a campaign of disinformation to keep the Americans and the Chinese apart. At the news of the first armed clashes between Soviet and Chinese soldiers in March 1969, an 'emotional' Anatoly Dobrynin, the Soviet ambassador in Washington, had told Kissinger that they should all be worried about China. That autumn, Dobrynin had conveyed a warning from Brezhnev to Nixon: it would be a 'very grave miscalculation' if 'someone' in the United States were tempted to profit from the rift between China and the Soviet Union at the latter's expense. Dobrynin had also persistently and anxiously questioned Kissinger in their private meetings about what the Americans were up to. The Soviet press was full of dire warnings about an alliance between the Chinese and 'world imperialism'. As Kissinger commented in his memoirs, 'it was heavy-handed Soviet diplomacy that made us think about our opportunities'.[3]

For all their concern, the Soviets had not expected a sudden breakthrough in the Sino-American relationship. The United States and the People's Republic, so they thought, had been enemies for too long, and the war in Vietnam remained to keep them apart. As a result, when Nixon pressed for an early summit with Brezhnev the Soviets procrastinated. Nixon needed it more than they did, they assumed, because an improved relationship with the Soviet Union would help his chances of re-election. They also hoped, by withholding the summit, to get major concessions from the Americans on West Berlin (still an issue between East and West) and on SALT, the major arms-control talks going on in Geneva.

A month before his secret trip to China, Kissinger had a meeting with Dobrynin, who, yet again, was evasive on setting a date for a Soviet–American summit. 'It was comforting', thought Kissinger, 'to hold cards of which the other side was unaware.' As he was on his way towards China, Kissinger got word that the Soviets had postponed the summit yet again. That freed him up to press for an early meeting between Nixon and the Chinese leadership. When Chou expressed a desire that Nixon should come to China after he had been to Moscow, possibly because the Chinese did not want to anger the Soviets unnecessarily, Kissinger was able to explain that, if Nixon visited Beijing before Moscow, it was not the Americans' doing but the Soviets'.[4]

The announcement of Kissinger's secret trip and, even worse, that Nixon himself was going to visit China came as a complete shock to most of the top Soviet leadership. (Their knowledge of the world outside the Soviet Union, said Dobrynin pityingly, was understandably limited since it came mainly from the columns of *Izvestia* and *Pravda*.) The mood in the Kremlin, where suspicion and fear of China ran deep, was one of confusion and, indeed, almost hysteria. Initial comment in the Soviet press talked darkly about anti-Sovietism and hinted that somehow the Israeli lobby in the United States was pushing American policy towards a rapprochement with China. The official reaction was terse and warned the United States against using its new contacts against the Soviet Union. Georgi Arbatov, the Soviet Union's leading expert on North America, urged his superiors to remain calm. With their approval, he published an article which argued that an American–Chinese summit was nothing to worry about in itself as long as the Americans were also intending to improve their relations with other socialist countries. If the United States were willing to work on such issues as arms control and settling regional conflicts, then the opening to China was a good thing. The message, as was intended, was heard by the Americans – who had, in any case, no intention of alienating the Soviets, merely of pressuring them.[5]

On his return from China, Kissinger immediately called Dobrynin to pass on a message from Nixon to Brezhnev: the United States remained committed to improving the relationship between their two countries. Nixon's trip to China was not directed against any third country. A few days later, Kissinger invited Dobrynin to dinner at the White House to discuss his trip and its implications. Kissinger was reassuring: the Chinese, he said, not entirely truthfully, had said very little about the Soviet Union and appeared to be more worried about the Japanese. Dobrynin asked, 'almost plaintively' said Kissinger, whether Soviet dithering over their summit with Nixon had persuaded the United States to take the initiative towards China.

Kissinger did not answer directly but pointed out that the Soviet response to repeated American requests for a summit had been 'grudging and petty'. Dobrynin, who secretly agreed, was, in Kissinger's description for Nixon, 'almost beside himself with protestations of goodwill'. The Soviet leaders were very serious in wanting a meeting. Could it happen before Nixon went to Beijing? Kissinger was firm; the summits should take place in the order in which they were announced. The most that Dobrynin could get was an agreement that the announcement for the Moscow summit would be made before Nixon's trip to China.[6]

Although Nixon and Kissinger later claimed that the announcement of Kissinger's trip brought the Soviet Union into a more accommodating frame of mind in other areas, the evidence is mixed. The negotiations over West Berlin (primarily about its political and actual links to West Germany) were virtually concluded by the time Kissinger went to Beijing. The SALT negotiations were going to move ahead significantly after July 1971, culminating in the final treaty which was signed in Moscow in May 1972, but agreements on certain key areas had already been reached in the spring of 1971. The most that can be said, perhaps, is that the Soviet Union became more aware of the need to work with the United States and even more sensitive to perceived slights. When Nixon gave his toast at the opening banquet in Beijing, he referred to the United States and China together solving the world's problems. 'That cut to the quick,' Brezhnev's personal interpreter remembered. 'Where was the Soviet Union in this equation?'[7]

The Japanese were also shocked by the new direction in American foreign policy because it threatened a bargain Japan had made with the United States in the early 1950s. When Japan regained its independence in 1952 after the American occupation, it agreed to be a part of the American Cold War coalition in Asia, promising, for example, to sign a treaty with Chiang Kai-shek's government in Taiwan. It also accepted continued American control of the island of Okinawa and allowed American bases on its own islands. At the same time, Japan would renounce its militarist past. The new Japanese constitution of 1946 specifically ruled out the use of force to settle international disputes. In return, the United States guaranteed Japan's defence with the

Security Treaty and allowed Japanese industry access to American markets. Although China was a more natural market for Japan, the ruling political party, the Liberal Democrats, bowed to what they felt was inevitable, at least for the time being, and accepted American limitations on trade with China and an outright ban on recognizing it. Asakai Koichiro, the Japanese ambassador in Washington in the late 1950s, had a recurring nightmare, though, that one day he would wake up and find that the United States had reversed its policy on China without telling any of its allies.

By the end of the 1960s, Japan was much stronger and more confident than when the bargain with the United States had first been struck. Vietnam had shaken Japanese confidence in American power, and the American control of Okinawa was becoming an increasingly tricky issue for Japanese public opinion especially when there were, from time to time, highly publicized incidents of rape or brutality against Japanese by American servicemen. On the American side, Congress and the American public were going through one of their periodic fits of antipathy towards Japan. An American ally, no matter what its constitution said, should lift some of the burden from the American taxpayer and do more to defend itself. Not only that, Japanese manufactures, once a byword for shoddiness, were now cutting into American markets as American consumers snapped up well-made Japanese electronics and textiles.

Nixon quite liked Japan; he had visited there often and knew many of the leading Japanese politicians. He watched its dramatic recovery from defeat, though, with a mixture of admiration and apprehension. 'The Japanese are all over Asia like lice,' he told Edward Heath. 'What must be done is to make sure we have a home for them.' A Japan going off in its own direction, as it had done before the Second World War, could only be dangerous to its neighbours and to American interests.

Kissinger, with his focus on Europe and Soviet–American rivalry, had never had reason to know much about Japan. Although in his memoirs, which he wrote in the late 1970s, he waxed lyrical about its mist-covered mountains and green valleys and its complex and subtle inhabitants with their unique society, in the early 1970s he was capable of the crudest generalizations. 'The Japanese', he told Chou, 'are capable of sudden and explosive changes. They went from feudalism to emperor worship in two to three years. They went from emperor worship to democracy in three months.' Kissinger was also bored by Japanese issues. He is said to have described Japanese officials as 'little Sony salesmen'. Moreover, since neither he nor Nixon were interested in economics, a power whose chief strength lay in its economy rather than in its military did not strike them as needing to be taken seriously. And, with the Middle Kingdom beckoning, Japan seemed, if not expendable, certainly less important than it had once been. Lack of attention rather than positive malice explains much of what went wrong with American policy towards Japan in the first years of the Nixon presidency.[8]

Sato Eisaku, who was prime minister from 1964 to 1972, remained convinced that it was in Japan's best interests to foster the relationship with the United States and prepared to renew the Security Treaty for another ten years. Nixon, for his part, recognized that the status of Okinawa was an unnecessary irritant, and negotiations over its return to Japan started in 1969. It was agreed that the Americans could continue to have bases there. Two other issues, unfortunately, got mixed in: whether or not the United States could station nuclear weapons there (a very sensitive issue in the only country in the world to have suffered a nuclear attack) and textiles. Kissinger persuaded Nixon that the two could be profitably linked, with the Americans giving up the nuclear weapons in exchange for a voluntary Japanese quota on its textile exports to the United States.

The deal appeared to have been struck by the time Sato arrived in Washington in November 1969. The Japanese Prime Minister had also made an oral commitment, which he repeated in Washington, to accept the limits the Americans wanted on textiles. Nixon promised to return Okinawa by 1972 and to withdraw nuclear weapons from American bases, and Sato had agreed in a secret letter that the Americans could bring them back to Okinawa in an emergency. There is a curious story, still not completely verified, that Nixon also hinted that the United States would be understanding if Japan decided to develop its own nuclear weapons. Another, equally curious addendum is that in their discussions in Beijing, according to Seymour Hersh, first Kissinger and then Nixon used the threat of allowing

Japan to become a nuclear power partly as a way to pressure the Chinese to work with the United States against the Soviet Union and to protect Japan. 'We told them,' Nixon apparently also said, when he testified to the Watergate Special Prosecution Force in 1975, 'if you try to keep us from protecting the Japanese, we would let them go nuclear.' If such stories are true, it shows a deeply ambivalent attitude on the part of Nixon and Kissinger towards a country which, they repeatedly said, was thoroughly capable of becoming an aggressive military power all over again.[9]

Sato was, it turned out, promising more than he could deliver on the textile issue in the face of furious opposition from Japanese textile manufacturers and their allies in the government. The Okinawa treaty moved ahead, but Nixon did not get the quota he wanted. Comments came out of the White House, perhaps from Nixon himself, suggesting that the United States was worried about Japan sliding back into militarism or going Communist. In private, Nixon talked about 'Jap betrayal'. As Kissinger prepared to leave on his secret trip to China in the summer of 1971, the United States' relations with Japan were already strained.[10]

For fear of leaks Nixon and Kissinger had decided not to inform their allies (or indeed their own State Department) about the trip until the day of Nixon's televised announcement. Alexis Johnson, who was Under-Secretary of State for Political Affairs, was summoned to San Clemente on 15 July where he found a frantic Rogers, 'left behind as usual by the President', trying to track down ambassadors in Washington, where the working day had already ended. When Johnson finally managed to get hold of the Japanese ambassador, Ushida Nobuhiko cried out, 'Alex, the Asakai nightmare has happened.' In Japan, Sato had three minutes' warning, and the American ambassador was lying in a barber's chair when he heard the news on an American armed forces broadcast. The Japanese were furious and humiliated. In Washington, the normally calm Ushida had a stormy interview with Marshall Green at the State Department in which he accused the United States of betraying a lack of trust towards Japan. Sato tried to put a brave face on it but he tearfully unburdened himself about the Americans to the Australian Prime Minister. 'I have done everything they asked but they have let me down.' Sato's own political position was seriously undermined and, in Johnson's opinion, the Japanese and American governments never recovered the trust and confidence they had formerly had in each other.[11]

The Japanese probably should have guessed that something was in the wind. The signs of a thaw between China and the United States were clearly visible by 1971 and American diplomats had tried to tip the Japanese off to expect more developments. 'If I had only listened more carefully to what you were saying,' a Japanese diplomat said disconsolately to Charles Freeman of the State Department, 'this would have not been the surprise that it was.' Chou had also apparently hinted that spring to a Japanese trade negotiator that the two countries were about to start serious discussions. For the Japanese, it was as much the way the Americans handled the announcement as the trip itself. A new word entered the Japanese language – *shokku*.[12]

And there were more to follow. On 15 August 1971 Nixon announced a package of measures to deal with inflation and with a growing American trade imbalance with the world. The United States stopped backing the dollar with gold, effectively devaluing its currency, and placed a surcharge on imports. Nixon knew that both measures would hurt Japan. 'We'll fix those bastards.' The second *shokku* led to the yen going sharply upwards against the dollar and to restrictions on Japanese exports to the United States. Then, in October, while Kissinger was on his second trip to China, Japanese delegates at the United Nations found themselves committed to support the American delegation in resisting Taiwan's expulsion at a time when the American government itself was abandoning the struggle. Sato's government, reasonably under the circumstances, decided that, given the American example, the time had come to push ahead to expand Japan's trading and diplomatic relations with mainland China.[13]

Nixon and Kissinger made a half-hearted effort to put things right with the Japanese. In September, they flew to Anchorage to meet the Emperor Hirohito when his plane refuelled on the way from Japan to Europe. Nixon described their meeting as an historic event, 'a spiritual bridge spanning East and West'. To Chou a month later, Kissinger was dismissive: 'Not a very profound conversation, Mr Prime Minister.' The Americans also invited Sato to Washington for a summit in

January 1972. In his private conversation with Nixon and Kissinger, Sato was polite but critical. Japan was rather concerned about Nixon's visit to China. Kissinger said that he had been very firm with the Chinese, who could be under no illusions but that the Americans intended to stand by their commitments to their friends. 'We have made no deal,' Nixon interjected. The announcement of Kissinger's trip, Sato went on, had come as a great shock to the Japanese people, who thought, wrongly of course, that it had been arranged behind Japan's back. Nixon was unapologetic; the important thing, in his view, was that on policy issues their two nations must consult fully. The Japanese, he noted, appeared to be moving quickly to establish full relations with the People's Republic of China. 'If Japan were to crawl, or to run, to Peking,' Nixon warned, 'its bargaining position would evaporate.' He was worried not so much that Japan would give away too much to get full diplomatic relations with China as that this would happen before the United States could do the same. In an election year, he did want not allies or Democrats taking the limelight.[14]

Sato left the United States pessimistic over the future of the Japanese–American relationship. His own political position had been irretrievably undermined by the series of *shokkus*. He resigned in the summer of 1972 and was replaced by Tanaka Kakuei, who moved rapidly to open up Japan's own relations with the People's Republic of China. Japan's relationship with the United States remained highly important, but as a senior official had said at the end of 1971, 'it will be necessary for us to recognize, once again, that Japan is an Asian nation'.[15]

If Japan felt tremors from the shift in American policy, Taiwan was hit by an earthquake. After Truman had guaranteed Taiwan's defence, its Guomindang rulers had confidently but unwisely assumed that the United States was their friend and protector in perpetuity. They had not noticed that a new generation of Americans, less affected by the early Cold War and the battle for Korea, was moving into influential positions in government, the media and the academic world. They had counted, too, on the ability of the China lobby to keep American governments in line. They had failed to see that it was slowly fading away, although they should perhaps have taken notice when its chief organizer abruptly resigned in 1969 and moved to

London to take up producing plays and when the *New York Times* referred to the 'once powerful China Lobby'. The Guomindang government did little to prepare its own citizens for the possibility that American allegiances might one day shift. An old and stubborn Chiang kept tight control on the media and refused to allow any consideration of such issues as dual membership for both his government and that of the mainland in the United Nations. 'There is no room for patriots and traitors to live together.'[16]

As the signs of a major shift in American policy – from Nixon's first use of the term People's Republic to ping-pong diplomacy – multiplied, the leadership in Taiwan drifted glumly along in a state of indecision. When Nixon made his announcement in the summer of 1971 that Kissinger had secretly visited Beijing, the first reaction in the capital, Taipei, was 'utter disbelief'. To James Shen, the Taiwanese ambassador in Washington, Kissinger was reassuring: in his conversations with Chou, he had stressed that the United States had no intention of turning its back on its loyal ally and friend. He had not made any secret deals with the Chinese over Taiwan. Just before he left on his second trip, Kissinger saw Shen again. He had no intention, he said, of bringing up the issue of Taiwan but it was possible that Chou might. In any case, Nixon was going to make completely clear that the American relationship with Taiwan was 'non-negotiable'. He himself, Kissinger went on, with his many friends in Taiwan, found going to China 'exceedingly painful'; he had no choice, however, but to accept the assignment. Was this, the ambassador wondered, sincere or a case of crocodile tears?

In October, shortly before Kissinger's second trip to China, Nixon sent Ronald Reagan, then Governor of California, to Taipei to talk to Chiang Kai-shek. Chiang sat like a stone, looking straight ahead. Reagan, who was a strong supporter of Taiwan, later said that he regretted helping Nixon out. Shortly after Reagan's visit, Taiwan was expelled from the United Nations. To add to Taiwan's humiliation, a number of countries indicated that they were going to switch their recognition to the People's Republic of China. Japan, Taiwan's prominent supporter and most important trading partner, hinted that it was starting negotiations with Beijing. For many Taiwanese, it was not just their status but their new-found prosperity which was threatened.[17]

From the Taiwanese perspective, there were only a few bright spots in 1971. The United States finally agreed to sell Taiwan's navy two submarines and to hold joint military training exercises, which had been in abeyance since 1968. In August, the USS *Oklahoma City*, flagship of the Seventh Fleet, visited a Taiwanese port. The authorities organized an enthusiastic welcome with singers, acrobats and dancers. Another event which occurred that month may have done even more to boost local morale. The Tainan Giants won the Little League World Series in baseball. Two-thirds of Taiwan's fourteen million inhabitants watched the games on television.[18]

Wild rumours came out of Taiwan. On his October visit, Kissinger, who had been alerted by American intelligence, passed on a warning to Chou that the Guomindang might use its American-made aircraft to cause trouble. 'We have a report that the Chinese Nationalists on the Taiwan General Staff are considering flying a R-104 reconnaissance aircraft over the mainland in order to disrupt our policy and our talks.' The American government was trying to put a stop to it. Such planes often came to harass them, Chou said, but the Chinese would assume that anything taking off from Taiwan was being flown by Guomindang pilots. As Nixon prepared to make his trip to China, the Chinese informed the Americans of reports that Chiang Kai-shek would use a plane painted with People's Republic markings to try and shoot down Air Force One. Chiang's more moderate son, Chiang Ching-kuo, promised that there would be no unusual incidents or manoeuvres in the Strait during Nixon's visit.[19]

The Taiwanese watched the Haldeman show in Beijing with gloomy fascination. (Some remained happily unaware: 'Oh, is that near Taipei?' asked a farmer's wife.) The press in Taiwan said that people all around the Pacific no longer trusted the United States as an ally. Nixon, so Shen thought, had made a great mistake in going to China at all. And why was Nixon so humble when he met Mao? He might as well have been on his knees doing the kow-tow to an emperor. The scene at the opening banquet, when Nixon went round the tables toasting everyone indiscriminately, was, in Shen's view, particularly demeaning. 'This was something no Oriental guest of honour with any sense of personal dignity would have done.' Shortly after Nixon's visit concluded, the Taiwanese government issued a defiant statement reaffirming its intention of overthrowing the illegitimate regime on the mainland. It might also look elsewhere for new friends. The Taiwanese Foreign Minister said he would not rule out 'shaking hands with the devil'. Rumours went around Taipei that the Soviets might lease one of Taiwan's outlying islands as a naval base.[20]

On the whole, the reaction of the government was less violent than it might have been. Most ordinary Taiwanese were mainly confused and uneasy about what the future held – partly, said an American diplomat, because their own government had done so little to prepare them for this moment. Their reaction to the Nixon visit, the Australian ambassador in Taipei reported, was one of 'essential helplessness in the face of events happening or to happen elsewhere'. Even the supporters of Taiwan's independence as a separate country shared the growing feeling of isolation.[21] Were they, as the American diplomat put it, 'an annoying fragment complicating the implementation of a grand American strategy devised in Washington'?

19

The Shanghai Communiqué

ON SATURDAY 26 FEBRUARY 1972, the American party prepared to leave Beijing for the last stage of the visit. Nixon's mood had not improved since the banquet the night before. As he sat in the airport waiting room, Chou politely called his attention to various pictures of China on the walls. Nixon tried to ignore him but was eventually forced to look about him. His smile grew strained, then disappeared. 'What the hell are you talking about?' he snapped. If the Chinese Prime Minister understood, he remained his usual imperturbable self.[1]

They were all flying together in a Chinese plane (this had caused great concern to the Secret Service) to Hangzhou, just south of Shanghai. The Chinese had insisted on putting this, one of China's most beautiful cities, on the itinerary. For its tree-covered hills and, above all, its West Lake, with its bridges, pavilions and temples, Hangzhou had been a favourite subject of China's writers and artists for centuries. Mao spent much time at his villa by the lake, especially during the winter months; he had also planned much of the Cultural Revolution there. It was possible, or so the Americans hoped, that he might be available there for a second meeting with Nixon. It would give the visit even more significance; it would also appease Rogers, who was deeply aggrieved that he had been cut out of the one meeting in Beijing. Kissinger raised the matter with Chou and Qiao in their private talks but was told that the Chairman's bronchitis made it difficult. There was no second meeting.[2]

By way of compensation, the two sides held a second plenary session at the Beijing airport. The Chinese had originally scheduled fifteen minutes, but Nixon had asked that the meeting be stretched out to half an hour: 'It would make some of our people who have not had a chance to sit in on the private sessions feel that they have a part to play, too.' Nixon and Chou talked blandly about how good their talks had been. There were, of course, still differences between them but they had made a good start on finding common ground. Nixon also took the opportunity to warn the Chinese, yet again, not to believe what the American press or American politicians said.

Perhaps, said Chou, they should invite their foreign ministers to report on their own discussions. That, said Kissinger sardonically in his memoirs, did not take long. Rogers led off; his talks with Ji, the Chinese Foreign Minister, had been frank and friendly. And useful in clearing up misunderstandings. For example, when the Chinese had been concerned that they might need to be fingerprinted for visas to the United States, he had been able to make one quick phone call to Washington and reassure them that the procedure was no longer required. 'That's a very serious and earnest attitude,' Chou commented. No mention was made of the communiqué, even though its wording had finally, or so Nixon and Kissinger confidently thought, been settled the night before with the Chinese. He would only show it to Rogers in confidence, Kissinger assured Qiao, and then only when they reached Hangzhou.[3]

In his memoirs, Nixon made only a brief mention of any problems over the communiqué. Both sides, as already agreed, stated their positions over Taiwan, the Chinese at first rather belligerently in Nixon's opinion. 'Thanks largely to Kissinger's negotiating skill and Chou's common sense, the Chinese finally agreed to sufficiently modified language.' In his own memoirs, Kissinger devoted considerably more space to what he admitted were delicate and tricky negotiations. The transcripts of his talks, mainly with Qiao but occasionally with Chou present as well, show just how difficult they were.[4]

Qiao, who was a trusted colleague of Chou's, was, like his superior, clever, tough and, when he chose, charming. Like Chou, he came from an upper-class background and had studied and lived abroad, in Japan and then in Germany where he had done a doctorate in philosophy. He had first worked for Chou during the Civil War and had joined the Foreign Ministry after the Communists took power. Like Chou, Qiao was a skilled negotiator who had learned his craft in the negotiations at the end of the Korean War. More recently, he had headed the Chinese team negotiating with the Soviets after the confrontations of 1969. Kissinger found Qiao a worthy opponent, and his subordinate, Zhang Wenjin, a stubborn nuisance with a fondness for splitting hairs. Kissinger's own assistants, Winston Lord and John Holdridge, from the State Department, rarely intervened in the discussions. The Americans had no inkling of strains the men on the other side were under.

In 1967, as the Cultural Revolution was getting into full swing, Zhang, who was then ambassador in Pakistan, had been summoned back to Beijing along with many other diplomats. Radicals had seized him at the airport and clapped a dunce's cap on his head. They had then held him in the Foreign Ministry where he had been forced to kneel for hours on a wooden bench, holding his leather shoes, signs of his bourgeois failings, above his head. As a protégé of Chou's, Qiao had also been caught up in the disputes in the Foreign Ministry. His enemies had accused him of being a rightist, an all-purpose but damning label. (Later on, after Mao's death, he faced the completely different charge of being part of the Gang of Four.) His personal life was also complicated; his wife had died suddenly in 1970 and a year later he had fallen in love with a much younger woman in the Foreign Ministry. Zhang Hanzhi, who was extremely pretty and charming, was the daughter of an old friend of Mao's and something of a favourite of the Chairman's. She had once tried to teach him English and now worked as an interpreter for Chou. There was much gossip about her relationship with Qiao and it was not until the end of 1973 that they were given permission to marry. Not surprisingly, given the turmoil in his political and private lives, Qiao suffered from fits of depression and melancholy.[5]

While most of the communiqué had been settled on Kissinger's and Haig's earlier trips, three issues still remained: trade and exchanges, the recent conflict between India and Pakistan, and Taiwan. While the communiqué was unusual in that both sides were going to state their respective positions where they disagreed, they still had to settle the actual wording and set out those areas where in fact they did agree. In an intense series of meetings, in the intervals either in the morning or late at night when their presence was not required at the Nixon–Chou meetings or at social events, Kissinger and Qiao went over the communiqué line by line. They argued over words and grammar. Did 'should' imply a moral obligation, for example? Could Nixon endorse a common statement that talked about revolution in the world? (In this case, they agreed to refer merely to 'important changes and great upheavals'.) Should the American names to be listed as participants in the talks have middle initials? That one had to be referred to Nixon himself who ruled against initials.

Behind the quibbles lay real and important issues. Two great powers were taking a public stand on significant questions where they differed but also demonstrating that they had found some common ground. The words they used in the communiqué were going to be read and studied – in Moscow, Hanoi, Tokyo, in capital cities worldwide. And the commitments, to work on normalizing relations between China and the United States, while not binding, would be hard to break once made publicly. The transcripts of Kissinger's and Qiao's talks show masters of their craft at work. They assure each other that they do not want to be tricky. They swear that they are being completely frank with each other. They do much thinking aloud. It was a useful device, said Kissinger, because both sides could advance positions without being committed to them. At times they flatter each other shamelessly. 'Our efficiency', sighed Qiao, 'is not as high as yours.' The Chinese, said Kissinger, were so much more subtle than most Americans.[6]

On South Asia, one of the outstanding issues, the Americans wanted to say simply that the peoples of South Asia had the right to determine their own future without the threat of force and without outside interference, while the Chinese wanted to stress that India must obey the United Nations' resolutions and withdraw its forces from Pakistan's territory in Kashmir. After a brief discussion, both sides agreed on what was an unconventional way to have a joint communiqué: while there would be common statements, each would also have a separate section with its own wording.

The wording on trade and exchanges was also relatively easy to settle and here the two sides were able to agree that it was desirable to expand the contacts and understanding between their two peoples, whether through cultural and academic exchanges or through sport. The Chinese were nervous about allowing foreigners into China and not particularly interested in trade or tourism, but Kissinger was reassuring. The words in the communiqué would be window-dressing: 'we both know that basically they don't mean anything'. He was obliged by 'sentimental' public pressure back home to push for more contacts between their two countries. 'The maximum amount of bilateral trade possible between us, even if we make great efforts, is infinitesimal in terms of our total economy. And the exchanges, while they are important, will not change objective realities.' The Chinese were hardened revolutionaries; 'pedants' from American universities were not going to make any impression on them. These are interesting predictions viewed from our vantage point today: now Walmart's imports from China amount to some $18 billion a year and place that one company ahead of Canada, Russia and Australia as a trading partner with the People's Republic; and almost 900,000 Americans a year now visit China and many of China's new leaders hold degrees from American universities.[7]

Taiwan, inevitably, was the main cause of long hours of work late into the night and it was Taiwan that very nearly prevented any communiqué from being issued at all. The fundamental problem, which had not been solved on either of Kissinger's visits or on Haig's, was that the Chinese wanted the Americans to recognize that the island was an integral part of China. Moreover they wanted a firm deadline for the Americans to withdraw militarily from Taiwan. 'Since you are to acknowledge', Qiao said on the day the Nixon party arrived, 'that the Taiwan question is a question of the Chinese people themselves, then the logical and inescapable conclusion would be the final and complete withdrawal of American forces.' The Americans could not go that far; publicly abandoning Taiwan would cause major domestic problems for Nixon and also leave a bad impression with American allies around the world. Qiao cleverly countered with his own reference to public opinion: the Chinese people had 'very strong feelings' on the issue of Taiwan.

Kissinger fell back on the tactics he and Nixon had used before: he could and would make private commitments. Surely, he argued, the fact that the United States had kept its promise not to have nuclear weapons on Taiwan was evidence of the Americans' good faith. When Qiao pressed him for an acknowledgement in the communiqué that

Taiwan was a province of China, Kissinger resisted: 'We would like to find a formulation which is at least vaguer, not because it affects what we will do, which you know, but because it enables us to return without looking as though we have surrendered on this point.' On the other hand, when Kissinger wanted the Chinese to state clearly that they would not use force to join Taiwan with the mainland, Qiao dug his heels in. 'Frankly speaking, we cannot agree to that because it is a fundamental violation of our principle – that it is an internal affair.' Nevertheless, he pointed out, the Chinese were making a significant concession in not insisting that the United States renounce its defence treaty with Taiwan.[8]

During the week in Beijing, the two sides inched towards each other. As the time for Nixon's departure for Hangzhou drew closer, the pace of the meetings stepped up. On Friday, the last full day the Americans were in Beijing, Kissinger and Qiao held four meetings, not finishing up until the early hours of Saturday. The wording of the Chinese statement on Taiwan, which reiterated China's longstanding position that Taiwan was a part of China and its fate an internal matter, was agreed relatively quickly. Because the Americans were changing their position, however, virtually every word in the four sentences expressing the American view on Taiwan was the subject of intense bargaining. The Americans acknowledged that all Chinese, both those on the mainland and those on Taiwan, held that there was only one China and that Taiwan was part of it. The word 'acknowledge', though, later caused problems with some officials in the State Department who felt that the United States could have followed the Canadian example to simply 'take note of' the Chinese position. On the other hand, Kissinger managed to avoid using the word 'recognize', which would have implied that the United States accepted China's claims to sovereignty over Taiwan.[9]

Although the Chinese still had not renounced the use of force, they conceded that the Americans might indicate a link between a peaceful settlement of the issue with the withdrawal of American forces from Taiwan. Qiao fretted over the word 'withdrawal'; did it imply that some forces could be left behind? Kissinger agreed to say that the 'ultimate objective' of the United States was the withdrawal of 'all' American forces, but he managed to put it in the context of the reduction of tensions in the Taiwan Strait. Where Kissinger wanted to say that, with the prospect of a peaceful settlement of the issue by the Chinese themselves, the United States 'anticipates' withdrawing its forces, Qiao wanted the stronger 'will'. They finally compromised on 'affirms'. Nixon and Chou approved all the changes and, by Saturday morning, the communiqué was apparently finally done. Haldeman planned to release it to the American press, who were increasingly restless at the lack of hard news on the communiqué or anything else, on the Sunday night.[10]

They were not the only ones who were restless. Rogers and his advisers from the State Department were increasingly concerned about being left out of the negotiations on the communiqué. Holdridge, from State, who was part of the Kissinger team, had long since learned that his loyalties had to lie with Kissinger and did not leak any information on the progress of the talks. When the State Department put forward a suggestion for wording on Taiwan, Kissinger merely handed the confidential memorandum to Qiao as an example of the sort of pressures he had to deal with. From time to time, during that week in Beijing, Kissinger went through the motions of consulting Rogers and his aides, showing them excerpts from the communiqué, but none of them saw the completed version until their plane took off for Hangzhou. Nixon handed over the communiqué to Rogers during the flight. He himself was supposed to sit with Chou and, in his memoirs, claims that they were talking 'quite freely' to each other by this point. In fact, after a few perfunctory remarks, Nixon left his seat and moved up to spend the rest of the flight with Haldeman, grumbling about how difficult the press were and how he was fed up with Rogers.[11]

At Hangzhou, the Chinese called the Americans' attention to the new terminal building at the airport, built, so they announced proudly, in forty days by 10,000 workers. Observant reporters noticed that, along the main streets, shop windows were unusually full of consumer goods. Groups of brightly dressed children were playing, apparently oblivious to the motorcade rushing past. The Nixons' villa was on the island of Three Towers Reflecting the Moon. It was, Nixon recalled, 'a bit musty but clean'. Spring comes early to Hangzhou and the magnolias were already in bloom.[12]

In spite of his strictures, Nixon was obliged to do some more sight-seeing that afternoon. With Chou as their guide, he and Pat Nixon floated by boat across the lake to admire spots with names like Listening to Orioles Among the Willows. The scenery, Nixon said politely, looked 'like a postcard'. Officials accompanying the party chatted about a bowl of fruit on board. The pears tasted like apples, said an American. 'We have pears that taste like bananas, too,' a Chinese replied proudly. As they walked through Flower Park, Mrs Nixon giggled at a cage of lovebirds. 'Lovey dovey,' she remarked to Chou, who muttered something in Chinese. Nixon and Chou inspected one of the redwoods the Americans had presented to the Chinese people. Chou worried that it might be a bit crowded by other trees. Nixon thought the tree would grow slowly. Smiling for the cameras, the Nixons fed huge goldfish, with breadcrumbs thoughtfully provided by the Chinese. 'I never saw goldfish that big,' Nixon commented.

Kissinger – his labours, or so he thought, largely over – took the opportunity to stroll through one of the West Lake's most beautiful glades. As he was gazing at the water and the distant hills beyond, Walter Cronkite appeared, dressed, so Kissinger said, as though he was going on an arctic expedition and staggering under the weight of the cameras around his neck. The press were everywhere. 'It was a grisly afternoon,' said the experienced journalist and old China hand Theodore White, 'all organized for television crews and cameras, for symbolism and manipulation, with posts and positions roped off, stakeouts set, each journalist assigned his two square feet of observation.'

Nixon suddenly decided to call an impromptu press conference at his villa. The shivering journalists stood outside on a terrace while he apologized for the news blackout of the previous few days. The extreme secrecy, he assured them, was at the request of the Chinese. He understood the difficulties the press faced in doing their job. Indeed, he was going to write to their bosses and suggest they got a raise. After the White House photographers had snapped a group picture, he invited each journalist to step inside for an individual photograph with him.[13]

That night there was the inevitable banquet. Pat Nixon chatted brightly to the wife of a Chinese official while Nixon and Chou sat silently, with, said one journalist, 'the look of men who for the moment have had more than enough of one another'. Nixon and his host, the chair of the local revolutionary committee, exchanged toasts, 'mercifully brief for once'. Hangzhou, said Nixon, was rightly renowned all over the world. He hoped that the future of the Chinese and American peoples and their friendship would be equally bright and beautiful.

Behind the scenes, although Nixon may not yet have known it, a major storm was brewing over the communiqué. That afternoon, Rogers had shown the final version of communiqué to his advisers for the first time. They immediately raised a number of issues. The communiqué said that all Chinese on both sides of the Taiwan Strait maintained that Taiwan was a part of China. This ignored the existence of the large number of Taiwan's inhabitants who supported Taiwan's independence. Marshall Green, the senior official for East Asia, was particularly horrified at the section where the United States set out its responsibilities in Asia. 'Mr Secretary, there is a serious problem.' The communiqué listed American defence commitments to, for example, South Korea and Japan, but did not mention the treaty with Taiwan. This was all too similar to what had happened in 1950, just before the Korean War, when Dean Acheson, then Secretary of State, had made a speech in which he referred to the United States' defensive perimeter as running from the Aleutian Islands, near Alaska in the north, southwards to include the Philippines but, crucially, had not mentioned South Korea. Many people, at the time and since, believed that this sent a signal to Kim Il Sung of North Korea and his patron, Stalin, that the North could attack South Korea without fear of an American response. When Green pointed out the unfortunate parallel, Rogers exclaimed, 'My God, you're right.'[14]

In his memoirs, Kissinger dismissed all the concerns raised by the State Department as nitpicking and trivial. Years later his loyal assistant Winston Lord still maintained that the impetus behind the demands that the communiqué be amended came partly from the State Department's pique at being left out of the key negotiations in Beijing, and partly out of a desire to make mischief by insisting on difficult terms: 'they figured it would be more embarrassing to us if we didn't get them'. Some of the State Department's concerns, it is true, involved quite minor matters in the communiqué, but others, notably the implied renunciation of the United States' obligation to defend Taiwan, clearly did not. Rogers tried to contact Nixon in the late afternoon, but Haldeman said firmly that the President was resting and could not be disturbed. In any case, said Haldeman, Nixon had already approved the communiqué.[15]

At the banquet, Ron Ziegler, the press secretary, noticed that Green was in a grim mood and listened to his complaints. Ziegler may have contacted Haldeman. Rogers had also got through to Nixon himself. By the time the banquet ended, it had become clear that the communiqué could not be left as it was. 'All hell has broken loose over this,' John Scali, a White House press adviser, told Green late that night, 'and it is because of you.' In his villa, Nixon stormed about in his underwear. According to Kissinger, he threatened to deal with the State Department once and for all. Or was it, as Green suspected, that Kissinger had created an awkward situation with the wording on Taiwan which, if it were not rectified, was bound to cause a wave of opposition back in the United States?[16]

There was nothing for it but to send Kissinger back to reopen his discussions with Qiao late that Saturday evening. Kissinger was clearly embarrassed and, at first, tried to minimize the importance of the changes he was requesting. Rogers, he said, needed to feel that he and the State Department had contributed something to the final document. It would be a good idea to have them on side; a 'mutinous bureaucracy' could cause lots of trouble for him and for Nixon. Rogers and his colleagues had been fussing about words. 'All Chinese' sounded a bit ridiculous in English; perhaps the communiqué could just say 'the Chinese' on both sides of the Taiwan Strait. The sense was really the same. 'That's one point,' said Qiao noncommittally. 'Now will you please continue.' Kissinger brought up a few minor changes, in words or punctuation. He also asked whether they might include something in the communiqué about Rogers and Ji having useful talks as well as Nixon and Chou. Then he reached the crux of the matter.

The communiqué was a bit ambiguous, Kissinger said, when it came to the United States' commitments to its allies in Asia. It mentioned Japan and South Korea but not the Philippines or Thailand with which the United States also had defence treaties. Kissinger carefully did not bring up Taiwan. He appealed to Qiao: 'You see, it's also a problem for you because supposing we say these two, then every other ally in the whole Pacific will say "what about us?" and we will have to be issuing statements every day.' Perhaps, Kissinger suggested, they could solve the problem either by having the United States list all its commitments or by watering down the particular references to Japan and South Korea so that they did not appear to specify a military relationship.

Qiao heard Kissinger out and merely asked for a brief recess, as Kissinger assumed, no doubt correctly, to consult Chou. In private, Qiao was furious. The Chinese did not really need the communiqué at all. 'The United States comes to China and it needs the communiqué. Nixon can make his visit to China as a tourist.' When he returned, Qiao let the Americans see something of his anger. He had thought, he said, that they were meeting just to discuss a few matters of style. The document after all was finished and had been approved at the highest levels. 'When I sent you off early this morning I was relaxed thinking we had solved this.' The Chinese and the Americans had spent huge amounts of time and energy on the Taiwan issue ever since Kissinger's first visit in 1971. How could they reopen it now? Kissinger was deeply apologetic. His colleagues in the State Department did not realize how sincerely the Chinese had negotiated, how they had made concession after concession. 'If you persist in your position,' said Qiao, 'there will be no need for further discussions tonight. And we will discuss it again tomorrow and the result will be no communiqué.' The Chinese could not accept any of the American suggestions on Taiwan. 'Cannot be. Not a matter of words.'

In fact, he was prepared to negotiate. Both China and the United States now had a vested interest in demonstrating that they had taken a major step towards a more normal relationship. Not to issue a communiqué, after all the press reports that one was being negotiated, would mark Nixon's trip as a failure. As Saturday night turned into Sunday morning, the two men managed to find a compromise. Qiao agreed that the United States would not mention any of its commitments at all and simply refer to its 'close ties' and 'support' for South

Korea and its 'existing close bonds' with Japan. Kissinger for his part dropped his attempt to change 'all' Chinese to 'the' Chinese. Qiao took the occasion to extract another concession. There had been a slight mistake in translation, he said. A sentence to the effect that neither side 'will seek hegemony in the Asia–Pacific region' ought to have read neither side 'should'. In other words, instead of a promise, Qiao wanted a moral obligation. Kissinger got the point immediately: the revised wording would allow the Chinese to accuse the Americans of behaving badly whenever they chose. After more hard bargaining and a few more changes, the two sides finally had a deal to take to Nixon and Chou. Qiao permitted himself a rare joke. 'As to specific wordings, we can see to it that it is a very beautifully worded document.' Nixon was wakened early on the morning of 27 February and gave his approval. Chou called Mao's villa in Beijing and a secretary read the draft out to the Chairman. Mao also approved it.[17]

An exhausted Kissinger lashed out at Green later that day for getting Rogers stirred up over the communiqué. Green, for the first time in his association with Kissinger, snapped back. 'Since when was the Secretary of State offering constructive criticisms defined as poormouthing?' Rogers rightly had done his duty to advise the President. Kissinger backed down. In any case, Rogers was now back in line after Nixon ordered him to make sure that both he and the State Department gave their full support to the communiqué.

Nixon had another piece of welcome news that day when a press report came in from the United States that Senator Ed Muskie, the leading Democratic presidential candidate, had broken down in tears at a press conference in New Hampshire as he denied accusations that he had made racial slurs about the state's large French Canadian population. 'Rather fascinating,' was all Haldeman put in his diary. In fact Haldeman, and quite possibly Nixon himself, had a very good idea of what lay behind the story. Muskie, who had been attacking Nixon, with considerable success, on his failure to get the United States out of Vietnam, was a prime target of the Committee to Re-Elect the President, or CREEP as it was aptly known. CREEP, which reported directly to Nixon, carried out the usual campaign activities, such as raising funds and preparing materials, but it had another, darker side. One of its employees was a young California lawyer called Donald

Segretti who ran a corps of 'pranksters' to disrupt the Democratic campaign. Their pranks were not innocent: they forged letters on Democratic letterhead, printed phoney flyers and spread slanderous rumours about Democratic politicians. The story about Muskie's remarks in New Hampshire, along with another that his wife drank and had mental troubles, had been planted by the Segretti team. Muskie never recovered from that news conference in February 1972, but, in the long run, although Nixon could not know it as he savoured his triumph in China, another step had been taken towards the Watergate scandal.[18]

On the morning of Sunday 27 February, the Americans and the Chinese flew onwards on Chou's plane to Shanghai. A giant billboard in Chinese characters greeted them: 'We Will Certainly Liberate Taiwan'. The American party was housed in the elegant Jinjiang Hotel, which had been built as the Grosvenor Mansions by the tycoon Sir Victor Sassoon in the 1930s. Nixon was on the top floor, with Kissinger on the next floor down and then Rogers and his State Department advisers below that. 'The symbolism', said Green, 'escaped no one.'[19]

The Americans found the city a pleasant change after the austerity of Beijing and Hangzhou. Shanghai, the great sea port which had been one of the main centres for foreign trade and investment before the Communist takeover, had been badly neglected by the Communists who mistrusted its free and easy ways, its radical traditions and its cosmopolitanism, but it was still, as one American journalist wrote, 'a *real* city'. Even in 1972 Shanghai women dared to wear lipstick and bright clothes. Its streets bustled with crowds and its shops had a richer variety of goods than those in Beijing or Hangzhou. The Americans did not know the lengths to which the authorities had gone to tidy the city up; the locals had even been ordered to take their laundry in from the racks that hung outside each apartment.[20]

The local authorities in the Shanghai Revolutionary Committee had laid on a full programme for the Nixons. Pat Nixon watched children's activities at the Shanghai Children's Palace and was serenaded by a student band playing 'Can She Bake a Cherry-Pie, Billy Boy'. 'We study very hard in this place,' said her young guide, 'and then go back to our schools and teach the others as Chairman Mao told us.' A weary Nixon was taken off to visit the Shanghai Industrial Exhibition, formerly the Sino-Soviet Friendship Building, to admire the products of Chinese industry. Machinery could be dangerous, he said. 'Sometimes when you push the button it does not turn out all right.' He inspected Chinese typewriters and an early computer. 'I understand philosophy,' he commented to Chou, 'but computers are too complicated for me.' Chou admitted that he did not understand them either; 'but you have to pay attention to them'. Nixon looked up at the giant portraits of Communist luminaries. 'We don't see many pictures of Engels in America,' he noted. He peered through a magnifying glass at a minuscule piece of ivory engraved with a famous poem of Mao's about plum blossoms reaching their height of beauty just as they are about to disappear. Chou had quoted it to Nixon in Beijing and explained that it meant that those who start something may not always be there to enjoy the result. Nixon had taken the initiative to re-establish the United States' relations with China. 'You may not be there to see its success,' he had warned Nixon. 'A very unlikely event,' Kissinger had interjected hastily.[21]

While the Nixons were touring Shanghai, Kissinger was having one last meeting with Qiao on the communiqué. 'Is there any new question your side would like to raise?' asked Qiao sardonically. There was not. Kissinger did, however, have a request. He hoped the Chinese would exercise discretion in the way they discussed the communiqué. 'It would make the realization of our common objective immeasurably more difficult if Chinese domestic propaganda or Chinese foreign propaganda or Chinese friends were to represent this as a major American defeat, or as any American defeat.' Qiao nodded. Kissinger also wanted to alert the Chinese to a couple of things. He was probably going to have to visit Japan in the next few weeks. It would, however, be a visit of no particular importance. More importantly, he would be having a press conference with the American journalists later that afternoon in which he was bound to be asked some awkward questions about, for example, whether he and Nixon had made any secret deals with the Chinese or whether the communiqué included all the topics that had been discussed. The answer to both those questions would, of course, be 'No.' To general laughter, Kissinger added, 'Wherever possible I will try to tell the truth.'

The most difficult question he expected to get would be one about whether the American defence commitment to Taiwan was still in force. He was bound to say that, yes, the commitment was still valid but he would do so in as low key a way as possible. If any journalists tried to follow up, he would simply say that he was not prepared to make any further comment on such a sensitive issue while he was on China's soil. 'Are you certain this is what will happen?' asked Qiao. Kissinger, who had already planted the necessary question with a reporter from the *Los Angeles Times*, assured Qiao that he need not worry. Qiao said he understood the difficulties the United States faced over its treaty with Taiwan and he was most grateful for Kissinger's forewarning of how he intended to deal with the issue. 'We can only express the hope that you will be as prudent as possible.'[22]

At 5.30 in the afternoon, a tired and nervous Kissinger stood in the banquet hall of the Shanghai Industrial Exhibition to sketch out the main points of the communiqué for the assembled journalists. The press, who had been working long hours themselves filing stories back to the United States, were equally tired. Many had initially asked to stay on in China after Nixon left; when the rumour spread through their hotel later that night that Chinese officials were walking through their hotel to offer permission, they locked their doors in a panic.

As an olive branch, and because it was useful to associate the State Department publicly with the communiqué, Kissinger had asked Green to join him at the briefing. The crucial question came: why had the United States not reaffirmed its treaty commitment to Taiwan in the communiqué? Kissinger answered that, as Nixon had said earlier that year in his report on foreign policy to Congress, the United States was maintaining the treaty with Taiwan. He had nothing further to say and he would appreciate it if the journalists did not pursue the subject. Much to Nixon's and Haldeman's relief, the press reports were, if not wildly enthusiastic, reasonably positive. Among the White House staff, though, Pat Buchanan, later a prominent conservative critic of Nixon, was appalled at what he considered a sell-out.[23]

Kissinger also attempted to mollify the State Department by giving the impression at the press conference that Rogers had been involved at every step in the negotiation of the communiqué. Rogers himself may have been more soothed by the unexpected visit that Chou paid him that same afternoon. Chou was well aware of the divisions among the Americans and the hurt feelings on the State Department side. The Chinese interpreters had reported back to him on the angry comments from the State Department officials about the communiqué. Kissinger had also hinted broadly in a conversation just before they left Beijing that it might be a good idea to do something for 'those who feel neglected'. Chou agreed. He now told Rogers how much he regretted that his duties as prime minister of China had kept them from meeting more often. 'Secretary Rogers, you have done so much and we appreciate it.'²⁴

That night the Shanghai Revolutionary Committee put on a final banquet for the Americans. Rose Woods, Nixon's long-time and deeply conservative secretary, kept everyone waiting as she and Buchanan commiserated with each other. 'Don't rush me,' she snapped when she was told to hurry up. 'As long as we have sold out to these bastards, it doesn't make any difference.' Chou and Nixon did the usual round of toasts, perhaps knocking back more maotai than usual. The host, Zhang Chunqiao, who had risen to prominence during the Cultural Revolution and who was later to be tried along with Mao's wife as one of the Gang of Four, made a brief speech of welcome and toasted the friendship between the great Chinese and the great American peoples. Nixon replied with a carefully crafted metaphor about building bridges across 16,000 miles of ocean and twenty-two years of hostility. Under the influence of the maotai, or so Kissinger suspected, Nixon got carried away and suggested that the United States stood ready to defend China if any foreign power tried to attack it. Their joint communiqué, he said proudly, would make international headlines the next morning. After all, 'This was the week that changed the world.'²⁵

After the banquet, while most of the Americans watched a display of acrobatics, Kissinger went off to hand over to Qiao a last batch of top-secret military intelligence about Soviet forces. He would, he told Qiao, continue to send special information privately through Huang Hua, the Chinese ambassador at the United Nations. It would be best if the Chinese did not tell the State Department about this secret channel. The two men went back over the old familiar subject of Vietnam, with Kissinger saying how sincere the United States was in wanting to get out of its war and Qiao reiterating that the Chinese had no intention of interfering. It was well after midnight when they parted with sentiments of mutual esteem. 'Maybe you will have some rest tonight,' Qiao said.[26]

Kissinger still had one last duty to perform before he could get to his bed. Haldeman, who had been sitting up with an excited Nixon, called him in to the President's suite. The three of them sat there until after 2 a.m. as Nixon drank more maotai, going over the past week and praising Kissinger for his role in making the visit such a success. 'Sort of recapping problems and triumphs,' wrote Haldeman in his diary, 'the real breakthrough, the lack of understanding of what has been done, but the fact will come out eventually.' Kissinger felt that, as so often, Nixon was asking for reassurance. He and Haldeman gave it to him, moved, said Kissinger, in part by a longing to get to bed but also 'by an odd tenderness for this lonely, tortured, and insecure man'. The evening finally came to an end as the three stood on the terrace of Nixon's suite and took one last look at the great, dimly lit city lying below them.[27]

Many people went short of rest that night. Walter Cronkite, along with other American journalists, was wakened out of a deep sleep by a pounding on his door. Two army officers stepped in, presented him with a huge box of sweets, saluted and left. The Chinese had been convinced, ever since Kissinger's first visit, that all Americans loved sweets because the bowlfuls left out had been emptied every day as the Americans amassed souvenirs. The attendants at the Diaoyutai, where the Kissinger party stayed in Beijing, had reported, much to Mao's amusement, that the Americans ate not only the sweets but the wrappers too.[28]

On Monday morning, at Nixon's request, he had one last private meeting with Chou. He wanted, Nixon said, to reassure Chou that the record of their talks would remain secret, even from the rest of the American government. The two of them had made considerable progress in the past week; he hoped that when they disagreed in the future, as they must given that they represented such different countries, they would keep the rhetoric cool and not attack each other personally. Although the two of them had discussed other powers such as the Soviet Union, India and Japan, he also intended, Nixon said, to say virtually nothing about their discussions either to the American press or to the leaders of those countries. Chou agreed that their two countries should not attack each other unnecessarily but pointed out that there were still many areas where they disagreed. Taiwan, of course, but there China was prepared to wait. Vietnam was the most pressing issue. The Chinese were particularly sad because the Americans had continued their bombing. Kissinger intervened: he was sure that there had not been any bombing during the Nixon visit. Chou was polite but firm that there had been.[29]

As Nixon left the hotel, the staff lined up in order of their rank along the driveway. He was accompanied to the airport by Shanghai's revolutionary leader, Zhang, who took the opportunity to remind a foreigner, yet again, of China's century of humiliation. He pointed out a former golf course, now a children's park: before the Communist victory, he said, repeating the widely believed story, a sign had said 'No Chinese allowed'. Haldeman, who had gone off to buy miniature trees, nearly missed the motorcade. The press took off their long underwear with relief and piled it on Barbara Walters' bed as a last joke. While she waited in line to say goodbye to Chou, a hotel attendant rushed up with a large and very smelly package for her.[30]

As the American planes took off, a Chinese worker hauled down the American flag and all over Shanghai, people rushed to hang their laundry out of their windows. Charles Freeman, from the State Department, remembers the mood on his plane as euphoric. 'We had accomplished our purpose, which was a strategic one. We had not given away very much on Taiwan. We had held our ground on other international issues. We had established the framework for a relationship.' The staff on the Zoo Plane, for the second-tier journalists, had decorated the cabin and laid in special meals and wines. The passengers settled into their seats and most did not wake again until the plane reached Anchorage. On his plane, Nixon continued to worry at his problems concerning Rogers and how to, as he put it to Haldeman, consign his Secretary of State to the deep freeze. He went over what Kissinger should say in a detailed background briefing to the press back in the United States. Haldeman, Nixon said, should make a note that Kissinger had been working very hard and, as a reward, Haldeman was to contact Bebe Rebozo and ask him for all the phone numbers of women under thirty in his little black book.[31]

Not all the Americans went directly home. Five journalists did stay on in China for a short period. Green and Holdridge went off to brief American allies throughout Asia and the Pacific. The Nixon visit, they were to say, had not altered anything; indeed their interests had been furthered by the reduction of tensions between the United States and China. This was not an easy sell. The South Korean Foreign Minister was not convinced by their assurances that Chou had told Nixon that China, which after all was a strong supporter of North Korea, wanted stability in the peninsula. In Taiwan, Chiang Kai-shek refused to meet Green and Freeman at all and sent his son instead. The young Chiang listened politely and had only a few questions. He probably had a very good idea of what had happened during the talks in China because one of the designated American interpreters, who was a close personal friend, had just been on a hunting trip with him.

The Japanese had not got over their earlier *shokkus* or the latest one when the Shanghai communiqué was released. Sato, the Prime Minister, had walked out of a press conference mumbling angrily against Nixon. Green was unable to convince him that Nixon had not made secret agreements with China and that American friendship for Japan remained as strong as ever. In South Vietnam, Laos and Cambodia, where the governments depended on American support for their survival, the reaction was muted. The Thai, Indonesian and Malaysian governments were polite but sceptical.

In the Philippines, the Americans found an atmosphere close to hysteria. Imelda Marcos, the wife of the President, threatened to leave for Beijing immediately to establish a new relationship between her country and China. Green and the American ambassador were called before the Senate to explain why the United States was repudiating its former policies on Taiwan and the People's Republic of China. When they reached Singapore, Lee Kuan Yew, the Prime Minister, told Holdridge and Green that their country had 'just sprung the trap' on their friends. The reaction was much the same on their last stops in Australia and New Zealand. Green made a particularly bad impression on the Australians. As their senior foreign ministry official said, 'He was either consumed with personal vanity to such an extent that he believed a lot of the optimistic nonsense he talked or alternatively he was lying to bolster a bad case.'[32]

Such reactions were not sufficient to diminish the pleasure that Nixon took in his trip. Back in Washington, he had received a hero's welcome. Fifteen thousand people had turned out at Andrews Air Force Base to see his plane land. Although both he and Kissinger grumbled about it, the press coverage was generally favourable. In the polls, Nixon's popularity rose sharply to a 56 per cent approval rating, the highest he had enjoyed in over a year. Nearly 70 per cent of those polled believed that his trip would be useful. When Nixon met his cabinet the day after his return, he told them that the United States had a 'profound new relationship' with China. He now turned his attention back to the Soviet Union and the perennial sore of Vietnam, and at home he increasingly focused on the presidential election.[33]

Conclusion

Nixon's week in China in 1972 was the culmination of a long and delicate process as two old adversaries moved to establish contact with each other. As the last-minute negotiations over the Shanghai communiqué so clearly showed, the process could have gone badly wrong and the relationship might have slid back into the deep freeze. Both sides rightly felt both relief and a certain guarded optimism about what the future now held. The Chinese assumed that American concessions on Taiwan, in particular, would lead in due course to a solution of that issue as the United States wound down its military presence and ended its support for the government in Taipei. Taiwan, no one perhaps knew quite how, would be merged into the homeland. Equally important, from the Chinese perspective, their country had been recognized as a major power and could now move to take its rightful place on the world's stage. The Americans, for their part, hoped for a substantial realignment in the balance of power which would give them China, with its massive population, vast territories and enormous potential, as a counter-balance against the Soviet Union and also as a new means of pressuring North Vietnam.

At Andrews Air Force Base in Washington, Nixon arrived to an enthusiastic welcome organized by his Vice-President, Spiro Agnew. 'My God,' said Hugh Sidey of *Life*, 'it's like the arrival of the king.' At 98 per cent, Nixon's trip to China registered the highest public awareness of any event in the Gallup poll's history. The right-wing fulminated to little apparent effect. A furious Buchanan threatened to resign from the White House staff on the grounds that the United States had done a deal with a Communist regime and sold out its ally, Taiwan, but in the end he did not carry out his threat. The conservative journalist William F. Buckley, who had been brought along on the trip to win him over, publicly condemned the Shanghai communiqué and went off to support John Ashbrook of Ohio, a little-known Republican Congressman who was trying to stop Nixon's re-election.[1]

American allies murmured – a 'distinct whiff of "peace in our time",' said the British ambassador in Washington – but the overall position of the United States in the world seemed strengthened by its new relationship with China. True, North Vietnam suddenly attacked the South at the end of March 1972. On the other hand, when the United States resumed its heavy bombing of targets in South Vietnam and, for a brief period, of Hanoi and its port city of Haiphong, the Chinese protested but did nothing. In May, when Nixon went even further and mined Haiphong harbour to prevent much-needed Soviet supplies from reaching the North, the Soviet Union made a *pro forma* protest, but it did not attempt to break the blockade and, more importantly, did not cancel the approaching summit.

Kissinger and Nixon both assumed that a major factor in the Soviet Union's unwillingness to make an issue over Haiphong and to move ahead on détente was its obsession with the Chinese menace and a fear that the United States would draw closer to China. The evidence so far from the Soviet side is mixed. It is true that the Soviet Union was concerned about China. Indeed the Soviets continued their military preparations along the Soviet–Chinese border. Nevertheless, the chief Soviet concern in the early 1970s appears to have been Europe, where the Soviet Union wanted to get Western recognition of the borders left behind in the aftermath of the Second World War. That would confirm, or so it appeared at the time, both the division of Germany and Soviet control over its satellites in Eastern Europe.[2]

Nixon went to Moscow in May 1972 and the summit went ahead as planned in a generally friendly atmosphere The United States and the Soviet Union signed a major arms limitation agreement, SALT 1, and an agreement on the Basic Principles to govern their relations. The Soviets also suggested that the two sides formally promise not to use nuclear weapons against each other. That left the door open, though, for their use by, for example, the Soviet Union against China. Kissinger duly let the Chinese know about the Soviet proposal with the assurance that Nixon would accept it only if the Soviets promised as well not to use their weapons on China. Not surprisingly, the Chinese were alarmed both by this and by the overall progress of Soviet–American détente. When Kissinger made two more visits to Beijing, in February and then in November 1973, not only was he granted the honour of meetings with Mao but he was given a particularly friendly welcome. The Chinese took a major step towards normalization of relations by agreeing that the United States and China would establish liaison offices, in many ways indistinguishable from embassies, in each other's capitals.

Mao and Chou both expressed concern over the Soviet Union. Where Kissinger had once been rebuffed by the Chinese when he suggested a defensive alliance, he now found Mao talking about the need for a 'horizontal line' of countries stretching along the borders of the Soviet Union, from the United States, through China and into Europe, to contain Soviet power. 'The driving force on the Chinese side', Kissinger told Nixon after his November trip, 'remained their preoccupation with the Soviet Union.' The Chinese were counting on the United States as a counterweight. 'The key,' commented Nixon in the margin. The China card seemed to be working as both men had intended, to keep the Soviets in line and to bring the Chinese into the American camp.[3]

At the start of 1973, too, there was more good news for the Nixon administration when the war in Vietnam finally came to an end. Kissinger and his counterpart in Paris, Le Duc Tho, reached an agreement which allowed the United States to get out, leaving behind an apparently viable South Vietnam and peace for Laos and Cambodia as well. Taiwan felt a sudden chill, but, as James Shen, Taiwan's ambassador in Washington, commented sourly, selling South Vietnam out meant that his own country was temporarily safe: the United States could not be seen to be abandoning all its allies.[4]

By 1974, however, the China card appeared to be losing its effectiveness. Relations between the United States and the Soviet Union had been badly strained by the Yom Kippur War of October 1973 when the Americans backed Israel and the Soviets its Arab opponents, by the issue of Jewish emigration from the Soviet Union, and by the increasingly aggressive Soviet inroads into the Third World. And the Chinese no longer seemed as friendly. The small American mission in

Beijing found local officials obstructive and difficult and grew used to repeated lectures on offences it had unwittingly committed against the Chinese people. A detachment of Marines, assigned, as was standard practice, to guard the American mission, caused particular trouble. The Chinese objected to their uniforms, to their jogging in formation through the streets of Beijing, and, above all, to their bar, the Red-Ass Saloon, where lonely and bored foreigners crammed in to drink and listen to loud Western music. The Chinese insisted that the Marines leave.[5]

While Sino-American relations did not go back to what they had been before Nixon's visit, they did not move ahead either. The Shanghai communiqué had promised that China and the United States would continue to consult about the full normalization of relations, but that proved to be impossible in the mid-1970s because in each country there was a major leadership crisis: Nixon struggled to stay in office and Mao lay dying.

At his moment of greatest triumph, Nixon had embarked on the series of steps which led him to the Watergate scandal and his eventual disgrace. In June 1972, less than four months after his triumphant return from China, five men with strong links to CREEP, Nixon's campaign committee, and to the White House itself, were arrested trying to bug and burgle the Democratic campaign office in the Watergate complex in downtown Washington. The news made the papers, initially as a minor story. As reporters started to uncover direct connections between the Watergate burglars and the circles around Nixon, the reaction in the White House and the Nixon campaign was to shred documents, deny everything and try to keep a lid on the news. According to Haldeman, the first and fatal mistake was to treat Watergate as a potential public relations disaster. Each attempt to contain it merely led deeper into a full-blown cover-up as Nixon and many of those close to him committed illegal acts and seriously abused government power.[6]

In the run-up to the presidential election of 1972, however, the White House strategy appeared to be working. The major domestic news story was the Democratic campaign, which was imploding as anonymous tips revealed that the vice-presidential candidate, Senator Thomas Eagleton, had not disclosed that he had been treated for depression. Haldeman assured Nixon that, although the Watergate burglars and two of their superiors were going to be indicted that September, everything was under control. All the men had been paid off handsomely to keep quiet. The Justice Department was on side and did not intend to charge anyone else. At the *Washington Post*, though, a couple of junior reporters, Bob Woodward and Carl Bernstein, were starting to uncover some interesting details of payments made to the burglars from CREEP.[7]

Nixon was in a cheerful and confident mood that autumn. The Republican Convention had renominated him by a vote of 1,327 to 1 and the Democrats' candidate for president, George McGovern, was far behind in the polls. Nixon intended, so he said in interviews, to make the next four years even more successful than his first term. He had turned things around for the United States, with bold moves like his China initiative. The long-awaited peace in Vietnam was nearly at hand. In private he told his associates that he was going to get back at his enemies. 'They are asking for it and they are going to get it,' he told John Dean, the White House counsel. Even the Woodward and Bernstein story that October about Segretti and his 'pranksters' with their dirty tricks did not worry Nixon. 'Sue the sons of bitches,' he told Haldeman.[8]

Nixon won the election in November in a landslide. He happily made plans to overhaul the government and centralize decision-making even more in his office. *Time* magazine made him its man of the year in its New Year's issue of 1973. Nixon was pleased but also annoyed that he had to share the honour with Kissinger. On 9 January 1973, his sixtieth birthday, he received a present in a cable from Kissinger, who was in Paris: peace terms had finally been concluded with the North Vietnamese. Two days later Nixon wrote down his goal, both for the United States and for himself. He intended to pursue détente, including major new arms agreements with the Soviet Union. Perhaps he could get a settlement in the Middle East. And for the presidency, 'Restore respect for office.' That day the Watergate trial began.[9]

In the next year and a half, it all unravelled for Nixon. In February 1973 the Senate set up its own committee to investigate. In March, it made public a letter from the one burglar who had broken ranks stating that highly placed officials in the White House had known in advance of the break-in. The Justice Department began its own investigation of the original incident and the subsequent cover-up. More stories surfaced, of the destruction of evidence, of extensive and illegal wiretapping, and of other burglaries to find incriminating evidence against Nixon's enemies. In April, Nixon let Haldeman and Ehrlichman go, his Berlin Wall. It was too late to stop what was now a major scandal. As a Special Prosecutor began digging into the sorry story, the Senate Committee started its televised hearings. In August, it learned that Nixon had hours of tapes of conversations. When Archibald Cox, the Special Prosecutor, got a court order in October that the relevant ones be turned over, Nixon not only resisted but fired Cox. There was now talk of impeaching Nixon.

By 1973, according to Kissinger, Watergate was distracting Nixon and seriously harming the ability of the United States to conduct its foreign relations. Reports came in that spring that the Chinese were discreetly asking about how much authority Nixon still possessed. Nixon had always been bored by domestic issues; now he had to deal with them to the neglect of the international affairs he loved so much. Much to his displeasure, he had to let Kissinger take on a more prominent role. In August 1973 he grudgingly appointed him his Secretary of State. 'With the Watergate problem,' Nixon later told Kissinger's biographer, 'I didn't have any choices.'[10]

At the end of 1973, the White House released transcripts of part of the tapes but fought to keep the rest private. In July 1974, the Supreme Court ruled unanimously against Nixon. Three days later, the House Judiciary Committee approved the first of the articles of impeachment. On 8 August, Nixon announced his resignation to the nation. In his last conversations as president with Kissinger, he went over the great moments of his foreign policy including the opening to China. 'For some reason,' he wrote in his memoirs, 'the agony and the loss of what was about to happen became most acute for me during that conversation. I found myself more emotional than I had been at any time since the decision had been set in motion.' Nixon pulled out the bottle of old brandy which he and Kissinger had drunk from three years previously when they toasted Chou's letter inviting an American emissary to travel to China, but neither man had the heart to drink much. An emotional Nixon asked Kissinger for one last favour; would he kneel beside him for a silent prayer? Kissinger was deeply moved.[11]

Gerald Ford, who had succeeded the disgraced Agnew as vice-president and now found himself Nixon's successor, kept Kissinger on as Secretary of State but he was not prepared to move as fast as Kissinger wanted on China. American public opinion was cooling off after the initial excitement over Nixon's visit. Ford was concerned about the Republican right, which largely supported Taiwan and was not prepared to push for full normalization of relations with China, even if the Chinese had been willing on their side. A visit to China by Ford in 1975 produced little in the way of results. 'I think it was very useful,' said an American official, 'but I can't suggest why I think that.'[12]

The Chinese never really understood Watergate, just as they never really understood how democracies worked. In one of his last coherent conversations with Kissinger, Mao made light of it. 'Why is it in your country', he asked, 'you are always obsessed with that nonsensical Watergate issue?' To embarrassed laughter from the Chinese, his interpreter explained that she was watering down Mao's original expression which really meant 'breaking wind'. Watergate, Mao thought, was no reason to get rid of a president. While Mao's own power remained unassailable, he faced a challenge of another sort. His health was deteriorating rapidly. By the start of 1974, his eyesight was going and he had difficulty talking and swallowing. Saliva dribbled from his half-open mouth. In July, he finally agreed to be examined by a team of specialists. The doctors concluded that he had the rare and fatal disease of the nervous system known in English as Lou Gehrig's Disease. No one dared tell Mao himself, but it was clear to those around him that he had only a year, perhaps two, to live. Mao with his deep-rooted suspicion of doctors initially refused to have treatment of any sort.[13]

He also refused treatment to Chou, whose doctors had discovered in 1973 that he had cancer of the bladder. Chou looked perfectly healthy, Mao said; no need to make him uncomfortable with what were probably useless attempts to cure him. 'Leave the patient alone and let him live out his life happily,' Mao ordered. It was only in the following summer, when a pretty young laboratory technician coaxed Mao, that he agreed to let Chou have an operation. By then it was too late – Chou's cancer had spread rapidly. In March 1975, he went into hospital for yet another operation. There he stayed, working on with what strength he had left. He received foreign dignitaries and high-ranking Chinese Communists in his room. Kissinger saw him one last time. Chou refused to talk politics but he was not able to escape them, as it turned out, even in death.[14]

As Mao moved inexorably towards his own end, his colleagues and servants, as at the court of a dying emperor, jockeyed for power. Much of the infighting and intrigues went on behind the scenes, in the villas of the top leaders or government offices, but distorted reverberations reached the outside world. The press carried strange articles denouncing incorrect thought or work habits or this historical figure or that one. In 1973 a campaign flared up to attack Confucius, the great Chinese philosopher of the sixth century BC. He had supported feudalism, so it was said, and urged rulers to use experienced officials, even if their outlook was old fashioned. Somehow, improbably, Lin Biao, the disgraced, dead Defence Minister, was said to have had the same views. The real targets, hated by Jiang Qing and her coterie, were still alive: Deng Xiaoping, a Communist Party elder who had suddenly been called back from the countryside to become vice-premier, and Chou En-lai himself. Counterattacks, equally indirect, appeared, perhaps inspired by Chou. Jiang Qing was known to like Beethoven. An article in the *People's Daily* accused the Philadelphia Orchestra which had visited Beijing of playing counter-revolutionary Western music, especially Beethoven's Sixth Symphony.[15]

In the background, alternatively stirring up conflict and damping it down, lurked a reclusive and ailing Mao. He communicated with the outside world mainly through his young women assistants. By 1975, he was partly paralysed and could not stand on his own. Zhang Yufeng, once his mistress and now his chief nurse, fed him laboriously by spoon. At Mao's last Chinese New Year, in February 1976, the two of them celebrated alone. 'A faint smile', she recalled, 'crept over his old and weary face when he heard the firecrackers in the courtyard.' Only a select few visitors came to disturb his seclusion. Kissinger came one last time in the autumn of 1975. An American diplomat who spoke Chinese watched as Mao tried to speak: 'Despite my language ability, I couldn't follow the dialogue, but it seemed rather contrived. One grunt became many coherent English sentences, etc. Not necessarily phony, but surely padded out by Mao's female assistants.' Nixon, making one of his periodic trips to China, paid his last respects a few months later, and found it painful to see Mao's deterioration. 'Whatever one may think of him,' he said with admiration, 'no one can deny that he was a fighter to the end.'[16]

During Mao's death-watch, Chinese policy, both domestic and foreign, remained in a state of suspension. High-ranking Chinese tried simply to survive. Many developed convenient illnesses and checked themselves into hospital. Deng, in disgrace again, retired to south China where he was under the protection of the army. Qiao, who was increasingly nervous and depressed as he came under ever fiercer attacks, tried in vain to get himself posted abroad or be allowed to resign. At the start of 1976, Chou died. His death was marked by perfunctory ceremonies. Mao, who was too ill to attend his funeral, showed no emotion at the disappearance of one of his oldest and most faithful servants. The Chinese public, in what was an extraordinary and rare spontaneous outburst, showed what they felt during the traditional spring festival for paying respects to the dead: Tiananmen Square filled with crowds leaving wreaths. Mao, who was told about this by a furious Jiang Qing, appears to have given orders to suppress the demonstrations and remove the wreaths. By this point, since he could communicate only by grunts and scribbled characters, it is impossible to know how much he understood.[17]

In July 1976, a colossal earthquake shook the north of China. When dynasties fell in traditional China, nature, it was believed, often provided such signs. On 9 September, Mao finally died. His body, or what is left of it, still lies in its giant mausoleum in Tiananmen Square. Crowds of Chinese, who appear to be curious rather than sad, file by. Many have bought plastic flowers at the entrance which they leave by Mao's portrait as they make the traditional three bows of respect. Attendants whisk the flowers back outside where they are sold again. By the exit, there are more items for sale: postcards, buttons, boxes, scarves decorated with Mao's round red face and cigarette lighters in the shape of the Little Red Book.

Mao memorabilia, especially from the Cultural Revolution when the Mao cult reached its crazed peak, is for sale all over China. The government, though, has difficulty getting rid of the billions of copies of his works which sit mouldering in warehouses around China. People prefer Mao on T-shirts and New Year's greetings cards. Bars have karaoke versions of his favourite revolutionary songs. In the 1990s, Chinese television ran a Mao quiz show where teams competed to give Mao facts and Mao quotations. Mao has become kitsch. He has also become a talisman. Old women put his image over their stoves as their ancestors would have put the god of the kitchen, and taxi drivers have his picture on their dashboards to save them from accidents. In 1993, the new Maxim's in Beijing held a Mao birthday buffet; guests wore Mao suits and listened to excerpts from one of Jiang Qing's revolutionary operas.[18]

A month after Mao's death, his chosen successor Hua Guofeng and his allies in the armed forces made their move. Jiang Qing and her fellow radicals in the Gang of Four, along with many of their followers, were arrested. Gradually some of the more radical policies of the Cultural Revolution were put aside and China began to wake slowly out of its nightmare. Experienced officials and managers were brought back from exile; universities started to reopen; and official propaganda proclaimed that China must modernize itself. Deng Xiaoping returned from the south and gradually made himself the most powerful man in China. Hua was no match for him and by 1980 he had been forced on to the sidelines as Deng, who preferred to remain in the background, put his own men into office. The pace of change quickened; new economic zones were set up to encourage foreign investment; farmers were allowed to keep a greater share of what they produced; workers were given cash incentives to work harder; and an increasing amount of private enterprise was permitted, indeed encouraged. The government now had a new slogan: 'To Get Rich is Glorious'. Over the next two decades, China's Gross Domestic Product grew at almost 10 per cent per year, an extraordinary figure.

In 1980, as well, the Gang of Four were finally brought to trial. They were charged and convicted, conveniently for everyone involved, with all the crimes of the Cultural Revolution. Jiang Qing was portrayed as a demon, an unwomanly woman and modern-day empress, who had plotted to murder her own husband and seize power. Even her favourite American movie, *Gone with the Wind*, was hauled in as evidence to show that, like Scarlett O'Hara, she was out to bring men under her sway. Although Jiang was sentenced to death, the sentence was suspended and she was locked away in China's elite prison north of Beijing where, so it is said, she knitted sweaters and embroidered dolls, none of which could be sold because she always put her name on them. There are stories that she wrote her memoirs but that Deng, who feared what she could tell, ordered them to be destroyed. In 1991, she died, perhaps of cancer of the throat. The official news agency reported that she had hung herself with the belt of her trousers. Like much about Jiang, we will probably never know the truth. Her body has been cremated and the ashes have disappeared.

Qiao Guanhua's career came to an unhappy end in 1976 when he was dismissed in the purges that followed Mao's death. Although he had tried desperately to steer between the factions which tore the foreign ministry apart, he was accused both of making rightist mistakes and of taking part in the Gang of Four's conspiracies. He and his wife, Zhang Hanzhi, were held under arrest for the next two years and subjected to public meetings where they were criticized and manhandled. Qiao, who had tuberculosis, became increasingly feeble. As Deng began to consolidate his power, he was able to intervene and make sure that Qiao received medical treatment. In 1982, the last of the charges against Qiao were withdrawn. He died in 1983. His wife, who still lives in Beijing, refused to have him buried in the special plot for high-ranking ministers and his ashes are in the beautiful city of Suzhou in a tomb flanked by two pine trees from Geneva, a city where he had once been happy. Their daughter went to Vassar and edits a magazine in China devoted to profiles of celebrities and filled with advertisements for luxury goods.[19]

Henry Kissinger survived the turmoil of the Nixon White House and stayed on as Gerald Ford's Secretary of State. Ford, who trusted and admired him, gave him a free hand to run American foreign policy. In 1976, with the election of Jimmy Carter to the presidency, Kissinger found himself out of a job. He confidently expected that Harvard University would invite him back as a distinguished professor; when it only offered him his old post back, he turned it down with disdain and some bitterness. Life provided many compensations, though: an apartment in New York with his second wife Nancy, a country house in Connecticut, a circle of famous and powerful friends, well-paid consultancies for banks and television networks, and an enduring reputation as one of the United States' most brilliant and fascinating men. He continued to write: articles, columns, two gigantic volumes of memoirs and several books on international relations. When there were international crises, the press inevitably came calling; his comments were incisive, clear and amusing, but, although he continued to hope that he would be called back to office, especially when Ronald Reagan became president in 1980, the call never came. He increasingly devoted his time to his work as a high-level consultant. Kissinger and Associates, which still flourishes in New York, provides the sort of analysis and contacts with governments around the world for which companies are willing to pay handsomely. As China opened up as a field for trade and investment, Kissinger was much in demand to help get American business in the door. He was able to provide introductions to virtually every important official, including Deng himself.

He has been criticized for blurring the roles of commentator and consultant, for, to take one example, advocating restraint on the part of the American government in its reaction to the crackdown in Tiananmen Square in 1989 at a time when he had just established a company with a group of big American corporations to look for investments in China. He remains, as he has been for much of his life, a controversial figure who is widely admired and widely condemned. What both his defenders and his critics agree on is that he has never been dull.[20]

Richard Nixon left the White House in disgrace in 1974. In his resignation speech, as Kissinger put it, he admitted his mistakes but not his guilt. He reminded his audience of his efforts to make the world a safer and more stable place. 'This, more than anything, is what I hope will be my legacy to you, to our country, as I leave the presidency.' A month later, President Ford granted him a blanket pardon for anything he might have done. Unlike Qiao, Nixon lived long enough to see his reputation at least partly restored. He worked hard at it. He wrote his memoirs; they deal with Watergate but spend much more time on the great achievements of his presidency, including of course the opening to China. He continued to visit China and its leaders as a private citizen, and the Chinese, who regarded Watergate as a trivial domestic matter, always welcomed him as an honoured guest. He gradually started to give speeches and interviews again. He wrote books and articles, on foreign affairs or about the world leaders he had known. His last book, *Beyond Peace*, published shortly before his death, gave the United States advice on how to conduct itself in the post-Cold War world. Jimmy Carter consulted him; so did presidents Reagan, Bush senior and Clinton. In 1986, *Newsweek* ran a cover story: 'He's Back: the Rehabilitation of Richard Nixon'.[21]

In 1976, Pat Nixon suffered a stroke but did not tell anyone until Nixon found her struggling to make breakfast. She kept going with the strong sense of duty that had carried her through her life and died in 1993. When Nixon himself died in a New York hospital a year later, President Clinton proclaimed a national day of mourning. Nixon's coffin was carried from New York to California by the same Air Force One that had first taken him to China all those years before, and his funeral was organized by Ron Walker, the advance man for that momentous trip. He was buried beside Pat Nixon at the Richard M. Nixon Memorial Library near where he had grown up in Yorba Linda. As all the living former presidents, Ford, Carter, Reagan and Bush senior sat with their wives in the front row, Clinton asked Americans to forgive Nixon. 'May the day of judging President Nixon on anything less than his entire life and career come to a close.' An emotional Kissinger delivered the eulogy. He admitted Nixon's faults but praised him for his outstanding conduct of foreign policy. Nixon had never given up. 'In his solitude he envisaged a new international order that would reduce lingering enmities, strengthen historic friendships, and give new hope to mankind.'[22]

To the end, Nixon regarded the opening to China as one of his greatest achievements, perhaps the greatest. As he said on his last trip to China in 1993, 'I will be known historically for two things. Watergate and the opening to China . . . I don't mean to be pessimistic, but Watergate, that silly, silly thing, is going to rank up there historically with what I did here.' He hoped that his initiative had brought the United States and China into a working relationship which would benefit both and bring stability to Asia.[23]

Nixon and Kissinger both witnessed the full normalization of relations in the late 1970s, from the sidelines. By then, changes in China and the United States made it possible for the two countries to take another step forward in their relationship. Both were concerned about the Soviet Union, which was aggressively expanding its military and its influence. China was stirring out of the nightmare of the Cultural Revolution and Deng was firmly in control. The seeds of China's extraordinary development over the next two decades had been planted. Learning from the outside world, making money, individual initiative, all were not only permissible but encouraged. In 1977 when the new Democrat administration under Jimmy Carter took office in the United States determined to push ahead on normalization, it found a receptive audience in Beijing. The two sides agreed to establish full diplomatic relations. The United States cut its formal ties with Taiwan, withdrew the last of its troops, and gave notice that the defence treaty would be terminated. In January 1979, Deng was welcomed enthusiastically in the United States. American television audiences were charmed when he wore a cowboy hat in Texas and kissed little children. The White House gave him a twenty-one-gun salute and the band at the Kennedy Center played 'Getting to Know You'.[24]

Nixon also was around to witness the growing strains in the relationship between China and the United States in the late 1980s. Ever since they first made contact, relations between the two countries have had their ups and downs. Perhaps they are bound to be rivals, for each in its own way aspires to be a model for others. Each has a tendency to think it is right, that it is more moral than other nations. They have come to know each other well but they do not always understand each other. The Americans hope that the Chinese are becoming more like them; repeatedly they have been disappointed. The Chinese are repeatedly surprised by and suspicious of American concerns for democracy and human rights. American protests, notably after Chinese authorities brutally put down the pro-democracy movement in Tiananmen Square in 1989, strike them as interference on a par with that of the Western imperialists during the century of humiliation.

In April 1993, two decades after he had first been there, Nixon went back to Hangzhou. 'The growth of this place', he told his companions, 'is really unbelievable. And you know, I like to think that I had something to do with it.' Yet China's increasing prosperity has brought its own difficulties and caused tensions. American consumers love the prices of goods made in China; American labour and some American businesses do not. The United States' trade deficit with China grew sharply in the new century; in 2005 alone it neared $200 billion. As China's economy continues to expand rapidly, the Chinese government is moving to secure sources of raw materials, especially oil, in parts of Africa and Central Asia which the United States has till now considered its own. It is not just China's growing economic power that worries Americans. Chinese firms, many of them close to the military, are enthusiastic exporters, often to some of the most troubled parts of the world, of weapons, from handguns to missiles. And, according to official figures, China's defence budget has increased at least 10 per cent every year since the mid-1990s. In Washington, military planners have adopted what they describe as a long-range 'hedging strategy' to prepare for the eventuality that there might, one day, be a conflict between the United States and China. The United States has quietly been strengthening its forces in the Pacific and encouraging Japan to enhance its military establishment. The Soviet Union has gone but perhaps, so the pessimists think, there is a new Cold War in the making between the United States and China.[25]

Taiwan of course remains the major unsettled issue between the United States and China. It is neither independent nor a part of China. The Americans have never quite been able to give up their interest in it; the formal links have gone but the unofficial ones remain strong, whether through trade or personal contact or, from time to time, the sale of American military equipment. The Chinese have found this irritating and still maintain that Taiwan must be reunited with the Motherland. When leaders of Taiwan's lively independence movement visit the United States, the Chinese government reacts angrily. When the presidential election in 2004 brought a pro-independence candidate into office, the Chinese government responded with solemn warnings. Today in Taiwan there is talk of a compromise that will fudge reality, just as it has been fudged since 1972. Why not a thirty- to fifty-year 'interim agreement' under which Taiwan would give up on formal independence and China would renounce the use of force? The danger with such an ingenious solution is that it leaves the door open for trouble. What if hardline nationalists in China grow impatient with the lack of clarity about whether or not Taiwan belongs to China? There have already been plenty of warning shots: Chinese submarines in waters claimed by Taiwan, missile tests, planes in Taiwan airspace. What if Japan, whose own relations with China are troubled, decides that Taiwan must be defended? And what choices then will the United States face?

The present troubles between China and the United States tempt us to look backwards and wonder what mistakes might have been made in the past. It was probably a mistake for the United States to back the Guomindang for as long as it did, but, on the other hand, the risks of abandoning a longstanding ally were also great. It was a mistake on Mao's part that his new Communist regime in China threw in its lot with the Soviet Union and perhaps missed the chance of coming to an accommodation with the United States in 1949. There is always the question, though, of how ready the Americans would have been to talk to a new Communist regime in those tense early days of the Cold War. It is true that they were able to come to an accommodation with Tito's Yugoslavia but only after it was clear that he had broken with the Soviet Union. It is a pity that the Cold War and Korea and then Vietnam intervened to keep China and the United States apart for so long.

The breakthrough of the 1970s, most would agree now, was not only overdue; it was good for both countries and their new relationship had great potential, which still remains, to act as a stabilizing force in world politics. It is possible, though, to ask whether the United States was too eager and whether it gave away too much. Should, for example, Nixon have visited China first, without knowing whether or not he would see Mao, and without a firm agreement on the Shanghai communiqué? Should the Americans have handed over quite so much confidential material about the Soviets and, moreover, given the impression that the United States was eager to have an alliance with China against the Soviet Union?

American behaviour raised expectations among the Chinese which could not always be met. The China of the 1970s was both weak and apprehensive about its place in the world. The Americans may have unwittingly done more than merely reassure the Chinese leadership; they may have fed into the old Chinese belief that China was at the centre of the world. Did Kissinger have to be quite so deferential, even at times obsequious? The decision to use Chinese interpreters in his own and Nixon's conversations with the Chinese may have been politic, a gesture of reassurance. Was it necessary to explain away the presence of an American interpreter in the meetings? 'We will tell the press', Kissinger warned Chou, 'we have Mr Holdridge there to check on your interpreter. I apologize to your interpreter. It is only so our people won't say we put ourselves at your mercy – which we are doing.' When relations got on to a more normal footing, as they were bound to after those first euphoric moments in 1972, the Chinese were surprised when the Americans treated them as merely one power among several, suspicious when the White House and the State Department appeared to be following different policies, and were aggrieved when the United States was not able to live up to its promises. Nixon and Kissinger went too far, for example, in making assurances to China about withdrawing American forces from Taiwan, which they were not in the end able to keep.[26]

For Nixon and the Americans, the visit was a bold and dramatic move which placed Nixon himself in the centre of great events and the United States as the pivotal power between China and the Soviet Union. The China card did not produce as much as the Americans hoped for, but cards, particularly if they have a will of their own, usually do not. For a time the Soviet Union was more amenable in its negotiations with the United States, and unease about China certainly played a part in that. The North Vietnamese did not stop fighting and, in the end, gave way very little in the Paris negotiations to conclude the war. China's new relationship with the United States did, however, help to deepen the suspicion with which the Vietnamese regarded the Chinese and paved the way for the later war between China and a newly reunited Vietnam.

For the Chinese, there were also losses and gains as a result of the Nixon visit. They agreed to wait on Taiwan and they are still waiting.

On the other hand, the visit was an acknowledgement of China's importance in the world and marked the end to the isolation of the 1960s. Although the legacy of the Cultural Revolution was to lie heavily on China until Mao's death, the beginnings of the reawakening and revitalization of China after 1976 lie in this period.

We now take for granted that, whatever the ups and downs between China and the United States, there was bound to be a relationship, that the gap between 1949 and 1971 was an aberration which could not last. Yet we should remember that the long chill between the United States and Cuba has lasted for more than four decades and that with Iran for nearly three. Nixon's visit occurred because both sides came to the conclusion at the same time that it was a good idea. Yet it took individuals, four men in this case, to make it happen. Nixon and Mao, Kissinger and Chou. Two men who for all their faults possessed the necessary vision and determination and two men who had the talent, the patience and the skill to make the vision reality. In one of their conversations, Chou told Kissinger of an old Chinese proverb: 'The helmsman who knows how to guide the boat will guide it well through the waves. Otherwise he will be submerged by the waves. A far-sighted man will know how to till the helm.' Or as Mr Spock will say aboard his spaceship many centuries from now, there is an old Vulcan proverb, 'Only Nixon can go to China.'[27]

Appendix: The Communiqué

PRESIDENT RICHARD NIXON of the United States of America visited the People's Republic of China at the invitation of Premier Chou En-lai of the People's Republic of China from February 21 to February 28, 1972. Accompanying the President were Mrs. Nixon, U.S. Secretary of State William Rogers, Assistant to the President Dr. Henry Kissinger, and other American officials.

President Nixon met with Chairman Mao Tse-tung of the Communist Party of China on February 21. The two leaders had a serious and frank exchange of views on Sino-U.S. relations and world affairs.

During the visit, extensive, earnest, and frank discussions were held between President Nixon and Premier Chou En-lai on the normalization of relations between the United States of America and the People's Republic of China, as well as on other matters of interest to both sides. In addition, Secretary of State William Rogers and Foreign Minister Chi P'engfei held talks in the same spirit.

President Nixon and his party visited Peking and viewed cultural, industrial and agricultural sites, and they also toured Hangchow and Shanghai where, continuing discussions with Chinese leaders, they viewed similar places of interest.

The leaders of the People's Republic of China and the United States of America found it beneficial to have this opportunity, after so many years without contact, to present candidly to one another their views on a variety of issues. They reviewed the international situation in which important changes and great upheavals are taking place and expounded their respective positions and attitudes.

The U.S. side stated: Peace in Asia and peace in the world requires efforts both to reduce immediate tensions and to eliminate the basic causes of conflict. The United States will work for a just and secure peace: just, because it fulfills the aspirations of peoples and nations for freedom and progress; secure, because it removes the danger of foreign aggression. The United States supports individual freedom and social progress for all the peoples of the world, free of outside pressure or intervention. The United States believes that the effort to reduce tensions is served by improving communication between countries that have different ideologies so as to lessen the risks of confrontation through accident, miscalculation or misunderstanding. Countries should treat each other with mutual respect and be willing to compete peacefully, letting performance be the ultimate judge. No country should claim infallibility and each country should be prepared to re-examine its own attitudes for the common good. The United States stressed that the peoples of Indochina should be allowed to determine their destiny without outside intervention; its constant primary objective has been a negotiated solution; the eight-point proposal put forward by the Republic of Vietnam and the United States on January 27, 1972 represents a basis for the attainment of that objective; in the absence of a negotiated settlement the United States envisages the ultimate withdrawal of all U.S. forces from the region consistent with the aim of self-determination for each country of Indochina. The United States will maintain its close ties with and support for the Republic of Korea; the United States will support efforts of the Republic of Korea to seek a relaxation of tension and increased communication in the Korean peninsula. The United States places the highest value on its friendly relations with Japan; it will continue to develop the existing close bonds. Consistent with the United Nations Security Council Resolution of December 21, 1971, the United States favors the continuation of the cease-fire between India and Pakistan and the withdrawal of all military forces to within their own territories and to their own sides of the cease-fire line in Jammu and Kashmir; the United States supports the right of the peoples of South Asia to shape their own future in peace, free of military threat, and without having the area become the subject of great power rivalry.

The Chinese side stated: Wherever there is oppression, there is resistance. Countries want independence, nations want liberation and the people want revolution – this has become the irresistible trend of history. All nations, big or small, should be equal; big nations should not bully the small and strong nations should not bully the weak. China will never be a superpower and it opposes hegemony and power politics of any kind. The Chinese side stated that it firmly supports the struggles of all the oppressed people and nations for freedom and liberation and that the people of all countries have the right to choose their social systems according to their own wishes and the right to safeguard the independence, sovereignty and territorial integrity of their own countries and oppose foreign aggression, interference, control and subversion. All foreign troops should be withdrawn to their own countries.

The Chinese side expressed its firm support to the peoples of Vietnam, Laos, and Cambodia in their efforts for the attainment of their goal and its firm support to the seven-point proposal of the Provisional Revolutionary Government of the Republic of South Vietnam and the elaboration of February this year on the two key problems in the proposal, and to the Joint Declaration of the Summit Conference of the Indo-Chinese Peoples. It firmly supports the eight-point program for the peaceful unification of Korea put forward by the Government of the Democratic People's Republic of Korea on April 12, 1971, and the stand for the abolition of the 'U.N. Commission for the Unification and Rehabilitation of Korea.' It firmly opposes the revival and outward expansion of Japanese militarism and firmly supports the Japanese people's desire to build an independent, democratic, peaceful and neutral Japan. It firmly maintains that India and Pakistan should, in accordance with the United Nations resolutions on the India–Pakistan question, immediately withdraw all their forces to their respective territories and to their own sides of the cease-fire line in Jammu and Kashmir and firmly supports the Pakistan Government and people in their struggle to preserve their independence and sovereignty and the people of Jammu and Kashmir in their struggle for the right of self-determination.

There are essential differences between China and the United States in their social systems and foreign policies. However, the two sides agreed that countries, regardless of their social systems, should conduct their relations on the principles of respect for the sovereignty and territorial integrity of all states, nonaggression against other states, noninterference in the internal affairs of other states, equality and mutual benefit, and peaceful coexistence. International disputes should be settled on this basis, without resorting to the use or threat of force. The United States and the People's Republic of China are prepared to apply these principles to their mutual relations.

With these principles of international relations in mind the two sides stated that:
– progress toward the normalization of relations between China and the United States is in the interests of all countries;
– both wish to reduce the danger of international military conflict;
– neither should seek hegemony in the Asia-Pacific region and each is opposed to efforts by any other country or group of countries to establish such hegemony; and
– neither is prepared to negotiate on behalf of any third party or to enter into agreements or understandings with the other directed at other states.

Both sides are of the view that it would be against the interests of the peoples of the world for any major country to collude with another against other countries, or for major countries to divide up the world into spheres of interest.

The two sides reviewed the long-standing serious disputes between China and the United States. The Chinese side reaffirmed its position: The Taiwan question is the crucial question obstructing the normalization of relations between China and the United States; the Government of the People's Republic of China is the sole legal government of China; Taiwan is a province of China which has long been returned to the motherland; the liberation of Taiwan is China's internal affair in which no other country has the right to interfere; and all U.S. forces and military installations must be withdrawn from Taiwan. The Chinese Government firmly opposes any activities which aim at the creation of 'one China, one Taiwan . . . one China, two governments,' 'two Chinas,' and 'independent Taiwan' or advocate that 'the status of Taiwan remains to be determined.'

The U.S. side declared: The United States acknowledges that all Chinese on either side of the Taiwan Strait maintain there is but one China and that Taiwan is a part of China. The United States Government does not challenge that position. It reaffirms its interest in a peaceful settlement of the Taiwan question by the Chinese themselves. With this prospect in mind, it affirms the ultimate objective of the withdrawal of all U.S. forces and military installations from Taiwan. In the meantime, it will progressively reduce its forces and military installations on Taiwan as the tension in the area diminishes.

The two sides agreed that it is desirable to broaden the understanding between the two peoples. To this end, they discussed specific areas in such fields as science, technology, culture, sports and journalism, in which people-to-people contacts and exchanges would be mutually beneficial. Each side undertakes to facilitate the further development of such contacts and exchanges.

Both sides view bilateral trade as another area from which mutual benefit can be derived, and agreed that economic relations based on equality and mutual benefit are in the interest of the people of the two countries. They agree to facilitate the progressive development of trade between their two countries.

The two sides agreed that they will stay in contact through various channels, including the sending of a senior U.S. representative to Peking from time to time for concrete consultations to further the normalization of relations between the two countries and continue to exchange views on issues of common interest.

The two sides expressed the hope that the gains achieved during this visit would open up new prospects for the relations between the two countries. They believe that the normalization of relations between the two countries is not only in the interest of the Chinese and American peoples but also contributes to the relaxation of tension in Asia and the world.

President Nixon, Mrs. Nixon and the American party expressed their appreciation for the gracious hospitality shown them by the Government and people of the People's Republic of China.

Notes

KEY TO ABBREVIATIONS

CWIHP   Cold War International History Project
FRUS   *Foreign Relations of the United States*
NARA   National Archives and Records Administration (US)
NPM   Nixon Presidential Materials Project, National Archives and Records Administration [Archives II (College Park, Maryland), 2006; by 2008 these materials will be in the Nixon Presidential Library, Yorba Linda, California]
NSA   National Security Archive [http://www.gwu.edu/~nsarchiv/]
PCC   *Playing the China Card* [documentary]
PRO   Public Record Office (UK)
RN   *RN: The Memoirs of Richard Nixon*
USOH   US Foreign Affairs oral history collection
WHY   Kissinger, *The White House Years*

INTRODUCTION

1   *RN*, p. 580

CHAPTER 1: SETTING OUT

1   Remarks on Departure from the White House for a State Visit to the People's Republic of China, Richard Nixon, 17 February 1972, The Public Papers of Presidents of the United States, The American Presidency Project
2   USOH, Supplement, Lord; Thomas, *Front Row*, p. 187; *RN*, p. 559
3   *RN*, p. 559
4   USOH, Supplement, Lord
5   *RN*, p. 284; *FRUS, Foundations*, pp. 2–10; Memorandum of Conversation, 22 February 1972, 2.10 p.m.–6.00 p.m., NSA, Nixon's Trip to China: Records Now Completely Declassified, Doc. 1, p. 8
6   Hoff, p. 6; Nixon, 'Asia after Vietnam', pp. 121, 123; Richard Nixon, 20 January 1969, The Public Papers of Presidents of the United States, The American Presidency Project
7   Kissinger, *Diplomacy*, p. 729

8 White, p. 147
9 Brodie, p. 162; *FRUS, Foundations*, p. 43
10 USOH, Nichols; USOH, Green
11 *FRUS, Foundations*, p. 199; Memorandum for the President's Files, 'Briefing of the White House Staff on the July 15 Announcement of the President's Trip to Peking', 19 July 1971, NSA, Electronic Briefing Book No. 66, Doc. 41
12 *RN*, p. 1076; Ambrose, *Nixon: Triumph*, p. 26; Reeves, p. 145
13 *RN*, p. 45; Bundy, pp. 7–10; *FRUS, Foundations*, pp. 352, 142; Richard Nixon 20 January 1969, The Public Papers of Presidents of the United States, The American Presidency Project
14 See, for example, Reeves, p. 25; Aitken, p. 241
15 Reeves, p. 156; Wicker, *One of Us*, pp. 76, 79; Ambrose, *Nixon: Education*, p. 459
16 Wicker, *One of Us*, p. 686; Haldeman, *Diaries*, p. 293
17 Haldeman, *Ends*, p. 60; Aitken, p. 239; Ehrlichman, p. 313 n. 1
18 Cited in Wicker, 'Richard M. Nixon 1969–1974', p. 251; Brodie, p. 110
19 Cited in Wicker, 'Richard M. Nixon 1969–1974', p. 253; USOH, Supplement, Feldman; Garment, p. 387; Wicker, *One of Us*, p. 653
20 Summers, p. 40; Ambrose, *Nixon: Education*, p. 351; Garment, p. 299; Summers, p. 96; Valeriani, p. 75
21 Ambrose, *Nixon: Triumph*, p. 326; *RN*, p. 573
22 Ambrose, *Nixon: Education*, pp. 669–71
23 Cited in Ambrose, *Nixon: Education*, p. 359; Cited in Wicker, 'Richard M. Nixon 1969–1974', pp. 250, 252; Garment, p. 298
24 Ambrose, *Nixon: Triumph*, p. 326; Rather and Gates, p. 245; USOH, Freeman; Haldeman, *Ends*, p. 73
25 Ambrose, *Nixon: Triumph*, p. 254; Summers, p. 326
26 Ambrose, *Nixon: Triumph*, p. 254; Haldeman, *Diaries*, p. 283; Ehrlichman, p. 268; Haldeman, *Ends*, p. 73; Haldeman, *Diaries*, p. 89
27 Kimball, p. 9; Haldeman, *Ends*, p. 72
28 Haldeman, *Ends*, p. 65; Ehrlichman, p. 67
29 Aitken, p. 240; Wicker, *One of Us*, p. 653
30 Ehrlichman, p. 294; Kalb, p. 267
31 *WHY*, pp. 1051, 1051–2; Reeves, p. 433, endnote; *RN*, pp. 557–9; Garment, p. 245
32 Holdridge, pp. 77–8; *WHY*, p. 1051; Haldeman, *Diaries*, p. 410
33 Kraft, p. 10
34 Haldeman, *Diaries*, p. 412

CHAPTER 2: ARRIVAL

1 Author interview with John Fraser
2 Author interview with John Burns; Kalb, p. 266
3 John Burns in the *Globe and Mail*, 7 October 1971
4 Osborne, pp. 23, 28

5 Kalb, p. 267

6 Kraft, p. 20

7 Osborne, p. 22; *WHY*, p. 1055; Holdridge, pp. 83–4; Haldeman, *Diaries*, pp. 412–13; author interviews with Gordon Barass and John Fraser

8 Holdridge, p. 56; see also Frankel, p. 350

9 Chang and Halliday, pp. 569, 586

10 Short, *Dragon and the Bear*, p. 189; Leys, *Chinese Shadows*, p. 4

11 Brady, chs 4 and 5; Cradock, p. 27

12 Cradock, pp. 22–4; author interview with Gordon Barass

13 Author interviews with Gordon Barass and John Fraser

CHAPTER 3: CHOU EN-LAI

1 *RN*, p. 560

2 Wilson, *Chou*, pp. 22, 23

3 *Ibid.*, pp. 26, 24

4 Khrushchev, *Khrushchev Remembers* (1970), p. 372

5 Shao, pp. 6–15

6 Wilson, *Chou*, p. 35

7 *Ibid.*, pp. 40–1

8 Shao, p. 51; Wilson, *Chou*, p. 48

9 Wilson, *Chou*, p. 58 and ch. 5 *passim*

10 Chang and Halliday, p. 73; Han, pp. 79, 85; Wilson, *Chou*, p. 120

11 Chang and Halliday, pp. 116, 616; Jin, p. 207

12 Xu, p. 98; author interview with Zhang Hanzhi

13 Wilson, *Chou*, p. 17; *WHY*, pp. 743, 745, 744

14 Wilson, *Chou*, pp. 110–11; Chang and Halliday, pp. 107–8, 133; Li Zhisui, p. 510; Fang and Fang, pp. 62–4

15 Leys, *Burning Forest*, p. 155

16 Short, *Mao*, p. 419

17 Xu, p. 90

18 Fang and Fang, p. 100

19 Keith, pp. 24–5; Fang and Fang, p. 108; Memorandum of Conversation, 21 October 1971, 10.30 a.m.–1.45 p.m., NSA, Electronic Briefing Book No. 70, Doc. 11, p. 19

20 Keith, p. 30

CHAPTER 4: DIAOYUTAI

1 Haldeman, *Diaries*, p. 413; Chapin interview, *PCC* transcripts, roll 47, p. 14

2 Strober and Strober, p. 124

3 *RN*, pp. 1055, 341

4 *FRUS, Foundations*, pp. 45–6, 45

5 Kissinger, *World Restored*, Introduction; *WHY*, p. 191; *FRUS, Foundations*, p. 44

6 Fried, *Day of Dedication*, p. 287

7 Kissinger, *World Restored*, pp. 317–18, 326

8 *WHY*, p. 598; Kissinger, *World Restored*, p. 329; Fallaci, p. 41

9 Isaacson, p. 128

10 *RN*, pp. 340–1

11 *WHY*, pp. 12, 14; Haldeman, *Diaries*, p. 22

12 *RN*, p. 341

13 Isaacson, p. 29

14 *Ibid.*, p. 56n

15 Feeney, p. 165; USOH, Holdridge

16 Marshall Green in Strober and Strober, p. 125; Garment, pp. 186–7

17 Isaacson, pp. 100, 147

18 *Ibid.*, pp. 601–2

19 *Ibid.*, pp. 152–5; Hanhimäki, pp. 24–5; Bundy, pp. 54–5; Helms, pp. 382, 384

20 Isaacson, p. 193; Valeriani, p. 21

21 Valeriani, p. 14; Haldeman, *Diaries*, pp. 99, 189

22 Strober and Strober, p. 119; Price, p. 305; see also Hoff, pp. 152–3

23 Author interview with Kissinger; *WHY*, pp. 163–5; Isaacson, p. 126; see, for example, USOH, Kreisberg

24 Haig, p. 257; *FRUS, Foundations*, p. 81; Haldeman, *Ends*, p. 91

25 *RN*, pp. 544–50; *WHY*, pp. 163, 194; Haldeman, *Diaries*, p. 189; Strober and Strober, p. 124; Haldeman, *Ends*, p. 84; Ambrose, *Nixon: Triumph*, p. 480; Ehrlichman, pp. 310–11; Haldeman, *Diaries*, p. 555

26 Strober and Strober, p. 126; *RN*, p. 407; Hanhimäki, p. 26; Isaacson, p. 147

27 Isaacson, p. 145; Haldeman, *Ends*, p. 94; Isaacson, pp. 190–2; Strober and Strober, p. 125; Hoff, p. 155

28 Hoff, ch. 5; Isaacson, p. 140

29 Isaacson, p. 152; Dobrynin, pp. 198–200; Bundy, pp. 57–8

30 Conversation among President Nixon, Henry Kissinger and John Mitchell, 8 December 1971, Doc. 165, *FRUS, Nixon–Ford Administrations*, vol. E-7; Valeriani, p. 94; USOH, Holdridge; Kissinger, *World Restored*, p. 326; Chapin interview, *PCC* transcripts, roll 46, p. 14

31 *WHY*, p. 1055; Memorandum for Henry A. Kissinger, 6 August, 1971, NSA, Electronic Briefing Book No. 66, Doc. 35, p. 30; Memorandum of Conversation, 21 October 1971, NSA, Electronic Briefing Book No. 70, Doc. 11, pp. 3, 8

32 USOH, Thayer; USOH, Green, ch. VI

33 USOH, Freeman; Ambrose, *Nixon: Education*, p. 618; *RN*, p. 339; Ehrlichman, p. 297

34 Strober and Strober, p. 128; USOH, Freeman

35 Isaacson, p. 198

36 Hersh, pp. 32, 33

37 Haldeman, *Diaries*, pp. 289, 253–4; author interview with Kissinger; Haldeman, *Diaries*, pp. 253–4

38 Haldeman, *Diaries*, p. 413; USOH, Freeman
39 Memorandum of Conversation, 21 October 1971, 10.30 a.m.–1.45 p.m., NSA, Electronic Briefing Book No. 70, Doc. 11, p. 5

CHAPTER 5: MEETING WITH MAO

1 Li Zhisui, pp. 542–3, 547
2 *Ibid.*, pp. 551–2, 553–8
3 *Ibid.*, pp. 561–3
4 *Ibid.*, p. 563; USOH, Supplement, Lord
5 Garver, *Foreign Relations*, p. 9
6 Luo, p. 155
7 Schram, *Political Thought*, p. 256
8 Hunt, *Genesis*, ch. 1, for a discussion of this point
9 *WHY*, p. 1057; USOH, Supplement, Lord
10 Li Zhisui, p. 564; Haldeman, *Diaries*, p. 414
11 Kraft, p. 20
12 Li Zhisui, pp. 78–9; Chang and Halliday, p. 345
13 *WHY*, p. 1058
14 USOH, Supplement, Lord
15 *WHY*, p. 1059; *RN*, p. 560; Burr, ed., *Kissinger Transcripts*, pp. 59, 60; *WHY*, pp. 1063–4
16 Burr, ed., *Kissinger Transcripts*, pp. 65, 62, 61; Teng and Fairbank, p. 19
17 Burr, ed., *Kissinger Transcripts*, pp. 61, 62, 60, 63
18 *Ibid.*, pp. 59, 60
19 Li Zhisui, p. 565
20 Burr, ed., *Kissinger Transcripts*, p. 64
21 *Ibid.*, pp. 64, 65
22 *Ibid.*, p. 65; *Niksong dangnian fanghua xianwei renzhi de neimu*
23 Li Zhisui, p. 565; Heath, p. 495
24 Haldeman, *Diaries*, p. 414; USOH, Supplement, Lord; USOH, Freeman; *WHY*, p. 1057
25 *RN*, p. 561; Safire, p. 411; *WHY*, pp. 1058, 1059; author interview with Kissinger; USOH, Supplement, Lord
26 Strober and Strober, p. 136; *WHY*, p. 1061; Kalb, p. 270

CHAPTER 6: MAO TSE-TUNG

1 Burr, ed., *Kissinger Transcripts*, p. 65; Ambrose, *Nixon: Triumph*, p. 454
2 See, for example, Ambrose, *Nixon: Triumph*, p. 409; Li Zhisui, pp. 478–9
3 Short, *Mao*, pp. 60–1; *Mao Zedong on Diplomacy*, pp. 419–20
4 Teiwes, p. 1
5 Schram, *Mao Tse-tung*, p. 29
6 Short, *Mao*, p. 33
7 *Ibid.*, pp. 26–7, 33–4, 29

8 Chang and Halliday, p. 6
9 Short, *Mao*, p. 37
10 *Ibid.*, pp. 37, 55, 66; Schram, *Mao Tse-tung*, p. 25
11 Short, *Mao*, p. 57
12 Schram, *Political Thought*, p. 143
13 *Ibid*, p. 94
14 Chang and Halliday, p. 269; Khrushchev, *Khrushchev Remembers: The Last Testament* (1974), p. 249
15 Short, *Mao*, p. 60
16 *Ibid.*, p. 102
17 Chang and Halliday, p. 18
18 *Ibid.*, pp. 24–5
19 *Ibid.*, pp. 144, 158–60
20 Short, *Mao*, pp. 382, 395; Chang and Halliday, p. 279; Short, *Mao*, p. 396
21 Smedley, p. 170
22 Chang and Halliday, p. 632; Li Zhisui, pp. 120–1; Short, *Mao*, p. 434; Jin, p. 51; Quan, p. 43; Ji, p. 14.
23 Ross, 'From Lin Biao to Deng Xiaoping', p. 272; Chang and Halliday, p. 409
24 Short, *Mao*, p. 226; Chang and Halliday, pp. 83–91
25 Chang and Halliday, p. 346; Li Zhisui, pp. 363–4
26 Hunt, *Genesis*, p. 7; Khrushchev, *Khrushchev Remembers: The Last Testament* (1974), p. 252; Short, *Mao*, p. 70
27 Teiwes, p. 75; Fang and Fang, pp. 123–4; Jin, p. 74
28 Quan, pp. 44, 45–7; Li Zhisui, pp. 120–1; Chang and Halliday, p. 454; Schoenhals, p. 96
29 Short, *Mao*, p. 79; Chang and Halliday, p. 432n.
30 Schram, *Political Thought*, pp. 182, 253
31 Luo, p. 214
32 Li Zhisui, pp. 126, 107; Quan, pp. 90–2, 97, 99, 113, 115
33 Quan, p. 29; Li Zhisui, p. 99; Quan, p. 111
34 Short, *Mao*, p. 586; Quan, p. 153; Jin, p. 206; Li Zhisui, pp. 509–10, 560
35 Short, *Mao*, pp. 149, 298, 403, 422; Li Zhisui, pp. 109–10, 233, 369, 443
36 Author interview with Zhang Hanzhi
37 Author interview with John Fraser; Holdridge, p. 84; Kraft, p. 22; Osborne, p. 25

CHAPTER 7: THE LONG FREEZE

1 Memorandum of Conversation, 21 February 1972, NSA, Record of Historic Richard–Nixon–Chou En-lai Talks in February 1972 Now Declassified, pp. 4, 2, 6, 3, 5
2 *WHY*, p. 1070
3 Memorandum of Conversation, 21 February 1972, NSA, Record of Historic

Richard Nixon–Chou En-lai Talks in February 1972 Now Declassified, pp. 5, 9, 6, 4

4 He, pp. 145, 155

5 Carter, p. 40

6 Hunt, *Genesis*, p. 168; Friedman, pp. 59–60

7 He, p. 147

8 *Mao Zedong on Diplomacy*, pp. 46–7

9 Chen Jian, *Mao's China and the Cold War*, ch. 2 *passim*; *Mao Zedong on Diplomacy*, pp. 73, 85

10 *Mao Zedong on Diplomacy*, p. 88; Garver, *Foreign Relations*, p. 8

11 *Mao Zedong on Diplomacy*, pp. 81, 70

12 Chen Jian, *Mao's China and the Cold War*, p. 40; Xu, p. 180; Lowe, p. 111

13 Chang, pp. 50–9; USOH, Holloway

14 Chang, pp. 67, 68

15 *Ibid.*, p. 76

16 USOH, Kreisberg

17 USOH, Lutkins

18 USOH, Kreisberg

19 USOH, Green; USOH, Johnson

20 USOH, Levin

21 Zhai, *Dragon, the Lion and the Eagle*, pp. 7–8, 11; Shambaugh, p. 6

22 Arkush and Lee, pp. 254, 246ff

23 USOH, Thayer; see also USOH, Lacey; USOH, Lutkins; USOH, Johnson

24 USOH, Lutkins; USOH, Clough; USOH, Holdridge

25 He, p. 151

26 USOH, Clough; USOH, Supplement, David Fischer

27 USOH, Osborn; USOH, Holdridge; Luo, p. 162

28 USOH, Supplement, David Fischer

CHAPTER 8: BREAKING THE PATTERN

1 Memorandum of Conversation, 21 February 1972, NSA, Record of Historic Richard–Nixon–Chou En-lai Talks in February 1972 Now Declassified, p. 7

2 Garver, *Foreign Relations*, p. 155 and n. 28; Foot, 'Redefinitions', pp. 264–5

3 Shao, pp. 195–6

4 USOH, Grant

5 Cohen, pp. 190–1

6 USOH, Holdridge

7 Barnouin and Yu, p. 47

8 Chen Jian, *Mao's China and the Cold War*, pp. 221–9; Garver, *Foreign Relations*, pp. 291–2; *Mao Zedong on Diplomacy*, pp. 425, 426

9 Yan and Gao, p. 74; Barnouin and Yu, pp. 66–9; Brady, pp. 163–9

10 USOH, Green, ch. V, n.p.

11 Chen and Wilson, 'All Under the Heaven', pp. 164, 163

12 *RN*, p. 353; Haldeman, *Diaries*, p. 519

13 Haldeman, DVD, 13 May, 1 July 1971

14 Haldeman, *Diaries*, p. 73; *FRUS, Foundations*, p. 110

15 Aitken, p. 244; Haldeman, *Diaries*, p. 108

16 Ford Library, Lord; *FRUS, Foundations*, p. 151

17 *FRUS, Foundations*, p. 154

18 *Ibid.*, pp. 56–7, 122; *WHY*, pp. 129–30

19 *WHY*, p. 192; Kissinger, *Years of Upheaval*, p. 70

20 *FRUS, Foundations*, p. 154; *WHY*, pp. 164, 712, 763–70

CHAPTER 9: THE POLAR BEAR

1   Barnouin and Yu, pp. 108–9

2   USOH, Freeman

3   Khrushchev, *Khrushchev Remembers* (1970), p. 466; Khrushchev, *Khrushchev Remembers: The Last Testament* (1974), p. 245; Leys, *Chinese Shadows*, p. 181

4   Short, *Mao*, p. 421

5   Goncharov, Lewis and Xue, p. 8; Khrushchev, *Khrushchev Remembers* (1970), p. 462

6   Goncharov, Lewis and Xue, pp. 79–80

7   *Ibid.*, pp. 85–93; Short, *Mao*, p. 424

8   Goncharov, Lewis and Xue, pp. 127, 107–9

9   Zhihua, pp. 44–68; Chen Jian, *Mao's China and the Cold War*, pp. 58, 58–61

10 Khrushchev, *Khrushchev Remembers: The Last Testament* (1974), p. 249

11 Chen Jian, *Mao's China and the Cold War*, pp. 64–8; Khrushchev, *Khrushchev Remembers: The Last Testament* (1974), p. 250; Strong and Keyssar, pp. 503–4

12 Chen Jian, *Mao's China and the Cold War*, pp. 77–8; Yang Kuisong, pp. 18–19

13 Li Zhisui, p. 270; Share, p. 9; Taubman, p. 392

14 Schram, *Mao*, p. 291; Taubman, p. 341

15 Hsüeh and North, p. 22; Luo, p. 167; Chang and Halliday, p. 505

16 'Conversation between Mao Zedong and E. F. Hill', in *Mao Zedong on Diplomacy*, p. 424; Chen and Wilson, 'All Under the Heaven' pp. 159, 157–61; Yang Kuisong, pp. 36–7

17 Chang and Halliday, pp. 503–4; Naughton, pp. 351–86

18 Lilley, p. 146; USOH, Supplement, David Dean

19 Barnouin and Yu, p. 86

20 Garver, *Foreign Relations*, pp. 304–5

21 Ostermann, p. 186

22 Goldstein, p. 987 n. 9; Ostermann, p. 187; Yang Kuisong, p. 24

23 Goldstein, pp. 992–4, 992 n. 40, 994

24 Goldstein, p. 987; Barnouin and Yu, p. 89; Chang and Halliday, p. 570; Yang Kuisong, p. 27; USOH, Holdridge; Ma Jisen, p. 334; NIE 11/13–69: The USSR and China, p. 4, in National Intelligence Council, *Tracking the Dragon*

25 Goldstein, *passim*; Yang Kuisong, pp. 21, 30

26 Ostermann, pp. 187–8; Schaller, 'Détente', p. 368; Yang Kuisong, p. 32; Chang and Halliday, pp. 570–1; Garver, *China's Decision*, pp. 57, 58

27 Zhang Baijia, pp. 67–8; Whiting, p. 336; Yang Kuisong, p. 34; Wishnick, *Mending Fences*, p. 35; Hoff, p. 197; Whiting, p. 226

28 *WHY*, p. 184

29 Yang Kuisong, pp. 35, 35–6

30 *Ibid.*, p. 36; Barnouin and Yu, p. 91

31 Wishnick, 'In the Region and in the Center', p. 198; Yang Kuisong, pp. 37–9; Soviet Report on 11 September 1969 Kosygin–Zhou Meeting, *CWHIP Bulletin* 6–7, pp. 191–3; Luo, pp. 273–4

32 Yang Kuisong, p. 40; Soviet Report on 11 September 1969 Kosygin–Zhou Meeting, *CWHIP Bulletin* 6–7, p. 193; *WHY*, p. 185; Yang Kuisong, p. 39; Tyler, p. 77; Pollock, pp. 244–71

33 Yang Kuisong, p. 40

34 Chang and Halliday, p. 572; Yang Kuisong, pp. 40–1, 47–8; Ma Jisen, pp. 242–3; author interviews

35 Hsüeh and North, p. 25; Ma Jisen, p. 294

36 Luo, pp. 254–6

37 Zhang Baijia, p. 69; Luo, pp. 162, 166

38 Luo, pp. 272–3

39 Chen and Wilson, 'All Under the Heaven', pp. 166–8

40 *Ibid.*, pp. 170, 171; Ma Jisen, p. 301

41 Zhang Baijia, p. 71; Yang Kuisong, p. 43

42 Li Zhisui, p. 514; *WHY*, p. 182; Luo, p. 275

CHAPTER 10: THE BANQUET

1 USOH, Supplement, Lord

2 Xiong, 'Jiang Qing', p. 61

3 Author interview with John Burns; Cronkite, p. 322; NPM, Dwight Chapin Files, Box 28, Folder Memoranda to Official/Unofficial Parties

4 USOH, Freeman

5 Mancall, p. 24; *Financial Times*, 7/8 May 2005

6 Holdridge, p. 79; Walker, pp. 237, 409–10

7 Walker, p. 229; Chen and Hong, pp. 310–11; *WHY*, p. 1069; Haig, p. 259

8 NPM, Dwight Chapin Files, Box 28, Folder Memoranda to Official/Unofficial Parties; Haldeman, *Diaries*, p. 415; Holdridge, pp. 86–7

9 Author interview with John Burns; Haldeman, *Diaries*, p. 59; Garment, p. 111

10 Ehrlichman, pp. 263–4, 273–4; Greenberg, p. 128; Chapin interview, *PCC* transcripts, roll 46, p. 5

11 Greenberg, pp. 137, 146, 155; Ehrlichman, pp. 264–9

12 Memorandum of Conversation, 11 July 1971, 10.35 a.m.–11.55 a.m., NSA, Electronic Briefing Book No. 66, Doc. 38, p. 5; Greenberg, p. 276; Frankel, p. 349; Memorandum for Henry A. Kissinger, 6 August 1971,

'Conversations with Chou En-lai, 10 July afternoon sessions', NSA, Electronic Briefing Book No. 66, Doc. 35, pp. 18–19; Rather, *Camera Never Blinks*, p. 230

13 Wen, p. 1735
14 Holdridge, p. 70; author interview with Li Qin
15 Memorandum of Conversation, 23 October 1971, 9.05 p.m.–10.05 p.m., NSA Electronic Briefing Book No. 70, Doc. 14, p. 8; Memorandum of Meeting, 11.45 p.m., 7 January 1972, NSA Electronic Briefing Book No. 70, Doc. 25, p. 4; Haig, pp. 262–3
16 Walker, pp. 308, 21, 246; Halstead, p. 6
17 Halstead, p. 4
18 Halstead, p. 5
19 Thomas, *Dateline*, p. 139; Thomas, *Front Row*, p. 187; Kraft, p. 9
20 Thomas, *Dateline*, pp. 140–1; Walker, p. 84
21 Author interview with Yu Jiafu; Halstead, pp. 6–7
22 Hevia, p. 117 and ch. 5 *passim*
23 Text available at The American Presidency Project; Holdridge, p. 87
24 USOH, Freeman
25 Text available at The American Presidency Project
26 Haldeman, *Diaries* pp. 416, 415
27 Buckley, p. 87; quoted in Hersh, p. 495
28 Holdridge, p. 87; author interview with John Burns
29 Haldeman, *Diaries*, pp. 415–16

CHAPTER II: OPENING MOVES

1 *WHY*, p. 187
2 See Haig interview, *Nixon's China Game*, PBS website
3 Kissinger interview, *PCC* transcripts, 1/V, p. 2; *WHY*, pp. 189–90
4 USOH, Nichols
5 *Ibid.*
6 USOH, Holdridge
7 Secret Cable 427, 18 February 1969, NSA, China and the US, CH00055
8 *FRUS*, *Foundations*, p. 79
9 Department of State, Next Steps in China Policy, 6 October 1971, NSA, China and the US, CH00079; Walters, p. 526; Holdridge, p, 32; Aijazuddin, p. 3; Secret Cable 2547, 12 August 1969, NSA, China and the US, CH00075; Secret Cable 2618, 18 August 1969, NSA, China and the US, CH00077
10 National Security Study Memorandum, NSSM 14, 5 February 1969, NSA, China and the US, CH00043; *WHY*, p. 169; Hoff, pp. 196–7; Ma Jisen, p. 298
11 Mann, p. 22; Foot, 'Redefinitions', pp. 277–8, 280
12 Confidential Cable 1720, 9 June 1969, NSA, China and the US, CH00070; Chen Jian, *Mao's China and the Cold War*, p. 245; Mann, p. 62; Zhang Baijia, p. 68; Barnouin and Yu, pp. 99, 99–100

13 USOH, Supplement, Buche
14 Author interview with John Fraser; Robert Edmonds; Author interview with Chen Weiming
15 USOH, Jenkins; Ma Jisen, p. 326
16 Chen Jian, *Mao's China and the Cold War*, p. 250; *WHY*, p. 190; *RN*, p. 545
17 Chen Jian, *Mao's China and the Cold War*, pp. 250–2; Secret Memorandum of Conversation, 21 February 1970, NSA, China and the US, CH00143
18 Mann, p. 24; Holdridge, p. 37; *WHY*, pp. 684–5, 692; Chen Jian, *Mao's China and the Cold War*, p. 252
19 Safire, pp. 206–7; *RN*, p. 546
20 Walters, pp. 526–7
21 *Ibid.*, pp. 534–8, 529–30
22 Aijazzudin, p. 30; Ma Jisen, pp. 327–8; *WHY*, pp. 701–2; *Mao Zedong on Diplomacy*, p. 450; see, for example, Aijazuddin, pp. 58–9
23 *Mao Zedong on Diplomacy*, pp. 449–50; Holdridge, p. 41; *WHY*, pp. 702–3; *RN*, p. 547
24 Aijazuddin, pp. 42–3
25 *WHY*, pp. 701–2; *RN*, pp. 549–50; Aijazuddin, pp. 52–3; Memorandum of Conversation, 11 July 1971, 10.35 a.m.–11.55 a.m., NSA, Electronic Briefing Book No. 66, Doc. 38, p. 3; *WHY*, p. 736; Isaacson, pp. 338–9
26 *RN*, p. 548; *WHY*, pp. 704–5
27 Ma Jisen, pp. 328–9; Chen and Hong, pp. 250–5; Ma Jisen, p. 329
28 USOH, Levin; Boggan interview, *PCC* transcripts, 1/V, p. 1; Chen Jian, *Mao's China and the Cold War*, p. 260
29 Chen Jian, *Mao's China and the Cold War*, p. 261; Zhang Baijia, p. 73
30 Ma Jisen, p. 230; USOH, Cunningham; Brown interview, *PCC* transcripts, 1/V, p. 5
31 Boggan interview, *PCC* transcripts, 1/V, pp. 18–19
32 Barnouin and Yu, pp. 103–4; *WHY*, p. 710
33 *Globe and Mail*, 15 April 1971
34 *Ibid.*; Boggan interview, *PCC* transcripts, 1/V, pp. 18–20; Chen Jian, *Mao's China and the Cold War*, p. 262
35 *WHY*, p. 710; copy in NSA, Electronic Briefing Book No. 66, Doc. 15, Doc. 19
36 *RN*, p. 549; Haldeman, *Diaries*, p. 275; *WHY*, p. 721
37 *WHY*, pp. 716–17
38 Aijazuddin, pp. 58–9; Chen Jian, *Mao's China and the Cold War*, p. 263 n. 113; *WHY*, p. 725
39 Message for the Government of the People's Republic of China, 20 May 1971, NSA, Electronic Briefing Book No. 66, Doc. 24; Chen Jian, *Mao's China and the Cold War*, pp. 264–5
40 *WHY*, pp. 726–7; Haldeman, *Diaries*, p. 295; *RN*, pp. 551–2; Mann, p. 29
41 *RN*, p. 552

CHAPTER 12: THE SECRET VISIT

1 *RN*, p. 552
2 Aijazuddin, p. 67; *RN*, pp. 550; Isaacson, pp. 339–40; Haldeman, *Diaries*, p. 282; *WHY*, pp. 715–17; telecon The President/Mr. Kissinger, 8.18 p.m., 27 April 1971, NSA, Electronic Briefing Book No. 66, Doc. 18
3 *RN*, p. 550; *WHY*, pp. 717, 734
4 USOH, Supplement, Farland; *WHY*, p. 738; Kissinger interview, *PCC* transcripts, 1/V, p. 18
5 Hilaly to Kissinger, 19 June 1971, NSA, Electronic Briefing Book No. 66, Doc. 29; Aijazuddin, pp. 102–5; USOH, Supplement, Farland
6 Zhang Baijia, pp. 74–5; Chen Jian, *Mao's China and the Cold War*, pp. 262–5
7 NPM, NSC Files, For the President's Files (Winston Lord) China/Vietnam Negotiations, Box 850, Folder 3, pp. 1–5
8 Memorandum for the President's Files, 1 July 1971, NSA, Electronic Briefing Book No. 66, Doc. 33; *WHY*, pp. 735–6
9 *WHY*, pp. 728–9; Hersh, pp. 466–76
10 Aijazuddin, p. 81 n. 25
11 *WHY*, p. 725; Brown interview, *PCC* transcripts, 1/V, p. 12; Hanhimäki, pp. 116–20, 124; Bundy, p. 233
12 *WHY*, p. 729; Holdridge, p. 52
13 Author interview with Gordon Barass; USOH, Supplement, Lord
14 Wicker, *One of Us*, pp. 594–5; WHY, p. 749
15 Holdridge, p. 55; USOH, Supplement, Lord; *WHY*, p. 753
16 Haldeman, *Diaries*, pp. 289, 316
17 USOH, Holdridge; Chen and Hong, p. 266
18 Author interview with Zhang Hanzhi
19 Memorandum of Conversation, 9 July 1971, Afternoon and Evening, NSA, Electronic Briefing Book No. 66, Doc. 34
20 *Ibid*, p. 6
21 Memorandum of Conversation 10 July 1971, Afternoon, NSA, Electronic Briefing Book No. 66, Doc. 35, p. 2
22 Chen Jian, *Mao's China and the Cold War*, p. 267; Barnouin and Yu, p. 107
23 Memorandum for the President, 14 July 1971, NSA, Electronic Briefing Book No. 66, Doc. 40, p. 3; USOH, Supplement, Lord
24 Memorandum of Conversation, 10 July 1971, Afternoon, NSA, Electronic Briefing Book No. 66, Doc. 35, pp. 9, 2–13, 7
25 *Ibid.*, pp. 10, 13
26 *Ibid.*, pp. 14–18
27 *Ibid.*, pp. 18, 20
28 *Ibid.*, pp. 21, 32; USOH, Supplement, Lord; USOH, Holdridge, pp. 59–60
29 USOH, Supplement, Lord; Bundy, p. 241
30 *WHY*, p. 751
31 *Ibid.*, pp. 751–2

32 Memorandum of Conversation, 11 July 1971, Early Morning and Morning, NSA, Electronic Briefing Book No. 66, Doc. 37, pp. 1–2; *WHY*, pp. 751–3; Barnouin and Yu, pp. 107–8; Chen Jian, *Mao's China and the Cold War*, p. 268

33 Memorandum of Conversation, 11 July, 1971, 10.35 a.m.–11.55 a.m., NSA, Electronic Briefing Book No. 66, Doc. 38

34 *WHY*, p. 753; Memorandum for the President, 14 July 1971, NSA, Electronic Briefing Book No. 66, Doc. 40, p. 2

35 Memorandum for the President, 14 July 1971. NSA, Beijing–Washington, Doc. 40, pp. 5, 6, 26; *WHY*, pp. 1055–6; Memorandum for the President, 14 July 1971, NSA, Electronic Briefing Book No. 66, Doc. 40, p. 26; *WHY*, pp. 744–7; Valeriani, p. 95

36 USOH, Supplement, Farland; Green, in Green, Holdridge and Stokes

37 USOH, Supplement, Farland; *WHY*, pp. 755–6; Haig interview, *PCC* transcripts, 2, p. 5; Henry Kissinger to General Haig, 11 July 1971, NSA, Electronic Briefing Book No. 66, Doc. 39

38 *WHY*, p. 758; Haldeman, *Diaries*, pp. 318–20; Brandon, p. 278

39 *WHY*, p. 760; Ehrlichman, p. 293

40 USOH, Freeman; *WHY*, p. 761

41 Haldeman, *Diaries*, pp. 321, 323–4; *RN*, pp. 554–5; Bundy, pp. 240–1

42 Isaacson, p. 347; USOH, Galloway; Hanhimäki, pp. 144–5; Arbatov, p. 180; Wishnick, *Mending Fences*, pp. 58–9; Ma Jisen, p. 301

43 Hersh, p. 442; Kalb, p. 268

44 Chen Jian, *Mao's China and the Cold War*, p. 269; Hoxha, pp. 560, 577

45 Chen Jian, *Mao's China and the Cold War*, pp. 269–70

46 Schoenhals, p. 111 n. 108; Jin Qiu, pp. 80, 129, 135–6, 146; Li Zhisui, pp. 453–4

47 Jin Qiu, p. 146, ch. 7 *passim*; Chang and Halliday, pp. 580–3

48 Short, *Mao*, pp. 614–15; Li Zhisui, pp. 542–3; Ma Jisen, pp. 142–3, 355–6, 378, 401

49 See, for example, *WHY*, pp. 696–7, 768–9; Chen Jian, *Mao's China and the Cold War*, p. 270; Barnouin and Yu, p. 193; Burr, ed., *Kissinger Transcripts*, p. 61

50 Li Jie, pp. 60–1; Barnouin and Yu, p. 195; Kraft, p. 18; Li Danhui, p. 186; author interview with Yanhua Shi; Tao, Part II, p. 349

CHAPTER 13: GETTING READY

1 Walker, pp. 183, 148, 167, 94

2 USOH, Freeman

3 Walters, pp. 533–41; Memorandum of Conversation, 20 October 1971, 4.40–7.10 p.m., NSA, Electronic Briefing Book No. 70, Doc. 10, p. 7; *WHY*, p. 775

4 Memorandum of Conversation, 23 October 1971, 9.05 p.m.–10.05 p.m., NSA, Electronic Briefing Book No. 70, Doc. 14, p. 12

5 *WHY*, pp. 776–8; Diplomatic History Institute of the Chinese Ministry of Foreign Affairs, *Xin zhongguo wenjiao fengyun*, vol. 3, pp. 59–70 [available at NSA, Electronic Briefing Book No. 70, Doc. 21, p. 3]

6 Chapin interview, *PCC* transcripts, roll 46, pp. 9–10; Diplomatic History Institute of the Chinese Ministry of Foreign Affairs, *Xin zhongguo wenjiao fengyun*, vol. 3, pp. 59–70 [available at NSA, Electronic Briefing Book No. 70, Doc. 21, p. 6]; Chapin interview, *PCC* transcripts, roll 46, p. 28; *WHY*, p. 780

7 Memorandum of Conversation, 21 October 1971, 10.30 a.m.–1.45 p.m., NSA, Electronic Briefing Book No. 70, Doc. 11, pp. 8–9; Walker, p. 164

8 Memorandum of Conversation, 21 October 1971, 10.30 a.m.–1.45 pm., NSA, Electronic Briefing Book No. 70, Doc. 11, p. 3; *WHY*, p. 778

9 Memorandum of Conversation, 22 October 1971, 4.15 p.m.–8.28 p.m., NSA, Electronic Briefing Book No. 70, Doc. 13, p. 40; Diplomatic History Institute of the Chinese Ministry of Foreign Affairs, *Xin zhongguo wenjiao fengyun*, vol. 3, pp. 59–70 [available at NSA, Electronic Briefing Book No. 70, Doc. 21, pp. 7–8]; Chen Jian, *Mao's China and the Cold War*, pp. 271–2

10 Memorandum of Conversation, October 24, 1971, 10.28 a.m.–1.55 p.m., NSA, Electronic Briefing Book No. 70, Doc. 15, pp. 3–11

11 Diplomatic History Institute of the Chinese Ministry of Foreign Affairs, *Xin zhongguo wenjiao fengyun*, vol. 3, pp. 59–70 [available at NSA, Electronic Briefing Book No. 70, Doc. 21, pp. 9]; *WHY*, pp. 781–4; Memorandum of Conversation, 24 October 1971, 10.28 a.m.–1.55 p.m., NSA, Electronic Briefing Book No. 70, Doc. 15, p. 25; Memorandum of Conversation, 24 October 1971, 9.23 p.m.–11.20 p.m., NSA, Electronic Briefing Book No. 70, Doc. 16, pp. 3–11

12 Henry A. Kissinger, Memorandum for The President, from My October China Visit: Drafting the Communiqué, p. 5, in Briefing Books I and II, The NPM–NSC Files, For the President's Files (Winston Lord) China/Vietnam Negotiations, Box 846; *WHY*, pp. 782–4; Chen Jian, *Mao's China and the Cold War*, p. 272 n. 153

13 Chapin interview, *PCC* transcripts, roll 46, pp. 14–15

14 Bostdorff, pp. 31–56; Memorandum of Conversation, 10 July 1971, Afternoon, NSA, Electronic Briefing Book 66, Doc. 35, p. 17; Xiong, 'Mao Zedong', p. 13; USOH, Supplement, Feldman

15 NSSM 107 Issues paper: The Entire U.N. Membership Question and U.S.–China Policy, 9 February 1971, NSA, Collection: China and the United States, CH00201; NSSM-106: United States China Policy, NSA, Collection: China and the United States, CH00202; Memorandum of Conversation, 10 July 1971, Afternoon, NSA, Electronic Briefing Book No. 66, Doc. 35, p. 17

16 USOH, Supplement, Feldman; Christopher H. Phillips interview, *PCC* transcripts, 2/1

17 Conversation among President Nixon, Secretary of State William Rogers, and

National Security Adviser Henry Kissinger, 30 September 1971 and Conversation between President Nixon and National Security Adviser Henry Kissinger, 30 September 1971, NSA, Electronic Briefing Book No. 70, Documents 7 and 8

18 Phillips interview, *PCC* transcripts, 2, 2–3; Haldeman, *Diaries*, pp. 368–9

19 Cited in Isaacson, p. 352

20 Barnouin and Yu, p. 65; Xiong, 'Mao Zedong', pp. 18–19

21 Zhang Hanzhi, p. 279; USOH, Thayer; author interview with Yanhua Shi; Telegram from the Mission to the United Nations to the Department of State, 20 November 1971, *FRUS, United Nations, 1969–1972*, pp. 886–8

22 Memorandum of Conversation, 23 November 1971, 10.00 p.m.–11.55 p.m., NSA, Electronic Briefing Book No. 70, pp. 3–4, 10

23 Interview with Mohammad Khan, *Nixon's China Game*, PBS website

24 Van Hollen, pp. 339–61

25 See for example Paper Prepared by the National Security Council's Interdepartmental Group for Near East and South Asia for the Senior Review Group, Washington, undated [April 1971?], *FRUS, Nixon–Ford Administrations*, vol. E-7, Doc. 132; Study Prepared in Response to National Security Study Memorandum 133, Washington, 10 July 1971, *FRUS, Nixon–Ford Administrations*, vol. E-7, Doc. 140

26 *WHY*, pp. 860–1, 866–7

27 Memorandum of Conversation, 10 July 1971, 12.10 p.m.–6.00 p.m., NSA, Electronic Briefing Book No. 66, Doc. 35, p. 11; Memorandum for the President from Henry Kissinger, 14 July 1971, NSA, Electronic Briefing Book No. 66, Doc. 40, p. 20; Memorandum for the President from Henry A. Kissinger, 11 November 1972, NSA, Electronic Briefing Book No. 70, Doc. 20, p. 27

28 Conversation among President Nixon, Henry Kissinger and John Mitchell, 8 December 1971, *FRUS, Nixon–Ford Administrations*, vol. E-7, Doc. 165; Van Hollen, pp. 353–7

29 Conversation among President Nixon, Kissinger and Sultan Kahn, 15 November 1971, *FRUS, Nixon–Ford Administrations*, vol. E-7, Doc. 154

30 Conversation among President Nixon, Henry Kissinger and John Mitchell, 8 December 1971 and Conversation among President Nixon, Kissinger and Haig, Washington, 12 December 1971, *FRUS, Nixon–Ford Administrations*, vol. E-7, Docs 165 and 177

31 Conversation among President Nixon, Kissinger and Haig, Washington, 12 December 1971, *FRUS, Nixon–Ford Administrations*, vol. E-7, Doc. 177; Bundy, pp. 279–80 and n. 99; Memorandum of Conversation, 10 December 1971, NSA, Electronic Briefing Book No. 70, Doc. 23

32 *WHY*, pp. 913, 917–18; Isaacson, pp. 394–6; Haldeman, *Diaries*, pp. 391–7

33 Brown interview, *PCC* transcripts 1/V, pp. 13–15, 20–1; USOH, Freeman

34 'Nixon's Visit to China'; Barnouin and Yu, p. 109

35 Haig, pp. 263–4; author interview with Zhang Hanzhi, Beijing, 21 April 2005; interview with Zhang Hanzhi, *Nixon's China Game*, PBS website

36 Memorandum of Conversation, 25 October 1971, 9.50 p.m.–11.40 p.m., NSA, Electronic Briefing Book No. 70, Doc. 18, p. 14; Haig, pp. 259–61

37 Haig, pp. 260–1; Memorandum of Conversation, 3 January 1971, Midnight, NSA, Electronic Briefing Book No. 70, Doc. 24, pp. 1–2

38 Memorandum of Conversation, 3 January 1971, Midnight, NSA, Electronic Briefing Book No. 70, Doc. 24, pp. 4–6; 'Haig's Preparatory Mission for Nixon's Visit to China in January 1972', *Xin Zhonggjuo wenjiao fengyun*, vol. 3, pp. 71–82, translation available NSA, Electronic Briefing Book No. 70, Doc. 26

39 Author interview with Zhang Hanzhi; Memorandum of Conversation, 7 January 1971, 11.45 p.m., NSA, Electronic Briefing Book No. 70, Doc. 25, pp. 3–4, 6

40 Memorandum of Conversation, 3 January 1971, Midnight, NSA, Electronic Briefing Book No. 70, Doc. 24, pp. 6–7, 9

41 'Haig's Preparatory Mission for Nixon's Visit to China in January 1972', *Xin Zhonggjuo wenjiao fengyun*, vol. 3, pp. 71–82, translation available NSA, Electronic Briefing Book No. 70, Doc. 26; Memorandum of Conversation, 7 January 1971, 11.45 p.m., NSA, Electronic Briefing Book No. 70, Doc. 25, pp. 4–5

42 Author interview with Zhang Hanzhi; Haig interview, *PCC* transcripts, 2/33, p. 15

43 Walker, p. 9

CHAPTER 14: DOWN TO BUSINESS

1 *WHY*, pp. 1071–2

2 Haldeman, *Diaries*, p. 416

3 *WHY*, pp. 1070–1; *RN*, p. 570

4 *WHY*, p. 1070; Memorandum of Conversation, Monday 21 February 1972, 4.15 p.m.–5.30 p.m., NPM, National Security Council Files, HAK Office Files, Box 92, Country Files–Far East; Dr Kissinger's Meetings in the PRC during the Presidential Visit, February 1972, pp. 2–4

5 Chapin interview, *PCC* transcripts roll 47, p. 19; Ma Jisen, pp. 378–9

6 USOH, Freeman

7 Memorandum of Conversation, 24 February 1972, 5.15 p.m.– 8.05 p.m., NSA, Record of Historic Richard Nixon–Chou En-lai Talks in February 1972, Doc. 3, pp. 10–11

8 Memorandum of Conversation, 21 February 1972, 5.58 p.m.–6.55 p.m., NSA, Record of Historic Richard Nixon–Chou En-lai Talks in February 1972, Doc. 1

9 Solomon, p. 77

10 Reeves, p. 436; NPM, White House Special Files. President's Personal Files, Box 7, Folder 'China Notes'

11 Memorandum for the President from Henry A. Kissinger, Your Encounter

with the Chinese, 5 February 1972, pp. 1–3, NPM, National Security Council Office Files, For the President's Files (Winston Lord) China/Vietnam Negotiations, Box 847, Briefing Book V

12 Memorandum for the President, 19 February 1972, in NPM, National Security Council Office Files, For the President's Files (Winston Lord) China/Vietnam Negotiations, Box 847, Briefing Book IV

13 Memorandum of Conversation, 22 February 1972, 2.10 p.m.–6.00 p.m., NSA, Nixon's Trip to China: Records Now Completely Declassified, Doc. 1, pp. 4–5

14 *Ibid.*, pp. 6–7, 9–10, 11–12

15 *Ibid.*, pp. 17–18, 31

16 Kazuo, pp. 532–4

17 Memorandum of Conversation, 23 February 1972, 2.00 p.m.–6.00 p.m., NSA, Nixon's Trip to China: Records Now Completely Declassified, Doc. 2, pp. 2–11

18 See, for example, Memorandum of Conversation, 9 July 1971, 4.35 p.m.–11.20 p.m., NSA, Electronic Briefing Book No. 66, Doc. 34, p. 29; Memorandum of Conversation 11 July 1971, 10.35 a.m.–11.55 a.m., NSA, Electronic Briefing Book No. 66, Doc. 38, p. 14

19 Memorandum of Conversation, 23 February 1972, 2.00 p.m.–6.00 p.m., NSA, Nixon's Trip to China: Records Now Completely Declassified, Doc. 2, pp. 18–19; Memorandum of Conversation, 24 February 1972, 5.15 p.m.–8.05 p.m., NSA, Nixon's Trip to China: Records Now Completely Declassified, Doc. 3, pp. 26–7; Memorandum for the President, 11 November 1972, NSA, Electronic Briefing Book No. 70, Doc. 20, p. 4

20 Memorandum for the President from Henry A. Kissinger, 11 November 1971, NSA, Electronic Briefing Book No. 70, Doc. 20, pp. 4, 20–2; Memorandum of Conversation, 23 February 1972, 2.00 p.m.–6.00 p.m., NSA, Nixon's Trip to China: Records Now Completely Declassified, Doc. 2, pp. 16–17

21 Memorandum of Conversation, 22 February 1972, 2.10 p.m.–6.00 p.m., NSA, Nixon's Trip to China: Records Now Completely Declassified, Doc. 1, pp. 14–17; Memorandum of Conversation, 23 February 1972, 2.00 p.m.–6.00 p.m., NSA, Nixon's Trip to China: Records Now Completely Declassified, Doc. 2, pp. 3–4, 23–4, 26–7

22 Memorandum of Conversation, 22 February 1972, 2.10 p.m.–6.00 p.m., NSA, Nixon's Trip to China: Records Now Completely Declassified, Doc. 1, p. 13; Memorandum of Conversation, 23 February 1972, 2.00 p.m.–6.00 p.m., NSA, Nixon's Trip to China: Records Now Completely Declassified, Doc. 2, pp. 20–3, 28–31; Goh, pp. 475–502, 480

23 Topping, p. 396; Valeriani, p. 89

24 Memorandum of Conversation, 22 February 1972, 2.10 p.m.–6.00 p.m., NSA, Nixon's Trip to China: Records Now Completely Declassified, Doc. 1, pp. 14–15, 18–19

25 Memorandum of Conversation, 10 July 1971, Afternoon, NSA, Electronic Briefing Book No. 66, Doc. 35, pp. 28–9; Memorandum of Conversation, 11 July 1971, 10.35 a.m.–11.55 a.m., NSA, Electronic Briefing Book No. 66, Doc. 38, p. 9; NSA, Electronic Briefing Book No. 70, Doc. 13, p. 36; Lord to Kissinger, 15 December 1971, NSA, Electronic Briefing Book No. 70, Doc. 23, p. 2

26 Memorandum of Conversation, 23 February 1972, 9.35 a.m.-12.34 p.m., NSA, Nixon's Trip to China: Records Now Completely Declassified, Doc. 4, pp. 2–13

27 *Ibid.*, pp. 14–18

28 *Ibid.*, p. 20

29 *Ibid.*, pp. 13, 20; McFarlane, p. 151

30 *RN*, p. 568; Ambrose, *Nixon: Triumph*, p. 518; Haldeman, *Diaries*, p. 422

CHAPTER 15: THE IRRITANT: TAIWAN

1 NPM, White House Special Files, President's Personal Files, Box 7, Folder 'China Notes'; *WHY*, p. 705

2 *RN*, pp. 344, 523; *WHY*, pp. 705, 766; Yahuda, *passim*; Wang, pp. 157, 159–64

3 Memorandum of Conversation, 11 July 1971, 10.35 a.m.-11.55 a.m., NSA, Electronic Briefing Book No. 66, Doc. 38, p. 11; Memorandum of Conversation, 9 July 1971, Afternoon and Evening, NSA, Electronic Briefing Book No. 66, Doc. 34, p. 13; Green, Holdridge and Stokes, p. 124

4 Barnouin and Yu, p. 183

5 Fenby, pp. 498, 43, 387

6 *Ibid.*, 187; Spence, pp. 526–7, 529; Tucker, *Taiwan, Hong Kong, and the United States*, pp. 32–3; Memorandum of Conversation, 9 July 1971, Afternoon and Evening, NSA, Electronic Briefing Book No. 66, Doc. 34, pp. 9–10

7 Tucker, *Taiwan, Hong Kong, and the United States*, pp. 62–72; Garver, *Sino-American Alliance*, ch. 6

8 USOH, Holdridge

9 USOH, Osborn; USOH, Grant

10 USOH, Katrosh

11 Chen Jian, *Mao's China and the Cold War*, pp. 179–81; Tucker, *Taiwan, Hong Kong, and the United States*, pp. 42–3; *Mao Zedong on Diplomacy*, pp. 264–72; Taylor, p. 243; Garver, *Sino-American Alliance*, pp. 137–8; *Mao Zedong on Diplomacy*, p. 266

12 USOH, Green, ch. 1; Garver, *Sino-American Alliance*, p. 139; *Mao Zedong on Diplomacy*, p. 428

13 Chen Jian, *Mao's China and the Cold War*, p. 199; Tucker, *Taiwan, Hong Kong, and the United States*, p. 43

14 Memorandum of Conversation, 24 February 1972, 5.15 p.m.–8.05 p.m., NSA, Record of Historic Richard Nixon–Chou En-lai Talks in February 1972, Doc. 3, p. 7

15 *Ibid.*, pp. 14–15

16 Tucker, 'Taiwan Expendable?', p. 116

17 Taylor, p. 297; see also *FRUS, Foundations*, pp. 208–9; telecon, The President/Mr Kissinger, 18(?) April 1971, NSA, Electronic Briefing Book No. 145, Doc. 5; Memorandum for the President's File, 1 July 1971, NSA, Electronic Briefing Book No. 66, Doc. 33

18 NPM, NSC Files, For the President's Files (Winston Lord) China/Vietnam Negotiations, Box 850, Folder 3, p. 3; *WHY*, p. 749

19 PRO, FCO 21/824, Memorandum from L. J. Wilder, 30 July 1971; Romberg, p. 26

20 See, for example, Memorandum for the President from Henry A. Kissinger, 10(?) December 1970; NSA, Electronic Briefing Book No. 66, Doc. 6; Record of a Discussion with Mr. Henry Kissinger on 16 December 1970, Electronic Briefing Book No. 66, Doc. 7; Accinelli, pp. 11–25

21 See NSA, Electronic Briefing Book No. 66, Docs 34–8 and NSA, Electronic Briefing Book No. 70, Docs 10–15; Memorandum of Conversation, 9 July 1971, NSA, Electronic Briefing Book No. 66, Doc. 34, p. 16; Memorandum of Conversation, 10 July 1971, NSA, Electronic Briefing Book No. 66, Doc. 35, pp. 15–17, 19

22 NSA, Electronic Briefing Book No. 66, Doc. 34, pp. 12, 13; Doc. 38, p. 10; Memorandum of Conversation, 21 October 1971, NSA, Electronic Briefing Book No. 70, Doc. 11, pp. 13, 20–34; Barnouin and Yu, pp. 185–7

23 Chen Jian, *Mao's China and the Cold War*, p. 267; USOH, Green, ch. V

24 Memorandum of Conversation, 10 July 1971, NSA, Electronic Briefing Book 66, Doc. 35; Memorandum of Conversation, 11 July 1971, 10.35 a.m.–11.55 a.m., NSA, Electronic Briefing Book No. 66, Doc. 38, p. 10; Memorandum of Conversation, 24 October 1971, 10.28 a.m.–1.55 p.m., NSA, Electronic Briefing Book No. 70, Doc. 15, p. 25; Memorandum of Conversation, 24 October 1971, 9.23 p.m.–11.20 p.m., NSA, Electronic Briefing Book No. 70, Doc. 16, p. 8

25 Memorandum of Conversation, 26 October 1971, 5.30 a.m.–8.10 a.m., NSA, Electronic Briefing Book No. 70, Doc. 19, p. 10; Opening Statement – First Private Meeting with Prime Minister Chou En-lai, p. 2, NPM, NSC Files, For the President's Files (Winston Lord) China/Vietnam Negotiations, Box 847; Memorandum from Henry A. Kissinger to the President, 8 February 1972, Taiwan section, pp. 5 [Nixon handwritten comment], 8: Memorandum Henry A. Kissinger to the President, 7 February 1972, Taiwan, p. 2, Briefing Papers for the China Trip, Briefing Book V, NARA, From the NPM–NSC Files, For the President's Files (Winston Lord) China/Vietnam Negotiations, Box 847

26 NPM, White House Special Files, President's Personal Files, Box 7, Folder 'China Notes', 15 February 1972; Memorandum of Conversation, 22 February 1972, 2.10 p.m.–6.00 p.m., NSA, Nixon's Trip to China: Records

Now Completely Declassified, Doc. 1, pp. 4–5, 23; Memorandum of Conversation, 24 February 1972, 5.15 p.m.–8.05 p.m., NSA, Nixon's Trip to China: Records Now Completely Declassified, Doc. 3, p. 6

27 Memorandum of Conversation, 24 February 1972, 5.15 p.m.–8.05 p.m., NSA, Nixon's Trip to China: Records Now Completely Declassified, Doc. 3, pp. 10–12; Memorandum of Conversation, 22 February 1972, 2.10 p.m.–6.00 p.m., NSA, Nixon's Trip to China: Records Now Completely Declassified, Doc. 1, p. 6

28 Memorandum of Conversation, 28 February 1972, 8.30 a.m.–9.30 a.m., NSA, Nixon's Trip to China: Records Now Completely Declassified, Doc. 7, pp. 8–10

CHAPTER 16: INDOCHINA

1 NPM, White House Special Files, President's Personal Files, Box 7, Folder 'China Notes', 15 February 1972, p. 23

2 Bundy, pp. 78–9; Morris, pp. 12–15

3 Telecon, The President/Mr Kissinger, NSA, Electronic Briefing Book No. 145, Doc. 7, p. 3; Memorandum from Henry A. Kissinger to the President, 8 February 1972, Indochina, p. 4: Briefing Papers for the China Trip, Briefing Book V, NARA, From the NPM–NSC Files, For the President's Files (Winston Lord) China/Vietnam Negotiations, Box 847

4 Briefing Papers for the China Trip, Memorandum for the President from Henry A. Kissinger, 8 February 1972, Indochina/Vietnam, n.p., Briefing Book V, From the NPM–NSC Files, For the President's Files (Winston Lord) China/Vietnam Negotiations, Box 847; Li Danhui, p. 187

5 Memorandum of Conversation, 9 July 1971, Afternoon and Evening, NSA, Electronic Briefing Book No. 66, Doc. 34, p. 26; Westad *et al.*, p. 20; Yang Kuisong, p. 33; Qiang Zhai, *China and the Vietnam Wars*, p. 135

6 Westad, 'History, Memory, and the Languages of Alliance-Making', in Westad *et al.*, pp. 10–11

7 Chen Jian, 'China's Involvement in the Vietnam War', p. 385; Li Danhui, p. 177

8 Memorandum of Conversation, 22 February 1972, 2.10 p.m.–6.00 p.m., NSA, Nixon's Trip to China: Records Now Completely Declassified, Doc. 1, p. 21; Walters, p. 546; Mann, p. 39

9 Memorandum of Conversation, 9 July 1971, Afternoon and Evening, NSA, Electronic Briefing Book No. 66, Doc. 34, pp. 21–5, 30–4; Memorandum of Conversation, 10 July 1971, Afternoon, NSA, Electronic Briefing Book No. 66, Doc. 35, pp. 10, 23–4

10 Memorandum of Conversation, 21 October 1971, 10.30 a.m.–1.45 p.m., NSA, Electronic Briefing Book No. 70, Doc. 11, p. 17; Memorandum of Conversation, 21 October 1971, 4.42 p.m.–7.17 p.m., NSA, Electronic Briefing Book No. 70, Doc. 12, p. 21; Memorandum for the President from Henry A. Kissinger, Your Encounter with the Chinese, 5 February 1972, p. 6; Briefing Papers for the

China Trip, Briefing Book V, From the NPM–NSC Files, For the President's Files (Winston Lord) China/Vietnam Negotiations, Box 847

11 Memorandum of Conversation, 9 July 1971, Afternoon and Evening, NSA, Electronic Briefing Book No. 66, Doc. 34, pp. 33–4

12 My Talks with Chou En-lai, Memorandum for the President from Henry A. Kissinger, NSA, Electronic Briefing Book No. 66, Doc. 40, pp. 15–16; Zhai, *China and the Vietnam Wars*, p. 196; Westad *et al.*, p. 178

13 Yum, p. 75; Barnouin and Yu, p. 189

14 Zhai, *China and the Vietnam Wars*, pp. 197–8; Li Danhui, p. 194

15 Zhai, *China and the Vietnam Wars*, pp. 200, n. 38, 201

16 Memorandum of Conversation, 22 February 1972, 2.10 p.m.–6.00 p.m., NSA, Nixon's Trip to China: Records Now Completely Declassified, Doc. 1, pp. 22–27; Memorandum of Conversation, 24 February 1972, 5.15 p.m.–8.05 p.m., NSA, Nixon's Trip to China: Records Now Completely Declassified, Doc. 3, pp. 16–17

17 Memorandum of Conversation, 24 February 1972, 5.15 p.m.–8.05 p.m., NSA, Nixon's Trip to China: Records Now Completely Declassified, Doc. 3, pp. 22–3

18 *Ibid.*, pp. 16–19; Memorandum of Conversation, 28 February 1972, 8.30 a.m.–9.30 a.m., NSA, Nixon's Trip to China: Records Now Completely Declassified, Doc. 7, p. 8; Green, Holdridge and Stokes, p. 130: Haig, p. 261

19 Li Danhui, pp. 198–9, 199–202

20 Zhai, *China and the Vietnam Wars*, pp. 212–13

CHAPTER 17: HALDEMAN'S MASTERPIECE

1 Rather and Gates, p. 245; *Globe and Mail*, 28 February 2006

2 Kalb, p. 274; Haldeman, *Diaries*, pp. 363–4

3 Chancellor, p. 94

4 Cronkite, p. 324; Haldeman, *Diaries*, p. 419; Haldeman, DVD, 25 February 1972; *Globe and Mail*, 25 February 1972; Memorandum of Conversation, 26 February 1972, NSA, Record of Historic Richard Nixon–Chou En-lai Talks in February 1972, Doc. 6, p. 5

5 Halstead, p. 10

6 Haldeman, *Diaries*, p. 364; NPM, White House Special Files, Staff Member and Office Files, Dwight Chapin Files, Box 26

7 Ambrose, *Nixon: Education*, pp. 95, 585–6; Summers, p. 36; Ehrlichman, pp. 56–8; Walker, p. 183

8 Safire, p. 607; Ehrlichman, pp. 55–6; Hersh, p. 109; Summers, p. 35

9 Osborne, p. 29; Thomas, *Front Row*, p. 190; Reeves, p. 451; author interview with Zhang Hanzhi

10 Memorandum of Conversation, 22 February 1972, 2.10 p.m.–6.00 p.m., NSA, Nixon's Trip to China: Records Now Completely Declassified, Doc. 1, p. 1

11 Witke, *Comrade Chiang Ch'ing*, pp. 46–50; Witke, 'The Last Days of Madame

Mao', pp. 142, 144; Terrill, pp. 17–22

12 Witke, *Comrade Chiang Ch'ing*, p. 187; Terrill, pp. 135–6; Chang and Halliday, pp. 204–6

13 Li Zhisui, pp. 144, 254–60, 347–51, 370–1; Jin, pp.144–5

14 Witke, *Comrade Chiang Ch'ing*, p. 291; author interview with Zhang Hangzhi; Li Zhisui, pp. 451–2

15 Terrill, pp. 237, 239–41; 250–3

16 Author interview with Zhang Hanzhi; Chang and Halliday, p. 627; *RN*, p. 570; Witke, *Comrade Chiang Ch'ing*, p. 370

17 *RN*, p. 570; Haldeman, *Diaries*, p. 417; Walker, p. 40

18 Haldeman, *Diaries*, p. 418; Fang and Fang, pp. 117–18; *RN*, pp. 572, 577

19 Lovell, pp. 10–13, ch. 6, and *passim*

20 Cronkite, pp. 322–3; Kraft, p. 31; Chen and Hong, p. 313; Lovell, p. 11

21 Kraft, pp. 31–2

22 Haldeman, *Diaries*, p. 419; Haldeman, DVD, 25 February 1972; Kalb, pp. 276–7; author interview with John Burns

23 Memorandum of Conversation, 25 February 1972, 5.45 p.m.–6.45 p.m., NSA, Record of Historic Richard Nixon–Chou En-lai Talks in February 1972, Doc. 5; Lilley, pp. 167–8

24 Halstead, pp. 8–9; Kalb, p. 277; Walker, pp. 47, 154; Kraft, p. 34; *Globe and Mail*, 26 February 1972

CHAPTER 18: AUDIENCE REACTIONS

1 Doran and Lee, p. 730; USOH, Supplement, Galloway

2 Kraft, p. 29

3 Gaiduk, p. 228; *WHY*, pp. 172–3, 192–3, 268, 688; Arbatov, p. 180

4 Gaiduk, p. 229; Dobrynin, pp. 208, 217–18; *WHY*, pp. 731, 737; p. 8; Memorandum for the President, 14 July 1971, NSA, Electronic Briefing Book No. 66, Doc. 40, p. 8

5 Dobrynin, pp. 218–19, 225; Soviet Press Comments on President Nixon's Visit to China, 30 July 1971, PRO, FCO 21/824; Wishnick, *Mending Fences*, p. 59; Arbatov, pp. 180–2

6 Dobrynin, pp. 226–8; *WHY*, p. 766; *FRUS*, *Foundations*, pp. 327–8

7 Bundy, pp. 250–9; Strober and Strober, p. 132; Su, Chi, p. 562 n. 14

8 *FRUS*, *Foundations*, p. 353; Schaller, pp. 2–3; *WHY*, pp. 321–5; Memorandum of Conversation, 22 October 1971, NSA, Electronic Briefing Book No. 70, Doc. 13, p. 22

9 Schaller, 'The Nixon "Shocks"', p. 7; Bundy, pp. 142–4; Hersh, pp. 380–1; Giffard, pp. 170–1

10 Schaller, 'The Nixon "Shocks"', pp. 8–9

11 Schaller, 'The Nixon "Shocks"', pp. 11–12; Johnson, p. 554; Brown interview, PCC transcripts, 1/V, pp. 9–10

12 Schaller, 'The Nixon "Shocks"', p. 12; USOH, Freeman

13 Hoff, pp. 140–1; Reeves, p. 341; Schaller, 'The Nixon "Shocks"', p. 16

14 Memorandum of Conversation, 22 October 1971, 4.40 p.m.–7.10 p.m., NSA, Electronic Briefing Book No. 70, Doc. 13, p. 23; NPM, National Security Council Files, January 1972, Japan SATO San Clemente, Box 925, VIP Visits

15 Schaller, 'The Nixon "Shocks"', p. 17

16 Bachrack, pp. 261, 265; Tucker, 'Taiwan Expendable?', p. 129

17 Shen (Myers, ed.), pp. 70, 73–7; Tucker, 'Taiwan Expendable?', pp. 127, 132, 134; Mann interview, *PCC* transcripts, 1/V, roll 43, p. 13

18 Taylor, p. 307; Garver, *Sino-American Alliance*, pp. 276–7

19 Memorandum of Conversation, 23 October 1971, 9.05 p.m.–10.05 p.m., NSA, Electronic Briefing Book No. 70, Doc. 14, p. 2; Tucker, 'Taiwan Expendable?', p. 126; Walters, p. 546; author interview with Richard Solomon; Taylor, p. 308

20 Jacobs, p. 102; Shen (Myers, ed.), p. 79; Garver, *Sino-American Alliance*, p. 275; Kalb, p. 282; Taylor, p. 309

21 Doran and Lee, p. 696; USOH, Supplement, Gleysteen

CHAPTER 19: THE SHANGHAI COMMUNIQUÉ

1 Haldeman, DVD, 26 February 1972

2 Haldeman, *Diaries*, p. 418; *Globe and Mail*, 26 February, 1972; Memorandum of Conversation, 21 February 1972, 4.15 p.m.–5.30 p.m., p. 9, and Memorandum of Conversation, 25 February 1972, 9.34 a.m.-10.58 a.m., p. 10, NPM, National Security Council Files, HAK Office Files, Country Files–Far East, Box 92, Dr Kissinger's Meetings in the PRC during the Presidential Visit, February 1972

3 *WHY*, p. 1081; Memorandum of Conversation, 25 February 1972, 5.45 p.m.–6.45 p.m., NSA, Record of Historic Richard Nixon–Chou En-lai Talks in February 1972, Doc. 5, pp. 1–2; Memorandum of Conversation, Saturday 26 February 1972, NSA, Record of Historic Richard Nixon–Chou En-lai Talks in February 1972, Doc 6; Memorandum of Conversation, 25 February 1972, 4.50 p.m.–5.25 p.m. and Memorandum of Conversation, 25–26 February 1972, 10.30 p.m.–1.40 a.m., NPM, National Security Council Files, HAK Office Files, Country Files–Far East, Box 92, Dr Kissinger's Meetings in the PRC during the Presidential Visit, February 1972

4 *RN*, p. 571; *WHY*, pp. 1074–80

5 Ma Jisen, pp. 80–1, 88, 376–8, 379–80; Qiang, *China and the Vietnam Wars*, p. 100; *WHY*, p. 1054; Zhang Hanzhi, p. 10

6 Memorandum of Conversation, 24 February 1972, 9.59 a.m.–12.42 a. m., pp. 6, 19, NPM, National Security Council Files, HAK Office Files, Country Files–Far East, Box 92, Dr Kissinger's Meetings in the PRC during the Presidential Visit, February 1972; *WHY*, p. 1077

7 Memorandum of Conversation, Thursday 24 February 1972, 9.59 a.m.–12.42 a.m., p. 22, NPM, National Security Council Files, HAK Office

Files, Country Files–Far East, Box 92, Dr Kissinger's Meetings in the PRC during the Presidential Visit, February 1972

8 Memorandum of Conversation, Tuesday 22 February 1972, 10.05 a.m.–11.55 a.m., pp. 7–9, 10; Memorandum of Conversation, 24 February 1972, 9.59 a.m.–12.42 a.m., pp. 18, 20, NPM, National Security Council Files, HAK Office Files, Box 92, Country Files–Far East, Dr Kissinger's Meetings in the PRC during the Presidential Visit, February 1972

9 USOH, Supplement, Gleysteen; Garver, *Sino-American Alliance*, pp. 271–2

10 Memorandum of Conversation, Thursday 24 February 1972, 9.59 a.m.–12.42 a.m, p. 19, and Memorandum of Conversation, Friday 25 February 1972, 9.34 a.m.–10.58 a.m., pp. 7–8, NPM, National Security Council Files, HAK Office Files, Box 92, Country Files–Far East, Dr Kissinger's Meetings in the PRC during the Presidential Visit, February 1972; Haldeman, *Diaries*, pp. 419–21; *RN*, p. 572

11 Haldeman, DVD, 25 and 26 February 1972; Memorandum of Conversation, Tuesday 22 February 1972, 10.05 a.m.–11.55 a.m., p. 7, NPM, National Security Council Files, HAK Office Files, Box 92, Country Files–Far East, Dr Kissinger's Meetings in the PRC during the Presidential Visit, February 1972

12 *RN*, p. 573; *Globe and Mail*, 28 February 1972

13 Thomas, *Front Row*, p. 190; *New York Times*, 27 February 1972; *Globe and Mail*, 28 February 2006; Osborne, p. 29; *WHY*, p. 1082; Kraft, pp. 35–6

14 Tyler, pp. 138–9; USOH, Green, ch. VI

15 Tucker, *China Confidential*, p. 274; USOH, Green, ch. VI

16 USOH, Green, ch. VI; *WHY*, p. 1083; Tyler, p. 140

17 Memorandum of Conversation, Saturday 26 February–Sunday 27 February 1972, 10.20 p.m.–1.40 a.m., NPM, National Security Council Files, HAK Office Files, Box 92, Country Files–Far East, NSC, NPM, Dr Kissinger's Meetings in the PRC during the Presidential Visit, February 1972; *WHY*, pp. 1083–4; author interview with Zhang Hanzhi

18 USOH, Green, ch. VI; Haldeman, *Diaries*, p. 422

19 USOH, Green, ch. VI; *Globe and Mail*, 28 February 1972

20 Kraft, p. 37; Zhang Hanzhi, p. 256; *Globe and Mail*, 28 February 1972; *New York Times*, 28 February 1972

21 *Globe and Mail*, 28 February 1972; *New York Times*, 28 February 1972; Memorandum of Conversation, 23 February 1972, 2.00 p.m.–6.00 p.m., NSA, Nixon's Trip to China: Records Now Completely Declassified, Doc. 2, pp. 14–15

22 Memorandum of Conversation, 27 February 1972, 11.30 a.m.–1.55 p.m., pp. 7–8, 10–11, NPM, National Security Council Files, HAK Office Files, Country Files–Far East, Box 92, Dr Kissinger's Meetings in the PRC during the Presidential Visit, February 1972; Green, Holdridge and Stokes, pp. 146–7

23 Kalb, pp. 280–1; Kraft, pp. 38–9; Halstead, p. 10; *New York Times*, 28 February

1972; USOH, Green, ch. VI; Haldeman, *Diaries*, p. 422; Tyler, p. 143

24 Memorandum of Conversation, 25 February 1972, 4.50 p.m.–5.25 p.m., p. 6, NPM, National Security Council Files, HAK Office Files, Country Files–Far East, Box 92, Dr Kissinger's Meetings in the PRC during the Presidential Visit, February 1972; Zhang Hanzhi, pp. 251–2; author interview with Zhang Hanzhi

25 Tyler, p. 143; *WHY*, p. 1069

26 Memorandum of Conversation, Sunday 27 February–Monday 28 February 1972, 11.05 p.m.–12.30 a.m., pp. 1–3, NPM, National Security Council Files, HAK Office Files, Country Files–Far East, Box 92, Dr Kissinger's Meetings in the PRC during the Presidential Visit, February 1972

27 Haldeman, *Diaries*, p. 422; *WHY*, p. 1086

28 Cronkite, p. 325; author interview with Zhang Hanzhi

29 Memorandum of Conversation, Monday 28 February 1972, 8.30 a.m.–9.30 a.m., NSA, Record of Historic Richard Nixon–Chou En-lai Talks in February 1972, Doc. 7, pp. 3–5, 8–11

30 Holdridge, p. 95; Reeves, p. 457; Haldeman, DVD, 28 February 1972; Halstead, p. 10

31 *Globe and Mail*, 28 February 1972; Zhang Hanzhi, p. 256; USOH, Freeman; Halstead, p. 10; Haldeman, DVD, 28 February 1972

32 Holdridge, pp. 98–102; USOH, Green, ch. VII; Taylor, p. 308; USOH, Freeman; Welfield, p. 310; Doran and Lee, pp. 710, 731

33 Chancellor, p. 91; Haldeman, *Diaries*, p. 423

CONCLUSION

1 *Life*, 72/9 (10 March 1972), pp. 11–12; Foot, *Practice of Power*, p. 107; Tyler, pp. 143–4

2 Hamilton, p. 117; Bundy, pp. 314–21; *WHY*, pp. 1118–19, 1122, 1142, 1146; RN, pp. 881–3; Kozyrev, pp. 267–76

3 Bundy, pp. 322–7; Burr, ed., *Kissinger Transcripts*, pp. 68–70; Wang Zhongchun, pp. 158–64; Memorandum for the President from Henry A. Kissinger, 2 March 1973; Memorandum for the President from Henry A. Kissinger, 19 November 1973, NSA, China and the United States, 1960–1998, Doc. CH00259 and Doc. CH00277

4 Shen (Myers, ed.), pp. 13, 184–5

5 Holdridge, pp. 118–21, 124–6

6 Haldeman, *Diaries*, p. 472

7 Reeves, pp. 519–20, 526

8 *Ibid.*, pp. 527, 531–2

9 *Ibid.*, pp. 558–9

10 Kissinger, *Years of Upheaval*, p. 122; Isaacson, p. 503

11 RN, p. 1076; Kissinger, *Years of Upheaval*, p. 1210

12 Harding, pp. 48, 64

13 Memorandum for the President from Henry A. Kissinger, 19 November 1973, NSA, China and the United States, Doc. CH00277, pp. 4–5; Shambaugh, p. 177; Li Zhisui, pp. 580–1, 584–5

14 Li Zhisui, pp. 572–3, 582–3; author interview with Kissinger

15 Holdridge, pp. 143–50; Short, *Mao*, pp. 606–11

16 Short, *Mao*, pp. 621–2; USOH, Supplement, Gleysteen; Nixon, *Leaders*, p. 239

17 Ma Jisen, pp. 379–86; Short, *Mao*, pp. 620–4

18 Barmé, pp. 8–9, 22, 43, 46, 52, 196, 211

19 Ma Jisen, pp. 389–90, 399–400

20 Isaacson, pp. 708–9; ch. 33 *passim*

21 Kissinger, *Years of Upheaval*, p. 1212; *RN*, p. 1083; Summers, p. 485

22 Brodie, p. 470; Summers, pp. ix–xi; *New York Times*, 28 April 1994

23 Crowley, p. 159

24 Tyler, pp. 275–8

25 Crowley, p. 159; *Wall Street Journal*, 20 April 2006

26 Mann, chapters 1 and 2; Bundy, pp. 523–4; Memorandum of Conversation, Monday 21 February 1972, 4.15 p.m.–5.30 p.m., NPM, National Security Council Files, HAK Office Files, Box 92, Country Files–Far East, Dr Kissinger's Meetings in the PRC during the Presidential Visit, February 1972, p. 4

27 Memorandum of Conversation, 20 October 1971, 4.40 p.m.–7.10 p.m., NSA, Electronic Briefing Book No. 70, Doc. 10; *Star Trek VI: The Undiscovered Country*

Bibliography

Archival Sources

United Kingdom

Public Record Office, Surrey (PRO)
Foreign and Commmonwealth Office (FCO) 21: 818, 823, 824, 825, 828, 833,
982, 983

United States

The American Presidency Project http://www.presidency.ucsb.edu/index.php
    The Public Papers of the Presidents of the United States (Public Papers
    found on The American Presidency Project – or also at http://www.
    gpoaccess.gov/pubpapers/index.html)
National Archives and Records Administration (NARA)
    Nixon Presidential Materials Project (NPM) [Archives II (College Park,
    Maryland), 2006; by 2008 these materials will be in the Nixon Presidential
    Library, Yorba Linda, California]
    National Security Council Files (NSC)
        White House Special Files, Staff Member and Office Files, Dwight
        Chapin Files, Box 28
        Japan SATO San Clemente, Box 925
        'For the President's Files (Winston Lord) China/Vietnam Negotiations':
        Box 846, Box 847, Box 850
        HAK Office Files: Country Files–Far East, Box 92

The National Security Archive (NSA), The George Washington University,
Washington, DC, 2005
    Collection: China and the United States: From Hostility to Engagement,
    1960–1998
    U.S. Japan Project

Record of Historic Richard Nixon–Chou En-lai Talks in February 1972, Now Declassified

Nixon's Trip to China: Records Now Completely Declassified

Electronic Briefing Books
  Briefing Book 66: 'The Beijing–Washington Back–Channel and Henry Kissinger's Secret Trip to Beijing September 1970–July 1971'
  Briefing Book 70: 'Negotiating US Chinese Rapprochement'
  Briefing Book 145: 'New Documentary Reveals Secret U.S., Chinese Diplomacy Behind Nixon's Trip'

US Department of State
  Foreign Relations of the United States (FRUS) [Washington, DC, 2005] http://www.state.gov
    Nixon-Ford Administrations, vol. E-7, Documents on South Asia, 1969–1972

INTERVIEWS AND ORAL HISTORIES

Author Interviews

Gordon Barass, London, 14 July 2003
John Burns, Toronto, 7 November 2003
Chen Weiming, Shanghai, 24 April 2005
Robert Edmonds, Toronto, 1 January 2004
John Fraser, Ottawa, 8 February 2004
Edward Heath, Salisbury, UK, 2 December 2004
Jia Qingguo, Beijing, 19 April 2005
Henry Kissinger, Paris, 15 and 18 May 2003
Herbert Levin, New York, 6 November 2003
Li Qin, Beijing, 20 April 2005
Winston Lord, telecon, 19 July 2004
Arthur Menzies, Ottawa, 28 February 2005
Michael Richardson, London, 2 June 2004
Peter Rodman, Washington, 8 November 2004
Blair Seaborn, Ottawa, 28 February 2005
John Small, Ottawa, 28 February 2005
Yanhua Shi, Beijing, 20 April 2005
Richard Solomon, Washington, 9 November 2004
Yu Jaifu, Beijing, 20 April 2005
Zhang Hanzhi, Beijing, 21 April 2005

Frontline Diplomacy: The US Foreign Affairs oral history collection, ed. Marilyn Bentley and Marie Warner [USOH]

Ralph Clough
William J. Cunningham
David Dean
Charles Freeman
Lindsey Grant
Marshall Green
John H. Holdridge
Jerome K. Holloway
Walter E. Jenkins
Richard E. Johnson
Ralph J. Katrosh
Paul Kreisberg
John Lacey
Herbert Levin
Winston Lord
Larue Lutkins
Robert L. Nichols
David Osborn
Harry Thayer

Supplement

John A. Buche
Joseph S. Farland
Harvey Feldman
David Fischer
William J. Galloway
William H. Gleysteen
Winston Lord

Gerald R. Ford Library

Winston Lord interview, 19 October 1977

Playing the China Card: Nixon and Mao (Documentary) [PCC]

Transcripts, Archives, British Library of Political and Economic Science, London School of Economics

Tim Boggan
William Brown

Dwight Chapin
Henry A. Kissinger
Christopher H. Phillips

Nixon's China Game (Documentary)
PBS website http://www.pbs.org/wgbh/amex/china/index.html

Alexander Haig
Mohammad Khan
Zhang Hanzhi

BOOKS AND ARTICLES

Accinelli, Robert, 'In Pursuit of a Modus Vivendi: The Taiwan Issue and Sino-American Rapprochement, 1969–1972', in William C. Kirby, Robert S. Ross and Gong Li, eds, *Normalization of U.S.–China Relations: An International History.* Cambridge, MA, and London, 2005.

Aijazuddin, F. S., *From a Head, through a Head, to a Head: The Secret Channel between the US and China through Pakistan.* Karachi, 2000.

Aitken, Jonathan, 'The Nixon Character', *Presidential Studies Quarterly* 26/1 (Winter 1996): 239–48.

Ambrose, Stephen E., *Nixon: The Education of a Politician 1913–1962.* New York, 1987.

——, *Nixon: The Triumph of a Politician 1962–1972.* New York, 1989.

Arbatov, Georgi, *The System: An Insider's Life in Soviet Politics.* New York, 1992.

Arkush, R. David and Leo Ou-fan Lee, *Land without Ghosts: Chinese Impressions of America from the Mid-Nineteenth Century to the Present.* Berkeley, 1989.

Bachrack, Stanley D., *The Committee of One Million: China Lobby Politics, 1953–1971.* New York, 1976.

Barmé, Geremie R., *Shades of Mao: the Posthumous Cult of the Great Leader.* Armonk, NY, 1996.

Barnouin, Barbara and Changgen Yu, *Chinese Foreign Policy During the Cultural Revolution.* London and New York, 1998.

Bloodworth, Dennis and Ching Ping Bloodworth, *The Chinese Machiavelli: 3,000 Years of Chinese Statecraft.* New York, 1976.

Bostdorff, Denise M., 'The Evolution of a Diplomatic Surprise: Richard M. Nixon's Rhetoric on China, 1952–July 15, 1971', *Rhetoric & Public Affairs* 5/1 (March 2002): 31–56.

Brady, Anne-Marie, *Making the Foreign Serve China: Managing Foreigners in the People's Republic.* Lanham, 2003.

Brandon, Henry, *Special Relationships: A Foreign Correspondent's Memoirs from Roosevelt to Reagan.* New York, 1988.

Brodie, Fawn, *Richard Nixon, the Shaping of his Character.* New York, 1981.

Buckley, William F., *Inveighing We Will Go.* New York, 1972.

Bundy, William P., *A Tangled Web: The Making of Foreign Policy in the Nixon Presidency*. New York, 1998.

Burr, William., 'Sino American Relations, 1969: The Sino-Soviet Border War and Steps Towards Rapprochement' *Cold War History* 1/3 (2001): 73–112.

—— ed., *The Kissinger Transcripts: The Top Secret Talks with Beijing and Moscow*. New York, 1998.

Carter, Carolle J., *Mission to Yenan: American Liaison with the Chinese Communists 1944–1947*. Lexington, KY, 1997.

Chancellor, John, 'Prime Time in China: Who Produced the China Show?', *Foreign Policy*, 7 (Summer, 1972).

Chang, Gordon H., *Friends and Enemies: The United States, China, and the Soviet Union, 1948–1972*. Stanford, CA, 1990.

Chang, Jung and Jon Halliday. *Mao: The Unknown Story*. London, 2005.

Chen, Feng and Lin Hong, *Zhongmei Jiaofeng Dajishi, 1949–2001*. Beijing, 2001.

Chen, Jian, 'China's Involvement in the Vietnam War, 1965–69', *China Quarterly* 142 (June 1995): 356–87.

——, *Mao's China and the Cold War*. Chapel Hill, NC, 2001.

Chen, Jian and David L. Wilson. "All Under the Heaven Is Great Chaos": Beijing, the Sino-Soviet Border Clashes, and the Turn Toward Sino-American Rapprochement, 1968–69', *Cold War International History Project Bulletin* 11 (Winter 1998): 157–75.

Cohen, Warren I., *America's Response to China: A History of Sino-American Relations*. New York, 2000.

Cradock, Percy, *Experiences of China*. London, 1994.

Crowley, Monica, *Nixon in Winter*. New York, 1998.

Dobrynin, Anatoly, *In Confidence: Moscow's Ambassador to America's Six Cold War Presidents (1962–1986)*. New York, 1995.

Doran, Stuart and David Lee, eds, *Documents on Australian Foreign Policy: Australia and Recognition of the People's Republic of China, 1949–1972*. Canberra, 2002.

Edmonds, R. B. 'China Trip Diary 2004'. Unpublished, copy lent to author.

Ehrlichman, John, *Witness to Power: The Nixon Years*. New York, 1982.

Fallaci, Oriana, *Interview with History*, trans. John Shepley. New York, 1976.

Fang, Percy Jucheng and Lucy Guinong J. Fang, *Zhou Enlai: A Profile*. Beijing, 1986.

Feeney, Mark, *Nixon at the Movies*. Chicago, 2004.

Fenby, Jonathan, *Chiang Kai Shek: China's Generalissimo and the Nation He Lost*. New York, 2003.

Foot, Rosemary, *Practice of Power: American Relations with China since 1949*. Oxford, 1995.

——, 'Redefinitions: The Domestic Context of America's China Policy in the 1960s', in Robert S. Ross and Jiang Changbin, eds, *Re-Examining the Cold War: U.S.-China Diplomacy 1954–1973*. Cambridge, MA., 2001.

——, 'Prizes Won, Opportunities Lost: The US Normalization of Relations with

China, 1972–1979', in William C. Kirby, Robert S. Ross and Gong Li, *Normalization of U.S.–China Relations: An International History*. Cambridge, MA, 2005.

Foreign Relations of the United States, 1969–1976, vol. I: *Foundations of Foreign Policy, 1969–1972*, ed. Louis J. Smith and David H. Herschler. Washington, DC, 2003.

——, vol. V: *United Nations, 1969–1972*, ed. Evan M. Duncan. Washington, DC, 2004.

Frankel, Max, *The Times of my Life and my Life with the Times*. New York, 1999.

Fried, Albert, ed., *A Day of Dedication: The Essential Writings and Speeches of Woodrow Wilson*. New York, 1965.

Friedman, Edward, 'Maoist and Post-Mao Conceptualizations of China' in Samuel S. Kim, ed., *China and the World: Chinese Foreign Policy Faces the New Millennium*. Boulder, CO, 1998.

Gaiduk, Ilya V., *The Soviet Union and the Vietnam War*. Chicago, 1996.

Garment, Leonard, *Crazy Rhythm: My Journey from Brooklyn, Jazz and Wall Street to Nixon's White House, Watergate and Beyond*. New York, 1997.

Garver, John W., *China's Decision for Rapprochement with the United States 1968–1971*. Boulder, CO, 1982.

——, *Foreign Relations of the People's Republic of China*. Englewood Cliffs, NJ, 1993.

——, *The Sino-American Alliance: Nationalist China and American Cold War Strategy in Asia*. Armonk, NY, 1997.

Giffard, Sydney, *Japan among the Powers 1890–1990*. New Haven, CT, 1994.

Goh, Evelyn, *Constructing the U.S. Rapprochement with China, 1961–1974: From 'red menace' to 'tacit ally'*. Cambridge, 2005.

——, 'Nixon, Kissinger, and the 'Soviet Card' in the U.S. Opening to China, 1971–1974', *Diplomatic History* 29/3 (June 2005): 475–502.

Goldstein, Lyle J., 'Return to Zhenbao Island: Who Started Shooting and Why it Matters', *China Quarterly* 168 (December 2001): 985–97.

Goncharov, Sergei Nikolaevich, John W. Lewis and Xue Litai, *Uncertain Partners: Stalin, Mao, and the Korean War*. Stanford, CA, 1993.

Gong, Li, *Deng Xiaoping Yu Meiguo*. Beijing, 2004.

Green, Marshall, 'The Evolution of US–China Policy 1956–1975' in Marshall Green, John H. Holdridge and William N. Stokes, *War and Peace with China*, Bethesda, MD, 1994.

——, John H. Holdridge and William N. Stokes, *War and Peace with China*. Bethesda, MD, 1994.

Greenberg, David, *Nixon's Shadow: The History of an Image*. New York, 2003.

Haig, Alexander Meigs, with Charles McCarry, *Inner Circles: How America Changed the World: A Memoir*. New York, 1992.

Haldeman, Harry R., with Joseph DiMona, *The Ends of Power*. Montreal, 1978.

——, *The Haldeman Diaries: Inside the Nixon White House*. New York, 1994.

Hamilton, K. A., 'A "Week that Changed the World": Britain and Nixon's China Visit of 21–28 February 1972', *Diplomacy and Statecraft* 15/1 (March 2004): 117–135.

Han, Suyin, *Eldest Son: Zhou Enlai and the Making of Modern China, 1898–1976*. New York, 1994.

Hanhimäki, Jussi M., *The Flawed Architect: Henry Kissinger and American Foreign Policy*. New York, 2004.

Harding, Harry, *A Fragile Relationship: The United States and China since 1972*. Washington, DC, 1992.

He, Di, 'The Most Respected Enemy: Mao Zedong's Perception of the United States', *China Quarterly* 137 (1994): 144–58.

Heath, Edward, *The Course of my Life: My Autobiography*. London, 1998.

Helms, Richard, with William Hood, *A Look Over my Shoulder: A Life in the Central Intelligence Agency*. New York, 2003.

Hersh, Seymour M., *The Price of Power: Kissinger in the Nixon White House*. New York, 1983.

Hevia, James L., *Cherishing Guests from Afar: Qing Guest Ritual and the Macartney Embassy of 1793*. Durham, NC, 1995.

Hoff, Joan, *Nixon Reconsidered*. New York, 1994.

Holdridge, John H., *Crossing the Divide: An Insider's Account of the Normalization of U.S.–China Relations*. Lanham, MD, 1997.

Hoxha, Enver. *Reflections on China*, vol. I: *1962–1972, Extracts from the Political Diary*. Tirana, 1979.

Hsüeh, Chün-tu, ed., *China's Foreign Relations: New Perspectives*. New York, 1982.

Hsüeh, Chün-tu and Robert C. North, 'China and the Superpowers: Perception and Policy', in Chün-tu Hsüeh, ed., *China's Foreign Relations: New Perspectives*. New York, 1982.

Hunt, Michael H., *The Making of a Special Relationship: The United States and China to 1914*. New York, 1983.

——, *The Genesis of Chinese Communist Foreign Policy*. New York, 1996.

Hunt, Michael H. and Niu Jun, eds, *Toward a History of Chinese Communist Foreign Relations 1920s–1960s*. Washington, DC, 1995.

Isaacson, Walter, *Kissinger: A Biography*. New York, 1992.

Jacobs, J. Bruce, 'Taiwan 1972: Political Season', *Asian Survey* 13/1 (January, 1973): 102–12.

Ji, Chaozhu, 'Reminiscences of a Harvard Man Who Served for 17 Years as Premier Zhou Enlai's Principal Interpreter'. Unpublished paper presented at the China Institute, New York, 27 January 2004.

Jin, Qiu, *The Culture of Power: The Lin Biao Incident in the Cultural Revolution*. Stanford, CA, 1999.

Johnson, U. Alexis, *The Right Hand of Power*. Englewood Cliffs, NJ, 1984.

Kalb, Marvin L., *Kissinger*. Boston, 1974.

Kazuo, Ogura, 'The "Inscrutables" Negotiate with the "Inscrutables"; Chinese Negotiating Tactics vis-à-vis the Japanese', *China Quarterly* 79 (September 1979): 529–52.

Keith, Ronald C., *The Diplomacy of Zhou Enlai*. Basingstoke, 1989.

Kennedy, Scott S., ed., *China Cross Talk: The American Debate over China Policy since Normalization*. Lanham, MD, 2003.

Khrushchev, Nikita Sergeevich, *Khrushchev Remembers,* trans./ed. Strobe Talbott. Boston, 1970.

——, *Khrushchev Remembers: The Last Testament,* trans./ed. Strobe Talbott. Boston, 1974.

Kim, Samuel S., ed., *China and the World: Chinese Foreign Policy Faces the New Millennium*. Boulder, Colo., 1998.

Kimball, Jeffrey P., *Nixon's Vietnam War*. Lawrence, KS, 1998.

Kirby, William C., Robert S. Ross and Gong Li, eds., *Normalization of U.S.–China Relations: An International History*. Cambridge, MA, 2005.

Kissinger, Henry, A *World Restored: Metternich, Castlereagh and the Problems of Peace 1812–22*. Boston, 1973.

——, *The White House Years*. Boston, 1979.

——, *Years of Upheaval*. Boston, 1982.

——, *Diplomacy*. New York, 1994.

Kozyrev, Vitaly, 'Soviet Policy toward the United States and China', in William C. Kirby, Robert S. Ross and Gong Li., eds, *Normalization of U.S.–China Relations: An International History*. Cambridge, MA, 2005.

Kraft, Joseph, *The Chinese Difference*. New York, 1973.

Leys, Simon, *Chinese Shadows*. New York, 1977.

——, *The Burning Forest: Essays on Chinese Culture and Politics*. New York, 1985.

Li, Baojun, *Dangdai Zhongguo Waijiao Gailun*. Beijing 1999.

Li, Danhui, 'Vietnam and Chinese Policy toward the United States', in William C. Kirby, Robert S. Ross and Gong Li, eds, *Normalization of U.S.-China Relations: An International History*. Cambridge, MA. 2005.

Li, Jie, 'China's Domestic Politics and the Normalization of Sino-U.S. Relations, 1969–1979', in William C. Kirby, Robert S. Ross and Gong Li, eds, *Normalization of U.S.–China Relations: An International History*. Cambridge, MA, 2005.

Li, Zhisui, *The Private Life of Chairman Mao: The Memoirs of Mao's Personal Physician,* trans. Tai Hung-Chao. New York, 1994.

Lilley, James R., with Jeffrey Lilley. *China Hands: Nine Decades of Adventure, Espionage and Diplomacy in Asia*. New York, 2004.

Lovell, Julia. *The Great Wall: China against the World 1000 BC–AD 2000*. Toronto, 2006.

Lowe, Peter, *Containing the Cold War in Asia: British Policies towards Japan, China, and Korea, 1948–53*. New York, 1997.

Luo, Yingcai, *Chen Yi De Feichang Zhilu*. Beijing, 2004.

Ma, Jisen, *The Cultural Revolution in the Foreign Ministry of China*. Hong Kong, 2004.

McFarlane, Robert C., with Zofia Smardz, *Special Trust*. New York, 1994.

Mancall, Mark, 'The Persistence of Tradition in Chinese Foreign Policy', *Annals of the American Academy of Political and Social Science* 349 (September 1963): 14–26

Mann, James, *About Face: A History of America's Curious Relationship with China, from Nixon to Clinton*. New York, 1999.

Mao Zedong on Diplomacy. Beijing, 1998.

Mitter, Rana, *A Bitter Revolution: China's Struggle with the Modern World*. Oxford, 2004.

Morris, Stephen J., 'The Soviet–Chinese–Vietnamese Triangle in the 1970s: The View from Moscow', *Cold War International History Project Working Paper 25*. Washington, DC, 1999.

National Intelligence Council, *Tracking the Dragon: National Intelligence Estimates on China during the Era of Mao, 1948–1976*. Washington, DC, 2004.

Naughton, Barry, 'The Third Front: Defence Industrialization in the Chinese Interior', *China Quarterly* 115 (September 1988): 351–86.

Nixon, Richard M., 'Asia after Vietnam', *Foreign Affairs* 46/1 (October 1967): 111–36.

——, *The White House Transcripts: Submission of Recorded Presidential Conversations to the Committee on the Judiciary of the House of Representatives by President Richard Nixon*. New York, 1974.

——, *RN: The Memoirs of Richard Nixon*. New York, 1978

——, *Leaders*. New York, 1982.

Osborne, John, *The Fourth Year of the Nixon Watch*. New York, 1973.

Ostermann, Christian F., 'New Evidence on the Sino-Soviet Border Dispute 1969–71', *The Cold War in Asia: Cold War International History Project Bulletin 6–7* (Winter 1995/6): 188–90.

Pollock, Jonathan D., 'Chinese Attitudes towards Nuclear Weapons, 1964–9', *China Quarterly* 50 (April–June 1972): 244–71.

Price, Raymond, *With Nixon*. New York, 1977.

Quan, Yanchi, *Mao Zedong: Man, Not God*. Beijing, 1992.

Rather, Dan, with Mickey Herskowitz, *The Camera Never Blinks: Adventures of a TV Journalist*. New York, 1977.

Rather, Dan and Gary Paul Gates, *The Palace Guard*. New York, 1974.

Reeves, Richard, *President Nixon: Alone in the White House*. New York, 2001.

Robinson, Thomas W. and David Shambaugh, eds, *Chinese Foreign Policy: Theory and Practice*. Oxford, 1994.

Romberg, Alan D., *Rein in at the Brink of the Precipice: American Policy toward Taiwan and U.S.–PRC Relations*. Washington, DC, 2003.

Ross, Robert S., 'From Lin Biao to Deng Xiaoping: Elite Instability and China's U.S. Policy', *China Quarterly* 118 (June 1989): 265–99.

——, ed., *China, the United States and the Soviet Union: Tripolarity and Policy Making in the Cold War*. Armonk, NY, 1993.

Ross, Robert S. and Jiang Changbin, eds, *Re-Examining the Cold War: U.S.–China Diplomacy 1954–1973*. Cambridge, MA, 2001.

Safire, William, *Before the Fall: An Inside View of the Pre-Watergate White House*. Garden City, NY, 1977.

Schaller, Michael, *The United States and China in the Twentieth Century*, 2nd edn. New York, 1990.

——, 'The Nixon "Shocks" and U.S.–Japan Strategic Relations, 1969–1974', National Security Archives, U.S.–Japan Project, Working Paper 2, 1996.

——, 'Détente and the Strategic Triangle, Or "Drinking your Mao Tai and Having Your Vodka Too"', in Robert S. Ross and Jiang Changbin, eds, *Re-Examining the Cold War: U.S.–China Diplomacy 1954–1973*. Cambridge, MA, 2001.

Schoenhals, Michael, 'The Central Case Examination Group, 1966–79', *China Quarterly* 145 (March 1996): 87–111.

Schram, Stuart, *Mao Tse-tung*. London, 1967.

——, *The Political Thought of Mao Tse-tung*. New York, 1977.

Shambaugh, David L., *Beautiful Imperialist: China Perceives America, 1972–1990*. Princeton, NJ, 1991.

Shao, Kuo-kang, *Zhou Enlai and the Foundations of Chinese Foreign Policy*. New York, 1996.

Share, Michael, 'From Ideological Foe to Uncertain Friend: Soviet Relations with Taiwan, 1943–82', *Cold War History* 3/2 (January 2003): 1–34.

Shen, James H. C., Robert Myers, ed., *The U.S. & Free China: How the U.S. Sold Out Its Ally*. Washington, DC, 1983.

Short, Philip, *The Dragon and the Bear: China and Russia in the Eighties*. New York, 1982.

——, *Mao: A Life*. London, 2004.

Smedley, Agnes, *Battle Hymn of China*. New York, 1975.

Solomon, Richard H., *Chinese Negotiating Behavior: Pursuing Interests through 'Old Friends'*. Washington, DC, 1999.

Spence, Jonathan D., *The Search for Modern China*. New York, 1990.

Strober, Gerald S. and Deborah H. Strober. *Nixon: An Oral History of his Presidency*. New York, 1994.

Strong, Tracy B. and Helene Keyssar, 'Anna Louise Strong: Three Interviews with Chairman Mao Zedong', *China Quarterly* 103 (September 1985): 489–509.

Su, Chi, 'U.S. China Relations: Soviet Views and Policies', *Asian Survey* 23/5 (May 1983): 555–79.

Su, Ge, *Meiguo Duihua Zhengce Yu Taiwan Wenti*. Beijing, 1998.

Summers, Anthony. *Arrogance of Power: The Secret World of Richard Nixon*. New York, 2000.

Suri, Jeremi, *Power and Protest: Global Revolution and the Rise of Détente*. Cambridge, MA, 2003.

Tao, Wenzhao, *Zhongmei Guanxishi, 1972–2000*, Parts II and III. Shanghai, 2004.

Taubman, William, *Khrushchev: The Man and his Era*. New York, 2003.

Taylor, Jay, *The Generalissimo's Son: Chiang Ching-kuo and the Revolutions in China and Taiwan*. Cambridge, MA, 2000.

Teiwes, Frederick C., 'Mao and his Lieutenants', *Australian Journal of Chinese Affairs* 19/20 (January–July 1988): 1–80.

Teng, Ssu-Yü and John K. Fairbank, *China's Response to the West: A Documentary Survey, 1839–1923*. New York, 1967.

Terrill, Ross, *Madame Mao: The White-Boned Demon*. Stanford, CA, 1999.

Thomas, Helen, *Dateline: White House*. New York, 1975.

——, *Front Row at The White House: My Life and Times*. New York, 1999.

Topping, Seymour, *Journey between Two Chinas*. New York, 1972.

Tucker, Nancy Bernkopf, *Taiwan, Hong Kong, and the United States, 1945–1992: Uncertain Friendships*. New York, 1994.

——, *China Confidential: American Diplomats and Sino-American Relations 1945–1996*. New York, 2001.

——, 'Taiwan Expendable? Nixon and Kissinger Go to China', *Journal of American History* 92/1 (June 2005): 109–35.

——, ed, *Dangerous Strait: The U.S.–Taiwan–China Crisis*. New York, 2005.

Tyler, Patrick, *A Great Wall: Six Presidents and China: An Investigative History*. New York, 1999.

Valeriani, Richard, *Travels with Henry*. Boston, 1979.

Van Hollen, Christopher, 'The Tilt Policy Revisited: Nixon–Kissinger Geopolitics and South Asia', *Asian Survey*, 20/4 (April 1980): 339–61.

Walker, Anne Collins, *China Calls: Paving the Way for Nixon's Historic Journey to China*. Lanham, MD, 1992.

Walters, Vernon A., *Silent Missions*. Garden City, NY, 1978.

Wang, Zhongchun, 'The Soviet Factor in Sino-American Normalization, 1969–1979', in William C. Kirby, Robert S. Ross and Gong Li, eds, *Normalization of U.S.–China Relations: An International History*. Cambridge, MA, 2005.

Welfield, John, *An Empire in Eclipse: Japan in the Post-War American Alliance System: A Study in the Interaction of Domestic Politics and Foreign Policy*. London, 1988.

Wested, Odd Arne, 'History, Memory, and the Languages of Alliance-Making' in Odd Arne Westad, Chen Jian, Stein Tønnesson, Nguyen Vu Tungand and James G. Hershberg, eds, '77 Conversations Between Chinese and Foreign Leaders on the Wars in Indochina, 1964–1977', *Cold War International History Project Working Paper No. 22*. Washington, DC, May 1998: 8–19.

Westad, Odd Arne, Chen Jian, Stein Tønnesson, Nguyen Vu Tungand and James G. Hershberg, eds, '77 Conversations between Chinese and Foreign Leaders on the Wars in Indochina, 1964–1977', *Cold War International History Project Working Paper No. 22*. Washington, DC, 1998.

White, Theodore Harold, *America in Search of Itself: The Making of the President 1956–1980*. New York, 1982.

Whiting, Allen S., 'Review: Sino-American *Détente*', *China Quarterly* 82 (June 1980): 334–41

Wicker, Tom, *One of Us: Richard Nixon and the American Dream*. New York, 1991.

——, 'Richard M. Nixon 1969–1974', *Presidential Studies Quarterly* 26/1 (Winter 1996): 249–58.

Wilson, Dick, *Chou: The Story of Zhou Enlai 1898–1976*. London, 1984.

Wishnick, Elizabeth, 'In the Region and in the Center: Soviet Reactions to the Border Rift', *Cold War International History Project Bulletin*, 6–7 (Winter 1995/6): 194–201.

——, *Mending Fences: The Evolution of Moscow's China Policy from Brezhnev to Yeltsin*. Seattle, WA, 2001.

Witke, Roxane, *Comrade Chiang Ch'ing*. Boston, MA, 1977.

——, 'The Last Days of Madame Mao', *Vanity Fair* 54/12 (December, 1991): 134–53.

Xiang, Liling, *Zhongmei Guanxishi Quanbian*. Shanghai, 2002.

Xie, Yixian, ed, *Dangdai Zhongkuo Waijiao Shi, 1949–2001*, 2nd edn. Beijing, 2002.

Xiong, Xianghui, 'Jiang Qing Xiang Nikesong Xianyinqin', *Bainianchao*, 1 (1999).

——, 'Mao Zedong "meiyou xiangdao" de shengli: huiyi woguo huifu zai lianheguo xiwei de guocheng', *Bainianchao*, 1 (1999).

Xu, Jingli, *Jie Mi: Zhongguo Waijiao Dangan*. Beijing, 2005.

Yahuda, Michael, 'The Significance of Tripolarity in China's Policy toward the United States Since 1972', in Robert S. Ross, ed., *China, the United States and the Soviet Union: Tripolarity and Policy Making in the Cold War*. Armonk, NY, and London, 1993.

Yan, Jiaqi and Gao Gao, *Turbulent Decade: A History of the Cultural Revolution*, trans./ed. D. W. Y. Kwok. Honolulu, 1996.

Yan, Wen, *Chaoyue Duikang: Zhongmei Sanci Dachongtu*. Beijing, 1998.

Yang, Gongsu, *Dangdai Zhongkuo Waijiao Lilun Yi Shijan, 1949–2001*. Hong Kong, 2002.

Yang, Kuisong, 'Changes in Mao Zedong's Attitude toward the Indochina War, 1949–1973', *Cold War International History Project Working Paper No. 34*. Washington, DC, 2002.

Zhai, Qiang, *The Dragon, the Lion and the Eagle: Chinese–British–American Relations, 1949–1958*. Kent, Ohio, 1994.

——, *China and the Vietnam Wars, 1950–1975*. Chapel Hill, NC, 2000.

Zhang, Baijia, 'The Changing International Scene', in Robert S. Ross and Jiang Changbin, eds, *Re-Examining the Cold War: U.S.–China Diplomacy, 1954–1973*. Cambridge, MA, 2001.

Zhang, Hanzhi, *Chuanguo Houhou De Dahongmen*. Shanghai, 2002.

Zhihua, Shen, 'Sino-Soviet Relations and the Origins of the Korean War: Stalin's Strategic Goals in the Far East', *Journal of Cold War Studies* 2/2 (Spring 2000): 44–68.

CONTEMPORARY NEWSPAPERS

Financial Times (London)
Globe and Mail (Toronto)

Wall Street Journal (New York)
New York Times (New York)

WEBSITES

Halstead, Dirck, 'With Nixon in China: A Memoir', *Digital Journalist* 501 (January 2005), 15 July 2006. http://dirckhalstead.org.

The American Presidency Project, 1999–2005, John Wooley and Gerhard Peters, 15 July, 2006. http://www.presidency.ucsb.edu/index.php

Yum, Jennifer, 'A Tenuous Alliance: The Evolution of Sino-Vietnamese Relations in the Second Indochinese War', Wellesley College, *International Relations Council Journal* 2 (Spring 2005), 15 July 2006. http://www.wellesley.edu/Activities/homepage/ircj/currentissue.html

The National Security Archive, 1995–2006, The George Washington University, 15 July 2006. http://www.gwu.edu/~nsarchiv

Niksong dangnian fanghua xianwei renzhi de neimu. http://www.phoenixtv.com/home/news/society/200310/23/124559.html

'Nixon's China Game: Interview Transcripts', *PBS: The American Experience.* 2004–6. PBS Online by WGBH Educational Foundation, 15 July 2006. http://www.pbs.org/wgbh/amex/china/filmmore/reference/interview/index.html

US Department of State. The Office of Electronic Information, Bureau of Public Affairs. 15 July, 2006. http://www.state.gov

OTHER

Star Trek VI: The Undiscovered Country. Dir. Nicholas Meyer. Perf. William Shatner, Leonard Nimoy, DeForest Kelley. 1991. DVD. Paramount Pictures, 2004.

Haldeman Diaries, CD-ROM. New York: Sony Electronic Publishing, 1994.

Index

HK = Henry Kissinger
PRC = People's Republic of China
RN = Richard Nixon